CAMBRIDGE STUDIES
IN ENGLISH LEGAL HISTORY

Edited by
J.H. BAKER
Fellow of St Catharine's College, Cambridge

Sir William Scott's thirty years as judge of the High Court of Admiralty provide the basis of his reputation as the greatest of civilian (as opposed to common) lawyers. In this major study, the first for over seventy years, Professor Bourguignon analyzes his work as judge of the admiralty court in the light of the little-known, unpublished body of law which had been developed prior to his appointment. His term of office coincided with the Revolutionary and Napoleonic wars, and thus Scott had to hear and determine hundreds of cases involving the capture of vessels in time of war. These prize cases provided Scott with the opportunity to state and develop many aspects of the international law of war, especially the law of neutral and belligerent rights at sea. He also influenced the development of admiralty law in the cases which he heard of private disputes concerning maritime commerce. His career also throws fresh light on the training and practice of eighteenth-century civilian lawyers who dealt with issues of church or maritime law.

SIR WILLIAM SCOTT, LORD STOWELL

JUDGE OF THE HIGH COURT OF ADMIRALTY, 1798–1828

HENRY J. BOURGUIGNON

Professor, University of Toledo College of Law

The right of the
University of Cambridge
to print and sell
all manner of books
was granted by
Henry VIII in 1534.
The University has printed
and published continuously
since 1584.

CAMBRIDGE UNIVERSITY PRESS

Cambridge

New York   New Rochelle   Melbourne   Sydney

PUBLISHED BY THE PRESS SYNDICATE OF THE UNIVERSITY OF CAMBRIDGE
The Pitt Building, Trumpington Street, Cambridge, United Kingdom

CAMBRIDGE UNIVERSITY PRESS
The Edinburgh Building, Cambridge CB2 2RU, UK
40 West 20th Street, New York NY 10011–4211, USA
477 Williamstown Road, Port Melbourne, VIC 3207, Australia
Ruiz de Alarcón 13, 28014 Madrid, Spain
Dock House, The Waterfront, Cape Town 8001, South Africa

http://www.cambridge.org

© Cambridge University Press 1987

This book is in copyright. Subject to statutory exception
and to the provisions of relevant collective licensing agreements,
no reproduction of any part may take place without
the written permission of Cambridge University Press.

First published 1987
First paperback edition 2004

A catalogue record for this book is available from the British Library

Library of Congress Cataloguing in Publication data
Bourguignon, Henry J.
Sir William Scott, Lord Stowell, judge of the High
Court of Admiralty, 1798–1828.
(Cambridge studies in English legal history)
Bibliography.
Includes index.
1. Scott, William, Baron Stowell of Stowell Park,
1745–1836. 2. Judges – Great Britain – Biography.
3. Great Britain. High Court of Admiralty – History.
I. Title. II. Series.
KD621.S36B68   1987   343.41′096′0269 [B] 344.103960269 [B]   87-6377

ISBN 0 521 34076 4 hardback
ISBN 0 521 52688 4 paperback

In Memory of
Joseph Henry Smith
1913–1981

A Gentleman and A Scholar

CONTENTS

PREFACE

Sir William Scott, Lord Stowell, has been considered a good, perhaps even a great, judge. As a civilian he practiced, not in the courts of common law, but in the courts which followed the civil law, like the admiralty court and the church courts. This book evaluates his work as judge of the admiralty court where he presided for thirty years. Although he also sat for more than thirty years as judge of the London Consistory Court, this aspect of his work is only briefly mentioned. I have, throughout the book, referred to him as Scott, since that is what he was called during most of his long life. He did not become Lord Stowell until near the end of his active career when he was seventy-five years old.

When I first began this project, I decided not to write a full-scale, judicial biography of Scott as judge of the admiralty court. During my year of research in Great Britain this decision was confirmed when I was unable to locate any substantial collection of Scott's letters, personal papers or legal books. The various scattered letters and papers I found shed considerable light on his work, but could not provide enough detailed information for a complete judicial biography.

Scott has left, however, an immensely valuable collection of admiralty court decisions, called judgments. The ten and a half volumes of Scott's reported judgments provide the focal point for this study. His fame as a judge and as the greatest of the civilians rests primarily on these well-crafted opinions. In preparing these decisions Scott drew upon his entire background and training, his years of study and legal practice. His judicial character can be discovered most fully in these decisions. All the other manuscript and published materials used in this book are meant to make Scott's numerous judgments intelligible to today's readers.

I have written this book as an analysis of Scott's judicial character:

it is a study of Scott's work as admiralty judge. Neither Scott nor the admiralty court are well known. The first two chapters, therefore, provide an historical sketch of the admiralty court and a biographical summary of Scott's career.

Chapters 3, 4 and 5 form the central body of the book. In Chapter 3 I analyze Scott's work on the private, maritime litigation, the instance suits, which he heard. This chapter casts significant new light on the historical development of admiralty law.

Chapters 4 and 5 focus on Scott's prize cases, that is, the cases involving the capture of enemy property in time of war. More specifically, these chapters analyze those many prize decisions which raised legal issues concerning the international law of war. Chapters 4 and 5, therefore, treat such issues as neutral rights, blockade, contraband, colonial trade and nationality, which remained important in the history of international law.

Scott's fame as the greatest of the civilians derives in the first place from the fact that he sat as admiralty judge during the long wars with France and its continental allies. But more importantly, Scott's fame rests on his extraordinary ability to state thoughtfully and with clarity the reasons for his decisions. He used the opportunity of the many difficult, controversial and often unsettled issues which came before him during the long war years to demonstrate his judicial ability. The enormous number of prize judgments which Scott determined form the most significant part of his judicial work.

Chapter 4 is a detailed study of one doctrine of international law, nationality, while Chapter 5 is a survey of several international legal doctrines. In Chapter 4 I have studied one doctrine in depth to point out the complexity and the inadequacy of the state of the law prior to Scott's day. I have also used this detailed study to provide examples of Scott's participation in the process of the development of the law prior to the time he became admiralty judge. His work as judge will be better understood if we first appreciate his eighteen years of apprenticeship as a civilian advocate. Some of Scott's arguments before the court are recreated in Chapter 4 to exemplify his role as a leading civilian before he became judge. Because of this ample study of one area of the law of the prize court in Chapter 4, the other areas can be studied in Chapter 5 without the need for a similarly detailed analysis.

Even though I have devoted these two lengthy chapters to the discussion of prize law, I have had to omit many aspects of it. In order to keep the analysis of prize law within some reasonable limits, I have selected only those issues for discussion which retained some lasting significance in international law. These cases turned upon many issues of the legality of the capture. I have omitted, therefore, any discussion of questions of distribution of the lawful prizes among the various captors. Many legal disputes came before the prize court to determine to whom a lawful prize ship or cargo would be awarded, for example, suits between joint captors, or suits for awards for recapturing British property, or suits for the officers' share of a prize or for gun money. None of these numerous, and often unseemly, private squabbles over the division of the spoils of maritime warfare will be discussed in this book. Furthermore, many prize decisions turned on questions of procedure and evidence. I have likewise omitted any lengthy discussion of Scott's application of these procedural and evidentiary rules.

Chapter 6 offers a more reflective analysis of Scott's role as a judge. I have tried to distill from the many cases analyzed in Chapters 3, 4 and 5, and from other cases also, the philosophical principles and personal values which lay behind Scott's individual judgments. A sketch of Scott's judicial character is the elusive goal of Chapter 6.

Chapter 7 provides a brief coda to the book. In this chapter I have offered some testimony to the enormous influence Scott continued to have throughout the nineteenth century and at least up to the time of the First World War.

Some perceptive readers will be surprised at two specific aspects of Scott's work which I have omitted from this book. I have not discussed his role as one of the judges presiding over the trials of crimes committed on the high seas, the criminal sessions of admiralty, nor have I discussed Scott's decisions in the slave cases which happened to come before him. Both of these questions merit full discussion, and perhaps on some other occasion I will write an article on one or other topic. But either question would require extensive background discussion, since both belong properly, not to the history of the admiralty court, but to the history of criminal law or to the history of slave law respectively. This book deals with Scott's immensely significant role in the history of the admiralty court, not with the small part he played in the history of criminal law or slave law.

An extensive research project cannot be accomplished alone. Over the years during which I have done research and have written this book, I have received help and encouragement without which I could not have completed the project. In the first place, I am deeply grateful to the institutions which had enough confidence in this project to provide essential funds for travel and research. The American Council of Learned Societies, the American Bar Foundation, the American Philosophical Society and the University of Toledo have generously supported and made possible my research for this book.

I am likewise grateful to the quiet competence and willing but unobtrusive help of many librarians and archivists in Great Britain and the United States. Without the help of these professionals, who preserve and make accessible the past's written records, my research efforts would have failed to locate many valuable manuscripts, books and pamphlets. I especially want to thank Lt Col and Mrs H. E. Scott for allowing me to come into their home to study the letters and papers of Sir William Scott's brother, Lord Eldon. I owe a special debt of gratitude also to Mr J. Rochford, Registrar of the Admiralty, who generously made available for my research two important manuscript documents which are kept in his office. I would like to acknowledge permission from the Bodleian Library, Oxford, and from the Warden and Fellows of All Souls College, Oxford, to quote from manuscripts in their libraries.

I would like to express my thanks to my secretary, Mrs Lee Mayer, who typed and retyped most of the manuscript of this book. I have also been helped by a number of research assistants who have patiently performed many thankless chores I would not have had the patience to complete myself. My thanks to Charles Poplestein, Linda Burkholder, Marilyn Luipold, Marc C. Pawl, Angela Morin, Kathryn Mohr and Mark von Wahlde who have helped me continue and complete the project.

I owe a great debt to the legal historians and other legal scholars who have read and commented upon various chapters of this book. I am especially grateful to John W. Cairns, Ian Doolittle, Richard W. Edwards, Jr, James H. Kettner, Susan R. Martyn and Stephen Waddams who took the time to study different parts of this book. They have spotted errors I had overlooked and provided valuable suggestions and insights. Above all, I am indebted to D. E. C. Yale, the former editor of this series, for his help during my year of research in England and for his continued interest, perceptive criticism and consistent encouragement as he reviewed various chapters of the book. The errors and shortcomings which remain are all mine, but the book is certainly far better because of the generous help of these scholars in Great Britain and the United States.

ABBREVIATIONS

A.J.L.H.	*American Journal of Legal History*
Bl. *Comm.*	W. Blackstone, *Commentaries on the laws of England* (4 vols., Oxford, 1765–9). References are to 9th edition, London, 1783, which contains Blackstone's last alterations
Bod. Lib.	Bodleian Library, Oxford
Brit. Lib.	British Library, London
Cobbett	*Parliamentary history of England ... to ... 1803*, ed. W. Cobbett (36 vols., London, 1806–20)
D.N.B.	*Dictionary of National Biography*
Dod.	J. Dodson, *Reports of cases argued and determined in the High Court of Admiralty* (2 vols., London, 1815–28)
Edw.	T. Edwards, *Reports of cases determined in the High Court of Admiralty* (London, 1812)
E.H.R.	*English History Review*
Hag.	J. Haggard, *Reports of cases argued and determined in the High Court of Admiralty* (3 vols., London, 1825–40)
Hansard, 1st ser.	*Parliamentary debates ... 1803 to [1820]*, ed. T. C. Hansard (41 vols., London, 1812–20)
Hansard, 2nd ser.	*Parliamentary debates ... [1820–30]*, ed. T. C. Hansard (25 vols., London, 1820–30)
H.E.L.	W. Holdsworth, *A history of English law* (16 vols., London, 1922–66)
H.S.P.	Historical Society of Pennsylvania, Philadelphia

N.Y.H.S.	New York Historical Society
N.Y.P.L.	New York Public Library
P.R.O.	Public Record Office
R.A.	Office of Registrar of the Admiralty, Royal Courts of Justice, London
Rob.	C. Robinson, *Reports of cases argued and determined in the High Court of Admiralty* (6 vols., London, 1799–1808)
Seld. Soc.	Selden Society Publications

1

SURVEY OF ENGLISH ADMIRALTY
JURISDICTION: HOW DID IT VANISH?

If one were to reflect on the possible functions of a court with special expertise over maritime problems, one would probably surmise that such a court could be used in three broad areas: to settle the many and varied disputes which arose out of the commercial carriage of goods by sea; to reduce friction with foreign princes by adjudicating conflicts which grew out of the capture or plunder of the ships of other states especially in time of war; and to try, convict and sentence individuals for crimes committed aboard ships beyond the knowledge of any jury and outside the jurisdiction of any land-based court. We shall see that the English High Court of Admiralty had jurisdiction, differing in scope from time to time, in these three general areas. Its civil or instance jurisdiction, which ebbed and flowed with the royal favor and support, focused on the wide variety of disputes of the shipping industry, for example, cases involving chartering of vessels, contracts for carrying cargo, seamen's wages, collisions, supplies and repairs to vessels and disputes between part owners of vessels. Its prize jurisdiction concerned the legality of the capture of vessels and cargoes belonging to persons from other countries and the division of these spoils. Its criminal jurisdiction extended the king's peace to the high seas by punishing acts of piracy, homicides, assaults and other crimes committed on English ships at sea. Parliament could, of course, give the court other power, for example, hearing appeals from colonial vice-admiralty courts.

Long before there was an admiral or an admiral's court for the whole of England, local officials, known as keepers or wardens (*custos*), had discharged some of the duties later within the admiral's reach. In the twelfth century the Cinque Ports were organized and received special royal privileges. This confederation of ports provided the king with ships for service in the navy. By the fourteenth century the loose organization of these southeast fishing ports had already lost its *raison d'être* and its value to the king. Perhaps the Cinque Port system provided the model for the creation of other keepers appointed elsewhere in the thirteenth century. Before the creation of the office of one admiral for all England, admirals of the north, south and west were appointed with authority over the fleets and with functions similar to those of the keepers. These local coastal officials had responsibilities for preservation of peace at sea, for restricting piracy and capture of vessels belonging to foreigners and especially for the care for wrecks on the coast. In the sixteenth century vice-admirals, appointed for one or more counties, were expected to control pirates, impress seamen, enforce embargoes and inventory captured or wrecked ships. As late as the seventeenth century, some of these local officials obtained exemptions from the lord admiral's jurisdiction and were granted jurisdiction over such admiralty matters within their ports and coastal areas. These franchises, whether exempt from the admiral's power or as his subordinates, were viewed primarily as private sources of profit derived especially from wrecks. The local keepers or vice-admirals had strong incentives to connive with pirates and to engage in wrecking and pillage, whereas only a few inadequate means existed to rein in their greed. Where judicial authority was exercised by these vice-admirals or wardens, it appears that eventually a right of appeal to the High Court of Admiralty would lie. Compiled lists show that vice-admirals continued to exist in the eighteenth and even in the nineteenth centuries.[1]

The title admiral first appears in 1295, but the admiral's functions did not at first include the power to hear pleas and administer justice. These judicial roles are not mentioned till the mid-fourteenth century. Apparently the office of admiral was created largely in response to the complaints by foreign sovereigns about the piracies and spoils committed at sea and the frustrations of the injured parties when they sought justice in English courts. Prior to the creation of an admiralty court, matters such as piracy, spoil of wreck, capture of royal fish or obstruction of rivers were dealt with by a confusing array of tribunals: by the common law courts, or by the Chancellor or the King's Council, or by arbitration. Common law juries often showed local prejudice in favor of the native parties, even if the accused happened to be a pirate. The admiral probably did not receive authority to hold

---

[1] R. G. Marsden, 'The vice-admirals of the coast', *E.H.R.*, 22 and 23 (1907, 1908), 468–75, 736–57; 6 Wm IV c. 76; K. M. E. Murray, *The constitutional history of the Cinque Ports* (Manchester, 1935), 1–8, 205–30.

an independent court until after 1340. Prior to that time several English kings had claimed sovereignty of the sea, but had been unable to end the stream of complaints against English seamen for committing acts of piracy. Attempts at arbitration of claims made by the French, the Flemish and others had apparently not solved the problem. Edward III, therefore, extended the power of the admiral, which previously had been mainly disciplinary and administrative, so that the admiral could act in a judicial capacity and provide justice in piracy and other maritime cases. But even in the fifteenth century the English Crown had to confront the disastrous international consequences of lawless acts of piracy committed by English subjects.[2]

By 1360 the admiral's jurisdiction clearly included the power to hold pleas. Previously there had been several admirals, with disciplinary power for a particular expedition or a particular part of the fleet. In 1360 the entire fleet was entrusted to one admiral, whose patent contained a broad and ill-defined grant of maritime jurisdiction, with full power

of hearing plaints of all and singular the matters that touch the office of the admiral and of taking cognisance of maritime causes and of doing justice and of correcting and punishing offences and of imprisoning [offenders] and of setting at liberty prisoners who ought to be set at liberty and of doing all other things that appertain to the office of admiral as they ought to be done of right and according to the maritime law.[3]

The admiral also had authority to appoint a deputy, probably a judge for the newly created court.

A new court obviously needed some rules to guide its procedures and decisions. Apparently not long after the admiralty court began functioning, some individuals interested in the work of the court, perhaps officials of the court, began compiling materials which eventually became the *Black book of the admiralty*. The *Black book*, which in its final form dates from the fifteenth century, contained administrative regulations for the admiral and the fleet. It also gathered together whatever rules could be found for practice before the court, with clear influence from continental civil law practice. The *Black book* likewise contained earlier compilations of maritime law

---

[2] *Select pleas in the court of admiralty*, ed. R. G. Marsden (2 vols., London, 1892, 1897) (Seld. Soc., vols. 6 and 11), I, xi–xl; S. P. Pistono, 'Henry IV and the English Privateers', *E.H.R.*, 90 (1975), 322–30.

[3] *Select pleas*, I, xlii–xliii.

used in the ports of Europe and England. The Laws of Oleron, dating from the early thirteenth century and incorporated into the *Black book*, provided rules concerning the powers and liabilities of the master of a ship, the rights and responsibilities of the mariners, the rights and duties of shippers of cargo, charterers and owners of ships and pilots, and the liabilities in case of damage to cargo or collision. The Laws of Oleron had to be supplemented as maritime commerce expanded and these additional articles were also included in the *Black book*. The *Black book* provides convincing evidence that those involved with the admiralty court soon recognized the need to settle the uncertainty about questions of law and practice in a new court.[4]

It is not surprising that the procedures of the admiralty court, especially the lack of jury trial, should arouse some opposition. In 1371 Parliament received a petition complaining of the decay of the navy and of various grievances of mariners and merchants. Probably the petitioners had the admiralty court in mind when they objected that various people had been made to answer charges otherwise than upon the presentment of a jury according to the common law. The inquisition of Queenborough of 1375, which is included in the *Black book*, appears to have been an attempt to determine the maritime law to be administered in the admiralty court, perhaps in response to the complaints in the petition of 1371. Eventually Parliament acted in 1389 and again in 1391 to restrict and define the jurisdiction of the court of admiralty. The first statute provided that 'the admirals and their deputies shall not meddle from henceforth of any thing done within the realm, but only of a thing done upon the Sea', and the second was even more specific in insisting that 'of all manner of contracts, pleas, and quarrels, and all other things rising within the bodies of the countries, as well by land as by water, and also of wreck of the sea, the admiral's court shall have no manner of cognizance, power, nor jurisdiction'.[5] These two statutes must not have accomplished their purposes since in 1400 Parliament imposed a penalty, a right of action for double damages, against anyone who brought suit in the admiralty court in violation of the statutes of Richard II.[6]

Throughout the years of struggle and conflict of the fifteenth

---

[4] *Ibid.*, xliii–xliv; *Black book of the admiralty*, ed. T. Twiss (4 vols., London, 1871–6), I, xli–lxxi, 1–220; *H.E.L.*, 5, 120–7; T. J. Runyan, 'The Rolls of Oleran and the admiralty court in fourteenth century England', *A.J.L.H.*, 19 (1975), 95.

[5] 13 Rich. II c. 5; 15 Rich. II c. 3; *Select pleas*, I, xlvii–li.

[6] 2 Hen. IV c. 11.

century, the admiralty court remained weak and ineffective. It failed to accomplish its main purpose, reducing the conflict with foreign princes concerning piracy and spoil cases. With the accession of Henry VIII, and the expansion of foreign trade and heightened interest in exploration of the sixteenth century, the admiralty court played a larger role in determining maritime disputes. The records of the admiralty court begin in the 1520s, an indication of the new life breathed into the court by Henry VIII's interest. These early records suggest that the court's business was steadily increasing during the decades after 1520. It was not until the middle of the seventeenth century that the prize records were kept separate from the court's instance or civil records.[7]

Henry VIII intended to expand the jurisdiction of the admiralty court even beyond the limits expressed in the statutes of Richard II. After these statutes were passed, it had been the practice to include in the admiral's patent a clause expressly limiting his authority according to the terms of the statutes. Henry VIII's patents, however, contain a *non obstante* clause which was intended to override the effect of the statutes of Richard II: 'any statutes, acts, ordinances, or restrictions to the contrary passed, promulgated, ordained, or provided notwithstanding'. Other provisions in these patents likewise made clear the purpose of enhancing the jurisdiction of the admiral and his court. The patent of 1525, for instance, granted Henry VIII's son Henry, Duke of Richmond and Somerset, as admiral the power

of hearing and terminating plaints of all contracts between the owners and proprietors of ships and merchants or between any other vessels concerning anything to be done on the sea or beyond sea, and of all and singular contracts to be performed beyond sea, contracted beyond sea, and also in England, and of all other things that concern the office of the admiral.[8]

The vast reach of power bestowed by these patents will become more apparent when considered in light of the controversies of the seventeenth century over the proper limits to admiralty jurisdiction.

The seventeenth-century furor concerning the admiralty court's jurisdiction cannot be appreciated without a fairly full grasp of the court's power under the Tudors. As already indicated, the court's work touched three different areas: the civil or instance jurisdiction, criminal jurisdiction and prize cases. The instance jurisdiction, so-called because the suit was initiated at the instance of the private

[7] *Select pleas*, I, lvi, lx–lxiii.
[8] *Ibid.*, lvi–lix.

party, not, as in criminal cases, by the government, dealt with a broad range of mercantile, shipping and commercial matters. The court apparently had exercised jurisdiction over commercial cases since the end of the fourteenth century. Henry VIII understood that the heart of maritime commerce, the carriage of goods by sea, required expeditious determination in the admiralty court of the disputes between shippers and carriers over the damage to cargo or the delay of shipping.[9] During these years of wine and roses for the admiralty court under the encouraging eye of the Tudors, the court dealt with every phase of the shipping business: contracts entered into abroad, bills of exchange, commercial agencies abroad, charter parties, insurance, average, freight, cargo damage or delay, negligence by the master, crew or pilots in navigation and breach of the warranty of seaworthiness. Collision cases were rare, but not because the court's jurisdiction over them was doubted. Not until the next century did the court clearly take jurisdiction of salvage cases, since questions of wreck were within the authority of the vice-admirals of the coast and their chief source of profit. The vice-admirals were expected to take possession of and to preserve shipwrecked goods; the salvage which the owners might pay to recover the goods was a perquisite of the admiral or vice-admiral.[10] Even without undisputed jurisdiction over salvage cases, the admiralty court during the Tudor years had wide-ranging authority over the most lucrative aspects of the shipping business, a fact which had not escaped the notice of the common lawyers.

Practice before the admiralty court was monopolized by a small group of lawyers trained in the civil law, the civilian advocates, whose university training and professional association, Doctors' Commons,

[9] 32 Hen. VIII c. 14, s. 10. Perhaps the term instance was not used until the seventeenth century. In a draft 'Digest of the law of the British courts of admiralty', written in the early nineteenth century by Alexander Croke, a civilian and judge of the Nova Scotia vice-admiralty court, the compiler gave the following impression, apparently derived from the lore of Doctors' Commons, of the source of the name of the Instance Court: 'Of the Instance Court – This is so called because suits are commenced at the instance of a private party in contradistinction from the criminal jurisdiction. Where the King or the Lord Admiral are the prosecutors ex officio[.] [A]s in the Ecclesiastical Courts causes are either *instantiae* or *ex officio*. It is therefore, properly the *civil* court in opposition to the *criminal* court but the name is extended to all proceedings in the proper, original court of admiralty in contradistinction from the prize court, which depends upon a special and distinct commission. – In the ecclesiastical courts causes are said to be in *prima instantia*, in distinction from *appeals*.' Bod. Lib. MSS Add. C. 156. Italics in the original.
[10] *Select pleas*, I, lxvii–lxx; II, xix–xxxix.

will be considered later. Proctors, generally comparable to solicitors, represented clients in maritime cases, but not in court. The practitioners in the common law courts obviously resented their exclusion from the growing number of maritime cases. The arguments of each side concerning the scope of admiralty jurisdiction will be summarized below, since they reached their high point of intensity later during the seventeenth century. The reality of the dispute, however, centered more on grasping a share of the lucrative maritime practice than on subtle jurisdictional boundaries.

Long before Lord Coke led the attack against the admiralty court's instance jurisdiction the common law courts had interfered with the admiralty court's exercise of its jurisdiction. The earliest attempts to question or curtail admiralty jurisdiction were by way of *supersedeas* and *certiorari*, issuing from Chancery. When it became obvious that resort to the Chancery usually failed to achieve the purpose of limiting the admiralty jurisdiction, common lawyers looked to the common law courts to issue writs of prohibition forbidding the admiralty judge and parties to proceed in a particular case on the ground that the matter was beyond the admiralty court's jurisdiction. The civilians, of course, opposed this power of the common law courts to issue prohibitions. They contended that where the civil law, that is the law merchant or law maritime, applied, the admiralty court had exclusive jurisdiction. The prohibitions often cited the statutes of Richard II as a basis for preventing suits from being heard in the admiralty court where the matter in issue was not 'done upon the Sea'. Many of these prohibitions were issued in cases where a contract had allegedly been entered into in London or in one of the counties. As one might surmise, most maritime contracts were entered into on dry land, not at sea. By the beginning of the reign of James I, prohibitions were issued concerning almost every subject of which the admiralty court claimed jurisdiction, including collision on a river, piracy, bottomry bonds, wreck, ownership of a vessel and even prize.[11]

The second area over which the admiralty court exercised jurisdiction, crimes committed on the high seas, attracted parliamentary attention during the reign of Henry VIII and was molded by the acts of 1535 and 1536 into the general form it would retain for the next three centuries. The admiralty court earlier had tried individuals for crimes committed at sea. The statute of Richard II of 1391 confirmed

---

[11] *Ibid.*, II, xli–lvii; J. H. Baker, *The reports of Sir John Spelman* (2 vols., London, 1976, 1978) (Seld. Soc., vols. 93 and 94), II, 73, 75.

and defined the landward limits of this criminal jurisdiction. The admiral's court, under that act, had cognizance 'of the death of a man, and of a maihem done in great ships, being and hovering in the main stream of great rivers, only beneath the bridges of the same rivers nigh to the sea, and in none other places of the same rivers'.[12] Most likely the admiralty court employed civil law procedure and tried accused parties without a common law jury. The petition of 1371, mentioned above, had complained to Parliament that the court made parties answer charges without presentment of a jury, apparently referring to a grand jury. The preamble to the acts of 1535 and 1536, to be discussed immediately, implied that the admiralty court did not use a trial jury in criminal cases. It seems strange, therefore, that the *Black book* speaks in a number of places of conviction by twelve men, as though a common law jury were employed at least in some criminal trials in the admiralty court.[13] The act of 1536, whether accurately reflecting actual practice in the admiralty court or not, recited that persons who committed crimes at sea often escaped punishment because the trial before the admiralty judge was 'after the course of the civil laws, the nature whereof is that before any judgment of death can be given against the offenders, either they must plainly confess their offences (which they will never do without torture or pains), or else their offences be so plainly and directly proved by witnesses indifferent, such as saw their offences committed', which witnesses, the act stated, seldom survived to tell tales of the criminal acts since pirates were shrewd enough to kill all on-lookers. Parliament, therefore, enacted that 'all treasons felonies robberies murders and confederacies hereafter to be committed upon the sea, or in any other haven, river creek or place where the admiral or admirals have ... jurisdiction, shall be enquired, tried ... and judged ... as if [they] had been committed in or upon the land'. The trial, following the course of the common law, must be before the admiral or his deputy, the admiralty judge, and three or four other substantial persons appointed by the Lord Chancellor in a commission under the Great Seal. The act denied the benefit of clergy.[14] Further research would be necessary to determine whether the act correctly described the mode of criminal trial prior to the enactment. The suggestion of the use of torture,

[12] 15 Rich. II c. 3.
[13] This point was made by J. F. Stephen, *A history of the criminal law of England* (3 vols., London, 1883), II, 17.
[14] 27 Hen. VIII c. 4; 28 Hen. VIII c. 15.

though consonant with the practice of the civil law on the continent, calls for some verification from the records beyond this act, verification which has thus far not been produced.[15] As a result of this act, crimes committed at sea were thereafter tried, according to the rules of the common law, with a jury and before a special commission which included the admiralty judge and a common law judge. Some uniquely maritime flavor remained in these admiralty sessions, as, for instance, the occasional trial for piracy. The statutes of Henry VIII, however, make it necessary to view the criminal law of the admiralty court as a phase of the criminal law of England, rather than as a phase of the admiralty law.

The third area of jurisdiction of the admiralty court, prize jurisdiction, originated in the disciplinary power over seamen granted to the admirals by their fourteenth-century patents. This power was intended primarily to rid the coasts of pirates. Although there was a Royal Navy of sorts even earlier, for many centuries the king's power at sea depended much more upon privately armed vessels, the owners and crews of which sought primarily personal gain from making captures. These sea rovers, or privateers as they came to be called in the seventeenth century, cared little about legal subtleties; they were in fact barely distinguishable from pirates. It appears that by the fifteenth century it was customary for these private ships to keep the entire profit from their captures. If a capture was made by a naval vessel, the admiral and the king received a share of the prize. By the sixteenth century the admiral enjoyed a share of all captures taken by any ships under his command, probably representing the king's share of earlier days. Well into the sixteenth century the main function of the admiralty court was to assure that the admiral and the king received their proper share of the booty rather than to adjudicate nice questions of legality of the captures. Formal condemnation of prizes often was ignored before the sixteenth century; captors merely kept their prizes unless the owner complained to the king. Not until 1589 did the Privy Council order that all prizes captured be brought in for adjudication in the admiralty court.[16]

The king, thus, had conflicting interests to balance: his need to enhance the strength of his naval forces by using private ships and his

---

[15] J. H. Langbein, *Torture and the law of proof* (Chicago, 1976), 131, 188.

[16] R. G. Marsden, 'Early prize jurisdiction and prize law in England', *E.H.R.*, 24 (1909), 675–80; *Select pleas*, I, xl–xlii; E. S. Roscoe, *A history of the English prize court* (London, 1924), 1–11.

or his admiral's desire for a share of the property captured, and on the
other hand, his desire to avoid conflicts with foreign princes over the
lawless capture by Englishmen of property belonging to foreign
subjects. The earliest recorded judicial proceedings before the
admiral (1357) dealt with a dispute over a capture by an Englishman
of Portuguese goods from a French ship. Such questions of the
legality of the capture of foreign goods or vessels involved questions of
state. In spite of this early indication that the admiralty court acted as
a prize tribunal, for two centuries many such questions came before
the Council or the Chancellor or commissioners appointed *ad hoc*, if
they were adjudicated at all. In many cases which did come before the
admiralty court, the Lord High Admiral, a member of the Privy
Council, transmitted to the admiralty judge the petitions presented to
him or to the Privy Council by the foreign party who complained of
piratical attacks by English ships. The petitioning party in these spoil
or depredation suits was the injured foreign party and the captor was
the defendant; this distinguishes these cases from the later prize cases
for which the procedures were not settled until the seventeenth
century. Sometimes the judge received general instructions to do
justice in the case, but at other times the admiral or the Council
directed how the case should be dealt with. Since questions of state lay
behind these disputes, it is not surprising that the admiralty judge
frequently had little opportunity for exercising any discretion in
deciding the case.[17]

Under Elizabeth I plunder at sea became a major patriotic fascina-
tion and a significant aspect of foreign policy. These sea rovers, who
preyed especially upon Spanish shipping, generally carried letters of
reprisal to ward off the charge of piracy. Letters of reprisal, a self-help
remedy for merchants injured by foreign parties, were issued by the
High Court of Admiralty in time of peace to allow the bearer to seize
property belonging to subjects of a certain state in recompense for
alleged injuries suffered by the bearer at the hands of that state.
Reprisals at sea, with or without legal authority, had been common for
centuries. The admiralty court records for the late sixteenth century
included many *ex parte* proceedings called 'querelae' which founded a
claim for letters of reprisal. The injured party, with supporting
depositions, filed a pleading in the admiralty court alleging the loss
and requesting a letter of reprisal. The court promulgated a decree

[17] *Select pleas*, I, lxv–lxvi.

stating the amount of the losses sustained and licencing the injured party to recoup his losses by force from any property belonging to individuals of the state causing the alleged injury. But proof of loss in many cases became a legal fiction; letters of reprisal were bought and sold and local admiralty officials traded these commissions in exchange for a share in the venture. The line distinguishing sea rovers from pirates was often as thin as these questionable letters of reprisal.[18]

During the Tudor period some efforts were gradually made to control the lawlessness of sea rovers. Henry VIII, by his proclamation of 1543, seemed primarily interested in encouraging private parties to arm their vessels and capture French and Scottish property. He explicitly allowed the captors to enjoy the profit of all booty. There was no suggestion that the captors had to bring the prizes to the admiralty court for adjudication. The first surviving instructions for privateers (1585), while imposing some restrictions on their behavior, did not provide for adjudication of captures. The recognizance bond for good behavior of privateers, also dating from 1585, required that the captured Spanish property must be brought to some English port before breaking bulk. The prize property was to be inventoried and appraised and the inventory and appraisal returned to the admiralty court. The instructions and recognizance showed that the chief concern was that the admiral received his tenth. Although the recognizance forbade the privateer to attack any English or friendly vessels, it did not require the captors to bring the prize before the admiralty court to determine the captor's compliance with these terms. Finally in 1589 by Order in Council, captors were directed to keep all prizes safe and not sell, spoil, waste or diminish any part 'till judgment has been first passed in the High Court of Admiralty that the said goods are a lawful prize'. After this Order, prize sentences, usually on paper not parchment, occur frequently in the admiralty court records. Not until the middle of the seventeenth century were the prize records separated from the instance records. In 1665 an Order in Council provided the basic rules for the admiralty court in the adjudication of prizes.[19]

[18] *Ibid.*, lxvi–lxviii; R. Andrews, *Elizabethan privateering* (Cambridge, 1964), 3–31; *English privateering voyages to the West Indies, 1588–1595*, ed. R. Andrews (Cambridge, 1959), 2–12, 16–28.

[19] *Documents relating to law and custom of the sea*, ed. R. G. Marsden (2 vols., n.p., 1915), I, 155–8, 236–7, 243–5, 252; II, 53–7; *Select pleas*, II, xvii; R. G. Marsden, 'Prize Law in England', *E.H.R.*, 24 (1909), 681–90.

The procedure and practice of the admiralty court in the sixteenth century has not been studied in appropriate detail. We do know that the central feature of admiralty practice was the arrest of the person of the defendant or of his goods as security to assure that the judgment could be paid. The ship of the defendant or, just as frequently, some other goods belonging to defendant were arrested at the commencement of the suit. Apparently it made no difference whether the property arrested was the subject matter of the suit or not, as long as it belonged to the defendant and was within the admiral's jurisdiction. The defendant could secure the release of the ship or other property arrested by giving bail to satisfy the judgment, but if he failed to do so, the judgment, if against the defendant, proceeded against him as well as against his property arrested. The many forms of contract used by shippers and ship owners, for example, charter parties, bills of lading and bottomry bonds, frequently contained a clause explicitly binding the ship for the performance of the contract. In other cases the parties bound themselves with sureties for the performance of the contract. In any case, if the contract was breached, the ship or other goods of the defendant could be arrested, that is, placed in the custody of the court. This reliance upon arrest of goods or upon the bail put up in place of the arrested goods provided the admiralty court with the assurance that its judgments would not be ignored, comparable to the sequestration power of Chancery.[20]

Before discussing the century of warfare between the civil lawyers and the common lawyers over the proper boundary of admiralty jurisdiction, a brief description of the civilians and their professional association will identify the less known of the combatants. The law in the admiralty court and in the ecclesiastical courts was based on the civil law and the canon law with strong influence from the Roman law tradition. Those who practiced in these courts were trained in the civil and canon law, the more proficient of whom had the degree of doctor in the civil law from one of the universities. These doctors of civil law, at the end of the fifteenth century, formed a professional association called Doctors' Commons, which was a society for the mutual benefit of the members and provided a place for lodging and eating and a library near St Paul's in London. Although there was an important educational value in the close association of a small group of individuals with the same professional interests and background, Doctors'

---

[20] *Select pleas*, II, lxxi–lxxii.

Commons was not intended as an educational institution comparable to the Inns of Court. The members had studied civil law at a university prior to admission to Doctors' Commons. At first some members of Doctors' Commons did not have a doctoral degree and some were trained in foreign universities. Some were clerics and some laymen, some were proctors and some advocates. By 1600 all members of Doctors' Commons were laymen, professional lawyers, and all were trained at Oxford or Cambridge and had received doctoral degrees there. The line between the functions of proctors and advocates apparently was clearly drawn sometime during the seventeenth century, and thereafter only advocates were members of Doctors' Commons, that is, only those who argued in the courts. Proctors who were not doctors in civil law continued to function in the same ecclesiastical or admiralty courts in a role, as it was finally defined, comparable to attorneys or solicitors. After the doctors were admitted as advocates in the Court of Arches, they had to maintain a year of silence during which they could not practice before the court. Obviously civilians needed families who could support them through their years of university study and during the required year of silence. Doctors' Commons was really a club of civilians, restricted to a small clique of practitioners and judges, a dozen or so at any one time, who could discuss their common problems and promote their professional learning and opportunities.[21]

By the end of the sixteenth century the civilians had become closely associated with the Crown and the Anglican Church. Being a member of the court party had advantages as long as the monarch was strong and could rule effectively; such a close association with the government was less desirable as the debates of the seventeenth century questioned precisely where sovereignty reposed in the state. Most of the courts before which the civilians practiced did not provide ample or lucrative opportunities. A list of the types of courts they appeared in, along with the other offices they filled, shows convincingly how dependent they were on the patronage of the king, the Chancellor, the admiral and the bishops. They practiced in the admiralty court, the prerogative court, the Court of Arches, the consistory courts of dioceses, the Court of Chivalry and they held a variety of offices such as diplomats, privy councillors, king's advocates, members of High Court of Delegates, chancellors of dioceses, commissaries of bishops,

[21] G. D. Squibb, *Doctors' Commons* (Oxford, 1977), 3–42. This excellent book gives a much fuller picture of Doctors' Commons.

officials of archdeacons, registrars of courts, as well as academic positions at the universities, ecclesiastical positions, deans, rectors, vicars, archdeacons and bishops. Since the practice before the ecclesiastical courts provided limited opportunities, the civilians usually accepted at least one legal, academic or ecclesiastical position to supplement their practice. When civilians became members of Parliament, they supported the interests of the king, the government and the Church. They became exponents of royalist politics, wrote political treatises and tracts, gave lectures and sermons, often upholding a broad concept of absolute royal sovereignty. Furthermore, they were viewed as custodians of religious orthodoxy, upholders of the established Church. The episcopacy controlled a majority of the positions where the civilians served, and, more important, these ecclesiastical positions provided the stepping stones to non-ecclesiastical positions in the king's service. As the crises of the seventeenth century engulfed them, as they were buffeted by the prohibitions of the common lawyers and the anathemas of the Puritans, the civilians became even more dependent on the monarch and the Church for survival.[22]

Long before James VI of Scotland ascended the English throne and before Sir Edward Coke became Chief Justice of Common Pleas, prohibitions issued by the common law courts had become a major source of controversy between the common lawyers and the civilians. Prohibitions not only called in question the most important areas of admiralty jurisdiction, they also curtailed the civilians' practice in the church courts.[23] By the reign of Elizabeth I, the tension created by these jurisdictional conflicts had become severe enough to call for an attempted settlement of admiralty jurisdiction at a conference with the common law judges before the Privy Council. The conciliar arbitration of 1575 proved to be only a temporary settlement, more properly viewed as evidence of the symptoms than a cure of the illness. The admiralty judge Dr David Lewis complained first that the finality of admiralty court judgments had been destroyed by prohibitions granted long after judgment or after sentence on appeal to the Court of Delegates, even at the request of the party who had originally

[22] B. P. Levack, *The civil lawyers in England, 1603–1641, a political study* (Oxford, 1973), 16–178. The brief summary in the text does not do justice to the full and complex argument of this book.
[23] Baker, *Sir John Spelman*, II, 66–8, 240–2; *St. German's doctor and student*, eds. T. F. T. Plucknett and J. L. Barton (Seld. Soc., London, 1974, vol. 65), 232–3, 312–13.

invoked admiralty jurisdiction. It was agreed that no prohibition should be granted after sentence in the Court of Delegates and only if requested during the term following sentence in the admiralty court. This pledge touched a problem that remained unsettled long after the common lawyers had conveniently forgotten the agreement of 1575: whichever party lost in an admiralty suit had everything to gain by turning to Westminster Hall for a prohibition. By this collateral attack on the admiralty jurisdiction, he could effectively overturn the unfavorable admiralty judgment and hope for a more acceptable result if the case were ever tried at common law. The admiralty judge in 1575 also complained of the *ex parte* nature, without proof, of the petitions for prohibitions. It was agreed that prohibitions not be granted *ex parte*, that the admiralty judge and the opposing party be allowed to have counsel to oppose the grant of the prohibition. It was also agreed that the admiralty court had jurisdiction of all contracts arising beyond or upon the seas and jurisdiction for breach of charter parties for all overseas voyages, even though the charter party had been entered into in England. These two provisions of the settlement at least acknowledged the admiralty court's concurrent jurisdiction of a substantial amount of the contract cases dealing with maritime affairs. They did not cover contracts for supplies or repairs entered into in England, but would have assured the admiralty court of ample jurisdiction over maritime contracts if the common law courts had complied with the agreement. Finally, the admiralty judge objected to the use of *habeas corpus* to deliver those in custody at the command of the admiralty court. It was agreed that the common law courts would return the person to confinement in the admiral's jail upon a certificate of the cause of confinement.[24]

The limited victory for the admiralty court of the settlement of 1575 failed to protect the admiralty court from the prohibitions of the common law courts. At first, apparently, the common law courts merely had challenged admiralty jurisdiction where the suit concerned something that had occurred within the body of one of the counties, whether on a river or on land, such as the signing of a charter party in London. The common law courts could justify their own jurisdiction over such cases. By the seventeenth century, however, the common law courts had prohibited the admiralty court's jurisdiction over contracts entered into abroad. By using the nontraversable

[24] The 1575 settlement is reproduced in R. Zouch, *The jurisdiction of the admiralty of England* (London, 1663), 120–3.

fiction that these contracts had been entered into in Cheapside or in Middlesex, the common law courts sought to capture a larger share of the growing commercial business of the admiralty court. The Court of Common Pleas, by Hobart, C.J., surely no friend of the admiralty court, held that

[T]he Admiralty of England can hold no plea of any contract, but such as riseth upon the sea: no, though it rise upon any continent, port, or haven in the world, out of the King's dominions, for their jurisdiction is limited by the statutes to the seas only; for the admiral is for the sea, and the Court for maritime causes.[25]

Even where a contract was entered into at sea, the common law court held that suit in admiralty could be prohibited where the contract had been put in writing and sealed on land abroad. '[E]very libel in the Admiralty doth, and must lay the cause of suit super altum mare.'[26] The common law courts insisted on the precise language of the statutes of Richard II making admiralty jurisdiction turn solely on the place, on the high seas, and not on the nature of the subject matter, for example, a contract for furnishing, supplying or chartering a ship. As Coke had stated, '[B]elow the low water mark the Admiral has the sole and absolute jurisdiction.'[27] Admiralty jurisdiction depended solely on the test of location. A prohibition could lie whenever the admiralty court was called upon to enforce a contract entered into on land, whether in England or abroad, or which could be performed on land.[28]

In 1611 once again the Privy Council became involved in trying to settle the jurisdictional conflicts between the common law courts and the admiralty court. Lord Chancellor Ellesmere prepared a tract on prohibitions, largely concerned with prohibitions in ecclesiastical cases, an issue then more vehemently debated. The tract also included a brief discussion of Ellesmere's views on prohibitions in admiralty cases. He objected especially to the grant of prohibitions upon the mere suggestion of the party that the action had taken place on land

---

[25] *Don Diego Serviento de Acuna, Ambassador of Spain v. Bingley* (n.d.), 1 Hobart 78; the authority of this case was rejected at least for ancillary jurisdiction in a prize case, in *Radley v. Egglesfield* (1671), 2 Wm Saund. 259, by Hale, C.J. In *Susans v. Turner* (1597), Noy 67, the court authorized prohibitions against suits in admiralty upon the surmise that the contract had been entered into on the land in England.

[26] *Palmer v. Pope* (1611), 1 Hobart 212.

[27] *Constable's Case* (1601), 5 Co. Rep. 106.

[28] D. E. C. Yale, 'A view of the admiral jurisdiction: Sir Matthew Hale and the civilians', *Legal Hist. Studies* (1972). This precise and penetrating article has been helpful throughout the remainder of this chapter.

within the jurisdiction of the common law court. He thought that the petitioner should have to make such a suggestion on oath or else enter into a bond to prove the truth of the suggestion. He criticized the use of actions on the case founded on a false allegation of a trover, 'Supposing in some Cases, that some Goods or Marchandizes, that indeed neuer were in England; and in some Cases, that a Shipp itselfe was lost in Cheapside in London, or in some other place in Middlesex, and there found by the Defendant, and converted to his use.'[29] This practice of fictions not only injured the admiralty court, but also wounded the basic premise of the common law courts, that everything ought to be tried in its own proper county.

The conciliar arbitration of 1611 has been clouded by the report of the objections raised by the civilians in Coke's *Fourth institutes*.[30] It seems probable that some settlement similar to the one in 1575 was reached, but Coke denies that the judges of the common law courts ever agreed to any settlement in 1575 and his version of the 1611 meeting amounts to a point by point rebuttal of the objections raised by the civilians. Coke's replies to the civilian's objections, though undoubtedly tendentious, became the classic statement of the view of the common lawyers in their opposition to admiralty jurisdiction. Coke, who came to be viewed as an oracle of the common law, struck for the jugular in making his arguments against the jurisdiction of the admiralty court. The admiralty court, he acknowledged, could hear cases of contracts made upon the sea which is not within any county (thereby eliminating bays and rivers). Prohibitions had never been granted in such cases of contracts concerning maritime matters 'made or done upon the sea, taking that only to be the sea wherein the admirall hath jurisdiction, which is before by law described to be out of any county'. Contracts made beyond the sea, in some foreign country, were outside of the admiralty jurisdiction. He asserted, without foundation, that such contract suits could be tried by the constable and marshal. Furthermore, the admiralty court, according to Coke, was not a court of record and so could not take any

---

[29] 'Some notes, and remembrances, concerning prohibitions for staying of suites in the Ecclesiasticall Courts, and in the Courts of the Admiraltie' (1611), in *Law and politics in Jacobean England: the tracts of Lord Chancellor Ellesmere*, ed. L. A. Knafla (Cambridge, 1977), 293–4.

[30] E. Coke, *The fourth part of the institutes of the laws of England*, first published posthumously in 1641. The edition of 1797 is used here, 134–47. J. Godolphin, in *A view of the admiral iurisdiction* (London, 1661), 155–6, seems unsure of the terms of the 1611 settlement.

recognizance.[31] Since the admiralty practice depended completely on its use of stipulations for appearance of parties and for performance of judgments, Coke's argument would have crippled its entire operation. Charter parties, Coke continued, entered into within any county, even though to be performed on the seas or beyond the seas, must be determined in the common law courts, not in the admiralty court. The *non obstante* clauses in the admiral's patents under the Tudors used to override the effect of the statutes of Richard II were invalid and could not dispense with the statutes. Coke further insisted that the admiralty jurisdiction over actions done on the rivers near the sea applied only to those criminal acts mentioned in the statutes of Richard II (homicide and mayhem), and not to any civil actions, contracts, collisions, and so forth, which took place on the rivers. Anything done within the rivers, creeks and havens was within a county and thus triable at common law. After thus maiming the civilians, Coke concluded the section by pouring salt in the wound. The civilians' proper sphere ('naturall jurisdiction') consisted of cases of capture in time of war. The civilians, Coke taunted,

wanting in this blessed time of peace causes appertaining to their naturall jurisdiction, they now incroach upon the jurisdiction of the common-law, lest they should sit idle and reap no profit. And if a greater number of prohibitions (as they affirm) hath been granted since the great benefit of this happy peace, then before in time of hostility, it moveth from their own incroachments upon the jurisdiction of the common law.[32]

Coke undoubtedly touched the raw nerve when he hinted that the entire dispute concerned who should have the profits from commercial maritime litigation. Coke accurately described the civilians' financial dependence on this litigation but perhaps mistook the aggressors in the dispute.

The civilians, with their narrow sphere of practice, desperately

---

[31] See S. E. Thorne, 'Courts of record and Sir Edward Coke', *University of Toronto Law Journal*, 2 (1937), 24, for a thorough discussion of Coke's arguments concerning courts of record in a broader context than his debates concerning admiralty jurisdiction. Thorne questions the historical accuracy of Coke's view that only courts of record could fine and imprison. Many courts, including admiralty, did not have formal Latin records enrolled on parchment in accordance with the common law custom, yet they habitually exercised the power to fine or imprison. Coke, in his arguments against admiralty jurisdiction in the *Fourth institutes* added a third disability to courts not of record, not only did they lack the power to fine and imprison, they could not take recognizances.

[32] Coke, *Fourth institutes*, 136.

needed these commercial suits which they saw the common lawyers snatching from their grasp. The common lawyers, we now realize, commanded the stronger ground and captured as much of the territory as they wanted. The sad thing, looking back, is that the admiralty court, which in so many ways was better equipped to accommodate the growing commerce of the day, left the field crippled and in many ways useless to handle most commercial suits. How easy it would have been to allow common lawyers to practice alongside the civilians in the admiralty court, thereby ending the war of jurisdiction in which the real losers were the merchants. Conflicts of jurisdiction invariably increase the cost, delay the final determination and magnify the uncertainty for the clients. Opening the doors of the admiralty court to the common lawyers would have made it possible for the admiralty court to continue developing its expertise in determining maritime commercial suits without the debilitating interference from the common law courts.[33]

A final attempt at establishing admiralty jurisdiction on a firm basis was made under Charles I in 1633. The common law judges agreed that prohibitions should not be issued to prevent suits in admiralty involving the following subject matter: (1) contracts entered into or other acts done by persons beyond or on the sea; (2) freight, mariners' wages or breach of charter parties for overseas voyages (even though the charter party had been entered into within England); or (3) contracts for building, repairing, fitting out or salving vessels, provided the suit was *in rem* against the ship. Suits, on the other hand, to determine whether a charter party had been entered into or whether there had been a discharge or release were to be tried only in the common law courts. The admiralty court was also acknowledged to have concurrent jurisdiction of suits involving obstructions or nuisances in navigable rivers and contracts or torts done on these rivers if there was some connection with maritime navigation. Finally, the common law judges agreed not to use the writ of *habeas corpus* to release prisoners of the admiralty court if the cause of imprisonment were certified to be within the admiralty court's jurisdiction as defined

---

[33] The Court of Chancery survived intact from the challenges by the common law courts under the leadership of Coke, perhaps in part because common lawyers practiced in Chancery and served as Chancellors. See *Law and politics*, 155–81; J. H. Baker, *An introduction to English legal history* (London, 1979), 92–3. By the eighteenth century litigants in prize appeals before the Lords Commissioners for Prize Appeals were usually represented by a barrister and a civilian advocate. P.R.O. HCA 45 *passim*.

in the agreement.[34] This agreement went far to reduce for a time the friction between the courts, but certainly did not confirm the wide-ranging jurisdiction the admiralty court had tasted under the Tudors.

It appears that many of the merchants appreciated the advantages of trying their maritime disputes according to the civil law in the court of admiralty.[35] But even a merchant convinced of the merits of the admiralty court might be inclined to retain counsel to seek a prohibition at common law when he had already lost his suit in the admiralty court or had an indefensible position to maintain there. The decline of the instance jurisdiction of the admiralty court does not seem to have been caused by a change in the commercial community. It was rather the undermining of the finality of the judgments of the admiralty court which caused the decline. Merchants sooner or later must have discovered the expense, delay and uncertainty of admiralty suits which could be prohibited by the opposing party's suit at common law. The many clear advantages of bringing maritime suits in the admiralty court could not outweigh this crucial defect.

With the coming of the Civil War and the temporary end of the monarchy, the civilians found themselves without the support of the Crown. Surprisingly, the ordinances of the Interregnum preserved admiralty jurisdiction on a fairly broad basis. Probably the survival of the admiralty court through these troubled and threatening times is the strongest proof of the utility of the court to the commercial interests. Apparently the admiralty court continued to hear a significant number of instance cases. The Long Parliament noted the injury to commerce caused by jurisdictional disputes. Although the legislation was only temporary and required periodic reaffirmation, the admiralty jurisdiction was preserved largely as it had been by the conciliar settlement of 1633. The court could hear cases *in rem* for many of the contract causes which had previously been questioned by prohibitions, suits concerning those who repaired or supplied vessels, suits concerning charter parties or contracts for freight and

---

[34] Reproduced in Zouch, *Admiralty of England*, 122–5, and Godolphin, *Admiral iurisdiction*, 157–60.

[35] See the petition of February 18, 1632, 'Reasons why the merchants both English and others desire liberty to try their foraine contracts at ye civill law as formerly they have done', Brit. Lib., Add. MS 32,093, fo. 40. The hostility toward the civilians of many outside the merchant class is suggested by the broadside *The late will and testament of the Doctors Commons* (n.p., 1641). G. F. Steckley, 'Merchants and the admiralty court during the English Revolution', *A.J.L.H.*, 22 (1978), 137–75.

even foreign contracts with a maritime connection.[36]

After the return of the monarchy in 1660, the civilians took heart and started reasserting the arguments for a broadly based commercial jurisdiction in the admiralty court. The crux of their case turned on an economic argument. The nation is preserved from foreign invasion by its ships and shipping, they contended, which are likewise a source of wealth for the nation. Neither shipping nor trade can remain strong unless the welfare of merchants, ship owners, fitters and furnishers of ships, and mariners is properly preserved. Only an admiralty court, with settled jurisdiction and employing the civil and maritime law relied on by all other sea-faring nations, can preserve the welfare of the merchants, ship owners and the rest who engage in maritime commerce. The common law is so different from the civil and maritime laws that

if Maritime Causes (be they either for freight, wages, damages done to Merchants Goods, Building, Tackling, and furnishing of Ships, &c) should be here determined by the . . . [common law] of this Nation, and beyond the Seas by the Civil and Maritime Laws, they must necessarily receive many of them, a different; many of them a clean contrary Judgment.[37]

One civilian, John Godolphin, devoted five pages of his book to a listing of the general categories of admiralty jurisdiction he considered appropriate. The following extract from these pages captures the flavor of the expansive view of admiralty jurisdiction the civilians dreamed of:

Within the Cognizance of this Jurisdiction are all affairs that peculiarly concern the Lord high Admiral . . . all matters immediately relating to the Navies . . . Vessels of Trade, and the Owners thereof, . . . all affairs relating to Mariners, whether Ship-Officers or common Mariners, their Rights and Priviledges respectively; their office and duty; their wages; their offences . . . all affairs of Commanders at Sea, and their under-officers . . . all matters that concern Owners and Proprietors of ships . . . all Masters, Pilots, Steersmen,

---

[36] Yale, 'Sir Matthew Hale', 90–1. The preamble of the Ordinance of 1648 noted the many inconveniences to foreign and domestic commerce because of the uncertainty of jurisdiction for maritime causes. *Acts and ordinances of the Interregnum*, eds. C. Firth and T. Rait (3 vols., London, 1911), I, 1120. This Ordinance was continued in force under the Commonwealth. See *ibid.*, II, 510, 712, 902. G. F. Steckley, 'Instance cases at admiralty in 1657: a court "packed up with sutors"', *Journal of Legal History*, 7 (1986), 68–83.

[37] J. Exton, *The maritime dicaeologie, or sea jurisdiction of England* (London, 1664), 181, see also *Resons for setling admiralty-jurisdiction and giving encouragement to merchants, owners, commanders, masters of ships, materialmen and mariners* (n.p., 1690).

Boteswains, and other ship-Officers; all Ship-wrights, Fisher-men, Ferry-men, and the like; . . . all causes of Seizures and Captures, made at Sea . . . all Charter-parties, Cocquets, Bills of Lading, Sea-Commissions, Letters of safe Conduct, Factories, Invoyces, Skippers Rolls, Inventories, and other Ship-Papers . . . all causes of Fraight, Mariners wages, Load-manage, Port-charges, Pilotage, Anchorage . . . all causes of Maritime Contracts *indeed*, or *as it were* [*quasi?*] Contracts, whether upon or beyond the Seas; all causes of mony lent to Sea or upon the Sea . . . all causes of pawning, hypothecating, or pledging of the ship itself, or any part thereof, or her Lading . . . all causes of . . . casting goods over board; and Contributions either for Redemption of Ship or Lading in case of seizure by Enemies or Pyrats, or in case of good damnified, or disburdening of ships, or other chances, with Average . . . all causes of Naval Consort-ships, whether in War or Peace; Ensurance, Mandates, Procurations, Payments, . . . Discharges, Loans . . . Emptions, Venditions, Conventions, taking or letting to Fraight, Exchanges, Partner-ship, Factoridge, Passage-mony, and whatever is of Maritime nature either by way of *Navigation* upon the Sea, or of *Negotiation* at or beyond the Sea in the way of Marine Trade and Commerce.[38]

Godolphin's last point, that admiralty jurisdiction turned on the nature of the subject matter of litigation (everything touching maritime commerce), directly contradicted the key point of Coke's test of location for admiralty jurisdiction (on the high seas). Between these two extreme claims lay the vast sea of disputed jurisdiction with prohibitions, like mines, making passage hazardous for most admiralty suits.

The civilians contrasted the civil law relied on in the admiralty court with the common law to demonstrate the superiority of the civil law for suits concerning maritime commerce. The civil or maritime law is a branch of the law of nations and must be applied by all nations in cases concerning merchants. The civil law allowed suits by a joint owner or partner against his partner for an account, but the common law did not allow such a suit. The civil law would hear an action of debt upon a contract without a deed, whereas the common law would allow the defendant to wage his law and effectively bar the action. The admiralty court permitted joinder of parties, such as several mariners suing for their wages, or several underwriters being sued on an insurance policy. The common law courts made such suits far more expensive and burdensome by not allowing such joinder.[39]

---

[38] Godolphin, *Admiral iurisdiction*, 43–5. Italics in the original.
[39] Exton, *Maritime dicaeologie*, 41–4; Zouch, *Admiralty of England*, 8–9, 143–9.

The civilians traced the roots of their expansive assertions of jurisdiction to the medieval maritime codes, especially the Laws of Oleron. In these codes they pointed to the early discussions of rules for determining disputes concerning hiring vessels for sea voyages (charter parties), liability for the safe keeping and delivery of goods carried, questions of demurrage, freight, average, collision, pilotage and other mainstays of instance jurisdiction.[40] They tried desperately to interpret the statutes of Richard II, in light of the preambles, as merely corrective of specific abuses and not as definitions of the outer limit of admiralty jurisdiction (on the high seas). But the civilians, although they tried, could not get around the insistence by Coke and the common lawyers that the common law courts had the ultimate authority to interpret statutes.[41]

Coke's assertions concerning the scope of admiralty jurisdiction became the target for much of the civilians' writings. They laid claim to the whole range of contracts touching maritime navigation and commerce, whether entered into in England or in some foreign country or at sea. The life blood of overseas trading was channeled through these contracts, the charter parties, bills of lading, insurance policies, bottomry bonds, bills of sale of ships and other contracts concerning commercial carriage of goods by sea. Few of these contracts were entered into on the high seas, the limit Coke had stated. The civilians rejoined that contracts, being incorporeal,

> may more properly be said to arise from that, from which they are caused, or occasioned, than from the place where they happen to be made, and so Contracts, Pleas and Quarrels occasioned by the businesses of the County may be said to arise within the Body of the County, and Contracts, Pleas and Quarrels occasioned by the businesses of the Sea, may be said to arise from the Sea, in what places so ever they happen to be made, or Written.[42]

Jurisdiction should be determined by the place where the contract must be performed rather than where it was made.

The civilians, in the years after the restoration of the monarchy, were not satisfied with their scholarly, if somewhat overwrought and overconfident, tracts. They also labored for a legislative settlement of admiralty jurisdiction. Bills based largely on the 1633 conciliar settlement were introduced in 1662, 1663, 1670 and finally in 1685.

[40] Zouch, *Admiralty of England*, 30–4.
[41] *Ibid.*, 42–7; Godolphin, *Admiral iurisdiction*, 141–54; Yale, 'Sir Matthew Hale', 89.
[42] Zouch, *Admiralty of England*, 62.

None were successful. Charles II and James II had far more pressing concerns than using what power they had in Parliament to back these measures. The civilians had placed their trust in kings and bishops only to find that the ultimate power lay in Parliament and the common law.[43]

The most persuasive argument for settling the jurisdiction of the admiralty court was made by Sir Leoline Jenkins before the House of Lords in support of the 1670 bill. None of the civilians had expressed the need and usefulness of admiralty jurisdiction with the clarity and cogency nor the modesty that Jenkins brought to this speech. He had been judge of the High Court of Admiralty and had served the king as diplomat on several occasions. Jenkins firmly asserted that the maritime character of the case, not the mere locality, should determine admiralty jurisdiction. He retraced the familiar arguments of the civilians against a narrow, literal interpretation of the statutes of Richard II. In these statutes, 'there was no Design', he assured the Lords, 'to diminish the Admiral's proper Jurisdiction, but only to restrain the Innovations and Exorbitancies of it, and consequently, that he is still in Possession of the Cognisance of all maritime Causes as before those Statutes'.[44] Jenkins reviewed the terms of the bill before the Lords and tried to show the propriety of admiralty jurisdiction over each of the areas included, namely: foreign contracts, mariners' wages, freight, breach of charter party, contracts for building and supplying ships and supervision of the Royal Navy. The prohibition-induced uncertainty of the jurisdiction, Jenkins contended, caused delays and extraordinary expenses.

Nothing can be more pernicious to Sea-faring and trading Men, than *Delays* in their Law-Suits; and therefore every maritime Country in *Christendom*, has a separate Judicature for Differences among Merchants and Sea-faring Men: [Summary proceedings are essential in admiralty suits] since there is not one Cause in ten before that Court, but some of the Parties, or Witnesses in it, are pressing to go to Sea with the next Tide.[45]

Jenkins drew up a list of maritime cases where the common law was incompetent to proceed. For instance, if an English party tried to recover a debt from a foreign debtor and had his ship arrested by admiralty process and bail was accepted, the foreign party could seek a

---

[43] Yale, 'Sir Matthew Hale', 91–6.
[44] W. Wynne, *Life of Sir Leoline Jenkins* (2 vols., London, 1724), I, lxxviii.
[45] *Ibid.*, lxxxi–lxxxii. Italics in the original.

prohibition on the ground that the contract was made on land abroad, and the English debtor, with the vessel long departed, would be without a remedy at common law. The debtor was abroad, the ship had sailed and no other court would act against the bail. Or in the opposite situation, continued Jenkins, if the English merchant owed money to a foreign debtor who sued for it in the admiralty, the English debtor could fly to the common law and obtain a prohibition. The foreign creditor in his trial at law could produce only a copy of the contract and the debtor would deny its existence. The original contract was in a foreign notary's office. A copy attested by a notary could be accepted as evidence in the admiralty court, but not at common law, so the foreign debtor would lose his case since the foreign notary would not allow the original contract out of his office. Similarly, if a master of a ship should sue for freight, he might recover on the contract at common law. But if the shipper complained of damage due to improper stowage, embezzlement or delay by the master's fault, the common law could not make adjustments in the amount of freight due under the contract, as the admiralty court could. Witnesses at common law must be present for oral examination, whereas in admiralty their evidence could be taken in writing by a commission for taking depositions abroad. Particularly sad, Jenkins said, was the plight of the materialmen, the suppliers of provisions, tackle or repairs for the vessel. If they were not paid in time, they could have the ship arrested by the admiralty court and thereby compel the appearance of all the owners to answer for the ship. But if a prohibition should be granted, the remedy at common law would be against the master only, who had made the purchases and who in most cases could personally pay only a fraction of the debts.[46]

Despite the arguments of Jenkins and the tracts of the civilians, no bill passed and the jurisdiction of the admiralty court was never laid on a firm foundation. The civilians' monopoly of practice before the court of admiralty gave the common lawyers ample incentive to cripple the admiralty court's lucrative instance jurisdiction and to begin the process of accommodating commercial litigation in the common law courts. All the erudition and logic of the civilians' tracts and all the conviction and persuasive arguments of Jenkins' speech before the House of Lords could not change the fact that the common lawyers and the judges of the common law courts coveted the

---

[46] *Ibid.*, lxxxii–lxxxiii.

commercial litigation of the admiralty court and were determined to absorb it within the jurisdiction of their courts.

While the civilians were making speeches and writing tracts, the common lawyers were acting. Through the effective use of writs of prohibition, the most important areas of admiralty court jurisdiction over maritime commerce were taken over by the common law courts. Henry Rolle's *Abridgement*, which was contemporary with the civilian tracts already discussed, reiterated the extremely narrow interpretation of the admiralty court's jurisdiction over contracts which Hobart had pronounced half a century earlier. Admiralty jurisdiction extended only to contracts made on the sea, not to those entered into on land beyond the seas, nor even to contracts made at sea but sealed on land.[47] Sir Matthew Hale, Chief Justice of King's Bench from 1671 to 1676, wrote a treatise on maritime jurisdiction for his own use. He also concluded that the common law courts had broad jurisdiction over maritime commerce which left little room for exclusive admiralty jurisdiction.[48]

During these same years, the common law courts applied the rules stated earlier by Coke and Hobart further to restrict admiralty jurisdiction. Although one must use many of the seventeenth-century reports warily, the overall impression they create seems clear and accurate. In *Jurado v. Gregory* (1669) King's Bench put an end to the admiralty court's jurisdiction in suits concerning affreightment contracts, establishing that suits over contracts to receive and carry cargo entered into abroad on land must be brought exclusively in the common law courts.[49] *Gold v. Goodwin* in 1670 marked the end of the admiralty court's jurisdiction over cases involving general average.[50] King's Bench, in *Knight v. Berry* (1689), granted a prohibition in a suit between two groups of part owners of a vessel who disagreed whether to send the ship on a voyage. Though the admiralty court had frequently dealt with such disputes by requiring a bond from the majority owners to protect the minority against loss, King's Bench in

---

[47] H. Rolle, *Un abridgement des plusieurs cases et resolutions del common ley* (London, 1668). Rolle cites Hobart's cases *Don Diego Serviento de Acuna, Ambassador of Spain v. Bingley* (n.d.), 1 Hobart 78, and *Palmer v. Pope* (1611), 1 Hobart 212.

[48] Hale's manuscript treatise is discussed in Yale, 'Sir Matthew Hale', 102–8.

[49] (1669), 1 Ventris 32; 1 Lev. 267; 2 Keble 511, 610; 1 Sid. 418.

[50] (1670), 2 Keble 679.

this case denied the admiralty's jurisdiction.[51] The most profitable area of jurisdiction which the common law courts left to the civilians practicing in the admiralty court was prize, suits concerning the capture of property during time of war. The civilians certainly had ample reason to pray for a continual state of war. Apparently the common law courts even conceded to the admiralty court ancillary jurisdiction over non-prize issues which arose in a prize suit.[52] The admiralty court was also allowed to continue to hear suits by mariners (including mates, but not masters) for their wages, hardly the basis of a profitable practice.[53] Admiralty jurisdiction was also upheld in suits on contracts for supplies entered into aboard a ship at anchor.[54] King's Bench, after considerable debate, likewise refused to prohibit a suit in admiralty on a recognizance entered into in admiralty by a surety as bail for the property. The argument was made, but ultimately rejected, that since the admiralty court was not a court of record, it could not take a recognizance. This argument, probably derived from Coke's *Fourth institutes*, would have been a fatal blow to the admiralty court if it had been accepted.[55]

The once-flourishing admiralty court thus limped into the eighteenth century. Fortunately for the civilians, it was a century of frequent warfare, which assured them numerous, lucrative prize cases. The procedures for prize trials had been defined by Order in Council of 1665.[56] Parliament followed the basic outline of this Order in the various eighteenth-century prize acts. These statutes eliminated any doubt as to the admiralty court's competence to hear and determine prize cases.[57]

More important than these prize acts, the Lords Commissioners of Prize Appeals maintained a constant influence on the development of substantive and procedural prize law. This court of prize appeals reviewed the prize determinations of the High Court of Admiralty and the colonial vice-admiralty courts. In the seventeenth century the number of privy councillors who constituted the Lords Commission-

---

[51] (1689), Carthew 26; 1 Show. 13. Chancery apparently had conceded admiralty jurisdiction in such a case, *Anonymous* (1680), 2 Chan. Cas. 36.
[52] *Turner v. Neele* (1668), 1 Lev. 243.
[53] *Opy v. Child* (1693), 1 Salk. 31; *Bayly v. Grant* (1700), 1 Salk. 34.
[54] *Godfrey's Case* (1625), Latch. 11.
[55] *Par v. Evans* (1663), Raym. 78; 1 Keble 489, 500, 515, 542, 552; Coke, *Fourth institutes*, 135. See also fn. 31 above.
[56] *Documents relating to law of the sea*, I, 56.
[57] 6 Anne c. 37 (for the American plantations); 13 Geo. II c. 4; 17 Geo. II c. 34.

ers varied widely. By the mid-eighteenth century the common law judges, even though not privy councillors, were commissioned to sit as Lords Commissioners. The judges' objections to this commission were overriden by an act of Parliament clearly establishing the form and membership of the Lords Commissioners.[58] This act required, however, that a majority of the Lords Commissioners determining any case must be members of the Privy Council.

The Lords Commissioners, therefore, with only limited influence from the more political members of the Privy Council, shaped the body of law applied in the High Court of Admiralty in its prize sessions. Legal principles, more than bare reasons of state, underlay the judgments of the Lords Commissioners. These legal principles, however, supposedly derived from the amorphous law of nations, developed a noticeably British accent.[59]

Probably because of the strong influence of the common law judges on the Lords Commissioners, at least by the middle of the eighteenth century it became standard practice for a common law barrister to argue along with a civilian advocate in virtually every case heard by the Lords Commissioners.[60] The barristers, therefore, participated in the written and oral argument and shared in the fees from these

---

[58] 22 Geo. II c. 3. The membership and functions of the Lords Commissioners in the eighteenth century is best discussed in R. Pares, *Colonial blockade and neutral rights 1739–1763* (Oxford, 1938), 101–8.

In 1692 it appears that the Privy Council had heard and reversed a judgment of the Lords Commissioners in the case of the *Armes of Plymouth (Olsen)*, P.R.O. PC 2/75 fo. 13. The issue was debated in 1712. *Documents relating to law of the sea*, II, 227–9.

As late as 1787 it was still open to argument that a party who had lost before the Lords Commissioners had a right to seek further review before the Privy Council. See the petition of Commodore George Johnstone concerning the *Expedition against the Cape of Good Hope*, P.R.O. HCA 45/14 fo. 1. In this case it was determined that the government did not have the right to grant special commissions to review a determination by the Lords Commissioners.

Scott appeared before the Privy Council to argue for an appeal to that body from the Lords Commissioners on the petition of Lord Rodney in the *Captures by Lord Rodney at Eustatius* (Privy Council, 1787). Despite the lengthy and pedantic argument of Scott, the Privy Council declined to review. Arnold's Notes of Prize Appeals 1787. (This entire notebook is devoted to this appeal.) P.R.O. HCA 30/468.

[59] Pares, *Colonial blockade*, 102–8; G. Best, *Humanity in warfare* (New York, 1980), 67–74.

[60] H. Bourguignon, *The first federal court – the federal appellate prize court of the American Revolution, 1775–1787* (Philadelphia, 1977), 164.

During the period 1751–66 the Lords Commissioners heard and determined 234 prize appeals. The following list indicates the approximate number of appeals during these years from the various admiralty or vice-admiralty courts:

appellate prize cases. One need look no further for an explanation of the total lack of a challenge to the civilians' monopoly of prize cases. They simply did not have a monopoly of the most lucrative cases, those worth appealing to the Lords Commissioners.

The admiralty judge in the eighteenth century, besides a constant stream of prize cases, continued to sit, along with common law judges, in the rare criminal trials before the admiralty sessions. The admiralty sessions for trial of crimes committed on the high seas continued under the statute of Henry VIII, but apparently the number of criminal trials remained quite few. The admiralty judge, and one or more judges of the common law courts were named in the commissions issued under this statute. The language of this sixteenth-century statute had restricted the jurisdiction to 'treasons, felonies, robberies, murders and confederacies'.[61] At the very end of the eighteenth century, Parliament expanded the jurisdiction of the criminal sessions of admiralty to reach all offenses of whatever kind committed at sea.[62]

Finally, the instance jurisdiction of the admiralty court remained as an emaciated reminder of more bounteous days. Since the middle of the seventeenth century the admiralty court had developed different procedures, different records and separate sittings for its prize and its instance dockets. As Lord Mansfield observed in 1782, 'The Court of Admiralty is called the Instance Court; the other the Prize Court. The manner of proceeding is totally different. The whole system of

Jamaica	88	Rhode Island	3
English High Court		Pennsylvania	2
of Admiralty	41	Virginia	2
New York	23	Gibraltar	1
Antigua	19	Maryland	1
St Christophers	5	Montserrat	1
Newfoundland	3	North Carolina	1

These statistics are based on the carefully prepared indexes to the four volumes of Cases (printed summaries and arguments presented to the Lords Commissioners) which are in the Law Library of Congress, Washington, D.C., listed as Appeal Cases in Prize Causes. These four volumes of Cases, by the way, are far more complete and more carefully arranged than the comparable volumes in the P.R.O. HCA 45/1–5.

[61] 27 Hen. VIII c. 4; 28 Hen. VIII c. 15.

[62] 39 Geo. III c. 54. The records of the admiralty sessions for the end of the eighteenth century and the beginning of the nineteenth century indicate that only a few criminal cases were heard each year. All too often, it appears, serious charges failed to lead to a conviction because important witnesses were missing. P.R.O. HCA 1/27; 1/61; 1/87. See also the pamphlets, F. Vincent, *Proceedings in the High Court of Admiralty, held at Justice-Hall in the Old-Bailey on Saturday, March 30, 1782* (London, 1782), and *Trial of Captain John Kimber for the murder of two female negro slaves on board the Recovery, African slave ship ... 1792* (London, n.d.).

litigation and jurisprudence in the Prize Court, is peculiar to itself: it is no more like the Court of Admiralty, than it is to any Court in Westminster Hall.'[63]

The instance court in the eighteenth century survived on the scraps of litigation not tasty enough to tempt the common lawyers. It heard many suits for seamen's wages and a scattering of other cases involving damages (generally collision cases on the high seas), salvage, bottomry (suits on bonds entered into on the security of the ship to obtain funds for repairing or refitting the vessel), possession of the vessel (but not property or title) and pilotage.[64] Sir Nathaniel Lloyd, a civilian who was King's Advocate from 1715 to 1720, had taken notes from the calendars of the admiralty office. Observing the great decline in instance jurisdiction, he jotted in his common-place book: 'By perusing this callendar it will appear that the Admiralty had a large Jurisdiction. Quomodo evanuit?'[65]

---

[63] *Lindo v. Rodney and Another* (1782), 2 Dougl. 613, 614.
[64] Simpson MS in office of Registrar of the Admiralty (London). The date and authorship of this Manuscript is discussed in Appendix.
[65] Quoted in Yale, 'Sir Matthew Hale', 96.

2

SIR WILLIAM SCOTT –
A BIOGRAPHICAL SKETCH

William Scott was born on October 17, 1745 at his grandfather's country house at Heworth, three miles from Newcastle-upon-Tyne, but on the Durham side of the Tyne. His birth in Durham county, rather than in Newcastle where his parents' home was, resulted from the alarm in Newcastle at the advance of the Jacobite rebels. His mother shortly before the birth had left Newcastle, where the residents felt threatened, to the greater safety of Heworth. Mrs Scott gave birth to twins, William, the eldest son, and Barbara.[1]

Scott's father, William Scott of Newcastle was a coal-fitter, a trade which had occupied not only his father's family for at least two generations, but his mother's family also. Coal-fitters were middlemen between the producers of coal in the Tyne region and the ship owners who carried it to London. During the seventeenth century, many colliery owners had ceased dealing directly with the ship owners and instead negotiated with the fitters who bought through contracts with the mine owners for delivery at the piers. The fitter then found a shipmaster to purchase his coal, had it loaded in keels or coal barges for delivery aboard the ships, arranged for clearance of the coal and paid the taxes. Fitters often were interested in the mining business either as partners in the collieries or indirectly as money lenders or owners of royalties. Fitters, as middlemen, used their power of playing off one mine owner against another to buy coal at the lowest price and by close combination with other fitters forced up the price of the coal they sold to the shippers. The fitters of Newcastle were men of power and prestige in the community and, because of the intren-

---

[1] The standard biographical sources are: W. C. Townsend, 'The life of Lord Stowell', in *The lives of twelve eminent judges* (2 vols., London, 1846), II, 279–365; W. E. Surtees, *A sketch of the lives of Lords Stowell and Eldon* (London, 1846); J. A. Hamilton, 'Sir William Scott', in *D.N.B.*, and E. S. Roscoe, *Lord Stowell – his life and the development of English prize law* (Boston, 1916).

ched monopoly position, were shrewd dealers, willing and able to pursue their own profit.[2]

Scott thus grew up in an environment saturated with coal dust and salt water. He must have gained some familiarity with the shipping business from his father who not only bought and sold coal, but also was active in bringing in supplies such as wagon wheels and rails which he could sell to the coal producers. Scott's father is said to have kept a public house near the docks and to have speculated in shipping and maritime insurance. He owned a vessel, one hopes not a coal barge, named the *William and Barbara*, presumably after the twins.[3] In such an atmosphere, it is not surprising that the son grew up with shrewd, hardheaded business instincts.

At a time when education throughout England often meant sterile memorization of Roman and Greek writings, Scott was fortunate to have attended the Royal Free Grammar School of Newcastle during the years that Hugh Moises was headmaster. Moises, who had been a fellow at Peterhouse, Cambridge, accepted the headmastership at Newcastle in 1749 and turned a moribund institution into a thriving and stimulating grammar school. Scott received his basic education in the Latin and Greek classics from a master who loved these writings and could instill a similar appreciation for them in his students. But Moises also believed in incorporating lectures on science into the curriculum. Moral education was basic to Moises' scheme of education and his success in developing the minds and characters of his students is attested by the pupils' long-lasting respect and admiration for their master. In 1810, half a century after Scott had left the Newcastle grammar school, he composed the inscription for the monument to the memory of Moises which his students had placed in St Nicholas' Church, Newcastle.[4]

---

[2] J. U. Nef, *The rise of the British coal industry* (2 vols., London, 1932), II, 78–110; T. S. Ashton and J. Sykes, *The coal industry of the eighteenth century*, 2nd edn (Manchester, 1964), 195–6.

[3] Surtees, *Lords Stowell and Eldon*, 2–4; *Letters of William Scott father of Lords Stowell and Eldon* (Newcastle, 1848), 31–52. Scott's mother, by the way, gave birth to two more pairs of twins, including William's younger brother John, the future Lord Eldon, who also had a twin sister. Scott in a letter from Oxford in 1777 to his brother Henry expressed the philosophy of sheer, persistent determination he derived from his father: 'Remember that we all of us owe our present establishment in life to a conduct founded upon industry and frugality – upon unremitting attention to business, and seclusion from company. We inherit from our deceased father not only a provision, but what is more, an example.' Townsend, 'Life of Lord Stowell', 290.

[4] A. R. Laws, *Schola novocastrensis: a biographical history of the Royal Free Grammar School of Newcastle upon Tyne* (2 vols., Newcastle, 1932), II, 46–81.

In 1761 at the age of fifteen, Scott stood for and obtained a scholarship at Corpus Christi College, Oxford. Since the scholarship was for scholars from Durham, only the accident of his birth in Durham made him eligible.

The Oxford to which Scott eagerly set out in March 1761 has often been portrayed as largely devoid of worthwhile intellectual activity with its obsolete curriculum and port-drinking Tory dons. The detailed and uncomplimentary sketch by Edward Gibbon of the Oxford he had attended in 1752 has accounted in large measure for the unflattering portrait. Gibbon, years later, wrote in his memoirs of the idle and unprofitable fourteen months at Magdalen College:

> The schools of Oxford and Cambridge were founded in a dark age of false and barbarous science; and they are still tainted with the vices of their origin. Their primitive discipline was adapted to the education of priests and monks; and the government still remains in the hands of the Clergy, an order of men, whose manners are remote from the present World, and whose eyes are dazzled by the light of Philosophy. The legal incorporation of these societies by the charters of Popes and Kings had given them a monopoly of the public instruction; and the spirit of monopolists is narrow, lazy and oppressive: their work is more costly and less productive than that of independent artists; and the new improvements so eagerly grasped by the competition of freedom, are admitted with slow and sullen reluctance in those proud corporations, above the fear of a rival, and below the confession of an error . . .
>
> . . . I should applaud the institution, if the degrees of Batchelor or licentiate were bestowed as the reward of manly and successful study: if the name and rank of Doctor or Master were strictly reserved for the professors of science who have approved their title to the public esteem . . .
>
> . . . The fellows or monks of my time were decent easy men who supinely enjoyed the gifts of the founder: their days were filled by a series of uniform employments; the Chappel and the Hall, the Coffee house, and the common room, till they retired, weary, and well-satisfied, to a long slumber. From the toil of reading or thinking, or writing they had absolved their conscience, and the first shoots of learning and ingenuity withered on the ground without yielding any fruit to the owners or the public.[5]

Unfortunately Gibbon and other critics had solid grounds for condemning Oxford's medieval educational structure with its sterile disputations and archaic, wooden university degree requirements. Oxford in the eighteenth century, as Gibbon suggested, certainly had failings: fellows and senior tutors sunk in sloth and drunkenness; a requirement of celibacy for fellows at a time when celibacy had fallen

---

[5] E. Gibbon, *Memoirs of my life*, ed. G. A. Bonnard (New York, 1966), 48–52.

out of fashion; rare and listless lectures by professors who had little to contribute to learning even when they did lecture, and a basic goal of training clerics when anti-clericalism was growing more common. But recently Dame Lucy Sutherland has shown that Oxford in the eighteenth century had not completely quenched the lamp of learning.[6] The colleges, each with only fifteen or twenty students, continued to challenge these undergraduates. Many of the undergraduates, called foundationers or scholars, met regularly with tutors, and often, prodded or inspired by their tutors, read seriously the classical writers thought essential to an education as well as more recent scientific and mathematical writings. Most of the education depended on the development of habits of voracious and systematic readings. The intellectual life at Oxford, centered more in the colleges than at the University, had not died out when young William Scott arrived in 1761.

Gibbon's cynical and disdainful appraisal of the Oxford he remembered thus represents only part of the true picture, and it is unlikely that young Scott, with his northern accent and urgent sense of the need to prove himself, viewed Oxford with Gibbon's jaundiced eyes. For Scott, the challenge and inspiration of tutors in the college must have created an atmosphere of intellectual zest. Scott's notebooks from readings or lectures on chemistry and mineralogy show that he took his education seriously and thought that he was learning something of importance.[7]

Far more important to Scott must have been the lectures on English law which William Blackstone had started delivering just three years before Scott arrived at Oxford. These lectures marked a brilliant moment in Oxford's intellectual history, a total contrast to the usual fare provided in university lectures. Blackstone was not yet forty in 1761 and his *Commentaries* were not published until 1765. It is hard to imagine that Scott failed to attend Blackstone's lectures during these years. Even if Oxford had provided no other intellectual challenge for Scott, these lectures would have given him much to

---

[6] L. Sutherland, *The University of Oxford in the eighteenth century – a reconsideration* (Oxford, 1973), 4–28.

[7] Scott's notebook is in the Old Ashmolean, Oxford University, University College, MS 1. There is another notebook, apparently in Scott's hand, among the Eldon Papers, Encombe House. It contains notes from lectures or personal readings on Roman and Greek civilization, especially sculpture and coins. The frequent passages in French, Greek or Latin suggest the background Scott brought to Oxford and developed there.

digest. Perhaps Blackstone's lectures helped to instill that respect for the common law which Scott showed throughout life. Blackstone's influence might account for the fact that in 1762 Scott registered as a student at the Middle Temple. Blackstone began his course of lectures with broad background material on legal education and the nature of law in general. He managed to build an elaborate structure for his lecture course within which he was able to discuss almost every aspect of English law and legal institutions in a clear, concise and accurate style. Although Blackstone primarily sought to summarize the law of his day, a goal he eminently achieved, he also tried to place various legal doctrines within their proper historical context. Blackstone thus provided a more adequate grasp of English legal history than any other single source Scott could have found. Blackstone drew as readily on the continental authorities on Roman law as he did on the writings and reports on English law. Blackstone's lectures must have been a heady stimulant for a coal-fitter's son.[8]

Scott undoubtedly also attended the lectures of Thomas Bever, a fellow of All Souls, a doctor in the civil law, and a member of Doctors' Commons. Bever's lectures on jurisprudence and the civil law were begun in 1762. After several introductory lectures on jurisprudence, law in general and the history of Roman law, Bever proceeded to summarize some major topics of civil law, such as: man as a subject of obligation, natural law, equity, states, family, property, contracts, succession, civil injuries, forms and powers of civil government, the administration of justice and the law of nations. Though today his lectures make dull and overly pious reading, they were an attempt to acquaint his students with the best authorities ancient and modern on Roman law. Bever followed in the classical natural law school of Grotius and Pufendorf. One passage from Bever's lecture on the definition of law suffices to give the tone of his course and to place him clearly within the natural law tradition. He is commenting on a passage from Demosthenes in stating,

Law is then a general obligation of obedience incumbent upon the whole Race of Mankind . . . founded in the Conveniences inherent in its very nature; and

---

[8] *H.E.L.*, 12, 703–27; see also J. W. Cairns, 'Blackstone, an English institutist: legal literature and the rise of the nation state', *Oxford Journal of Legal Studies*, 4 (1984), 318–60. Scott obviously knew Blackstone personally. Boswell relates that Scott repeated to Johnson the gossip that 'Blackstone, a sober man, composed his *Commentaries* with a bottle of port before him.' *Boswell's life of Johnson*, ed. G. B. Hill, rev. L. Powell (6 vols., Oxford, 1934–50), IV, 91.

which Mankind, independently of their Duty, will find their advantage in submitting to ... But this is further enforced upon them not barely in consequence of the positive Authority of God, from whom it is derived, but chiefly because it proceeds likewise from the Bounty, and Love of God to Mankind, and is designed by him for their good ... And beside the Precepts which God himself hath given us, i.e. such as he hath either expressly revealed, or hath enabled us to comprehend by the Light of Reason, he hath likewise endued some Individuals with a superior Degree of intellectual Power and Wisdom, to render them capable of framing Laws for the Security and Economy of Civil Government; with a view therefore to this End, Human Law is ... to obviate and rectify all those Evils and Inconveniences that Society feels, either from the voluntary or involuntary Misconduct of its Members ... And from a thorough sense of the advantage and Happiness of having a settled Rule of Conduct, Men have bound themselves to obedience by a common Covenant, necessarily implied, upon the first Coalition of any Number in one regular Community; and Law then becomes the properest Cement of this Union ... Thus in this concise and beautiful Passage is set forth the whole Rationale of our Acquiescence under, and submission to, all Civil Institutions. For you see plainly from hence, that all Laws of what kind soever, whether Divine and Natural, or Human and Positive, proceed from the same sublime original; the former immediately, either by express Revelation, or the Dictates of Reason; the latter mediately, thro' the Channel of Human Understanding.[9]

We can probably safely assume that Scott faithfully attended the entire course of more than thirty mind-numbing lectures. Bever, of course, introduced his students also to the law of nations which, he explained, derived from the same law of nature which God in the act of creation had engraved in the minds and hearts of men. The relations between civilized nations, he argued, must be regulated by the fixed rules derived from natural reason. This typically eighteenth-century collection of axiomatic maxims acquiesced in by the nations of Europe impressed a lasting mark on Scott. Throughout his life he seems to have accepted as too obvious to question the natural law view of the universe, with all the stars and planets, the states and each individual obliged to carry out their preordained movement. In discussing his many judicial decisions, it will be obvious that his thinking on international law remained fixed within this law of nations frame of reference. When Bever treated the courts which followed in the civil law tradition, he could not resist reopening what one would

[9] T. Bever, 'A course of lectures on jurisprudence and civil law read in the Vinerian Law School', Codrington Library, All Souls College, Oxford, MS 109c, vol. III, lecture V, pp. 4–5. I am indebted to Mr Ian Doolittle of Christ Church for calling this manuscript to my attention.

have thought was a long lost war, the debate over the proper jurisdiction of the admiralty and ecclesiastical courts and the impropriety of prohibitions from the common law courts.[10] Scott took his B.A. degree in November 1764 and in December of that year was elected to a Durham fellowship at University College to which he was admitted in June 1765. He continued as a fellow and tutor at University College until 1776. He received his master's degree in 1767 and then turned toward the civil law as a profession. He received the bachelor's degree in civil law in 1772 and the doctorate in 1779. In 1774 the university convocation elected him to be Camden Reader of Ancient History. He continued giving these lectures until his career in law was assured. He kept terms at the Middle Temple starting in 1777 and enrolled as an advocate of Doctors' Commons in 1779 after receiving the D.C.L. The next year he was called to the bar by the Middle Temple. In 1781 he married Maria Anne, the eldest daughter of John Bagnall of Earley Court, Berkshire. Scott, then thirty-five years old, took a residence with his wife at Doctors' Commons, and began his life's work as a civilian, but without yet completely renouncing his university source of income. He continued to hold his Camden readership until 1785.[11]

During his twenty years at Oxford, Scott laid the groundwork for his future career as a civilian by broad reading in the works of Roman law and the continental classics on the law of nations.[12] He must also have read a recently published English work on the civil law by John Taylor which fitted closely with the approach of Thomas Bever. Taylor surveyed the usual topics of Roman law with the customary

[10] *Ibid.*, 26–8. See also, *ibid.*, lecture VII, and T. Bever, 'A history of the legal polity of the Roman state, and of the rise, progress and extent of the Roman law', Codrington Library, MS 110, Chapter IV, 230–7.

Blackstone's lecture on the nature of laws in general reinforced this natural law, law of nations approach. Bl. *Comm.*, I, 38–62.

[11] See Townsend, 'Life of Lord Stowell', 284–93; Roscoe, *Lord Stowell*, ix. Scott had taken chambers at the Middle Temple earlier to keep terms. He entertained Samuel Johnson there on April 10, 1778, *Life of Johnson*, III, 261–2.

[12] Among the readings for the Bachelor of Civil Law degree was an elementary introduction to the civil law by Robert Eden, a product of the Newcastle Grammar School and fellow at University College, *Jurisprudentia philologica sive elementa juris civilis* (Oxford, 1744). Eden followed the order of Justinian in discussing the topics of the civil law. He went beyond a summary of the text and introduced historical notes, quotations from the classics and made some effort to point out English parallels. I am indebted to an unpublished article by the late Dame Lucy Sutherland which pointed out that Eden was usually read by students preparing for the Bachelor of Civil Law degree. The article is now with Sutherland's literary executor, Dr Anne Whiteman of Lady Margaret Hall.

string of quotations from Roman and Greek writers. Like Bever and the whole law of nations school, Taylor instilled the view that states were bound to restrict their dealings with other states by naturally knowable canons of conduct. Taylor discussed the law of nations as 'That unwritten, general, reasonable and clear Obligation, which links separate Communities together, like Individuals. It is still the Dictate of Right Reason, applied to the Wants and Services, the Exigencies and Necessities of Societies.'[13]

It is said that Scott's lectures as Camden Reader of Ancient History were superbly crafted and well received. The broad and detailed grasp of classical antiquity he derived from preparing these lectures enhanced his own sense of the context within which Roman law had developed. Scott apparently ordered that his lectures not be published and the manuscript cannot now be located. Even Gibbon acknowledged Scott's ability as a tutor and lecturer.[14]

Although Scott resigned his Camden readership in 1785, thereby severing a significant tie to Oxford, the University always remained a large part of his life. In 1791 Scott, his younger brother John, the future Lord Eldon, and Robert Chambers, who succeeded Blackstone as Vinerian lecturer, organized a dining club in London. The two Scotts and Chambers had all come to Oxford from the Royal Free Grammar School in Newcastle and all became fellows at University College. All the members of the dining club had spent some time at University College and had been instructed by one of the Scotts or by Chambers. But eighteenth-century dining clubs were not just opportunities for college reunions. Membership was restricted to like-minded men who would discuss the profound issues of the day without introducing any jarring discord. This University College Dining Club retained a distinctly Tory flavor and perhaps the outbreak of the French Revolution just two years earlier had provided the stimulus to bring together men who were unanimous in expressing their horror at developments in France. The association with their

---

[13] J. Taylor, *Elements of civil law* (Cambridge, 1755), 128.
[14] Gibbon, in his *Memoirs*, 65–6, wrote: 'At a more recent period many students have been attracted by the merit and reputation of Sir William Scott, then a tutor in University College, and now conspicuous in the profession of the Civil law: my personal acquaintance with that Gentleman has inspired me with a just esteem for his abilities and knowledge; and I am assured that his Lectures on history would compose, were they given to the public, a most valuable treatise.'

former students also provided the Scotts with access to persons of wealth and power who could further their careers. For instance, the three sons of the Bouverie family, including the second Earl of Radnor, had entered University College under William Scott's aegis. It is not surprising that Scott between 1790 and 1801 sat for the Bouverie pocket-borough of Downton and thus received his introduction to Parliament.[15]

During the years Scott was dividing his time between Oxford and London, he became associated with Samuel Johnson and his circle of friends. Robert Chambers introduced Scott to Johnson at Oxford and in 1778 Scott was elected a member of Johnson's Club. Johnson, then nearing seventy, must have recognized in Scott, in his early thirties, the young man he had so wanted to be, a talented, articulate person with an Oxford education and a future in law. Access to the Club introduced Scott to many of the bright intellectual and political lights of London society such as: Joshua Reynolds, Edward Gibbon, Adam Smith, Charles James Fox, William Windham, R. B. Sheridan, Edmund Burke and, of course, James Boswell. Johnson's respect for Scott continued till the end of his life; he named Scott one of the executors of his will. Scott shared many more moments of socializing and serious conversation with Johnson and his circle than Boswell has recorded. The approval and friendship of this diverse, elite group bolstered Scott's sense of confidence and accomplishment.[16]

In 1780 Scott had not only been admitted by the Middle Temple as a barrister but had also completed the year of silence required of new members of Doctors' Commons so that he could begin practice as a civilian advocate. Although there is no record of the reasons inclining Scott to decide to pursue a career as a civilian, two possible reasons spring to mind: lack of competition among rival civilians and the American war. During the twenty years after 1760 only seven civilians including Scott were admitted to membership in Doctors' Commons. Four of these civilians had retired before Scott was admitted to

[15] L. Mitchell, 'The first univ. dining club', *University College Record* (Oxford, 1970), 351–8.
[16] W. J. Bate, *Samuel Johnson* (New York, 1979), 84–111, 345, 366, 463–4, 504–5; *Life of Johnson*, I, 479; III, 261–9; IV, 91; V, 109 fn. 5. In a 1777 letter to his brother Henry, Scott mentioned in passing: 'I have had my friend Johnson staying with me for a fortnight.' Townsend, 'Life of Lord Stowell', 290. Scott's difficulties arising from his appointment as an executor of Johnson's will are narrated by Scott in a letter to Lady Inchiquin, 1794, Beinecke Library, Yale University, Osborne File.

practice.[17] Even though Doctors' Commons had always consisted of only a few civilians, there was clearly room for younger blood. Secondly, the American war, as all wars, brought a large number of lucrative prize cases before the admiralty court. In his first year of practice as a civilian, Scott wrote, 'I believe our rulers would be very glad of a peace; but it is not to be had without a general peace, which I sincerely wish for, though my own interest will suffer considerably by it. I am exceedingly oppressed with business, and shall remain so for these three weeks.'[18]

Scott's career as a civilian follows the *cursus honorum* of the seventeenth-century civilian so well that one can only marvel at how little had changed in more than a century. He began his civilian career with the necessary university credentials. He received his earliest income from his positions at Oxford. He espoused Tory politics and strongly supported the king's government and the Church on whose patronage he relied to supplement his income from practice before the admiralty court and the ecclesiastical courts. His brother John noted in a letter in 1783 that Scott had received a sinecure from the Archbishop of Canterbury which would give him more than £400 a year for life.[19] Within the next few years, Scott had been appointed by the Archbishop to several more offices, which he held till he was made a peer more than a quarter of a century later.[20] In 1782 he was appointed advocate for the Lords Commissioners of the Admiralty,

[17] G. D. Squibb, *Doctors' Commons* (Oxford, 1977), 193–4. A contemporary civilian assessed Scott's motives for becoming a civilian as follows: 'When he first entered the precincts of the university, he had not formed the intention of cultivating the civil law, but, hearing that the advocates in Doctors' Commons were not very numerous, and that a man of talents might easily obtain a great share of the emoluments attendant upon their practice, he readily took the hint; and the rapid flow of business with which he was gratified demonstrated the justness of the predictive remark.' [C. Coote], *Sketches of the lives and characters of eminent English civilians* (London, 1804), 128.

[18] Townsend, 'Life of Lord Stowell', 293. Townsend gives neither the exact date nor the recipient of this letter. Scott had also the added security from a substantial inheritance, some £20,000, when his father had died in 1776. *Ibid.*, 289.

[19] *Ibid.*, 293. The reference presumably is to the office of Register or Clerk of the Faculties, January 3, 1783, which he resigned April 13, 1790. Lambeth Palace Library, Act Books, 11/335; 12/159.

[20] On July 11, 1785, Scott was appointed Consistorial Commissary General of the Diocese of Canterbury, which he resigned August 15, 1821; on October 22, 1785 he was appointed Official to the Archdeacon of Canterbury, which he resigned February 26, 1822; on September 24, 1788 he was appointed Vicar General in Spirituals and Official Principal to the Lord Archbishop of Canterbury, which he resigned August 15, 1821. Lambeth Palace Library, Act Books, 11/401, 404, 410; 12/104; 14/368, 371, 408.

the first of many positions he received from the government. By 1788 he had made a sufficiently favorable impression to be appointed by the Bishop of London as judge of the Consistory Court of the Diocese of London. That same year he was appointed to the lucrative position of King's Advocate, the official who represented the government's interest before the admiralty court and the ecclesiastical courts. He was also knighted in that year, and so by the age of forty-three he had already shown that he would be at the head of his profession as a civilian advocate.[21]

This first decade of his legal career was marked by events which must have permanently colored Scott's thinking. The long national agony of the American war, ending with the world turned upside-down, was sensed as a traumatic personal loss by Scott.[22] During the Gordon Riots Scott and his brother John had to flee for safety and feared that the Inns of Court and Doctors' Commons would be destroyed. After the riots, as he walked with Dr Johnson through the burned out areas near Newgate, his native conservativism must have been greatly reinforced.[23] He viewed with alarm the quibbling politics and tottering ministries of the early years of the decade, and must have been shaken by the crisis at the end of the decade brought on by the king's insanity and the debate over the appointment of the Prince of Wales as regent. He received an education in political realities and corruption when he served briefly as counsel for the prosecution in the impeachment proceedings against Warren Hastings.[24] In the summer of 1789 the French Revolution began the long process of change in international relations which would occupy Scott's energy for many years as judge of the admiralty court.

Scott's eighteen years of admiralty practice before he became judge of the High Court of Admiralty in 1798 can be viewed in the notebooks of two younger civilians, John Nicholl and James Henry Arnold, who were admitted to Doctors' Commons in 1785 and 1787 respectively.[25] Nicholl began his first notebook in 1781, shortly after

[21] Townsend, 'Life of Lord Stowell', 305.
[22] Scott wrote in an overwrought letter to his brother [Henry?] that at the news of Burgoyne's defeat, he and his brother and sister had 'mingled our tears for two days together, being English folks of the old stamp, and retaining, in spite of modern patriotism, some affection and reverence for the name of Old England'. *Ibid.*, 291.
[23] 'People's minds are heartily sickened of licentious notions', Scott wrote to his brother Henry after the riots. *Ibid.*, 299–300.
[24] *The correspondence of Edmund Burke*, ed. R. B. McDowell and J. A. Woods (10 vols., Chicago, 1958–78), V, 324, 398; VI, 174.
[25] Squibb, *Doctors' Commons*, 195.

42   *Sir William Scott*

Scott began practice. The notes, apparently for private use, were taken when the admiralty court was sitting and include summaries of the arguments of counsel and the unreported opinions of the judge. Some of the notes were taken at sessions of the Lords Commissioners for Prize Appeals, the appellate court for prize cases. From these notebooks, especially Nicholl's notebooks, it is evident that Scott, even in the early 1780s, was already one of the two or three leading civilians in admiralty practice. By the 1790s when Scott had been made King's Advocate, he appeared in the vast majority of cases summarized in Nicholl's notebooks. He argued about 150 cases between 1793 and 1797.[26]

The quality of Scott's work as a civilian is more important than mere numbers in evaluating his preparation for the role of judge of the admiralty court. In 1793 Scott, as the King's Advocate, represented the interests of the naval captors of a Spanish ship which had previously been captured by the French and held by them for fourteen days. The Spanish owners claimed the vessel as neutral property. Scott had to argue that it had become French property and so was enemy property liable to capture by the English when taken. In the course of his lengthy argument, he cited Roman law, a wide variety of continental writers on Roman law, maritime law and the law of nations,[27] various English authorities,[28] common law reports,[29] prior unreported admiralty cases, as well as English and Spanish statutes.

---

[26] Nicholl's Notebooks, 1781–92, 1793–7, P.R.O. HCA 30/464; Arnold's Notebooks, 1787–97, P.R.O. HCA 30/468. These notebooks are briefly discussed in C. J. B. Gaskoin, 'Prize case notes in the days of Stowell', *British Yearbook of International Law*, 4 (1923–4), 78–89.

[27] Although the references in the notes are incomplete, it appears that Scott referred among other works to: H. Grotius, *De jure belli ac pacis* (Paris, 1625); C. van Bynkershoek, *Quaestionum juris publici libri duo* (Amsterdam, 1747); J. Burlamaqui, *Principles of natural and politic law* (London, 1752); J. G. Heineccius, *Elementa juris naturae et gentium* (Halle, 1746); E. de Vattel, *Le droit des gens* (3 vols., London, 1758); J. Voet, *Commentarius ad pandectas*, 5th edn (Hague, 1726); R. J. Valin, *Nouveau commentaire sur l'ordonnance de la marine* (New Rochelle, 1776); F. J. d'Abreu, *Tratado juridico-politico, sobre pressas de mar, y calidades, que deben concurrin para hacerse legitamamente el corso* (Cadiz, 1746).

[28] Scott referred to Magna Charta; C. Molloy, *De jure maritimo et navali* (London, 1676); M. Postlethwayt, *Universal dictionary of trade and commerce* (London, 1751); W. Wynne, *Life of Sir Leoline Jenkins* (2 vols., London, 1724).

[29] Scott cited cases from: Y.B. Edw. IV; J. T. Atkyns, *Reports, Court of Chancery* (3 vols., London, 1765–8); J. Keble, *Reports, King's Bench* (3 vols., London, 1685); H. Rolle, *Les reports de divers cases, Banke le Roy* (London, 1675–6); E. Bulstrode, *Reports in King's Bench* (London, 1657–9).

Scott's argument in this case, as well as in other cases,[30] shows the breadth of his study of the sources of international law. Since the other counsel in the case, French Laurence and Maurice Swabey, were equally intent on displaying their broad erudition, Scott's discursive style apparently followed the ordinary practice in a significant admiralty case. The long arguments, with their scholarly references to old writers on the law of nations, obviously did not impress the admiralty judge, Sir James Marriott. He commented, in giving his judgment, that it was almost time to dispense with Grotius, the bible of the civilians, and that he was not bound by ancient precedents or opinions but only by principles and reasons.[31] Notwithstanding these deflating comments by the judge, Scott's performance demonstrated the technical proficiency in prize law he had achieved during his years of study and practice.

In 1782, at the beginning of his years of practice, Scott had the extraordinary opportunity as a civilian to present arguments before King's Bench. That court had heard arguments from barristers on a case involving a ransom bill. A British vessel had been captured by a French privateer during the American Revolution. The British ship had been released upon execution of an agreement to pay £2,000 to the French privateer. This ransom bill was secured by a hostage released by another British ship. The ransom bill, however, had been concealed. Suit was brought in King's Bench by the French privateer on the ransom bill. Lord Mansfield, dissatisfied after hearing the barristers on this case, requested argument by civilians. Dr William Wynne, more than twenty years Scott's senior as a civilian, spoke for the French plaintiff. Scott argued cogently for the defendant. Lord Mansfield obviously was not convinced by Scott's argument, with its many learned citations, that King's Bench lacked jurisdiction to decide a prize case. Mansfield would have merely enforced the agreement as a contract, despite Scott's insistence that it was a

---

[30] For instance, *Jacobus* (1785), argued before Lords Commissioners for Prize Appeals, Nicholl's Notebook, 1781–92, P.R.O. HCA 30/464, and *Captures by Lord Rodney at Eustatius* (Privy Council, 1787), Arnold's Notes of Prize Appeals, P.R.O. HCA 30/468.

[31] St Iago, Nicholl's Notebook, 1793–7, P.R.O. HCA 30/464. Scott's argument is noted fos. 16–29, Laurence and Swabey's arguments from fos. 48–59. The court's judgment begins at fo. 59. Scott probably was not surprised at Marriott's derogatory comments. Marriott by this time was getting old and infirm, and in the opinion of a contemporary civilian, he was 'incapable of a correct and satisfactory performance of the duties of his office ... He was less deficient in talents than in soundness of judgment.' [Coote], *English civilians*, 124–5.

contract founded in violence. The court, however, refused to go along with Lord Mansfield, so the case was referred to Exchequer Chamber. Ultimately it was held that an enemy alien could not bring suit in a British court.[32] The memory of this rare occasion to appear before Lord Mansfield and the Court of King's Bench must have remained long in Scott's memory. He obviously rose quickly to the top of the tiny band of civilians.

His years as a tutor and lecturer at Oxford developed in Scott scholarly habits which he retained throughout his busy career. While he was judge of the admiralty court, he acquired a manuscript copy of the *Black book of the admiralty* which had originally been made for Sir Leoline Jenkins in the seventeenth century and had come into the hands of Sir James Marriott, Scott's predecessor in the admiralty court. This manuscript, now in the library of the Inner Temple, includes one page, folded to form four sides, on which Scott wrote his conclusions as to the dates and relationship of the various documents which make up the *Black book*. The surprising thing is that he had the time and interest to try to piece together the clues to the origins and authorship of the *Black book*, which dated from the fourteenth and fifteenth centuries.[33] Most of its contents were far removed from the immediate realities of the prize cases which were flooding his court.

As a civilian Scott devoted much of his time to ecclesiastical questions. He sat as judge of the Consistory Court of London from 1788 till his elevation to a peerage in 1821. Many of his more notable judgments have been reported in the two volumes of Haggard's *Reports of cases in the Consistory Court of London*. These cases show that even in his earliest consistory cases, Scott had developed the clear, precise yet graceful style of writing which would be so characteristic of his admiralty judgments ten years later. One does not have to know anything about the election or authority of churchwardens,

---

[32] *Anthon v. Fisher* (1782), 3 Dougl. 166; Nicholl's Notebook, 1781–92, P.R.O. HCA 30/464.

[33] Inner Temple Library, Misc. MS, 56. There is a note opposite to the title page which explains: 'Mr. Alliston presents respectfully to Sir William Scott among the Books bequeathed to him by the late Sir James Marriott were two volumes which A. sends herewith and begs Sir William's acceptance of them if they are of any use Freemans Court, Cornl – 15th May 1809.' Sir Leoline Jenkins, for whom this copy of the *Black book* had been made, gave it to the library of Doctors' Commons. *Ibid.*, 71. There is no indication how it came into the possession of Marriott. Scott's eductated hunches as to the dating of the main parts of the *Black book* correspond rather closely with the much fuller discussion of the question in *Black book of the admiralty*, ed. T. Twiss (4 vols., London, 1871–6), I, xxx–lxx.

faculties for repairing or modifying churches, validity of marriages, restitution of marital rights or grounds for divorce to be able to read and understand these Consistory Court judgments. Haggard has reported about seventy of Scott's consistory judgments, but there undoubtedly were many more unreported cases Scott dealt with during his thirty-three years as judge.[34]

A clearer glimpse of Scott's day-to-day work as a civilian can be derived from an office notebook he kept for about a year and a half in 1788 and 1789, just at the time he had been appointed King's Advocate and judge of the Consistory Court. The notebook, in Scott's hand, has survived in the office of the Registrar of the Admiralty. Scott kept notes of the legal activities he engaged in during this period, the opinions he wrote as counsel, a few letters he received on legal matters, summaries of the arguments and judgments in cases either before him as judge or before another judge in other courts. His notes provide a sketch of his practice till on page 167 he noted 'So much business came on that I have been under a necessity of desisting for 3 Months or more.' His notetaking ended a few pages after this notation.[35]

Since these notes were taken during years when the country was at peace, the vast majority of Scott's work dealt with questions of wills, marriage matters and other questions of ecclesiastical law. There are about eighty-nine opinions he wrote for his clients. In these opinions as counsel he discussed, sometimes briefly and sometimes quite fully, such questions as: Does a parson forfeit his living when he leases the rectory for the benefit of creditors? Is it simony for a parson of two benefices to sell one to a clergyman? Are the fish in a pond, if kept for profit or sale, tithable? Is a perpetual curate removable at pleasure? How should one proceed in propounding an imperfect instrument bequeathing securities which have been lost? If a man of landed property has been denied by the ministers and churchwardens the assignment of a pew, can the Consistory Court grant one? Where the crew of a privateer captured by the Americans recovered possession of the ship and the insurers gave them a considerable sum as salvage, what is the rule for distribution among the crew members? If a fellow

---

[34] J. Haggard, *Reports of cases ... in the Consistory Court of London* (2 vols., London, 1822). Haggard filled out his second volume with judgments from other ecclesiastical judges prior to or contemporary with Scott.
[35] R.A., Stowell's Notebook. This notebook is described briefly in the Appendix, below.

of St Catharine's College, Cambridge, married during the term, can the master immediately declare a vacancy and insist on an election? Whether a holographic will should be propounded? Does the town of Newcastle have admiralty jurisdiction by its charter over some anchors and cables which had been lost in a storm and were recovered by some local inhabitants? Where an Englishman dies in Florida leaving a will, and where the appointed executor obtained a sort of probate from the Spanish commandant at Mobile, and where the executor received voluntary payments in a large amount under the foreign probate from some English debtors of the estate, can the brother of the deceased bring suit to challenge the release given to these debtors by the executor? What rights does an executor have to the crops of a rector who died after having sown, ploughed and tilled his glebe? Whether an incomplete and unexecuted will of a testator who began it three days before his sudden death should be proved in place of or as a codicil to a previous, executed will? Whether a patron can pull down a church which is in ruins in order to rebuild it and in the meantime fit up a convenient building for the use of the parish without a licence from the ordinary, and can the minister safely officiate in the temporary church without a licence? Whether the merchant who advanced £500 to the captain of a Dutch ship to pay the salvors who rescued it when stranded has a lien upon the ship or only a personal remedy against the Dutch captain? Were the dying words of a clergyman, written down by a fellow clergyman and signed by five witnesses who heard the words, sufficient to make a nuncupative will? Can an unexecuted will which the testator had read and approved while ill but did not execute be propounded and what is the proper procedure for bringing this paper to the attention of the court? Can a man marry his former wife's sister and are their children legitimate? Can the ordinary grant permission for the building of a public road through part of the churchyard when the members of the parish are opposed? If churchwardens have themselves paid money for the repair of the church and the vestry imposed on the parishioners a rate for the reimbursement of these expenses, what remedy do the churchwardens have to obtain reimbursement after the church court held that the rate was invalid because the vestry was called without adequate notice?[36]

This sampling from the opinions as counsel which Scott prepared

---

[36] R.A., Stowell's Notebook, 2, 3, 17, 25, 29, 32, 37, 39, 42, 54, 58, 64, 80, 82, 84, 88, 91, 104, 111, 133.

during the year and a half he recorded his practice in a notebook reveals his day-to-day work as a civilian. Though many of the issues today sound quaint, such questions, often of little moment, filled part of the civilian's life and provided a slight addition to his other sources of income.

Scott's practice notebook also recorded the arguments and judgments in cases he attended in such courts as the Prerogative Court or the Court of Arches. He is careful to note the precedents cited by counsel and the reasons given by the judge for his judgment. Since few, if any, of these cases were reported, it was only through this close attention to what happened in court that the civilians could develop a sense for the law that was applied in the ecclesiastical and admiralty courts. The notebook gives us an accurate impression of the practice of the small cosy coterie of civilians which remained basically unchanged when Charles Dickens, sixty years later, described that 'mighty snug little party' known as Doctors' Commons. One day Scott sat as judge, another day he represented clients or attended court while other civilians were counsel and judges, who might have been deputies, surrogates or some other official of the court on another occasion. As Dickens wrote,

You shall go [to Doctors' Commons] one day, and find them blundering through half the nautical terms in Young's Dictionary, apropos of the 'Nancy' having run down the 'Sarah Jane', or Mr. Peggotty and the Yarmouth boatmen having put off in a gale of wind with an anchor and cable to the 'Nelson' Indiamen in distress; and you shall go there another day, and find them deep in the evidence, pro and con, respecting a clergyman who has misbehaved himself; and you shall find the judge in the nautical case, the advocate in the clergyman case, or contrariwise. They are like actors: now a man's a judge, and now he is not a judge; now he's one thing, now he's another! now he's something else, change and change about; but it's always a very pleasant, profitable little affair of private theatricals, presented to an uncommonly select audience.[37]

Through the entries of this notebook Scott displayed his continuing effort to develop his grasp of the law. He recorded the precedents cited during the arguments, often including cases decided at common law.[38] He listed the common law authorities he intended to use, apparently in preparation for a case he was to argue.[39] He copied into

[37] C. Dickens, *David Copperfield*, ed. N. Burgis (Oxford, 1981), 292.
[38] E.g. argument in *Booth v. Panter* (1788), Prerogative Court, R.A., Stowell's Notebook, 6.
[39] List of citations concerning revocation of wills. *Ibid.*, 82.

the notebook a letter he had received from Henry Cowper, reporter of King's Bench cases at the time of Lord Mansfield. Scott apparently had asked Cowper whether in a reported decision Cowper had accurately represented Mansfield's words. Cowper, of course, assured Scott that the reported version was perfectly correct and also sent along his own version of the judgment in another case touching the same point which had been reported inaccurately by a different reporter.[40] The precise issue which concerned Scott in this exchange with Cowper is summarized in the notes; it is less important than Scott's persistent pursuit, demonstrated by this letter, of an ever more accurate understanding of the law. At the back of the notebook Scott wrote nearly thirty pages of notes of old prize appeal cases he had extracted from some other source. There is no indication of the date at which he did this work, nor of the sources he used. He probably worked from some annotated copies of the case files for the Lords Commissioners for Prize Appeals, or perhaps from the notebooks of earlier civilians. He summarized the judgments of some 135 prize appeals.[41] Although these summaries are brief and probably of use to no one but Scott, they again indicate the seriousness with which he sought professional development.

[40] Letter from Henry Cowper, February 5, 1789, discussing *Rich v. Coe* (1777), 2 Cowp. 636, and sending a copy of his notes concerning *Wilkins and others v. Carmichael* (1779), 1 Dougl. 101, R.A., Stowell's Notebook, 60–2. *Rich* involved a suit against the owners of a vessel by materialmen and repairmen who had provisioned and repaired it on order of the master who had chartered the vessel. Scott questioned the statement in Mansfield's opinion that 'Whoever supplies a ship with necessaries, has a treble security. 1. The person of the master. 2. The specific ship. 3. The personal security of the owners, whether they know of the supply or not.' Cowper assured Scott that he too had been surprised when Mansfield had used the words 'the specific ship' (implying an *in rem* remedy) but had reported the opinion as rendered, even though he thought it wrong. Cowper sent along his own notes of *Wilkins* which he said were fuller than the opinion as reported by Douglas and which, Cowper claimed, effectively overruled *Rich*. *Wilkins* had also raised the issue of a materialman's lien on the ship. Douglas had reported Mansfield as saying: '[I]f there was any lien originally, it was only in the carpenter.' Cowper stated that, according to his own notes, Mansfield had said: '[T]he only creditor who c[oul]d have a Lien upon the ship is the Builder or Carpenter who has the ship in his Possession *in the dock*[.] The Rest had no lien.' (Italics are in the Stowell notebook.) The type of mechanic's lien remedy implied in Cowper's version of *Wilkins* is obviously wholly different from the language in *Rich* which seemed to imply an *in rem* remedy against the ship at common law.

[41] Under the heading 'Adm Prize Appeals', Scott wrote one sentence summaries of the decrees of the Lords Commissioners for Prize Appeals. Most of the prize cases came from the years 1740–50, but a significant number came from the period 1701–10. R.A., Stowell's Notebook, 300–29.

The office of King's Advocate, which Scott held for ten years prior to his appointment as judge of the admiralty court, gave him opportunities not only to represent the government's interests in court, but also to draft opinions for the Foreign Office on a wide variety of questions such as neutral rights, trade with a belligerent's colonies, treaty interpretation, impressment, domicile of merchants trading in various countries and the rights of parties in prize cases. Well over a hundred of his opinions to the Foreign Office have been compiled. During the years Scott was King's Advocate, his brother John served first as Solicitor General and later as Attorney General. Thus, some of these opinions to the Foreign Office were signed by the two Scott brothers, as two of the law officers of the Crown. The government obviously respected Scott's opinion on such issues since even after he became admiralty judge it occasionally sought his advice on a number of issues.[42]

In October 1798, when Scott had just turned fifty-three, his long and varied apprenticeship ended. He was appointed to serve as judge of the High Court of Admiralty in place of Sir James Marriott who had become too infirm to continue as judge. Scott would continue to serve as judge of the admiralty court for twenty-nine eventful years. The king was informed of Scott's appointment and was told that he was 'in every point of view ... the most proper person to fill that office'.[43] Scott certainly was the right man for the admiralty court. Practically everything he had done in his many years of education and legal experience seemed in retrospect to have laid the groundwork for these years as admiralty judge. His Tory politics undoubtedly did not hurt his chances. Furthermore, Scott took over this office at a critical moment in the nation's history, in the early years of the long and mortal struggle with France for survival. If Scott had presided over

---

[42] *Law officers' opinions to the Foreign Office*, ed. C. Parry (97 vols., Westmead, England, 1970–3), I, pp. 224–420, 540; XXV, pp. 3–38; XXVIII, pp. 13–16; XXXVI, pp. 115–63; XXXIX, p. 106; XLI, pp. 2–13; LIV, pp. 2–4, 308; LXI, pp. 2–26, 43; LXII, p. 52; LXVI, p. 5; LXXVIII, pp. 2–7; LXXXVIII, p. 2. Some of his opinions to the government on other topics are reproduced in *The later correspondence of George III*, ed. A. Aspinall (5 vols., Cambridge, 1966–70), e.g. nos. 1024, 2770, 3513; see also Lord Liverpool to Wm Scott, John Nicholl and Christopher Robinson, March 14, 1814. Brit. Lib., Add. MS 38,256, fo. 355.

[43] Marriott was given a pension of £2,000 per year to induce him to retire. *Correspondence of George III*, no. 1859.

the admiralty court in time of peace, he would have been as long forgotten as Sir Thomas Salusbury or Dr Stephen Lushington.[44] At a crucial moment in history he brought a mature, seasoned judgment to confront novel and momentous issues of international relations. His fame rests entirely upon his success as admiralty judge.

Many who have read Scott's judgments in the reports of the Consistory Court or the admiralty court have expressed admiration for the simplicity, clarity and grace of his expression. It is clear, however, that he was a diffident speaker, whether he was presenting his arguments in court or speaking in Parliament. When he began his practice as a civilian he insisted on writing out his arguments in full and reading them to the court. He apparently developed some confidence so that written speeches were no longer necessary, but he never achieved the fluency of a good public speaker. One observer who had been impressed by the 'precision and elegance in [Scott's] recorded opinions', attended the admiralty court in 1819 to hear him deliver his judgment. The observer was disappointed. 'It was extemporaneous, or delivered without any notes that were perceptible from my position', he noted, 'neither was it long; but his elocution did not appear to me the best; his manner was hesitating; his sentences more than once got entangled, and his words were sometimes recalled that others might be substituted.'[45] Scott, undoubtedly aware of the limitation of his oral delivery, spent much time preparing his judgments for publication. On occasion he stopped the press to correct a single line or to worry over the correct punctuation.[46] One has the impression that he consciously thought of himself as a Mansfield of prize law, articulating the principles for an entire body of law.

Scott's thirty years as a member of Parliament merit at least a brief mention in this biographical sketch. As early as 1779 he had expressed an interest in obtaining a seat in Parliament, a convenient stepping

---

[44] Salusbury was judge of the admiralty court, 1751–73; Lushington, judge, 1838–67.
　　Lord Grenville, the Foreign Secretary, congratulated Scott on his appointment as admiralty judge. The appointment, he wrote prophetically, 'will not only retrieve the nearly lost character of the Court of Admiralty, but will place it on a much higher footing than it has hitherto stood'. Grenville to Scott, October 27, 1798, Beinecke Library, Yale University, Osborne File.

[45] The American ambassador Richard Rush, whose observations are reproduced in 'Sir William Scott a hundred years ago', *Juridical Rev.*, 35 (1923), 239, 241. See also Surtees, *Lords Stowell and Eldon*, 66.

[46] Townsend, 'Life of Lord Stowell', 320.

stone for a young lawyer. In 1780 he sought to represent Oxford University, but the University predictably selected an older person to fill the seat. In 1784 Scott was chosen to represent the pocket-borough of Downton, but was unseated on petition. Finally, in 1790 he was selected for Downton, as already mentioned, with the influence of the Bouverie family whose sons he had tutored at Oxford. He sat for Downton until 1801 when he was grave enough to be selected to represent Oxford University. He held that seat till 1821 when he was given a peerage and took his seat in the House of Lords.[47]

Scott spoke more frequently in Parliament than is usually thought. He joined in the debate on issues which lay within the areas of his special expertise. He spoke most frequently on questions which touched the Church of England, invariably defending its rights and generally opposing reforms affecting the ecclesiastical authorities. Scott's bill to compel the residence of the lower clergy in their parishes was viewed by some clergy as a means of crushing the curates under the feet of absentee bishops.[48] He spoke at length and with special fervor in opposing Catholic emancipation in Ireland on the ground of national self-defense. Scott viewed the removal of legal incapacities for Irish Catholics as dangerous to the state and the Church of England. 'It is a question fraught with danger to the nation', he told

---

[47] *Ibid.*, 306–10; Mitchell, 'Dining club', 355.

[48] On the clergy non-residence bill, see Cobbett, XXXV, 1549 (1801); XXXVI, 463, 492, 889, 1514 (1802–3); Hansard, 1st ser. IV, 612 (1805). Scott's principal speech on this bill was published as a pamphlet: *Substance of the speech of ... Sir William Scott ... upon a motion for leave to bring in a bill relative to non-residence of the clergy* (London, 1802). Opponents of the bill also spoke out in pamphlets: T. Trim, *Ecclesiastical dignities, ecclesiastical grievances ... with observations on Sir William Scott's residence bill* (London, n.d.); *A letter to Sir William Scott upon his curate's bill* (London, 1803).

Scott also spoke on such topics as: the monastic institutions bill, the adultery prevention bill, the inferior ecclesiastical courts bill, the clergy penalties bill, the chapel exemption bill, the tithes law amendment bill, the new churches building bill and (as Lord Stowell in the House of Lords) the marriage act amendment bill; Cobbett, XXXV, 304, 316, 359 (1800); Hansard 1st ser. XXI, 306–9 (1812); XXIII, 806–7 (1812); XXV, 761–2 (1813); XXVI, 311–12, 706–7 (1813); XXVII, 360–1, 741 (1814); XXXI, 851–3 (1815); XXXIV, 689–90 (1816); XXXVI, 124–5 (1817); XXXVII, 552–3, 1131–2 (1818); Hansard, 2nd ser. VII, 428, 1132–7 (1818); VIII, 124 (1823); IX, 661–4 (1823).

Scott wrote the Archbishop of Canterbury, February 7, 1812, stating that he had opposed an inquiry into the practices of the ecclesiastical courts. He reminded the Archbishop that the civilians had studiously avoided mentioning in Parliament the

Parliament, 'and one which hazards the setting fire to the country.'[49]

Scott displayed irritation and touchiness when any suggestion of undue delay, excessive fees or mishandling of funds affected the admiralty court and its officials. He repeatedly sprang to the defense of the King's Proctor, the King's Advocate and the civilians in general. Scott insisted that any accusations could undermine the respect and authority of the admiralty court in the eyes of parties from neutral nations.[50]

Scott opposed reform of education or the Church or anything at all that remotely bore the scent of reform. In a letter to the American Supreme Court Justice, Joseph Story, Scott expressed the philosophy he shared with his brother John, Lord Eldon. He wrote that they resisted reform altogether, moderate reform even more strenuously than what he called the violent kind. He felt that violent reform would never take place unless moderate reform had first made a breach in the constitution. Once such a breach was made, he feared, the violent reformers would all rush in.[51]

At least as early as 1805 there were rumors at Oxford that Scott was to be awarded a peerage, but nothing came of the rumors for some years.[52] Perhaps one reason for the reluctance to grant him a peerage

serious imperfections in the ecclesiastical courts out of fear of precipitating radical reform. Nonetheless, Scott said that the issue was now before Parliament and the Church must accept some reform of its court system. Beinecke Library, Yale University, Osborne File.

[49] Hansard, 1st ser. XXII, 862 (1812). Scott's major speeches on Catholic emancipation are: Hansard, 1st ser. IV, 966 (1805); XVII, 182–7 (1810); XXII, 860–6 (1812); XXIV, 1006–18 (1813). Scott even opposed a bill which would have exempted Irish potato farmers from paying a tithe on potatoes for the support of the Church of England. Hansard, 1st ser. XXIII, 943–4 (1812).

Scott also wrote to the Vice-Chancellor of Oxford urging him to send a petition to Parliament in response to the Catholic petitions. He insisted that the University should oppose 'so dangerous a measure' as Catholic emancipation. Scott to Vice-Chancellor, March 14, 1807, Harvard Law Library.

[50] See the debates over the prize agency bill, the admiralty registrar's bill, and discussions of abuses in the admiralty court and the conduct of the prize court, Hansard, 1st ser. IV, 61–5 (1804); V, 136–7 (1805); XV, 13–15, 472–4 (1810); XIX, 477–9 (1811); XX, 1001 (1811); XXIII, 627–8 (1812); XXVI, 245 (1813).

Scott was also involved in the preparation of a bill for the regulation of the vice-admiralty courts. Scott to Rufus King, April 18, April 19, May 4, May 21, 1801, N.Y.H.S., Rufus King Papers, vol. 54, fos. 375–9.

[51] Scott to Joseph Story, n.d. (apparently in 1820), Humanities Research Center, University of Texas at Austin. See also, Scott to Rev. Dr Butler, November 30, 1820. Brit. Lib., Add. MS 34,585, fo. 53.

[52] A group of letters concerning a possible successor to Scott as member for Oxford University is collected in Brit. Lib., Add. MS 37,909.

was that no civilian had ever been so honored. Scott craved the honor and earnestly solicited it from Lord Liverpool. At the end of the war in a letter to Lord Liverpool, who then headed the cabinet, Scott poured out his feelings in requesting consideration for a peerage. Though the letter grates on a present sense of proprieties, it was probably not extraordinary in Scott's day. Only an extensive quotation from the letter will capture the depth of Scott's desire for this reward. After excusing himself for troubling Liverpool, Scott began by insisting that his constituents in Oxford had begun a canvass to replace him in Parliament based on their expectation that he would be honored 'with a Call to the other House of Parliament'. Although Scott tried to quell these rumors in Oxford, he said they persisted. Scott continued,

Your Lordship will not suppose that I am absurd enough to build Pretensions to such a distinction upon any grounds which such Expectations and Rumours can furnish. I cannot but be well aware that they must rest upon other Foundations – those of Public Merits and Services – which It is not for me to assert in my own Case, but for my Country and those who conduct its Government to judge . . . whether they exist – to estimate their Value, if they are so found – and to submit them, if satisfactory in Both Respects, to the Royal Consideration. But may I be permitted, under shelter of this Observation, to represent, that if, during many (much the greater Part of) the most eventful years which the History of the World has witnessed, I have conducted a species of Jurisdiction highly delicate in itself and affecting the most important Concerns of the Country in a manner that has neither impaired its Interests or its Honour, if I have now attended for sixteen years the Business of almost every department of His Majesty's Privy Council, if I have, for a much longer term, uniformly supported in Parliament those Plans of Policy which I had Reason to suppose were honoured with the Royal approbation as most conducive to the Publick Welfare, I may venture to look back upon my Publick Conduct as not entirely destitute of good deserving; at the same time that my own Estimation of my own Claims might fall far short of producing the Expectation of such a Mark of the Royal Favour, if it was not sustained by the Testimonies of favourable opinions which I have occasionally received – Opinions, which I have some Reason to consider as not confined to this Country, but as generally prevailing amongst the subjects of other States who have attended to the Conduct of Great Britain as represented in its Tribunals of International Law during these extended and protracted Hostilities. By the Concurrence of such opinions I am encouraged to hope that I have not been wholly unsuccessful in my Endeavours to establish a system that should permanently connect some of the most essential Interests of my Country with the most undisputed Principles of General Justice.

In applying to your Lordship with the Request that my Claims, whatever they may be, may not be entirely unconsidered, I am not conscious that I violate any delicacy in stating that the Hopes of receiving such a distinction have been at different times excited in me by favourable Intimations from those who have directed His Majesty's Councils; and that the prevailing Expectation which induces me to trouble your Lordship at the present, furnishes at least a proof that the Publick would not receive it with any feelings of surprise or dissatisfaction.[53]

A touch of envy of his younger brother John, already a baron, would have been readily understandable. Scott's hint that some appropriate honor had been promised by the government must raise questions of governmental attempts to influence his judicial independence. Finally, upon the occasion of the coronation of George IV, Scott was created Baron Stowell of Stowell Park. At the age of seventy-six he thus took a seat in the House of Lords, but seldom participated actively in debate.[54]

A few words about Scott's personal and family life will fill out this impressionistic picture of his life. Apparently his first romance with the daughter of a wealthy wholesale grocer in Newcastle had led only to frustration. The girl's father sought a more exalted marriage for his daughter.[55] When he was thirty-five and his prospects in legal practice were better, Scott married Anna Maria, the eldest daughter and co-heir of John Bagnall of Earley Court, Berkshire. When his father-in-law died, Earley Court became Scott's principal residence outside London.[56] Scott lived with his wife till her death in 1809. They had four children, but two died in infancy. In reading the letters which have survived, we can occasionally catch a brief glimpse of a relaxed Scott, enjoying a holiday with his family at Ramsgate or expressing his excitement at the races.[57] Scott's son and daughter, William and Mary Anne, lived to adulthood, but only Mary Anne survived her father. Scott had refused to allow his son William a sufficient allowance to

---

[53] Scott to Liverpool, June 27, 1814, Brit. Lib., Add. MS 38,258, fo. 100. Liverpool's reply of August 4, 1814 made it clear that Scott could not expect a peerage in the immediate future. *Ibid.*, fo. 261.

Requests for a peerage appear to have been common enough, see for instance, Brit. Lib., Add. MS 31,232, fo. 302; Add. MS 38,191, fos. 161, 165; Add. MS 38,192, fo. 51; Add. MS 38,193, fo. 192. It is much more difficult to find examples of sitting judges pleading for a peerage.

[54] Townsend, 'Life of Lord Stowell', 340.

[55] Surtees, *Lords Stowell and Eldon*, 26.

[56] Townsend, 'Life of Lord Stowell', 306.

[57] Scott to Rufus King, August 12, 1801, N.Y.H.S., Rufus King Papers; Scott to [Wm Howley], August 28, 1818. In this letter Scott added the note: 'It is the Race Week! Sweepstakes & Handicaps every day! Balls, Plays & Concerts every night.' Beinecke Library, Yale University, Osborne File.

marry the girl of his choice and the son apparently became an alcoholic and died shortly before Scott himself died, at a time when Scott was too senile to be aware of anything.[58]

When he was a widower of sixty-seven, Scott met the Marchioness of Sligo under bizarre circumstances, and she soon became his second wife.[59] This unhappy interlude lasted only five years. These two older persons, set in their personal habits, could not make the adjustments necessary for married life. His tight-fisted management of the finances never met with her approval. Scott heard of his second wife's death in 1817 while he was traveling alone in Switzerland, yet he remained in Switzerland for several more weeks.[60]

Throughout life it appears that he maintained close ties with his brother John, who was appointed Lord Chief Justice of Common Pleas in 1799 and Lord Chancellor, 1801 to 1806 and again in 1807 to 1827. John had previously served as Solicitor General and Attorney General. He was given the title Baron Eldon in 1799 at the time he was made Chief Justice and, on the occasion of the coronation of George IV he was made Earl Eldon.[61] In all English legal history, it is impossible to find brothers who had both risen to comparable heights of the legal profession. Although few of William's letters to John have survived, a large collection of John's letters to William have been preserved by the Scott family.[62] Since most of John's letters to his brother are signed Eldon, that name will be followed here.

The letters of Eldon to his brother are filled with bits of personal news, illnesses, family problems, expressions of exhaustion from work and a few unexpected insights, such as mention of Scott's favorite pastime, fishing. In the later years the brothers corresponded nearly every day and in the 1820s and early 30s the letters are filled

[58] Townsend, 'Life of Lord Stowell', 328.

[59] Scott, while presiding over the criminal sessions of admiralty at Old Bailey, had the son of the dowager Lady Sligo as a defendant. The young Marquis of Sligo, in the midst of the Napoleonic war, had bribed two seamen to desert the Royal Navy so that they could serve on his own yacht. Scott was paternal but severe in sentencing the Marquis (£5,000 fine plus four months in Newgate). Because of this strange incident Scott met Lady Sligo who apparently admired the way he had dealt with her son. P.R.O. HCA 1/87, fos. 36–7; Townsend, 'Life of Lord Stowell', 328–30.

[60] Townsend, 'Life of Lord Stowell', 330–1; Surtees, *Lords Stowell and Eldon*, 133–5.

[61] Surtees, *Lords Stowell and Eldon*, 84–91, 124.

[62] These letters are at the Scott home, Encombe, Corfe Castle, Dorset. Lt Col H. L. Scott generously made these letters available for my research.

with political gossip and dire predictions of the likely results of various proposed reforms.

Since both brothers were so completely immersed in their legal careers, a number of letters contain references to their mutual professional interests. Eldon, in 1799, congratulated his brother, who had been admiralty judge for just a year, on his success in completing so much court business. Apparently Scott's predecessor had left the admiralty docket badly in arrears. In an undated letter, probably from 1809, Eldon advised his brother not to think of resigning his admiralty court position to assume the offices of Dean of the Arches and judge of the Prerogative Court, which ranked higher professionally than judge of the admiralty court.[63] Eldon urged his brother not to give up his present position 'merely because a Junior [John Nicholl] will have professional Rank beyond the Judge of the Admiralty'. He reminded his brother of the crucial importance of the admiralty judge in the time of national need. In another letter Eldon asked his brother if he had ever heard that Lord Northington had held, along with Mansfield, the doctrine 'once free, a Slave was always free'. If so, where did Northington state the opinion? In 1802 Eldon queried his brother concerning an application he had received for a prohibition to the court of prize appeals. He had denied the prohibition, but felt uneasy since nobody was in town to be consulted. Eldon in an undated letter discussed his understanding of two poorly drafted statutes, Lord Liverpool's Register Acts, which concerned registration of ships. Eldon occasionally showed his irritation, as when his brother apparently had asked his intervention in a particular case. Eldon told his brother:

I know very well that you like others do not mean to countenance any notion in any body who writes to you that they have Claims, or that I do not do my duty – but I am positively sure that such is the Inference they will draw from you and their Interposition, however slight – and I hope, therefore, you will allow me in the warmest Affection, to request that I may not have you made the Channel of Communication about my Causes.

In another undated letter Eldon told his brother not to be concerned about an application for an injunction he had received concerning an admiralty case. He assured his brother that all parties agreed that 'all

---

[63] Sir William Wynne stepped down from the two offices in 1809 and was replaced by Sir John Nicholl.

which has been done at your Court is perfectly right'. It was not a case of conflict of jurisdiction at all, Eldon insisted, but only a request for equitable relief after judgment on the ground of discovery of new facts.[64]

Scott's abiding belief in the law of nations comes out dramatically in these letters he exchanged with his brother. After Waterloo in 1815 the question arose of how the allies should dispose of Bonaparte. Although we have only Eldon's letters to his brother, it is clear Scott had insisted that the law of nations required that Bonaparte as a French subject be delivered to his French sovereign, Louis XVIII. Eldon, the practical politician, found the suggestion utterly unfeasible. '[N]o one of the Allies would have listened for a Moment to his being delivered up.' Eldon clearly rejected Scott's arguments and advised him, '[I]f you can't make this a Casus exceptionis or omissus within the Law of Nations founded upon Necessity you will not readily know what to say upon it.'[65] Scott thus, even in private correspondence with his brother on a highly controversial question which would have divided the most astute commentators on the law of nations, maintained an unpopular position because he thought it derived from the law of nations. The law of nations, which he had studied half a century earlier at Oxford and had applied for many years as judge of the admiralty court, remained a vivid reality with

---

[64] These letters, all preserved at Encombe, are in the files of letters (more than 500 letters) which Eldon wrote to his brother. The entire collection of Eldon Papers at Encombe is, of course, much more extensive than these files.

[65] Eldon to Wm Scott, October 6, 1815, Encombe Papers. See also another letter, dated only 1815, by Eldon to Wm Scott discussing the different views on the proper treatment of Bonaparte. Scott apparently did not make his position public in the debate on the effective detention of Bonaparte. *Annual Register*, 1816, 30–2.

In an earlier letter Eldon vaguely discussed advice Scott had given concerning Guadaloupe. Eldon said that Scott had indicated he would not support Eldon's action as not agreeable to the law of nations. Eldon continued: 'The foreign Secretary, too, does not like a business, which he understands you think contrary to that law ... If you have altered your mind as to the Law of Nations about Guad[alou]pe & will support us in the House of Commons ... say so in a short line.' January 1813, Encombe Papers.

Another clear example of Scott's strong convictions concerning the law of nations comes out in a letter Scott wrote as King's Advocate. He had been asked by the Secretary of War about an incident at St Lucia. Scott set up the law of nations as the norm for judging an English general who had been accused of compelling a contribution from the surrendered inhabitants of St Lucia. Scott in his advice to the government concluded: 'But with respect to the peaceable Inhabitants of a settled Country, not bearing arms, nor inclosed in any fortified Place, and willing to give

discernible rules binding upon all civilized governments. For Scott the law of nations was not entirely a facade he used to convince foreign parties that his judgments were compelled by a supernational body of rules.

These letters allow a slight glimpse of the types of matters the two brothers, the Lord Chancellor and the admiralty judge, talked about when they had time together. We catch a faint echo of the long hours the two brothers must have spent through their extraordinarily long professional careers, sipping port and debating legal issues.

Sir William Scott, Lord Stowell, continued as admiralty judge till he was eighty-two. During the Christmas vacation, in February 1828, after twenty-nine years of service, he retired. His sight and his voice were failing, but his mind continued to be clear for several more years. He lived for eight more years, but increasing senility made him less and less aware or able to understand what was going on around him. Because of his inability to grasp its significance, he was not informed of the death of his only surviving son, William, in 1835 and was thus unable to alter his will. He continued to live at his country home, Earley Court. Scott died at the age of ninety on January 28, 1836 and was buried at Sonning, near Reading.[66]

submission, the immediate Plunder of the Property of such Persons, I take to be not permitted by the Modern Law of Nations, and consequently, that a Ransom or Composition ought not to be demanded.' Wm Scott to Dundas, June 1, 1794, Brit. Lib., Add. MS 38,353, fo. 88. See also Scott to Grenville, December 24, 1794, P.R.O. FO 83,2204, fo. 38.

[66] Townsend, 'Life of Lord Stowell', 352. The will of Lord Stowell can be found in P.R.O. Prob. 11/1859/190. By the third and last codicil dated November 12, 1831, Stowell left to his son all his books and personal papers. These invaluable papers and books could not be located during my research.

3

THE LAW OF THE INSTANCE COURT

Sir William Scott, who late in life became Lord Stowell, is principally remembered for his numerous judgments as judge of the prize court in which he discussed and developed many facets of international law. As admiralty judge he also heard and determined a steady trickle of commercial maritime disputes brought by private parties who invoked the court's instance jurisdiction. Some of these instance judgments influenced the development of admiralty law. This chapter will analyze these instance decisions in light of the law the admiralty court applied fifty or seventy-five years earlier. The chief source for comparing Scott's judgments with eighteenth-century instance law is a draft abridgment of admiralty law, both instance and prize, which was prepared by Sir Edward Simpson, a civilian, about the middle of the eighteenth century. Scott had acquired this manuscript notebook, which is more fully described in the Appendix. In three cases he explicitly relied on it when giving his decision.[1]

The admiralty court in the eighteenth and early nineteenth centuries, despite the earlier prohibitions of the common law courts,

---

[1] This notebook now in the office of the Registrar of the Admiralty, London, will be cited as R.A., Simpson MS.

W. Welwood, a Scottish civilian, had published *An abridgement of all sea-laws* (London, 1613) to attract the attention of the new English King. It relies on authorities of Roman law, early compilations of sea law such as the Laws of Oleron, and Scottish law, but generally ignores the law or practice of the English High Court of Admiralty. It would have been a somewhat useful book for seamen, masters and merchants, but not for a judge of the admiralty court.

The most significant and useful source information about shipping law was C. Abbott (the future Lord Tenterden), *A treatise of the law relative to merchant ships and seamen* (Philadelphia, 1802). (The Philadelphia edition of that year has been used in this chapter.) Abbott consolidated the statute and common law material on shipping into a clear and concise treatise. He referred occasionally to reported admiralty court judgments from the first three volumes of Robinson's *Reports* of

continued to hear some of the disputes which arose from the maritime commerce of the nation. But without the enormous business generated by the capture of vessels in time of war, the prize cases, the admiralty court remained largely an idle, backwater court. Since they received no fixed salaries, the court's officials had to survive on a lean harvest of fees whenever the misfortune of peace occurred. Prior to the French wars the principal registrar received only £111 for the year 1792 from the fees of his offices as registrar of the courts of admiralty, prize appeals and delegates. In 1797, during the war, he received £10,340 from the fees of the admiralty court and an additional £1,024 as registrar of the court of prize appeals. The office of registrar of the Court of Delegates brought him only £20. Similarly in 1792 the marshal of the admiralty court received only £221 from the fees of his office, whereas in 1797 during the war he received £4,210.[2]

The table shows graphically the substantial drop in the business of the admiralty court after 1815 when the last of the wartime prize cases were gradually working their way through the court.[3] This list, which

Scott's decisions. Abbott also referred to the history of maritime law and to the treatises by continental authorities.

Abbott's treatise was expanded by F. L. Holt's *A system of the shipping and navigation laws of Great Britain*, 2nd edn (2 vols., London, 1824). (The 1824 edition will be referred to in this chapter.) Since Holt appeared toward the end of Scott's tenure as judge, it included more references to his admiralty court decisions. Holt, as Abbott, was primarily a treatise based on statutes and common law opinions.

Scott's predecessor as admiralty judge, Sir James Marriott, published a small compilation of forms used in the admiralty court, *Formulare instrumentorum: or, a formulary of authentic instruments, writs, and standing orders, used in the High Courts of Admiralty of Great Britain, of prize and instance* (London, 1802).

A. Browne published his lectures on the civil law delivered at the University of Dublin under the title *A compendious view of the civil law, and of the law of the admiralty*, 2nd edn (2 vols., London, 1802). The second volume which discussed the admiralty court relied on some general treatises on maritime law and on a narrow range of common law cases. Browne's lectures were of much more use to his students than to Scott, to whom the treatise was dedicated.

Throughout this chapter there will be references to personal notebooks of civilians who compiled notes of admiralty cases for their own use. One such manuscript notebook by Sir William Burrell has been published in 1885 by R. G. Marsden and is cited as Burrell. Burrell's notebook included reports of admiralty judgments, instance and prize, from the years 1758–74, with a few records from later years.

[2] *Courts of justice the report of the select committee appointed by the House of Commons to enquire into the establishment of the courts of justice* ... (London, 1799), 13; *Report of the commissioners for examining into the duties, salaries, and emoluments of the officers, clerks and ministers of the several courts of justice* ..., R. Com. Rep., 1824 (240), 9–16. Figures for total incomes are not available in the second report for the Napoleonic years.

[3] *Salaries and retired allowances to judges*, R. Com. Rep., 1833 (230), 3.

	Number of cases tried	Number of days on which the court sat for business
1793	403	47
1794	824	75
1795	1,693	60
1796	818	52
1797	671	73
1798	880	54
1799	1,470	74
1800	1,420	78
1801	1,634	105
1802	518	63
1803	1,125	59
1804	1,144	83
1805	1,175	87
1806	2,286	115
1807	1,789	99
1808	1,532	88
1809	1,161	55
1810	1,388	91
1811	1,082	77
1812	813	51
1813	944	49
1814	525	59
1815	413	39
1816	185	37
1817	128	30
1818	83	38
1819	69	37
1820	51	28
1821	57	26
1822	64	38
1823	83	33
1824	53	29
1825	86	36
1826	93	32
1827	105	32
1828	76	34
1829	66	36
1830	39	30
1831	54	32
1832	37	28

Note: Scott was judge of the admiralty court from 1798 through the year 1827.

was prepared by the deputy registrar in 1833, includes both the prize and the instance cases actually tried by the court. By consulting the indexes of the instance court assignation books, it is possible to identify about 75 instance cases filed in 1800, about 130 filed in 1810 and about 110 filed in 1820.[4] Many of these instance cases were dismissed or settled. These figures for instance cases filed thus give only a rough idea of the portion of the cases in the table which were actually tried as instance cases. They confirm, however, that the instance court dealt with only a fairly insignificant number of cases each year.

A more careful tabulation of the instance cases filed for the years 1799 to 1802 indicates that most of these cases fell into five categories. During these four years seventy-three cases were filed for mariners' wages, forty-five cases of civil salvage or derelict, thirty cases of bottomry bonds, twelve cases of damage (which included collision cases), and eleven cases of possession.[5] There were also a number of other cases filed including occasional appeals to the High Court of Admiralty from the various vice-admiralty courts in Navigation Act cases. These revenue cases, which occupied a small proportion of the docket, will not be discussed. They generally involved questions of factual disputes and statutory interpretation. The commercial maritime disputes within the court's authority, the five categories of cases already mentioned, provide the materials for this study of instance jurisdiction.

This work is about Scott as admiralty judge. His reliance on prior decided cases, therefore, or his independence of such precedents should remain the primary point of interest. Prior to Scott's years as judge, no admiralty judgments had been published. If it is necessary to reconstruct from manuscript sources the contours of the instance law as the admiralty court applied it in the eighteenth century, the purpose is not to write a treatise on admiralty law from that period, but rather to make it vividly clear that the court had developed a full, complex, subtle body of law long before Scott became judge and that he knew of and relied on that unpublished body of law in most of his instance judgments. Of course, Scott did not always find the stormy

---

[4] P.R.O. HCA 6/44, 45; 6/58; 7/1; 7/13, 14. Since the assignation books include many entries for most of the cases indexed and many of the cases are continued in the indexes for two or more years, it is difficult to give precise figures for the number of cases filed in any one year.

[5] P.R.O. HCA 6/44, 45.

channels marked by precedent. Since he had a thorough grasp of the social and economic realities of the shipping industry, he had occasion to discuss the broader policy reasons behind some of his judgments. Scott's unique contribution can only be grasped by this detailed comparison and contrast with past admiralty practice. Although eighteenth-century civilians undoubtedly had access to personal notebooks and other compilations of cases, only a few of these have been located and analyzed for this study. These meager manuscript sources will provide some clues to the law applied by the instance court prior to Scott's day as judge.

SUITS FOR MARINERS' WAGES

The merchant seamen, like their counterparts on the land, lived in a structured society. The crew before the mast (the ship's boys, the ordinary seamen and the able seamen) were differentiated largely by age and experience. The higher-ranking members of the crew, the cook, the carpenter, the boatswain, one or two mates, the surgeon and perhaps a gunner, and, in larger vessels, a sailmaker, caulker and others, had, or were supposed to have, specialized skills needed in service of the vessel and crew. Above them all was the master, who perhaps had worked his way from the lower ranks or more likely had been appointed by the owners because of his relationship or connections.

The lower ranks of common seamen came from the lower ranks of society, children of laborers, farmhands or seamen, those dissatisfied or unemployed on land. Those with some native cleverness and ambition could advance by slow steps from ship's boy to mate. Seamen earned their wages, occasionally as a share of the ship's earnings, but more frequently either as wages determined by the voyage on shorter trips or by the month on the longer voyages to the Baltic, Russia, Spain, the Mediterranean, America, Africa and the East Indies. Although the wages were probably higher than these men could have earned on land and there was, at least at first, the excitement and adventure of seeing new places, the life of the seaman was hard and dangerous. There was constant risk of wrecks, fires, collisions, storms, sickness, strange diseases, beatings and death at sea. The life aboard a naval vessel was even harsher. The additional risks from severe naval discipline, sea battles, capture and indefinite periods at sea induced many common seamen to avoid naval service. In time of war merchant seamen often jumped ship and forfeited their wages rather than face the press gangs which waited for arriving cargo vessels.

Although most modestly intelligent mariners could in time take the steps from ship's boy to boatswain, carpenter or even mate, the final step from first mate to master usually stopped their upward progress. The master's station placed him in a different position in society, with the possibility of earning a large salary and even achieving substantial wealth. The master, instead of being a constantly supervised subordinate, was the trusted agent and representative of the owners of the ship with vast responsibility not only for the navigation and maintenance of the vessel but often for the entire commercial interest of the owners and shippers. His actions, wise, foolish or criminal, usually bound the owners legally. Those who had invested in the vessel or cargo could be ruined by the master, far beyond their control, who could wreck the ship, cause immense damage to other ships or unwisely squander or abscond with the proceeds. While the master had absolute discretion and authority over his ship's crew, normally only the owners could select a master. Ownership of ships was ordinarily shared by many part owners in order to spread the risk of loss. The management usually fell to one or a few managing partners whose most important decisions were the purchase of a safe vessel, the choice of a profitable voyage and the selection of a competent, sober, trustworthy, resourceful master. Only if a mate could raise enough money to purchase a substantial share of the vessel could he ordinarily hope to become a master. The nephew or younger son of a merchant, or the son of a respected master had the best chance of being chosen by the owners as master. As the ship disappeared over the horizon, the owners had few means of rescuing the master if he were incompetent or restraining him if he were dishonest.[6]

This brief description of the role of masters and seamen within the shipping industry will provide the setting for the analysis of the suits for seamen's wages. These suits, the most common instance suits in the eighteenth and early nineteenth centuries, will be studied under

---

[6] R. Davis, *The rise of the English shipping industry in the seventeenth and eighteenth centuries* (London, 1962), 110–74. The duties of the master are discussed by Abbott, *Merchant ships*, 145–61.

several headings: the jurisdictional limits of the admiralty court; the nature and rules of interpretation of the mariners' contracts; the duties of the parties to the contract; and the grounds for forfeiture of mariners' wages. Finally this section will consider the judicial protection of the seamen Scott provided as admiralty judge and the sources relied on by him when he was not guided by precedent. Some brief suggestion of the prior state of the law will precede the analysis of Scott's judgments.

Jurisdictional limits

A half century before Scott became admiralty judge, it was settled that common law courts would not prohibit suits by seamen for wages. If the mate became master during the voyage, he could sue in the admiralty court for wages as mate. On the other hand, if a seaman signed on as mate and was wrongfully demoted to common seaman, he could recover his wages in admiralty as mate. But if the mariner's contract happened to be under seal, he could not sue in the admiralty court.[7] The mariners had the option of bringing suit against the ship, the owners or the master.[8] The master could sue in the admiralty court to recover apprentices' wages due to him or to recover advances he had made of mariners' wages.[9] The master could not sue for his wages in the admiralty court, but the civilians apparently thought that he could recover his wages in that court from the remaining proceeds from the sale of the vessel once it had been arrested and sold in a suit by the seamen for their wages.[10] It likewise seems clear that the admiralty court in the eighteenth century did hear suits for wages by

---

[7] R.A., Simpson MS 76, 251; *Davis v. Rotch* (1766), Burrell 20. The basic common law cases on point were *Ragg v. King* (1729), 2 Strange 858; *Read v. Chapman* (1731–2), 2 Strange 937; *Day v. Searle* (1732), 2 Strange 968. If a mariner had brought suit for wages in Common Pleas and subsequently brought suit in admiralty, he had to produce a release of the common law suit before the admiralty court would proceed. Lincoln's Inn Library, Misc. MS 147, 40.

[8] R.A., Simpson MS 246. If the ship had been lost or sold abroad, the seamen could sue the master or owners. *Ibid.*, fos. 29, 358.

[9] *Ibid.*, fos. 246, 310. If the apprentice deserted, the master forfeited the wages due. *Clarke v. Royal Duke* (1766), Burrell 17.

[10] R.A., Simpson MS 79, 291, 340; *Holland v. Money* (1767–8), Burrell 62, 76, arising from sale of the *Royal Charlotte*. This dubious procedure might have arisen from the case of *Barber and Philpot v. Wharton* (1726), 2 Ld. Raym. 1452, also reported as *Baker v. Wharton* (1726), 1 Barn. K.B. 2, in which King's Bench ultimately refused to grant a prohibition to stay an admiralty suit by a master for his wages. The rule for

British or even foreign seamen earned by service on foreign vessels. In such suits the court apparently contacted the consul of the foreign nation.[11]

By 1798 when Scott became admiralty judge, the limits of the court's authority had been well marked. Scott no longer fought the stale battles with the common law courts over jurisdiction. He knew perfectly well that

Suits for wages, due to mariners of our own country, have been said to be entertained by the Court of Admiralty, more from a kind of toleration founded upon the general convenience of the practice, than by any direct jurisdiction properly belonging to it, although the exercise of such a jurisdiction has existed from the first establishment of such a Court.[12]

The law reflected the sharp distinction in the shipping industry between seamen and masters. A master could not bring suit in the admiralty court for his wages, Scott said, 'because he is supposed to stand on the security of his personal contract with his owner, not relating to the bottom of the ship'.[13] The admiralty court could properly entertain a suit by a chief mate who was described as commander of the vessel because it was clear that he actually served as mate.[14] But if a mate had been promoted during the voyage to serve as master, he could only sue in the admiralty court as mate and must exclude the *quantum meruit* due as master, even though Scott was convinced that he had no chance of recovering at common law as master because of the insolvency of the owners. Scott knew that prohibitions had been granted in such suits.[15] Scott would not allow

the prohibition was discharged apparently because the admiralty court had already proceeded to sentence and it did not appear from the libel that the contract had been entered into on land. But, from a civilian's private digest of this case, it appears that the master had brought suit against the proceeds from the sale of the vessel after it had been arrested in a suit for mariners' wages. Lincoln's Inn Library, Misc. MS 147, 92. Perhaps the denial of a prohibition in this case led the civilians to think that the common law would allow suits by masters against the proceeds in the admiralty court from a suit by seamen for their wages.

[11] *Rachel* (1789), Arnold's Notebook, 1789, 57, P.R.O. HCA 30/470; *Sullivan* (1795), Nicholl's Notebook, 1793–7, 214, P.R.O. HCA 30/464; see also, J. Digges-Latouche, *Collections of cases, memorials, addresses and proceedings in Parliament relating to ... admiralty-courts* (London, 1757), 815.

[12] *Courtney (English)* (1810), Edw. 239, 240.

[13] *Favourite (Nicholas de Jersey)* (1799), 2 Rob. 232, 237. Abbott, *Merchant ships*, 288–9, citing the *Favourite*.

[14] *Lord Hobart (Gamage)* (1815), 2 Dod. 100, 104.

[15] *Favourite (Nicholas de Jersey)* (1799), 2 Rob. 232, 238. Similarly Scott, fearing a prohibition, refused jurisdiction where the seaman was suing to recover a share of the profits from a whaling voyage. *Sydney Cove (Fudge)* (1815), 2 Dod. 11, 12.

this mate to bring suit as master against the proceeds from the sale of the vessel which remained in the registry of the court.[16] As already mentioned, this mode of circumventing jurisdictional limits had apparently been tolerated in the mid-eighteenth century. Scott viewed the jurisdictional barrier more seriously. Although a carpenter clearly could sue in admiralty for his wages, Scott refused to allow a surgeon to do so since '[T]he contract of this gentleman is, in other respects, very different to the common contract of mariners for their wages.'[17]

One of the advantages of admiralty jurisdiction over seamen's wages was the freedom for many crew members to join in one suit.[18] This in part explains why suits at common law were not profitable for the common lawyers.

The admiralty court's power, Scott held, also reached suits by British or foreign seamen belonging to foreign vessels, even where the ship belonged to enemy aliens.[19] These suits by foreign seamen were allowed in the admiralty court to prevent a failure of justice where wages were due based on general maritime law. In such cases the court, Scott stated, had 'with the consent of the accredited agent of their own Government, entertained proceedings for wages at the suit of foreign seamen, against foreign Vessels in which they have served,

---

[16] *Favourite (Nicholas de Jersey)* (1799), 2 Rob. 232, 239. Scott said that no precedent had been found permitting a master to be paid his wages from the proceeds in the registry.

[17] *Lord Hobart (Gamage)* (1815), 2 Dod. 100, 104. Scott probably was aware that King's Bench had refused to grant a prohibition to a suit in the admiralty court by a surgeon. The court, in the opinion by Ryder, C.J., had held that the surgeon was obliged to assist in navigating the ship if called on by the master. Thus he should be considered a mariner. *Mills v. Long* (1754), Sayer 136. Scott was perhaps thinking of the Mills case in the surgeon's suit against the *Lord Hobart*, a post office packet, when he insisted on the unique character there of the surgeon's contract. 'The engagement which he has entered into is of a *mixed nature*, being made partly with His Majesty's post office and partly with the owners of the vessel'. 2 Dod. 104–5. Italics in the original.

[18] *Madonna D'Idra (Papaghica)* (1811), 1 Dod. 37, 39.

[19] *Vrow Mina (Behrends)* (1813), 1 Dod. 234; *Frederick (Bodom)* (1813), 1 Dod. 266, 267; *Maria Theresa (Phillips)* (1813), 1 Dod. 303, 304. All three cases involved American seamen. See also *Rosa (Rahden)* (1814), an unpublished judgment by Scott, Bod. Lib., 9 Monk Bretton Dep. A 141.
 Scott allowed suit by a British seaman who had signed on a British vessel in Britain. The vessel, however, had been transferred abroad to a foreign registry. Scott insisted: 'It can never be allowed that the owner shall, by selling his ship in a distant part of the world, divest the seaman of his wages earned under a contract entered into with himself in this country.' *Batavia alias Unity* (1822), 2 Dod. 500, 502.

such vessels being in the ports of this kingdom'.[20] Jurisdiction over
the vessel was thus essential to the court's jurisdiction over seamen
from foreign vessels. Although the court could enforce the general
maritime law, where the wage contract arose from the particular law
of a foreign country, the admiralty court, fearing a prohibition,
refused jurisdiction to enforce the foreign law.[21] In cases involving
English crews and English vessels, the mariners had an option to
select the party to be sued for wages. 'For the wages of mariners the
master is liable, the ship is liable, and the owner is liable.'[22]

Nature and interpretation of the mariners' contract

The admiralty court in the eighteenth century refused to enforce a
mariners' contract which included a clause by which the seamen, in
case the ship was lost on the homeward voyage, agreed not to demand
wages earned by delivery of cargo to the outward ports. The court
held such contracts void in law. The admiralty court, unlike the
common law courts, applied equitable principles in construing the
contract favorably to the mariners.[23] In a passage from the Simpson
notebook, which Scott explicitly referred to, it was stated that the
admiralty court in the eighteenth century, despite the language of the
statute for regulating seamen's contracts, could act as a court of equity

[20] *Courtney (English)* (1810), Edw. 239, 241; see also *Wilhelm Frederick (Noorman)*
(1823), 1 Hag. 138, 141.
[21] *Courtney (English)* (1810), Edw. 239, 241.
[22] *Jack Park (Little)* (1802), 4 Rob. 308, 310–11; *Lady Ann (Wardell)* (1810), Edw.
235. Where a seaman had requested to be paid abroad by bill of exchange rather than
in cash, he could not subsequently sue the owners or the ship when the bill was
refused because of the bankruptcy of the owners. *William Money (Jackson)* (1827),
2 Hag. 136.
[23] R.A., Simpson MS 267, 366. This apparently referred to the ship *Willing*, which was
affirmed by the Court of Delegates in 1724. Lincoln's Inn Library, Misc. MS 147,
221–3.
   The case of *Cutter v. Powell* (1795), 6 T.R. 320 shows the refusal of King's Bench
to apply equitable principles. Cutter had agreed to serve as second mate on the
Governor Parry on its voyage from Jamaica to Liverpool. Instead of merely signing
on as second mate, he was given a note that he would be paid 30 guineas if he did his
duty until the ship arrived at Liverpool. The unusually large amount is perhaps
explained by the desperate plight of a vessel which lost crew members in a foreign
port. The note probably explains why the case was brought in the common law court.
Unfortunately Cutter died at sea. King's Bench refused to compel the owners to pay
for the services Cutter had rendered, on a *pro rata* basis, since the note stipulated
that he must continue to serve until the ship arrived at Liverpool. The administratrix
received nothing although Cutter had served on board for six weeks.

and judge the reasonableness of the terms.[24] Apparently the admiralty
court had disallowed a wage contract which was properly signed
where there was no proof that it had been read to the seamen or that
they knew the contents.[25]

Long before Scott's day the admiralty court had repeated the old
axiom that freight is the mother of wages.[26] Where the ship was lost on
the homeward voyage, wages remained due to the seamen to the last
delivery port where freight had been earned.[27] Even if no freight had
been earned, if there had been any advantage to one of the owners
from carrying cargo free, the mariners apparently were entitled to
their wages.[28] As the admiralty court held in 1783, in a case which
Scott had appeared as counsel, freight and wages always go hand in
hand.[29] It was settled that the ship was hypothecated to the mariners
for their wages and that this lien attached to every part of the vessel as
an encouragement to the seamen to save whatever they could. This
lien was preferred to all other claims against the ship.[30]

Scott, as judge, knew perfectly well the old maxim that freight is the
mother of wages. He refused, however, to allow this old, simplistic
cliché to be used by the owners to deprive the seamen of their wages
where the cargo, and therefore the freight, had been lost but the
seamen had managed to save part of the vessel from wreck. Scott's
analysis of the basis of the mariners' right to wages was far more
adequate than the old axiom. Commenting on it, Scott insisted, 'The
maxim, though generally received, like most other maxims delivered
in figurative terms, certainly is not formed with real and strict
accuracy. For the natural and legal parents of wages are the mariner's
contract, and the performance of the service covenanted therein; they
in fact generate the title to wages.'[31] Scott agreed that where the

---

[24] R.A., Simpson MS 367, explicitly quoted by Scott in *Minerva* (*Bell*) (1825), 1 Hag.
347, 357. The two passages are set out below in the Appendix, p. 292. The statute
referred to was 2 Geo. II c. 36.

[25] R.A., Simpson MS 45; Lincoln's Inn Library, Misc. MS 147, 122.

[26] R.A., Simpson MS 295, 296, 338, 366, 372.

[27] *Ibid.*, fos. 218, 247. Where the ship had been destroyed by governmental order to
prevent it from falling into the hands of the enemy, the court ordered payment of
wages and costs. *Bennett v. Buggin* (1766), Burrell 24.

[28] R.A., Simpson MS 296–7, 339.

[29] *Nanny* (1783), Nicholl's Notebook, 1781–92, No. 32, P.R.O. HCA 30/464. Even
though Scott as counsel had argued in the *Nanny* that the seamen's wages should
diminish by 1/8th as a payment of average for salvage on the return voyage, the court
refused to deduct a portion of the salvage award since freight had been earned.

[30] R.A., Simpson MS 288, 289, 294.

[31] *Neptune* (*Clark*) (1824), 1 Hag. 227, 232.

voyage was successful and freight earned, the workmen were entitled to their stipulated wages. But he refused to accept the axiom in the opposite situation. It could not be used universally to mean 'that where no freight is due, no wages are due'.[32] The seamen could use the principle as a sword, but the owners could not always use it as a shield. Scott provided a more precise explanation of the relation between freight and seamen's wages when he said:

The freight being the only security of the mariner, the Courts have been justly anxious to uphold his lien upon it. Whenever freight is earned, his title to wages becomes vested, though the time of payment may, from causes of necessity or convenience, be postponed. Where a voyage is divided by various ports of delivery, a proportional claim attaches at each of such ports; and the Courts have upheld that title against all attempts to evade or invade it.[33]

By statute the mariners' contract had to be in writing, 'to render the agreement as distinct and definitive as possible', as Scott observed, and 'to prevent any part of it from resting in parol or vague conversation'.[34] Even if there had been no statute, Scott maintained that the court would have insisted on the same requirement. This written contract had to contain only two essential terms, 'on the part of the ship-owner – a description of the intended voyage; ... on the part of the seaman – engaging for the rate of wages which he was content to accept for his services on that voyage'.[35] But where the mate was promoted during the voyage to be chief mate, and performed the services of chief mate, he was entitled to be paid *quantum meruit* as chief mate, even though the alteration of the contract had not been noted in writing.[36] The wage contract did not fail for want of mutuality. Under certain circumstances the master could discharge the seamen or alter the voyage, even though the seamen were not free to dissolve the contract.[37]

It was well settled, Scott said, 'that wages form an indelible and perpetual lien on the ship, and follow her wherever she goes'.[38] This lien could be enforced in the admiralty court against a British vessel even after sale to a foreign owner.[39] But where the wage claim was

[32] *Ibid.*
[33] *Juliana (Ogilvie)* (1822), 2 Dod. 504, 510.
[34] *Isabella (Brand)* (1799), 2 Rob. 241, 243. The controlling statute was 2 Geo. II c. 36, s. 1, made perpetual by 2 Geo. III c. 31.
[35] *Minerva (Bell)* (1825), 1 Hag. 347, 353.
[36] *Providence (Herd)* (1825), 1 Hag. 391, 393.
[37] *Elizabeth (Gull)* (1819), 2 Dod. 403, 408.
[38] *Leander (Murray)* (1808), Edw. 35, 36.
[39] *Batavia alias Unity* (1822), 2 Dod. 500, 502.

based on an illegal expedition (to participate in a South American revolution), Scott refused to enforce the lien against innocent purchasers of the vessel.[40] This lien for seamen's wages 'was sacred as long as a single plank of the ship remained'.[41] Or as Scott later said with greater precision where only part of the vessel had been saved, 'A part separated by a storm is not disengaged by that accident from that lien. If it be recovered, it is recovered as a part of the primitive pledge mortgaged to the mariner.'[42] The lien for mariners' wages took precedence over other liens, such as bottomry bonds.[43]

Where the terms of the written contract were incomplete, Scott admitted parol evidence.[44] Contract terms must be interpreted in light of customary practice. Where a wage contract stated the voyage to be to New South Wales and India *or elsewhere*, Scott rejected the unlimited description of the intended voyage. Contract terms, he said, 'must receive a reasonable construction, a construction which ... must be, to a certain extent, conformable to the necessities of commerce'.[45] If the written terms of the contract were oppressive to the seaman (that the crew forfeited all wages on a long voyage to many ports, if the vessel did not return safe to London), Scott asserted equitable power to reform the contract despite some common law authority to the contrary. 'This Court', Scott said, 'certainly does not claim the character of a court of general equity; but it is bound, by its commission and constitution, to determine the cases submitted to its cognizance upon equitable principles, and according to the rules of natural justice.'[46] The disparity of the parties to the mariners' wage contract had to be considered in construing terms that bore harshly on

[40] *Leander (Murray)* (1808), Edw. 35, 38.
[41] *Sydney Cove (Fudge)* (1815), 2 Dod. 11, 13.
[42] *Neptune (Clark)* (1824), 1 Hag. 227, 238.
[43] *Madonna D'Idra (Papaghica)* (1811), 1 Dod. 37, 40.
[44] *Harvey (Peach)* (1827), 2 Hag. 79, 82.
[45] *Minerva (Bell)* (1825), 1 Hag. 347, 361. See also *George Home (Young)* (1825), 1 Hag. 370, 375.
[46] *Juliana (Ogilvie)* (1822), 2 Dod. 504, 521. In this case Scott explicitly rejected Abbott's interpretation of several common law cases which Abbott claimed had upheld the validity of bonds entered into by seamen conditioned on the seaman not demanding any wages until the ship's return to London. Scott's reading of the key common law case was quite different from Abbott's. Scott said that the House of Lords had not disapproved of the admiralty court's award of the wages, notwithstanding the bond. In the *Juliana* a condition had been inserted into the articles signed by the seamen: they could demand no wages for the outward voyage unless the ship returned safely to London. Abbott thought such a condition was valid unless obtained by oppression or fraud. Abbott, *Merchant ships*, 276–7. Scott, in the case of

the far more helpless party.[47] The admiralty court must refuse to enforce illegal contracts.[48] Scott, however, refused to find an illegal contract when he was confronted with the case of a female suing for wages as a cook and steward. After he swallowed hard several times and preached a short sermon on the proper place of women, he ultimately concluded that she must be paid for the services she had rendered. 'I find great difficulty in arriving at the conclusion that a female can be entitled to nothing for that service which would be remunerated in a man. It does not appear to me that the sex alone creates a legal and total disqualification.'[49]

Duties of the parties to the contract

Before Scott became admiralty judge the court had insisted that by statute the master was obliged to bring the seamen back to England.[50] If a seaman was discharged abroad without just cause before the end of the agreed voyage, the owners were obliged to pay him his whole wages until the return of the ship. But if he entered into the service of another ship, his wages earned there could mitigate the amount due under the original contract.[51] If the master wrongfully demoted the

the *Juliana*, carefully analyzed the common law cases and concluded that they had not decided the issue which was then before him. Scott reiterated the basic principle of admiralty law, that the seaman has a wage lien on any freight earned. 'Where a voyage is divided by various ports of delivery', he insisted, 'a proportional claim attaches at each of such ports; and the Courts have upheld that title against all attempts to evade or invade it.' 2 Dod. 510.

[47] *Minerva (Bell)* (1825), 1 Hag. 347, 355.
[48] *Vanguard (Pince)* (1805), 6 Rob. 207, 210 (wage contracts earned in illegal slave trade); *Benjamin Franklin (Wicks)* (1806), 6 Rob. 350 (wage contract of British pilot for aiding enemy ship).
[49] *Jane & Matilda (Chandler)* (1823), 1 Hag. 187, 194. After judgment in this case, the assignee of the bankrupt ship owners filed a bill in Chancery to obtain an injunction against Scott's judgment on the ground of collusion to defraud the estate. Scott's brother, Lord Eldon, the Chancellor, wrote to Scott to assure him that no one was questioning his handling of the case. '[A]ll, which has been done at your Court is perfectly right.' Eldon said that it turned out that there was a conspiracy between the master and the female cook, who was probably his wife, and that the master was to receive the benefit of the cook's judgment. Eldon soothed his brother's sensitivity by assuring him that 'The application asks for no process, that can be addressed to your Court – it treats as right all that has been done in it – tho it alleges that subseq[uen]t discovery may require injunction ag[ains]t the Man & Woman.' N.d. Encombe House. One marvels at the acuity of Chancery in ferreting out this conspiracy between husband and wife.
[50] R.A., Simpson MS 77. The statute referred to was 11 & 12 Wm III c. 7.
[51] R.A., Simpson MS 41, 278.

mate, the mate was entitled to his full wages as mate.[52] Where the vessel had been detained by a foreign power, the owners were obliged to pay only a half of the wages for the time of detention.[53] If a mariner was discharged for just cause, the owners apparently had to pay him his wages until the time of discharge, though, as we shall see, some grounds for discharge were sufficiently serious to cause complete forfeiture of wages.[54]

The court in the eighteenth century had not fully settled the obligation of the owners to care for injured seamen. In one place it was noted that if a carpenter became blind during the voyage he was entitled to wages only to the time he lost his sight unless he continued to perform as an ordinary seaman, in which case he should receive wages as such.[55] Nonetheless the seed of the doctrine of maintenance and cure had already started to germinate. If a seaman was injured by unskillfulness or carelessness, the owners were obliged to take care of him at the expense of the ship and to pay his wages while the voyage continued. But if the injury was caused by his own fault, such as his drunkenness or stupidity, the seaman was not entitled to wages while in the hospital or for the homeward voyage, unless he continued to do his duty. The court applied a presumption that the seaman was not at fault in causing the injury. If the owners alleged that the seaman had been at fault, the seaman was allowed to examine witnesses to the contrary. The owners' proof of fault had to be very clear.[56] The limits to the duty to care for an injured seaman appear in the case of the *Tower Hill*.[57] A seaman had his leg broken in Maryland when a hogshead of tobacco fell on him. The master left him in Maryland and returned to England. The following year when the same vessel returned to Maryland, the master allowed the seaman to return home to England but not under contract. When he sued for his wages till the end of the second voyage and for his lodging in Maryland, the admiralty court held that wages after such accidents had never been extended beyond the original voyage. The court thus allowed him

[52] *Ibid.*, fo. 76.
[53] *Ibid.*, fo. 376.
[54] *Ibid.*, fo. 278.
[55] *Ibid.*, fo. 279.
[56] *Ibid.*, fo. 112. Similarly, if a seaman was taken hostage to assure ransom for the vessel, he was entitled to wages and subsistence for the time of his captivity. *Earl of Dunmore* (1785), Nicholl's Notebook, 1781–92, No. 98, P.R.O. HCA 30/464. Scott was counsel in this case.
[57] *Tower Hill* (1727); Lincoln's Inn Library, Misc. MS 147, 124.

wages only until the ship returned to England the first time without the injured seaman. The doctrine of maintenance and cure, therefore, had clear but undeveloped roots in the eighteenth century.[58]

The mariners' duties in the eighteenth century included the duty to remain aboard till the vessel was safely moored and, if it was the immemorial custom in a particular voyage, to help unload the cargo.[59] Even if the master altered the voyage, the seamen were obliged to continue to obey orders.[60]

In cases dealing with the duties of the parties to the contract, Scott, as judge, followed the general outline of the law the admiralty court had applied in the eighteenth century.

The owners of the ship, through their master, had the obligation to make known to the crew the intended destination of the voyage. As Scott expressed the duty, '[T]he law makes the demand in favour of the mariner, that the voyage for which he contracts shall be made known to him.'[61] The owners, therefore, could not enforce a contract against the seamen in which the voyage was described as from London to New South Wales and India *and elsewhere* with return to some port in Europe.[62] The owners also had the obligation not to discharge a seaman in a foreign country, or, if such discharge was necessary for serious reasons, to pay his fare for the voyage home and to pay him wages until he returned home.[63] Subsistence while in a foreign port was considered as part of the seamen's wages.[64] Scott did not have occasion to discuss the duty of the owners to care for the injured

---

[58] After 1696 seamen were forced to contribute to support of Greenwich Hospital even though this hospital was exclusively for naval pensioners. Old or injured merchant seamen, who had not served at some time in the navy, received some attention from the Seamen's Hospitals in the leading port cities, but if maimed or disabled they probably had to rely on the poor laws like any other paupers. Apparently those sick or injured abroad had even less assistance. Davis, *Shipping industry*, 157. The common law courts had determined that the sick or disabled seaman was still entitled to his wages for the course of the voyage. Holt, *Navigation laws*, 272.

[59] R.A., Simpson MS 31, 285. The court was quite uncertain whether the duties of the crew of a ship carrying potatoes included the duty of shoveling the potatoes into sacks and hoisting the sacks out of the hold. The court found the mariners' demand for added compensation was excessive, but said that, in the absence of custom, the matter should in the future be determined by agreement. *Swinney v. Tinker* (1774), Burrell 139, 145.

[60] R.A., Simpson MS 39.

[61] *George Home (Young)* (1825), 1 Hag. 370, 375.

[62] *Minerva (Bell)* (1825), 1 Hag. 347, 359.

[63] *Elizabeth (Gull)* (1819), 2 Dod. 403, 405, 412; *Robinett v. Exeter* (1799), 2 Rob. 261, 262.

[64] *Madonna D'Idra (Papaghica)* (1811), 1 Dod. 37, 40.

seaman, the doctrine of maintenance and cure. He surely would have followed the norms of care outlined in the eighteenth century. The owners also had the duty to pay the mariners' wages, even when there was a dispute at common law as to which parties were the owners.[65] Although Scott allowed the master considerable freedom to maintain discipline on the ship, the master had the duty not to treat the crew with undue harshness or brutality.[66]

The basic duty of the seaman was performance of the services he had contracted to perform. 'In order to maintain a claim of this kind', Scott said, 'a mariner must prove one of two points, either the performance of the contract, or that some circumstances had intervened, which would equitably discharge him from the obligation of the contract, and continue to him the benefit of a legal and virtual performance.'[67] This meant that the seamen could not leave the vessel when it arrived in the roadstead at the end of the voyage, but only when the vessel was safely moored in the port of destination. 'The obligation of mariners is for the whole voyage, in the river as well as at sea; and if the port lies high up the river, a very considerable portion of their services may remain to be performed in the river.'[68] The crew was obliged not only to moor the ship but to unload the cargo.[69] The crew likewise had the duty to save as much of the vessel and cargo as it could in case of shipwreck. Seamen could not, therefore, recover salvage for service, however extraordinary, to their own vessel.[70] Furthermore, the seamen could not protect themselves by insurance from loss due to shipwreck as the owner could.[71]

Forfeiture of wages

It was settled in the eighteenth century that a seaman who was unable to perform the services he signed on for must be paid only for those services he actually performed.[72] If the carpenter was so unskillful that the master had to hire another carpenter to do his work, the amount paid to the second carpenter could be deducted from the

[65] *St. Johan (Havemeyer)* (1825), 1 Hag. 334, 338.
[66] *Minerva (Bell)* (1825), 1 Hag. 347, 368.
[67] *Pearl (Denton)* (1804), 5 Rob. 224, 227.
[68] *Ibid.*, 228.
[69] *Baltic Merchant (Smith)* (1809), Edw. 86, 91.
[70] *Neptune (Clark)* (1824), 1 Hag. 227, 236.
[71] *Ibid.*, 239.
[72] R.A., Simpson MS 42, 237, 336; Lincoln's Inn Library, Misc. MS 147, 115.

wages of the first.[73] It was apparently not settled whether leaving a ship before it was moored was desertion resulting in forfeiture of the whole of the seaman's wages (as Scott later held), or merely in the statutory penalty of forfeiture of a month's wages (as Simpson was inclined to believe).[74] It was held in the eighteenth century to be a desertion if the seaman stayed ashore without leave, or if he left the ship for fear of ill-treatment, or if he left the ship in fear of impressment.[75] But if the ill-treatment was so severe that the seaman reasonably feared for his life, or if the captain's own delays were responsible for the seaman's departure, then leaving the ship was not desertion.[76] It was not a justifiable reason for leaving the ship that the master had altered the destination, and so wages were forfeited.[77] It was desertion to leave a ship when it was in distress, but not if it was given up as lost.[78]

This law applied by the admiralty court in the eighteenth century provided the legal framework within which Scott determined those particular cases which came before him as judge. A seaman forfeited his wages, Scott held, if he failed to perform the services he had agreed to perform under the contract. Providing more precise definitions, Scott stated that a seaman might be properly discharged: (1) for neglect of duty which, he said, amounted to 'that habitual inattention to the ordinary duties of his station that might expose the ship to danger'; or (2) for proven disobedience of commands, even though the orders had been given with 'less personal civility ... than would excuse something of an hesitation of obedience, in other modes of life'; or (3) for drunkenness which is more than 'a single act of intemperance'.[79] Scott showed his realistic grasp of life at sea by not decreeing a forfeiture of wages for occasional drunkenness, but only

---

[73] R.A., Simpson MS 339.

[74] *Ibid.*, fos. 319, 362.

[75] *Ibid.*, fos. 22, 360.

[76] *Gray v. Gill* (1784), Nicholl's Notebook, 1781–92, No. 65, P.R.O. HCA 30/464; see also Lincoln's Inn Library, Misc. MS 147, 117. In *Fell v. Dorothy* (1766), Burrell 9, the court allowed wages for the half of the voyage completed. The captain had known that some of his crew were under prior contract to return to the Greenland Service when the season opened. The captain's delays had been the cause of their departure prior to completion of this voyage.

[77] R.A., Simpson MS 43, 44, 76, 172, 361.

[78] *Ibid.*, fos. 78, 280, 298; Lincoln's Inn Library, Misc. MS 147, 118.

[79] *Robinett v. Exeter* (1799), 2 Rob. 261, 263–5; *Frederick (Hearn)* (1823), 1 Hag. 211, 213–16.

for habitual drunkenness.[80] A seaman also forfeited his wages for desertion, which was 'the wilful quitting of the ship without the consent of the master'.[81] Scott held it was a desertion justifying forfeiture of the whole wages for a seaman to leave the ship after it had arrived at the port of London on return from the long voyage to the West Indies. The ship was lashed alongside another ship until it could proceed the last half mile to the West India Docks. Scott clearly defined the end of a voyage, prior to which unconsented departure would be desertion. '[T]he voyage is not completed by the mere fact of arrival; the act of mooring is an act to be done by the crew, and their duty extends to the time of the unlivery of the cargo.'[82] The owners did not even have to prove any actual damage from such desertion just prior to the mooring of the vessel.[83] Even if the crew member had gone ashore with permission of the master, it was a desertion for him to refuse to return to the ship when ordered to do so.[84] On the other hand, it was not desertion for a seaman to leave the vessel if he had not received provisions,[85] nor if he left the ship after the end of the agreed voyage but before a slight prolongation of the voyage. After a trip from London to Australia and back to London, the agreed voyage, the master received instructions to proceed to Rotterdam. The seaman did not desert when he refused to serve after London, the agreed end of the voyage.[86] Likewise Scott held it was not desertion when a seaman got so drunk while ashore on leave that he did not return to the ship promptly when his leave expired.[87]

[80] *New Phoenix* (*Lewthwaite*) (1823), 1 Hag. 198, 200; *Lady Campbell* (*Beetham*) (1826), 2 Hag. 5, 9.

[81] *Pearl* (*Denton*) (1804), 5 Rob. 224, 228.

[82] *Baltic Merchant* (*Smith*) (1809), Edw. 86, 91. By statute a seaman was to forfeit one month's pay to Greenwich Hospital if he left his ship without a discharge. 2 Geo. III c. 36. Scott in this case interpreted the statutory forfeiture to Greenwich Hospital as not restricting the right of the ship owners to the forfeited wages to make up for the loss they had sustained by the desertion. Scott considered the common law case *Frontine v. Frost* (1802), 3 Bos. & Pul. 302. After discussing *Frontine* 'with very learned persons who were interested in that judgment', he concluded that the owners of a ship were not barred by 2 Geo. II c. 36 from the right to which they were entitled under the law prior to the statute. The ship owner, therefore, could still make a set off against the wages for the loss he sustained when the seaman left the ship before it was docked and unloaded.

[83] *Phoenix* (*Holmon*) (1814), unpublished, Bod. Lib., 9 Monk Bretton Dep. A 75.

[84] *Bulmer* (*Brown*) (1823), 1 Hag. 163, 167.

[85] *Castilia* (*Stewart*) (1822), 1 Hag. 59, 60.

[86] *Countess of Harcourt* (*Bunn*) (1824), 1 Hag. 248, 249.

[87] *Ealing Grove* (*Falconer*) (1826), 2 Hag. 15, 22.

Judicial protection of seamen

On reading through the many judgments Scott rendered and the notes
of prior admiralty court determinations which have survived, one gets
the impression, and it may well be no more than a hunch, that Scott
was somewhat more concerned than his predecessors to protect the
interests of seamen. The difference may be entirely due to the fact that
Scott's judgments remain in final, polished, published form while the
judgments of his precedessors can only be pieced together from the
notes of practitioners. One can easily dismiss the paternalistic rhetoric
of Scott's opinions: 'The common mariner is easy and careless,
illiterate, and unthinking; he has no such resources, in his own
intelligence and experience in habits of business.'[88] Far more significant in confirming the impression of Scott's sympathy for the legal
rights of seamen are the outcomes of the forty-three suits for seamen's
wages among Scott's published judgments. Although in many cases
the owners must have settled wage claims prior to suit and litigated
only those in which they thought they had a legitimate defense,
nonetheless Scott sided with the seaman's wage claim in some thirty-
two of the forty-three reported cases. In many of these cases he also
decreed the expenses of the litigation against the owners. Such a risk
of paying costs of litigation would induce many others to settle before
trial any claims to which they had a doubtful defense.

Scott's occasional harsh words for the flinty owners also confirm the
impression. 'I am by no means inclined to sustain the objection which
has been taken on the part of the owner, who has derived great
advantage from the labour of these men, and now, against all justice
and conscience, refuses to pay them the stipulated reward for their
services.'[89] Scott had occasion to remind the owners in one case, who,
he insisted with a straight face, 'are respectable persons', that the
members of their crew

> have a country, and a home, and possibly wives and families; and that the
> banishment of such men to remote regions of the globe, for an indetermined
> course of time, and occupation against their consent, and in defiance of a
> solemn contract ... is a practice which, however approved by those who
> profit by it, most other men will be apt to think is much more easy to be
> described than to be defended.[90]

In another case Scott went out of his way to comment on the 'laxity

[88] *Juliana (Ogilvie)* (1822), 2 Dod. 504, 509.
[89] *Frederick (Bodom)* (1813), 1 Dod. 266, 267.
[90] *Minerva (Bell)* (1825), 1 Hag. 347, 369.

and inaccuracy both about the structure and execution of the mariners' contract', a practice which he insisted must be corrected. Although the seaman could not read or write, the contract had not been read to him. The owners had allowed only one mariner at a time to execute the contract without any witnesses present. Scott concluded: '[I]t would take me up a very inconvenient time to point out half the impertinences with which [the contract] is stuffed, and which it is high time should be corrected.'[91]

But certainly Scott never forgot the legitimate interests and rights of the ship owners. If, indeed, the impression is correct that he approached cases involving mariners' wages with greater sensitivity than his predecessors, he surely never forgot the larger policy questions concerning the shipping industry. As he said:

I know and feel the partiality which the maritime law entertains for this class of men, but it must not overrule all consideration of justice to other classes, particularly to merchants, their employers; for what is oppressive to the merchant cannot but be injurious to the mariner. The seaman cannot be ultimately benefited by that which, as far as it operates, must operate to the discouragement of navigation.[92]

Today we would probably describe Scott as having a keen insight into the industrial relations of the shipping industry. He knew the hardships and risks faced by the workers and he effectively protected their interests. But he also knew that no commercial vessels would sail without rather risky investments of venture capital. He decided these cases, not by rote application of precedent, but by thoughtful and sensitive application of precedent in light of the economic and social policies affecting the shipping industry.

Sources relied on by Scott

Precedent surely was important for Scott. All that has been said in this analysis of the wage cases should demonstrate that Scott did not approach these instance cases as if he wrote on a blank page. A full, complex body of precedent had been developed and the civilians made it their business to preserve and pass on this unreported tradition. In the vast majority of cases Scott decided, he was, at least implicitly,

---

[91] *George Home (Young)* (1825), 1 Hag. 370, 377–8.
[92] *Elizabeth (Gull)* (1819), 2 Dod. 403, 406.

conscious of the framework provided by this law developed over centuries by the admiralty court. Scott himself stated his approach in searching for sources. If relevant admiralty court precedents could not be found, he turned to the commentators on the law merchant or the common law reports. 'I have looked', he said, 'with some anxiety to find, if possible, a decided case, or a rule of authority that could be applied to the discretionary powers of a master in such circumstances; but I have found none, either in the books of foreign jurists or in reports of decided cases at common law, or in MSS. cases.'[93] In another case Scott discussed at length prior precedents of the admiralty court, the courts of common law and the Scottish Court of Sessions. When he reached his conclusion, it was based on 'the judgment of the Court of Admiralty, of the Courts of Common Law, of the Court of Chancery, and of the House of Lords, so far as they have been called to the consideration of the subject'.[94]

SUITS FOR POSSESSION

Ownership of merchant vessels at the end of the eighteenth century remained largely determined by the desire to spread the risk. Few individuals owned ships outright. Most commonly merchants, who were engaged in various businesses or trades, became part owners (usually in fractions of eighths, sixteenths, thirty-seconds or even sixty-fourths) and used a small portion of their time and capital seeking profit from partial ownership of a ship. Often there was a large number of partners, who could freely transfer their shares in a ship, with the management of the ship in the hands of one or two partners, or perhaps in the hands of the master who was also a part owner. Since the rate of shipping losses due to storm, negligent navigation or other mishaps remained high well into the nineteenth century, the incentive to risk only a part of one's capital in any given venture was strong. The owners, in effect, employed a primitive form of incorporation of each ship, in an attempt to limit their liability to their share of the vessel.

---

[93] *Ibid.*, 409.

[94] *Juliana (Ogilvie)* (1822), 2 Dod. 504, 511–22. He also relied on the commentary of '[M]y highly venerated friend, Lord Chief Justice Abbot [*sic*]', i.e. Abbott, *Merchant ships*.

The managing partner usually determined the voyage and this decision was based largely on his contacts in the intended ports of call.
These factors or agents abroad, in an era lacking all means of rapid
communication, enabled the ship owners and cargo shippers to sell
their cargoes and obtain supplies for the ship and cargoes for the
return voyage. Disputes between part owners could sometimes be
settled by the admiralty court.[95]

Jurisdictional limits

The admiralty court in the mid-eighteenth century distinguished, as
Scott later did, between cases of possession within admiralty jurisdiction and cases of property or title, which lay exclusively within the
jurisdiction of the common law courts. The owners of a vessel had
delivered possession to one Samuel Brooks upon his payment of one-
fourth of the purchase price and a promise to pay the rest within
fourteen days. Alas, Brooks did not pay the remainder and planned to
sail off with the ship. The original owners asked Sir George Lee, a
prominent civilian, how they could regain possession. Lee, in 1747,
prepared an opinion as counsel in which he said:

[F]ormerly it was the constant Practice of the Adm[iral]ty Court to grant
Warrants to arrest ships in point of property and if that practice was still in use
this ship might be stopt from proceeding on her intended Expedition & Mr.
Samuel Brooks might be dispossessed of her and the owners would not be
obliged to accept Bail for the remainder of the purchase money[.] [B]ut of late
years *so many* Prohibitions having been granted in those cases, the Jurisdiction seems to be settled in the Courts of Common Law.[96]

Because title to the vessel was at issue, Lee was saying, the common
law courts had exclusive jurisdiction. Suits for possession, in contrast
to such suits for property, involved the management or control of the
ship. In the eighteenth century it was apparently settled that a master
who was also part owner could not be removed by authority of the
admiralty court, except for misbehavior. The reason given was that he
was in possession of his own property. A master who was not a part
owner could be removed at the pleasure of the majority owners by suit

---

[95] Davis, *Shipping industry*, 81–109. For early discussions of disputes between part
owners of ships, see Welwood, *Sea-laws*, 40–1; C. Molloy, *De jure maritimo et
navali* (London, 1676); 192–3.
[96] H.S.P. Sir George Lee Opinions. (Words in italics were crossed out by Lee.)

in the admiralty court.[97] The court in the eighteenth century seems to have been ambivalent in refusing to hear cases brought by part owners to account for the profits of a voyage, because a 'prohib[itio]n will now be granted & redress must be had in Law or Equity'.[98] By Scott's day, this point was settled. He refused to hear a case of possession which would involve an examination of accounts.

The admiralty court, when Scott became judge, continued to distinguish between disputes over the title to a ship and disputes about possession. Although the distinction remained unruly, Scott added some precision when he insisted

> It is certainly true that this Court did formerly entertain questions of title to a much greater extent than it has lately been in the habit of doing. In former times, indeed, it decided without reserve upon all questions of disputed title, which the parties thought proper to bring before it for adjudication. After the Restoration, however, it was informed by other courts, that such matters were not properly cognizable here; and, since that time, it has been very abstemious in the interposition of its authority. The jurisdiction over *causes of possession* was still retained: and although the higher tribunals of the country denied the right of this Court to interfere *in mere questions of disputed title* no intimation was ever given by them that the Court must abandon its jurisdiction over *causes of possession*.[99]

The admiralty court had jurisdiction to inquire into questions of title only when such questions arose ancillary to a dispute over possession. The court had to consider questions of title in such cases only to assure that it could safely decree possession to one party or the other.[100] The admiralty court would not consider questions of equitable titles to the ship,[101] nor disputes about possession which would draw the court

---

[97] R.A., Simpson MS 263, 274–5, 384. *Adams and others v. Crouch* (1771), Burrell 110. In *Meeke and others v. Lord Holland* (1774), Burrell 145, the court refused to dispossess the master in possession where it appeared merely one half (eight-sixteenths) of the owners wanted to change masters. See also the *Springer* (1784), Nicholl's Notebook, 1781–92, No. 63, P.R.O. HCA 30/464.

[98] R.A., Simpson MS 103, 382.

[99] *Warrior (Peache)* (1818), 2 Dod. 288, 289. Italics in the original. Scott had made the same point in *Aurora (Thomson)* (1800), 3 Rob. 133, 136. For a discussion of common law cases involving questions of title, see Holt, *Navigation laws*, 183–95.

[100] *Warrior (Peache)* (1818), 2 Dod. 288, 289. In *Experimento (Garcia)* (1815), 2 Dod. 38, 42, Scott stated that, where British subjects claimed a ship which had sailed to a British port in possession of and as the property of foreigners, the admiralty court had the power to inquire 'a little into the title by which the property is held'. Scott feared that if the British claimant could not obtain justice in the English admiralty court, he certainly could not obtain it elsewhere.

[101] *Sisters* (1804), 5 Rob. 155, 158.

into an examination of the partners' accounts.[102] Scott laid it down as a rule that the court would consider petitions to transfer possession of a ship only in simple cases, such as where possession had been acquired by fraud or violence or by a party representing a minority of the owners. The court could determine questions of possession only 'in cases which speak for themselves ... but in those which, being complex, require a long and minute investigation, it cannot proceed with safety'.[103] The court, therefore, lacked the power to sever interests between bankrupt and solvent partners.[104] Scott displayed none of the old time-time fervor to protect and enhance the admiralty court's instance jurisdiction. He did bring clarity of analysis, however, where before there had been confused generalizations.

The admiralty court, according to Scott, could hear cases of possession involving foreign parties and foreign vessels, but only with the consent of the parties and at the behest of the foreign minister. But Scott refused to be drawn into a review of the propriety or correctness of foreign decrees concerning ownership. 'Heavy indeed', Scott said, 'would be the task imposed on this Court, were it to undertake to rectify all the errors, that parties may be disposed to impute to foreign jurisdictions.'[105] Although the court often entertained suits involving British ships to dispossess the master, who might be part owner, at the request of the majority partners, it was extremely reluctant to hear such a suit to dispossess a foreign master and part owner.[106] But where the master of a foreign vessel had for five years refused to return the vessel to its home port at the order of a large majority of the owners, and where there was a foreign judicial decree ordering the master to deliver the vessel to the majority owners, Scott reluctantly assumed jurisdiction to determine the question of possession.[107] Scott was sensitive to such cases which must be decided by the legal rules of different countries, not according to the *jus gentium*. Since piracy, however, was a crime against the *jus gentium*, Scott concluded the admiralty court had jurisdiction to determine whether proceeds from

---

[102] *Guardian (Beaton)* (1800), 3 Rob. 93, 94.
[103] *Pitt (Crosse)* (1824), 1 Hag. 240, 244. Scott likewise refused to adjudicate a suit for possession of the ship's register because of great uncertainty as to legal ownership of the ship. *Frances of Leith (Syme)* (1820), 2 Dod. 420, 424.
[104] *Jefferson (Dennis)* (1799), 1 Rob. 325, 327.
[105] *Martin of Norfolk (M'Crohan)* (1802), 4 Rob. 293, 301.
[106] *Johan and Siegmund (Niegel)* (1810), Edw. 242, 243.
[107] *Reuter (Lange)* (1811), 1 Dod. 22, 23.

the sale of the property taken by pirates, which was in the court's control, should be restored to the original foreign owner.[108]

Although the evidence located remains quite sketchy, once again it appears that Scott was not breaking new ground in his judgments in cases of possession. It was settled in the eighteenth century, for instance, that if a master could not raise money to repair the ship by hypothecating it in a foreign port the ship could be sold by court decree. If the foreign court had proper jurisdiction and its decree was not appealed from, its decree of sale bound the English admiralty court. Redress could only be had against the master. The adjudication of the foreign court created as good a title as any conveyance from the original owners. Apparently the common law courts had granted prohibitions where the admiralty court reviewed the propriety of a foreign decree.[109] Prior to the time of the statute of 1786 regulating ship registries, the admiralty court apparently recognized other titles not based on the names in the bill of sale. Even though only one partner's name appeared in the bill of sale, other partners who had paid their shares for building the vessel were considered part owners entitled to share in the profits of a voyage. If the recorded partner sent the ship on a voyage, he was answerable to the unrecorded partners for any loss and had to pay them their share of any profits.[110]

Before the admiralty court would decree possession to a party, Scott, as judge, insisted on some clear and convincing proof of title. Between British parties Scott looked for a clear and absolute conveyance of the ship proved by a valid title deed. Proof of a security interest in the vessel, 'a disputable, or an incomplete, and inchoate title', did not suffice as a basis for the court to award possession.[111] In a case in which it was alleged that one Charnock had purchased a ship as trustee for Kirkpatrick, Scott concluded that under the universal maritime law, as well as under British statute law, the bill of sale was the proper title. Although there was written proof that Charnock intended to transfer the vessel when the account was settled, Charnock remained in possession of the only legal title. Scott held the

---

[108] *Hercules* (*Chitty*) (1819), 2 Dod. 353, 376. This case was considered by Scott as a *causa spolii civilis et maritima*, a quaint category, but obviously similar to causes of possession.

[109] R.A., Simpson MS 312, 349.

[110] *Ibid.*, fos. 275, 382.

[111] *Aurora* (*Thomson*) (1800), 3 Rob. 133, 139.

court was bound to decide on the legal title.[112] Title to a vessel based on the decree of a foreign court was not easily impeached.[113] Even a title based on a governmental act of the Barbary States could not be readily overturned. Scott said, '[W]e must presume it was done regularly in their way, and according to the established custom of that part of the world.' Undoubtedly the delay of the original owners in challenging the transfer by the Algerines influenced Scott in this case.[114] Laches worked to cure defective titles. As Scott said, '[A] title which may have been originally faulty, must of necessity become unimpeachable by great lapse of time.'[115] Peace treaties also tended to quiet titles of possession which arose out of the war. 'Treaties of peace are intended to bury in oblivion all complaints; and if grievances are not brought forward at the time when peace is concluded, it must be presumed that it is not intended to bring them forward at any future time.'[116] If a vessel was sold abroad by the master without the owners' authority, but out of true necessity, and if the whole transaction was done in the best faith and for the benefit of the owners, the court would strain hard to uphold the title. Even a slight suspicion of collusion between the master and the purchasers, however, would induce the court to restore the vessel to the original owners.[117]

A fairly frequent type of suit, analogous to a suit for possession, enabled the admiralty court in the eighteenth century to settle disputes between part owners who could not agree whether the ship should set out on a voyage or not. The admiralty court decreed that

[112] *Sisters* (1804), 5 Rob. 155, 159. The applicable statutes, which required all transfers of vessels to be by written bill of sale, were 26 Geo. III c. 60 and 34 Geo. III c. 68. Perhaps it was in the context of this case that Scott and his brother, Lord Eldon, had discussed Lord Liverpool's Register Acts. Eldon's undated letter to Scott asserts 'There are not two worse drawn Acts in the Statute Book' than these two. Eldon continued: 'The effect of the Acts I have apprehended to be this – that the Persons; whom you call *the owners*, are *not* Owners, and, those, who are called *Trustees* or Agents, are not Trustees or *Agents*, but are de Jure, under the effect of the Acts, the *only* Owners. That is, the effect of the Acts is that the persons, whose Names appear in the Register, are in Law & Equity the Owners of the Vessell, & that the Acts do not admit of any Averment that those, who bought the Vessell with their Money if their Names are not in [the] *Reg*[iste]*r* are the Owners.' Encombe House. Italics in the original.
[113] *Martin of Norfolk (M'Crohan)* (1802), 4 Rob. 293, 300; *Warrior (Peache)* (1818), 2 Dod. 288, 295; *Granger (Van Dyke)* (1812), unpublished, Bod. Lib., 6 Monk Bretton Dep.
[114] *Helena (Heslop)* (1801), 4 Rob. 3, 6.
[115] *Molly (Eadie)* (1814), 1 Dod. 394, 395.
[116] *Ibid.*, 396.
[117] *Fanny and Elmira (Hicks)* (1809), Edw. 117, 118.

such a vessel was to be appraised and that the owners in possession who fitted it out had to give security to restore it at the end of the voyage and to reimburse the other partners in case of loss. The admiralty court could not order sale of the vessel. The court's policy was to assure that ships did not lie idle because of disagreements between the partners. At the same time the dissenting partners were protected from loss on the venture, but could not share in the profits.[118]

Near the end of his years as admiralty judge, Scott said in such a case, '[S]hips were made to plough the ocean, and not to rot by the wall.'[119] The admiralty court in this case remained willing to require that security be given for the safe return of the vessel to protect the interest of the dissenting partners. But Scott, unwilling to expand the court's jurisdiction, refused to use such a suit as a means of examining accounts between the partners.

BOTTOMRY BONDS

Bottomry bonds were an invention of necessity in early maritime commerce. The master of a ship in need of repair or refitting in a distant port had to find something he could provide as collateral for a loan. Without rapid communication and international banking facilities, the master could seldom borrow money on his own credit or even on the credit of the owners of the vessel, unless they happened to be well known in that port. Pledging the hull itself, the bottom, or occasionally pledging the cargo, were the only expedients for the master. The foreign lender, however, who lost his entire loan if the vessel foundered and was lost at sea, felt justified in charging high interest rates for loans based on the sole security of the hull.[120] The practice of lending money or advancing credit to a master in a foreign port under circumstances of necessity with reliance on the credit of

---

[118] This practice is clearly discussed in the seventeenth century. W. Wynne, *Life of Sir Leoline Jenkins* (2 vols., London, 1724), II, 792. See also R.A., Simpson MS 103, 179, 273–5, 382; Lincoln's Inn Library, Misc. MS 147, 114. H.S.P. Lee Admiralty Opinions. Abbott, *Merchant ships*, 60–2, and Holt, *Navigation laws*, 199–206, give the common law cases confirming admiralty jurisdiction.

[119] *Apollo (Tenant)* (1824), 1 Hag. 306, 312. Scott borrowed from Abbott, without citation, the little remark about ships being intended to plough the ocean. *Merchant ships*, 58. Perhaps it was a commonplace within the shipping industry.

[120] Davis, *Shipping industry*, 84, suggests that 36% was the ordinary rate in the seventeenth century: Bl. *Comm.*, II, 457, 458.

the ship itself was well established in the seventeenth century and had origins which went back centuries earlier.[121]

The nature and form of bottomry bonds

Bottomry bonds in the eighteenth century were considered debts of the highest nature, and along with mariners' wages, were preferred over all other debts.[122] The master in a foreign port, even a master who had just taken command by appointment or succession, could pledge or hypothecate the ship for necessaries in order to proceed with the voyage. The ship itself was bound by the bond, but only if the money was used for the vessel, not for the master's personal needs. Apparently the lenders could recover on the bond even if the master had embezzled the money. As long as the master remained in possession of the ship he had the power to borrow money abroad on the credit of the ship, even if he had privately promised the owners not to pledge the vessel. The lender abroad could not know of such private agreements.[123] The master had authority to pledge the ship as security for a loan only for necessary repairs or supplies to enable the ship to complete the voyage. Bottomry bonds, therefore, could be valid only if entered into abroad and only in cases of necessity.[124] Despite exceptions the ordinary rule was: if the ship was fitted out with new rigging in the Thames, the owners, not the ship, were liable at common law.[125] The admiralty court in the eighteenth century evaded the jurisdictional limits by allowing suit on a contract made in England before the start of the voyage. The admiralty court had held that, though such a suit was not within admiralty jurisdiction, if the ship had been arrested and sold in a suit for mariners' wages, the court

[121] Molloy, *De jure maritimo*, 282; *Black book of the admiralty*, ed. T. Twiss (4 vols., London, 1871–6), I, 89.
[122] R.A., Simpson MS 12, 349. Simpson thought that a bottomry bond entered into abroad for necessary repairs had priority even over seamen's wages. *Ibid.*, fo. 56.
[123] *Ibid.*, fos. 177, 390.
[124] *Ibid.*, fos. 289, 291. In *Day v. Wolfe* (1768), Burrell 88, the court upheld the bottomry bond, apparently on the ground that the master had no other way of raising money for necessary repairs.
[125] R.A., Simpson MS 178, 391. Scott's sometimes erratic precedessor, Judge Marriott, took jurisdiction of a case where the owner had mortgaged the ship within England, *Providence* (1783), Nicholl's Notebook, 1781–92, No. 73, P.R.O. HCA 30/464, also noted in Burrell 330. In this case Scott had argued against admiralty jurisdiction. But Marriott denied jurisdiction over a bottomry bond entered into abroad where all the parties were foreigners and the vessel had a foreign registry. *St. Francisco de Paulo* (1793), Nicholl's Notebook, 1793–7, 29, P.R.O. HCA 30/464.

could decree the money due to the builders, repairers and suppliers from what remained of the proceeds.[126]

Scott, as admiralty judge, obviously knew the basic contours of the judicially developed law of bottomry bonds. He summed up the basic elements required for a valid bottomry bond in saying:

> Where the master cannot procure the necessary supplies on the personal credit of himself or his employers, there can be no doubt that he is at liberty to pledge the ship itself, by way of security, to the lender, and to stipulate for the payment of interest after a rate which, in cases of bonds granted under other circumstances, would be deemed usurious.[127]

Such bonds the admiralty court considered sacred; they had to be upheld in the interests of the commercial world. The common law courts acknowledged that the admiralty court had jurisdiction over bottomry bonds entered into abroad since the common law courts could not give a remedy against the ship itself.[128]

Scott further delineated the essential traits of bottomry bonds by specifically discussing each characteristic within the concrete factual setting of different cases.

In the first place, bottomry bonds had to be entered into by the master. Even where the original master had deserted abroad and the consignees of the cargo there had appointed a new master, this master had the authority to give a bond to these same consignees in order to raise money for the repairs needed by the ship. Scott recognized the possibility of collusion in such a situation but found none in this case and upheld the bottomry bond. Since the consignees did not know the ship owners, they had no obligation to lend the money without

---

[126] R.A., Simpson MS 56, 57, 288; *Mackenzie v. Ogilvie* (1774), Burrell 124, 134, 137. In the case of *John (Jackson)* (1801), 3 Rob. 288, Scott permitted suit by London materialmen against the proceeds (£700) which remained in the registry of the court after the ship had been sold in a suit by seamen for their wages. Scott was reluctant to allow this suit and did so only after learning that the ship was American, its master was dead and its owner insolvent. Scott insisted on searching for a precedent and when he found the case of *Adventure (Clap)* from 1763, he allowed payment out of the proceeds, but only because he had concluded 'that it has continued to be the practice of this Court to allow material men to sue against remaining proceeds in the registry, notwithstanding that prohibitions have been obtained on *original suits* instituted by them'. *John (Jackson)* (1801), 3 Rob. 290.

Where no proceeds were in the registry of the court, Scott refused to take jurisdiction, even though the owner and master were resident in a foreign country and not likely to return to England. *Fanny and Elmira* (1811), unpublished, Bod. Lib., 5 Monk Bretton Dep. 360.

[127] *Hero (Howard)* (1817), 2 Dod. 139, 142.

[128] *Rhadamanthe (Mayer)* (1813), 1 Dod. 201, 203; *Gratitudine (Mazzola)* (1801), 3 Rob. 240, 268; see also Abbott, *Merchant ships*, 103–4.

looking to the ship itself as security.[129] By general maritime law, Scott asserted, the master had the right to borrow money in a foreign port for the use of the ship, '[A]s long as he remains the ostensible master, exercising all the functions of that situation, he has the authority attached to it.'[130]

Secondly, bottomry bonds had to be based on the credit of the ship, not the owner. If the foreign lender looked to the security of the owners of the vessel, for example, by accepting a bill of exchange drawn on a London firm, they could not later arrest the ship and seek to recover in a suit in admiralty. Bottomry bonds Scott said, 'are founded on a security of a very different kind, upon the ship where there is a failure of personal security, in order to enable the master to supply himself, in a foreign port'.[131] As long as the lender looked to the credit of the ship, a bottomry bond was valid even on the security of a transport vessel in the service of the government.[132]

Thirdly, bottomry loans had to be made in a foreign port. A loan, or credit advance, if entered into in England, could not provide the basis for a suit in the admiralty court. Prohibitions had been granted in such cases. But for the purpose of sustaining a bottomry bond, Scott was willing to consider Jersey a foreign port.[133] The crucial point was that the loan had been made for the needs of the ship 'in a place where the master was unknown, and without credit'. Where the owner was resident in the foreign country, but in a different province and inaccessible to the master, the bottomry bond entered into by the master was valid.[134]

Fourthly, the bottomry loan had to be made in a situation of necessity. The validity of bottomry bonds turned on the law of

---

[129] *Alexander (Tate)* (1812), 1 Dod. 278, 280.
[130] *Jane (Birkley)* (1814), 1 Dod. 461, 464.
[131] *Augusta (De Bluhn)* (1813), 1 Dod. 283, 286–7.
[132] *Jane (Birkley)* (1814), 1 Dod. 461, 462.
[133] *Barbara (Chegwin)* (1801), 4 Rob. 1, 2. Scott, in theory, considered Ireland a foreign port for purposes of bottomry bonds. *Rhadamanthe (Mayer)* (1813), 1 Dod. 201, 205. The jurisdictional limit barring the admiralty court from hearing suits involving contracts entered into in England had been settled by such cases as *Watkinson v. Bernadiston* (1726), 2 P. Wms. 368. The reason was that the courts presumed that the money had been advanced on the credit of the owners, not the ship. See also Abbott, *Merchant ships*, 91–8.

Scott in 1783 had argued as counsel that bonds entered into in England were merely personal. They did not bind the ship unless entered into in a foreign port. Though he argued that the admiralty court lacked jurisdiction in this case, the court took jurisdiction. *Providence* (1783), Burrell 330, see fn. 125 above.
[134] *Ysabel (Bozo)* (1812), 1 Dod. 273, 274.

necessity. They must 'arise out of the destitute situation of the master in a foreign port, unable to obtain the necessary supplies for his vessel on the personal credit of himself or his employers'.[135] Scott realistically viewed necessity as the touchstone of the cases of bottomry. '[N]ecessity creates the law, it supersedes rules; and whatever is *reasonable* and *just* in such cases, is likewise *legal*.'[136] Thus if the foreign lender elected to lend on security of the cargo rather than of the ship alone, the master could also pledge the cargo.[137] The advances had to be for the repairs and outfitting of the ship, not for the general maritime transactions of the ship owners.[138] If there were no other alternatives, the master could borrow money even from the agent of the owners abroad and grant a bottomry bond for security.[139]

Fifthly, the lender had to assume the risk of loss if the vessel failed to return to its intended port. In the case of the *Atlas*,[140] Scott consciously developed a new dimension of the law of bottomry bonds. Since the case demonstrates Scott's cautious approach when confronted with a novel question, a somewhat fuller discussion is justified. Scott ultimately held that the bond was not a valid bottomry bond, enforceable in admiralty, unless the lender assumed the sea risk.

The master of the *Atlas* while in Calcutta had granted a bond, labeled a bottomry bond, but it did not pledge the vessel as the sole security. It was an absolute and indefeasible bond, which had to be paid even if the *Atlas* were lost at sea. The *Atlas* was wrecked, sunk and raised and it limped back to London, greatly diminished in value. Scott considered for the first time whether such a bond could be enforced in the admiralty court. Scott was aware that in a number of cases the admiralty court had enforced bottomry bonds which lacked explicit assumption by the lender of the risk of loss at sea, but in none of them had this point been argued or considered by the court. In one case decided by his predecessor, Sir James Marriott, in which Scott had acted as counsel, the admiralty court passed over the jurisdic-

---

[135] *Rhadamanthe (Mayer)* (1813), 1 Dod. 201, 206. Scott had made these same points in his argument as counsel in *Count Dillon* (1787), Arnold's Notebook, 1787, P.R.O. HCA 30/470.

[136] *Gratitudine (Mazzola)* (1801), 3 Rob. 240, 266. Italics in the original.

[137] *Ibid.*, 262. These loans, with the cargo as security, were called *respondentia* bonds. It was later asserted by counsel that the *Gratitudine* was the first case in which the court upheld a bond hypothecating the cargo. *Prince Regent* (1821), unpublished opinion, Bod. Lib., 12 Monk Bretton Dep.

[138] *Belvidere (Marsh)* (1813), 1 Dod. 353, 358.

[139] *Hero (Howard)* (1817), 2 Dod. 139, 144.

[140] *Atlas (Clark)* (1827), 2 Hag. 48.

tional question and upheld the validity of the bond. When this same case was brought before King's Bench, the judges waived the jurisdictional issue and did not decide it one way or the other.[141]

Faced, therefore, with a case in which he could derive no guidance from precedent, Scott began by precisely defining the issue. From this definition, however, the ultimate conclusion inexorably followed. Bottomry bonds, he said,

> are founded upon sea risk, and are defeasible by the destruction of the ship in the course of her voyage, on which account alone the high interest is allowed ... [B]ut this bond is not defeasible by any such casualty: whether the ship sinks or swims, whether she arrives at her destined port or is lost in the ocean, it makes no real difference in the bond.[142]

After defining bottomry bonds, he traced their origins to the Roman contract called *foenus nauticum* or *usura maritima* in which high interest rates were allowed to reimburse the lender for the hazard of the sea. The gamble of the lender provided Scott with the policy argument which justified the high interest rates typical for bottomry bonds. The bond on the *Atlas*, however, involved no such gamble; this bond did not pledge the vessel itself as the sole security, regardless of what happened to the ship, the money had to be paid.

Even if the common law courts could not grant relief since the contract had been entered into in India, Scott insisted in the case of the *Atlas*, this fact did not establish the jurisdiction of the admiralty court. '[T]his Court is not a general receiver, nor is it empowered to entertain derelict jurisdictions.'[143] Although the parties did not object to admiralty court jurisdiction, Scott knew that the consent of the parties could not create jurisdiction. Scott discussed the case with 'two very eminent professors of common law, for whose legal talents I entertain the highest respect', but they could only point out the difficulties of the common law courts hearing such a case. Scott, even at the end of his long judicial career, remained reluctant to expand the admiralty court's jurisdiction. He insisted that 'The civil law Courts have no right to usurp an authority, merely because a common law court does not possess it; it must have a more direct and positive foundation.'[144] The only foundation for instance jurisdiction, Scott

---

[141] *Ladbroke v. Crickett* (1788), 2 Term Rep. 649.
[142] *Atlas (Clark)* (1827), 2 Hag. 48, 52. Scott might have been thinking of a passage in Abbott, *Merchant ships*, 102, which is quite similar.
[143] *Atlas (Clark)* (1827), 2 Hag. 48, 56.
[144] *Ibid.*, 62.

said, was authorized usage and established authority. Scott concluded that this bond, where the lender did not assume the sea risk, was not within the jurisdiction of the admiralty court. He was particularly reluctant to consider the bond in this case, since it involved many questions turning on oriental mercantile practice. The High Court of Delegates affirmed Scott's judgment in the case of the *Atlas*.[145] Scott, unlike his predecessors, here lacks all trace of grasping to enhance the admiralty court's jurisdiction. He recognized that the old wars with the common law courts had long since been lost and were better forgotten.

Finally, Scott did not place much emphasis on the form of bottomry bonds. They were expressed differently in various parts of the world.[146] Although counsel invariably paraded objections to the form of the bonds, Scott just as invariably overruled them.[147] Some written instrument was necessary; a mere affidavit that money had been advanced for the use of the ship would not suffice.[148] Since bottomry bonds had to rest on the security of the ship, they could clearly be distinguished from bills of exchange.[149]

Effects of bottomry bonds

Some of the legal effects can today be gleaned from the remaining eighteenth-century sources. A bottomry bond was treated as a lien on the ship and anyone who bought the ship from a private owner purchased it subject to that encumbrance. The debt on bottomry bonds followed the ship and the ship was answerable for the demands of the bond holders. But by this lien or hypothecation of the ship the property was not transferred to the lender. He only had an action against the ship to satisfy the money loaned.[150] In 1765 the judge of the admiralty court, Sir Thomas Salusbury, held that the bond which was first in time should be paid first. A few years later, however, the

---

[145] *Ibid.*, 73.
[146] *Ibid.*, 55; see also Abbott, *Merchant ships*, 103.
[147] *Nelson (Brown)* (1823), 1 Hag. 169, 177. Scott, himself, when arguing as counsel, had raised such an objection to the form of a bond, but the court dismissed his objection as a mere nullity. *Grace* (1796), Burrell 333, 334.
[148] *Belvidere (Marsh)* (1813), 1 Dod. 353, 356; *Sydney Cove (Fudge)* (1815), 2 Dod. 1, 6.
[149] *Eenrom (Fronier)* (1799), 2 Rob. 1, 5.
[150] R.A., Simpson MS 176, 349, 364, 393.

rule appears to have been settled that the later bond was ordinarily paid first.[151]

Scott, as judge, continued to treat the bottomry bond as a lien on the vessel, but shed considerable light on the meaning of such a lien. The lender by a lien acquired no title to property in the vessel, but a *jus in rem*, 'an interest directly and visibly residing in the substance of the thing itself'.[152] Scott doubted whether the master had the power to bind the owners personally beyond the value of their vessel.[153] The bottomry bond could also bind the ship's freight, even freight earned on a subsequent voyage.[154] The bond also attached to the ship's sails and rigging even if they had been removed from the ship.[155] In a case in which Scott analyzed at length the admiralty and common law precedents, as well as the commentators on the *lex mercatoria*, he concluded that the master, in cases of necessity, could also bind the cargo for the repair of the ship.[156] Such a bond, Scott said, could be sued on in admiralty. A bottomry bond was a negotiable instrument, which could be sued on, except in cases of laches, by the person acquiring it.[157]

As between several holders of bottomry bonds, Scott agreed that the last in time had priority in payment. He explained this inversion of the ordinary principle of security interests by observing: 'In this species of security, which is entered into under the pressure of necessity, the order of payment is very properly reversed, since, without the subsidiary aid of a later bond, the property would be totally lost, both to the owners and the former bond-holders.'[158] Even where there was just a slight difference in time between two bottomry bonds, the later received priority.[159] But if the several lenders had acted in privity with each other and advanced the money on the same

[151] *Dunlap v. Proceeds of the Neptune* (1769), Burrell 97. Sir George Hay, the judge of the admiralty court, clearly stated: 'But if in the same voyage the master takes up money at different ports, the posterior bond is preferred.' *Mackenzie v. Ogilvie* (1774), Burrell 134, 138.
[152] *Tobago (De Witte)* (1804), 5 Rob. 218, 222; *Eenrom (Fronier)* (1799), 2 Rob. 1, 5.
[153] *Gratitudine (Mazzola)* (1801), 3 Rob. 240, 274.
[154] *Jacob (Baer)* (1802), 4 Rob. 245, 250.
[155] *Alexander (Tate)* (1812), 1 Dod. 278, 282.
[156] *Gratitudine (Mazzola)* (1801), 3 Rob. 240, 271.
[157] *Rebecca (Maddick)* (1804), 5 Rob. 102, 104.
[158] *Rhadamanthe (Mayer)* (1813), 1 Dod. 201, 204; see also Abbott, *Merchant ships*, 105.
[159] *Betsey (Hay)* (1813), 1 Dod. 289, 290.

invitation and for the same repairs, the bond holders received payment *pro rata* without any preference.[160]

Equitable power to reform bottomry bonds

In the few sources which have been located from the eighteenth century, no discussion was found of the equitable power of the court to alter the terms of the agreement. Scott, following his ordinary practice when confronted by the lack of precedents, made explicit the non-judicial authorities and the policy reasons he considered in reaching his decision.

Scott clearly held that the admiralty court had some equitable power to reform bottomry bonds. For instance, where a bottomry bond included a £600 loan which had been secured by a bill of exchange and therefore on the personal credit of the ship owners, Scott had no difficulty upholding the remaining portions of the bond while holding the personal loan invalid as a bottomry bond. 'It is not necessary here that a bond should be either good or bad *in toto*: In the equitable proceedings in this Court, it may be good in part and bad in part.'[161] Scott considered it within the power of the court to question exorbitant interest rates (45% in one case) and to refer the issue to the registrar and merchants to determine the reasonableness of the rate.[162]

Scott found few precedents on the power of the court to reduce excessive interest rates. As he often did when he had to pilot through waters uncharted by precedent, Scott explicitly set out the basis of his reasoning process. In this passage once again Scott's grasp of the actual details of the shipping industry clearly appears. He explicitly balances the factors calling for an equitable reduction of the interest rate on behalf of the owners against the factors calling for a strict judicial enforcement of the bond as written on behalf of the foreign lenders. When he decided on policy grounds, he spelled out the policies which influenced his decision.

I have endeavoured to find in the authorities, ancient as well as modern, the regulations, if any, which have been allowed to Courts in restraining any exorbitance of maritime interest. But I do not find any, either in more ancient writers, or in the later authorities, such as *Emerigon* and *Pothier*, and the

---

[160] *Exeter (Whitford)* (1799), 1 Rob. 173, 177.
[161] *Augusta (De Bluhn)* (1813), 1 Dod. 283, 288.
[162] *Ysabel (Bozo)* (1812), 1 Dod. 273, 277.

modern writers upon maritime and commercial law. There have been a few instances, though a very few, in which this Court has exercised, with great caution, a control, in the way of a reduction of the stipulated interest, where it appeared exorbitant; and I think it rather difficult to say that no such power exists. The contract, even if made by the owner himself, may be a contract made under an undue advantage taken of his distress. But it is generally not made by the owner, but by the master who represents him; and not by special appointment of him for that purpose, but only by the operation of law acting upon an emergent and unprovided necessity, probably sometimes incurred not with the greatest prudence, considering that it is to impose the payment of an obligation upon another person; and, therefore, where there is a manifest want of such prudence, it requires some degree of correction. At the same time, a Court, in a distant part of the globe, can form only an imperfect measure of the distress existing, and of the difficulty of obtaining the needful supplies at the place where they are furnished. The money is to be advanced for persons unknown and resident in a foreign country; it is to be advanced upon an adventure which may totally fail of success, and the money may be irrecoverably lost. Upon all these considerations, a Court should be inclined to take the agreement as it stands, and not to disturb it, unless it be somehow vitiated by the party who objects to it ... [T]he presumption is in favour of the original contract.[163]

Such careful and explicit weighing of the relevant interests and policies characterized Scott's judgments when he could not find the comfort of precedent to guide him. It would be hard to expect more of a judge than such reasoned and clearly articulated decision-making.

In other cases, however, Scott had no difficulty holding a bottomry bond partially valid, while voiding some part of it, for instance, for fraud.[164] Similarly when Scott noted that a heavy commission had been charged for the loan, he referred the question to the 'Registrar properly assisted' to determine whether or not it was a proper charge.[165] Usually, however, the bond stood as drawn. The overriding interests of the shipping industry called for the assured enforceability of bottomry bonds. If the bond was drafted in legal form clearly binding on the parties, Scott refused to refer it to the registrar

---

[163] *Zodiac (Scott)* (1825), 1 Hag. 320, 326–7.
[164] *Tartar (Tharp)* (1822), 1 Hag. 1, 14; *Nelson (Brown)* (1823), 1 Hag. 169, 176.
 Scott also altered the strict terms of a bottomry bond to allow recovery by the bond holders. The master of the *Neptunus* had entered into a bottomry bond in Lisbon. Recovery under the bond was conditioned on the ship's return to London. The *Neptunus*, shattered by storm, could only struggle as far as Plymouth where it was proclaimed unfit to proceed to London. Scott, nonetheless, allowed the bond holders to recover against the remains of the ship, its cargo and freight. *Neptunus (Ley)* (1803), unreported, Arnold's Notebook, 1802–3, P.R.O. HCA 30/473; same case, Burrell 335.
[165] *Gratitudine (Mazzola)* (1801), 3 Rob. 240, 277.

assisted by merchants. 'These bonds have always been regarded as matter of serious obligation', Scott commented, 'protected by the terms of agreement between the lender and the borrower; nothing else is looked to but what the lender demands and the borrower agrees to; nobody has a right to alter that agreement.'[166]

SUITS FOR DAMAGES

As the shipping industry expanded enormously in the seventeenth and eighteenth centuries, one would expect reports of significant numbers of collisions between vessels and personal injuries aboard them. Collisions had been a matter of concern to the industry for centuries.[167] As the rivers and harbors became crowded with ships of all sizes and conditions, there surely must have been many instances of property damage. But collisions occurring there were within the body of the counties and thus within the jurisdiction of the common law courts. On the vast highways of the seas apparently collisions were infrequent. It is not surprising, therefore, to find only a few cases of collision noted in the early admiralty records.[168]

One doctrine of maritime collision law did have clearly traceable eighteenth-century roots. The equal division of damages where both vessels were at fault, the *rusticum judicium*, can be traced to the seventeenth century.[169] It was certainly settled in the eighteenth century that where 'Both ships seem to be in fault the loss of the Ship & Cargo must be equally born by the Master and Owners of both Vessels allowance being made for the damage the other has sustained.'[170]

---

[166] *Jane Vilet (Tindell)* (1827), 2 Hag. 92, 93.

[167] Laws of Oleron, s. 15 *Black book*, I, 109; Welwood, *Sea-laws*, 48.

[168] Apparently the volume of collision cases increased in the seventeenth century. *Select pleas in the court of admiralty*, ed. R. G. Marsden (2 vols., London, 1892, 1897) (Seld. Soc., vols. 6 and 11), II, lxxiii–lxxxv. Prohibitions were granted for collisions in the Thames, *Dorrington's Case* (1616), Moore 916, even though it was obvious that the common law courts could give no remedy, *Velthasen v. Ormsley* (1789), 3 Term Rep. 315. On prohibitions granted against suits in the admiralty court concerning collisions in the rivers, see R.A., Simpson MS 57.

[169] R. G. Marsden, *A treatise on the law of collisions at sea*, 7th edn (London, 1919), 156–69. *Harbyn v. Berry* (1648), Burrell 235, shows that the idea of equally divided damages went back at least to the mid-seventeenth century.

[170] R.A., Simpson MS 335.

Collisions

Scott, before he became judge, knew the legal rules applied by the admiralty court in collision cases. He had served as counsel for the owners of a large cargo vessel, the *Lynn*, which at night had run down and sunk a fishing smack at anchor in a bay.[171] Where the fault lay on one side only, he conceded, that vessel must be liable for all the consequences of the collision. But if the collision was caused without fault, then the damage must be borne by the vessel sustaining the harm. He argued, as an example, that if a vessel was totally ungovernable, it was not liable for the injury it caused. The damage, he asserted, was *damnum absque injuria*. The court, however, determined that the *Lynn* was governable and that there was no custom requiring lights on anchored fishing vessels. Therefore, since the *Lynn* was under sail and could have altered its course to avoid the collision, it must pay full damages and costs.

The court applied fairly simple rules of the road to determine liability in collision cases. In cases in which Scott had acted as counsel the following rules were stated: the moving ship was bound to avoid a ship at rest; a ship going before the wind must give way to ships beating against the wind; and unloaded or light ships must give way to heavy or loaded ships. The nautical facts in such cases were often determined by a reference to some of the brethren of Trinity House.[172]

Few of Scott's reported opinions as judge dealt with cases of collision. In his best-known judgment on the subject, Scott considered a collision a mile and a half off the southeast coast of England between the *Industry*, an 89-ton coal-carrying brig, and the *Woodrop-Sims*, a 520-ton American merchant vessel.[173] The *Industry* sank immediately, but its crew was picked up by the *Woodrop-Sims*. Since the factual dispute concerning liability involved questions best

---

[171] *Lynn* (1791), Arnold's Notebook, 1791, 38, P.R.O. HCA 30/470.

[172] *Ibid.*; *Sunnicide* (1783), Nicholl's Notebook, 1781–92, Nos. 33 and 72, P.R.O. HCA 30/464.

Trinity House had been first chartered under Henry VIII as a guild for protecting navigation on the coasts and rivers. The Trinity House brethren became responsible for pilotage and maintenance of lights and beacons and for providing charitable services for seamen. Among the elder brethren of Trinity House were some professional, experienced seamen and retired captains who were thoroughly conversant with the details of navigation. H. P. Mead, *Trinity House* (London, 1947), provides a rough sketch of the institution.

[173] *Woodrop-Sims (Jones)* (1815), 2 Dod. 83.

resolved by persons with nautical skill, Scott was assisted by two members of Trinity House. Relying on customary rules of the road, he instructed the Trinity masters as a common law judge would a jury:

> It is incumbent on you to determine whether proper measures of precaution were taken by the vessel which unfortunately ran the other down. The law imposes upon the vessel having the wind free, the obligation of taking proper measures to get out of the way of a vessel that is close-hauled, and of shewing that it has done so, if not, the owners of it are responsible for the loss which ensues.[174]

As the *Woodrop-Sims* was sailing with a free wind, the Trinity brethren had little difficulty in finding it liable, as the vessel burdened with the duty to keep clear of the *Industry*. Perhaps such simple rules of the road prevented most collisions and often determined, without the need for litigation, the liability where a collision had occurred. In this case the simple rule kept the Trinity brethren from having to consider the more difficult factual dispute as to the alleged negligence of the master and crew of the *Industry* in failing to maintain a proper lookout and in putting the helm hard to port rather than hard to starboard immediately before the collision.[175]

This case, however, is not remembered for the specific determination of liability, but rather for the broad discussion of liability applicable to any case of collision. Scott divided collision cases into four categories. First, in cases where the accident was caused by a storm or some other superhuman force, neither vessel would be at fault and each party must bear its own loss. Secondly, if the collision resulted from the fault of both ships, Scott stated that 'In such a case, the rule of law is, that the loss must be apportioned between them, as having been occasioned by the fault of both of them.'[176] This is the closest Scott came to endorsing the well-established *rusticum judicium* of equally divided damages where both vessels had been at fault. Scott, however, spoke only of apportionment of damages, which might have been interpreted to mean apportionment according to

---

[174] *Ibid.*, 2 Dod. 86–7. Scott relied on Trinity Masters in many other cases involving nautical questions, e.g. *Thames* (*Drummond*) (1805), 5 Rob. 345, 347; *Mary Ann* (*Ferrier*) (1823), 1 Hag. 158.

[175] *Woodrop-Sims* (*Jones*) (1815), 2 Dod. 83, 84 (argument of counsel).

[176] *Ibid.*, 85. See also *Lord Melville* (*Hollisbudton*) (1816), unpublished Bod. Lib., 6 Monk Bretton Dep. A 13.

degree of fault. Scott went on to point out, as a third possibility, that the vessel which suffered the loss might be completely at fault. If so, it must bear its own loss. Finally, if the fault lay entirely with the ship which caused the collision, the injured ship was entitled to full compensation from it.

Scott elsewhere qualified this final point, entitlement to full compensation, when he discussed the statutory limitation of liability to the value of the ship, tackle, apparel, furniture and freight. Although the ancient maritime law required full compensation from the negligent party causing a collision, England, Scott said, had followed the lead of Holland in limiting the owners' liability to the value of their property which they had exposed to hazard. Although the statute in its operative clause did not use the term 'appurtenances', Scott interpreted the statute to expose the appurtenances of a ship to liability in collision cases. Thus where a collision resulted from 'a want of that attention and vigilance which is due to the security of other vessels', the owners of the ship causing the accident were liable to the extent of the value of the ship and also of its 'indispensable instruments, without which the ship cannot execute its mission, and perform its functions'.[177]

In the few cases which came before him, Scott had occasion to determine several perennial problems in collision law. He held that a fishing smack, run down by another vessel, could not only recover actual damages for the loss of the smack and its cargo of fish, but also consequential damages for the loss of payment of salvage. At the time of the accident the smack was towing a disabled foreign ship.[178] He also held that the owners of a vessel causing a collision were liable even for the negligence of a pilot. 'The parties who suffer are entitled to have their remedy against the vessel that occasioned the damage, and are not under the necessity of looking to the pilot, from whom redress is not always to be had, for compensation.'[179] In the last reported case Scott decided as admiralty judge, he held that the owners of the ship at fault were liable also for interest on the amount of the unpaid damage claim if payment had been delayed.[180]

Scott's few decisions in this area reflect, but in some respects alter

---

[177] *Dundee (Holmes)* (1823), 1 Hag. 109, 121, 122; 53 Geo. III c. 159.
[178] *Betsey Caines (Wilson)* (1826), 2 Hag. 28, 30; see also *Yorkshireman (Furman)* (1827), 2 Hag. 30.
[179] *Neptune the Second* (1814), 1 Dod. 467.
[180] *Dundee (Holmes)* (1827), 2 Hag. 137, 143.

and clarify, the law of the eighteenth century. As already indicated, the *rusticum judicium* doctrine of divided damages had been settled long before Scott became judge. Perhaps Scott was attempting to soften the harshness of this rule of equal division of damages where both ships were at fault. He certainly must have been aware that his predecessor had decided two cases and that the Court of Delegates had decided a third, all in 1789, applying the rule of equally divided damages.[181] If, by speaking only of apportionment of damages, rather than equal division of damages, Scott intended to introduce a system of damages proportional to fault, his efforts proved unsuccessful.[182]

In discussing the rule of divided damages, Scott made another subtle modification of the prior law. When he prepared his decision in the *Woodrop-Sims*, Scott probably had consulted the Simpson notebook, which stated:

Rule in Damage Causes[:] where damage done by fault or neglect of Crew of other Ship it will be liable to whole Damage[.] But where both in fault or it is uncertain which Ship occasioned the damage – half damages are to be allowed – but where either the Ship damaged was in fault or it was done by violence of Storm & other Ship could not avoid it the Ship must bear its own loss.[183]

Scott's four categories of collision cases parallel this passage, but he spoke, as we have seen, of apportioned damages rather than equally divided damages, and he applied this rule only in cases where both parties were at fault, not where fault was uncertain. In restricting the rule of divided damages to cases where both ships were at fault, Scott was successful in settling the law for the future.[184]

There is no indication that Scott heard any cases where the collision had occurred in one of England's rivers or harbors, cases within the jurisdiction of the common law courts. Scott's predecessor, Judge Marriott, apparently lacked Scott's deferential attitude toward the common law courts. Marriott, in tones echoing the civilians of the seventeenth century, refused to dismiss a case of a collision which had occurred in the Thames. He feared the foreign ship would sail away if not arrested. When reminded of prohibitions in such cases, he observed that they had been granted without sufficient consideration by enemies to the prerogative of the Crown attempting to clip the

---

[181] The cases are discussed in Marsden, *Collisions at sea*, 163–5. The two admiralty court cases are: *Wildman v. Blakes* (1789), Burrell 332, and *Nelson v. Fawcett* (1789), Burrell 332. Scott was counsel in the latter case.

[182] Marsden, *Collisions at sea*, 166–7.

[183] R.A., Simpson MS 207; see also 332.

[184] Marsden, *Collisions at sea*, 166.

wings of the admiralty court.[185] Scott, it seems, never tried to reopen the old wounds of distant battles between the common law courts and the prerogative courts.

Scott perhaps clarified the law concerning the liability of the owner of a vessel for a collision caused by the negligence of a pilot, but he certainly was not creating new law. In the mid-eighteenth century Simpson was quite unsure whether the owners of a vessel had a remedy against a pilot for harm caused to their vessel by the pilot's negligence. Simpson, after some hesitation, concluded that cargo shippers could sue the owners or master of a ship for damage to the cargo caused by the fault of a pilot. The owners could then try to recover from the pilot.[186] Scott was more definite in a collision case in announcing as '[T]he true rule of law ... [that] The owners are responsible to the injured party for the acts of the pilot, and they must be left to recover the amount as well as they can against him.'[187]

In the eighteenth century the admiralty court had granted consequential damages, but rarely and apparently only if the damage had been caused voluntarily.[188] Scott again slightly modified and clarified the law by allowing consequential damages where the collision had been caused merely by negligence.[189]

Personal injuries

In the eighteenth century the admiralty court had already made the distinction between cases of immoderate correction of seamen (damages and costs awarded) and cases of moderate correction (no foundation for a damage action).[190] This distinction guided Scott in cases he heard concerning punishment of crew members.

When the captain of an East Indiaman was sued for damages for striking, kicking and ordering a public flagellation of a black cuddy cook, Scott awarded damages of £100 and costs. Although punish-

---

[185] *Vrow Maria* (1798), Nicholl's Notebook, 1797–9, 140, P.R.O. HCA 30/464. It was clear that actions for damages in navigable rivers, even below the first bridge, lay at common law. R.A., Simpson MS 57. Sir George Hay, admiralty judge, however, took jurisdiction in a case of collision which occurred near the Isle of Dogs in the Thames. *Fairless v. Thorsen* (1774), Burrell 130.

[186] R.A., Simpson MS 149, 175. It was settled that the owners were liable for the negligence of the master or the crew. *Ibid.*, fos. 305, 332.

[187] *Neptune the Second* (1814), 1 Dod. 467.

[188] R.A., Simpson MS 205–6.

[189] *Betsey Caines (Wilson)* (1826), 2 Hag. 28, 30.

[190] R.A., Simpson MS 20.

ment by the master of a vessel was within the law, Scott insisted that it must be applied with moderation and that '[I]n all cases which will admit of the delay proper for inquiry, due inquiry should precede the act of punishment; and, therefore, that the party charged should have the benefit of that rule of universal justice, of being heard in his own defence.'[191] Here Scott introduced, apparently without precedent, a requirement of minimal due process aboard ship. On the other hand, where Scott found that the punishment inflicted on a seaman was commensurate to the offense committed, that it was imposed only after a formal inquiry by the officers, that it was ordered by due authority and administered with proper moderation, Scott decided that the seaman was not entitled to damages.[192] Perhaps Scott's influence on admiralty law can best be seen in such subtle yet effective changes as insisting that even at sea the accused should have the opportunity to speak in his own defense.

An assault while at sea by the master against a passenger confronted Scott with a question he had not considered before.[193] Counsel pointed out that in the argument before King's Bench in *Le Caux v. Eden*, it had been contended that the admiralty court, without the aid of a jury, lacked the ability to estimate personal sufferings and assess compensation for them.[194] Scott, as always, uneasy without the guidance of precedent, asked the registrar to consult the records. The registrar reported on his findings after searching back to 1730. Scott concluded that the admiralty court could award damages for such an injury committed on the high seas. Reiterating his consistent pattern of following precedent, Scott stated:

I should be unwilling to entertain an action of this sort on such a mere general principle, if it did not appear to be sanctioned by the pre-existing practice of the Court ... But since the Registrar has reported several instances, in which the Court seems to have proceeded in causes of damage, between persons who were not connected by any relation, arising from official situations on board

[191] *Agincourt (Mahon)* (1824), 1 Hag. 271, 274. The cuddy cook prepared meals for the captain and passengers. In *Enchantress (Killoch)* (1825), 1 Hag. 395, 397, Scott awarded £120 and costs to a seaman for the aggravated and unmanly cruelty of the captain.

[192] *Lowther Castle (Baker)* (1825), 1 Hag. 384, 385.

[193] *Ruckers (Carey)* (1801), 4 Rob. 73.

[194] *Le Caux v. Eden* (1781), 2 Dougl. 595, 598. Scott, or possibly the reporter, added a footnote discussing the role of a jury in admiralty proceedings. *Ruckers (Carey)* (1801), 4 Rob. 73, 74.

the ship, I am not enabled to say, that the Court can refuse to receive the libel.[195]

Scott here did not find a precedent strictly on point. The precedents found by the registrar had not considered the case of a passenger assaulted by a master. Nonetheless Scott was willing to award damages once he was satisfied that the admiralty court had previously awarded damages to parties who were not part of the ship's company.

SUITS FOR SALVAGE

The common law has not deemed it appropriate to compel the owner of a business to pay a reward to a passerby who reported a fire on the business premises or helped to extinguish it. Much less has the common law ever imposed a lien on the business enterprise or its merchandise to assure payment of such a reward. The admiralty court's different treatment of salvage awards can be explained by the particular needs of the shipping industry, at least in its early periods of development. It seems trite to observe that the shipping industry was structured around the ship. Diverse individuals became part owners of one vessel, each owner often holding only a small fraction of the ownership. Some of these individuals might also be part owners of other vessels, but usually with a different group of partners. The ship was ordinarily the only tie which bound a group of investors together. This ship, the physical expression of their relationship, of necessity had to set out on voyages if it was to make a profit, but this meant that the partners, unless they sailed as master or passenger, had to watch their whole firm slip out of their control and beyond their ability to aid it in distress or to protect it from perils. At a time when insurance was only beginning to be available, the primary concern of the owners was to spread the risk among many owners and to reduce the risk of total loss.[196] This sense of insecurity of the ship owners as their fragile vessel departed on each voyage upon the often unfriendly seas explains the early development of the law of salvage. Ship owners had every reason to pay a reward to any party who voluntarily helped their ship when in need. It was surely in the interest of the shipping industry to have a body of law which encouraged individuals to save

[195] *Ruckers (Carey)* (1801), 4 Rob. 73, 76.
[196] Davis, *Shipping industry*, 81–109.

their vessels and which threatened to punish those who took advantage of a ship's distress to pillage it. The admiralty law, unlike the common law, thus created the clear expectation that volunteers who aided a ship in trouble would be rewarded and that heroes would be rewarded generously. This law at least increased the likelihood that something of their venture would be restored to the ship owners, precisely because the law compelled them to pay a suitable reward to those who voluntarily helped in saving it. Such was the heart of the law of salvage which had been in the process of development for hundreds of years before Scott became judge of the admiralty court.[197]

The salvage service

The distinction between military salvage due for restoring a ship recaptured from the enemy and civil salvage for rescuing a vessel from distress was established in the eighteenth century.[198] It was also clear in the eighteenth century that a suit for civil salvage could be brought either *in rem* or *in personam*. It was considered preferable to bring a salvage suit *in rem*, since otherwise the salvor would have the burden of proof to establish ownership of the salvaged vessel.[199]

It appears that the tension between the admiralty court and the common law courts over wrecks had not been resolved in the eighteenth century. Simpson in one place explicitly states that the admiralty court did not have jurisdiction over cases of wreck if the wreck had been claimed by the lord of the manor where it was found. '[N]either can [the] Court of Adm[iralt]y [take jurisdiction] in case of dispute whether it be Wreck or not [to] determine [the issue], but if it be claimed as such by [the] Lord of [the] Manor, it must be tried at Common Law.'[200] But elsewhere Simpson stated that a ship stranded on the coast did not become wreck and no right accrued to

[197] E. Benedict, *Admiralty: the law of salvage*, ed. M. J. Norris, 7th edn (New York, 1980), 3A, 1–2 to 1–17.
[198] R.A., Simpson MS 94–7, 164–7, 182–5, 252–5.
[199] *Ibid.*, fo. 254.
[200] *Ibid.*, fo. 399. In this context Simpson provided a definition of high and low water marks which was crucial in defining wreck. 'High & low Water Mark [is] to be taken according to the ordinary & natural course of the Sea & not as it may flow higher or ebb lower on account of Wind or other accidents[.] [Wha]t we call high Water Mark is described Quantum hibernus fluctus maximus excurrit & the low Water Mark on the contrary extends as far as the Summer ebb generally leaves the Shore dry which is within the bounds of the Manor[.] [A]s the Hull of [the] Ship &c is lodged within those bounds it belongs to the Lord of the Manor & not to the Adm[ira]l[.]' *Ibid.*

the lord of the manor, but only salvage to those who assisted in saving the ship.[201]

One would think from Simpson's confused comments that the low water mark was the dividing line between admiralty jurisdiction over stranded vessels and common law jurisdiction over wrecks.[202] Sir George Lee, however, in 1746 wrote an opinion as counsel in which he considered the rights to a vessel which had been driven by storm onto the shore of a manor explicitly stated to be above the low water mark. His response confirms the jurisdictional tension. He wrote:

Cases of Wreck are under the Jurisdiction of the Common Law. The Admiralty Court has no Cognizance and can not give any Relief therein. I think it is clear that this is not a Case of Wreck and consequently that Mr Sheppard is not intitled to this ship & cargo as such[.] [T]his ship appears to me to be stranded[.][203]

Apparently the admiralty court remained willing to assert jurisdiction in such cases, even though its jurisdiction could have been challenged. Shortly before Scott became admiralty judge, his predecessor heard a case of a vessel which had been stranded on the Isle of Wight. When counsel raised the question of the court's jurisdiction, James Marriott, the admiralty judge, brusquely replied that he had no intention of prohibiting himself.[204]

The admiralty court in the eighteenth century had sketched some aspects of the law of civil salvage. The court, for example, had held that mariners could not receive salvage for saving their own vessel from shipwreck or distress. It was their duty to do their utmost to save the ship and cargo.[205] Only those who actually assisted the ship in distress could claim a salvage award.[206] Well before Scott's day the admiralty court had likewise considered cases of derelict, a vessel abandoned at sea. Those who saved a derelict and brought it into port

---

[201] *Ibid.*, fo. 166.
[202] *Ibid.*, fo. 220.
[203] H.S.P. Lee Admiralty Opinions.
[204] *Crescent* (*Hodgson*) (1798), Nicholl's Notebook, 1797–9, P.R.O. HCA 30/464.
[205] R.A., Simpson MS 334, 345. In 1725 Henry Penrice, judge of the admiralty court, apparently was willing to consider an extraordinary reward for a crew in a suit by mariners for wages and salvage for navigating a leaky vessel back to England at great risk to their lives. This case is distinguishable since the mariners' ship had been seized, pillaged and sunk by pirates who ordered the crew aboard the leaky vessel which they eventually brought back to England. They clearly had no wage contract to sail the second vessel at all, much less in its dangerous condition. Lincoln's Inn Library, Misc. MS 147, 97.
[206] R.A., Simpson MS 252, 346.

merited a salvage award, but the derelict itself, if not claimed within a year and a day, became the property of the king as a perquisite of the admiralty. Wherever in the world abandoned property was found by British subjects, it belonged to the king, 'For he has [the] same right as Lord of the Seas to all Derelicts & Treasure Trove as he has in his own dominions unless claimed by Lords [of a manor] by grant from the Crown.'[207]

In the eighteenth-century sources consulted, there is no mention of the question of a salvage award for saving life at sea. Perhaps this occurred seldom where there was not also property salvage. Since Simpson's notebook sought comprehensive coverage of questions of admiralty law, it is surprising that he never mentioned the question of life salvage if he had been aware of any discussion of it by the court.

Cases of salvage provided an appropriate context for questioning the evidentiary rule barring the admissibility of testimony from interested parties. In the eighteenth century the rule that any person interested in the litigation should not be allowed to testify was usually applied in common law as well as in civil law courts.[208] In cases of salvage, however, ordinarily only the saving crew and the saved crew witnessed the salvage act. Without testimony from interested parties there often could be no testimony at all.

Scott had occasion as counsel to discuss the admissibility of testimony of a salvage crew. A 500-ton whaling vessel, with forty-two men aboard, signaled distress from where it lay anchored off the Norfolk coast. A fishing vessel, with a small crew, saved the whaling vessel and its crew. When the salvors brought suit for their salvage award, counsel for the owners of the whaling vessel objected that there was no competent evidence of the salvage since the salvors were all interested parties. Scott, arguing for the salvors, replied that counsel for the 'opulent owners' was trying to narrow the rules of evidence in the admiralty court to conform to the rules appropriately applied at common law. Since the only available evidence must come from the persons saved or the salvors, all equally interested parties, Scott argued that evidentiary rules must necessarily be lax. But he added with a refreshingly realistic view of the question, such testimony was open to observation on the credibility of the witnesses.

The necessity which he contended overrode the ordinary rules simply meant that there were witnesses without whose testimony

---

[207] *Ibid.*, fos. 107–8, 362; H.S.P. Lee Admiralty Opinions.
[208] *H.E.L.*, IX, 193–7; G. Gilbert, *Law of Evidence* (Dublin, 1754), 86–7.

material facts could not be proved. The court accepted Scott's argument from necessity and ruled that the testimony could be introduced.[209]

In order to delineate the scope of the admiralty court's jurisdiction in salvage cases, Scott, when he became judge, following the long tradition of the court, made several fundamental distinctions. First of all, he said, it was necessary to distinguish civil salvage from military salvage. Military salvage, which was within the admiralty court's prize jurisdiction, involved the rescuing of property from the enemy, usually the recapture of a British vessel which had previously fallen into the hands of the enemy. Civil salvage, on the other hand, involved preserving a vessel from some need or casualty or peril of the sea. Civil salvage was within the court's instance jurisdiction.[210] A second distinction had traditionally been made between cases of wreck where the vessel had been driven on the shore and cases of salvage where the vessel was on the sea below the low water mark. Although, as already mentioned, cases of wreck had previously been thought to be within the exclusive jurisdiction of the common law courts, Scott heard such a case. The vessel was clearly on the beach, '[S]o that any one could walk round the hulk without a wet foot', but neither the parties nor Scott questioned admiralty jurisdiction.[211] Scott apparently felt secure in the knowledge that his predecessors had continued to hear such cases despite possible jurisdictional challenges. Scott usually avoided treading on disputed terrain.

Although saving a derelict was considered a case of salvage, some distinct principles were involved. In a case of derelict, where the ship had been abandoned at sea by the master and crew without any hope of recovery, Scott followed well-settled precedent in holding that the property saved became the possession of the sovereign if no owner claimed it within a year and a day. The parties who had saved the derelict were entitled to a salvage award for their efforts, but did not

---

[209] *Pitt* (1789), Arnold's Notebook, 1789, 20 and 40, P.R.O. HCA 30/470. Counsel for the owners of the saved ship referred to such common law sources as Blackstone and Gilbert, see fn. 208.

[210] *Franklin* (*Goodrich*) (1801), 4 Rob. 147, 149; *Louisa* (*Higginbotham*) (1813), 1 Dod. 317, 318.
    Scott took jurisdiction, as a case of civil salvage, of a Dutch naval vessel which had been saved and brought to a British port by a British vessel. *Prins Frederik* (*Van Senden*) (1820), 2 Dod. 451, 482.

[211] *Augusta* or *Eugenie* (*Louvel*) (1822), 1 Hag. 16, 18. The common law courts held that admiralty jurisdiction extended only to salvage performed at sea. Abbott, *Merchant ships*, 249–56.

become owners of the derelict.[212]

In one case counsel had argued strenuously that admiralty jurisdiction in salvage cases had to be *in rem*, based on the arrest of the ship. Scott rejected the argument. Salvage suits could thus be based on *in personam* jurisdiction over the owners, although this must have been a rare occurrence.[213] At least as to other would-be salvors, the salvor in possession of a vessel had a lien. 'Those who have obtained possession of a ship as salvors', Scott said, 'have a legal interest, which cannot be divested before adjudication takes place in a court possessed of competent authority; and it is not for the King's officers, or any other persons, on the ground of superior authority, to dispossess them without cause.'[214]

The basic principle of determining whether an act of assistance merited a salvage award was that it must be a voluntary act of service to a vessel in need. Thus, regardless of their perils, the crew of a vessel could not be considered salvors for protecting their own ship from wreck. Scott defined a salvor as 'A person who, without any particular relation to a ship in distress, proffers useful service, and gives it as a volunteer adventurer, without any pre-existing covenant that connected him with the duty of employing himself for the preservation of that ship.'[215] Scott here summed up and restated with greater precision the prior law on the subject.

No salvage, therefore, was due to a naval officer who had extricated a hired transport vessel from a harbor, under the enemy's guns, after it became grounded and had to be abandoned by crew and troops.[216] Such was his duty. Similarly a naval vessel merited no salvage for providing a fishing vessel with information concerning its location and distance from land. Those who sought a salvage award, Scott observed, 'were bound to communicate such information; it was not more an act of humanity than of duty, and what the master of the fishing smack had a right to expect from any vessel that he might have fallen in with'.[217] Furthermore, since it was 'the bounden duty of the

---

[212] *Aquila (Lunsden)* (1798), 1 Rob. 37, 41. In his judgment in this case Scott explicitly relied on the Simpson MS; cf. Appendix, p. 291 below.

[213] *Hope (Horncastle)* (1801), 3 Rob. 215, 217.

[214] *Blenden Hall (Barr)* (1814), 1 Dod. 414, 416; *Maria (Kilstrom)* (1809), Edw. 175, 177.

[215] *Neptune (Clark)* (1824), 1 Hag. 227, 236.

[216] *Belle (Betts)* (1809), Edw. 66, 69. Although there were overtones of military salvage, the court considered this as a case of civil salvage.

[217] *Maria (Kilstrom)* (1809), Edw. 175, 178.

crew to give every assistance in their power to prevent or quell a mutiny', a crew which had subdued a mutiny had earned no salvage award.[218] Scott, in this mutiny case, was unsure enough to request a search for precedents, but when none were found, he dismissed the suit for salvage. Scott likewise dismissed a claim for salvage by the crew of a vessel which had assisted another vessel in distress. These two ships had sailed as consorts, 'under a special agreement to give mutual protection'. Since there was a contract duty to give aid, no salvage award could be granted.[219]

Pilots could not claim a salvage award unless they rendered truly extraordinary service to the vessel they were piloting. Scott conceded:

It may be, in an extraordinary case, difficult to distinguish a case of pilotage from a case of salvage, properly so called; for it is possible that the safe conduct of a ship into a port, under circumstances of extreme danger and personal exertion, may exalt a pilotage service into something of a salvage service. But in general they are distinguishable enough, and the pilot, though he contributes to the safety of the ship, is not to claim as a legal salvor.[220]

The magistrate who claimed salvage for sending fifteen men to protect a stranded ship from plunder received short shrift from Scott.[221] The magistrate's duty was clear. Even a passenger aboard a vessel where there was a common danger had a duty to give all the assistance he could. Scott could find no case where a passenger had received a salvage award.[222]

A wide range of voluntary services could provide a basis for a salvage award. Where the crew of one vessel rescued a slave ship from the insurgent slaves who had complete possession, Scott considered the service as meritorious as recovering a ship from pirates.[223] But where a naval vessel rescued a convict vessel from control of the convicts and the mutinous crew, Scott refused to allow salvage. He considered even such a service to be within the duties of the naval officers and crew.

[K]ing's ships may acquire a title to civil salvage by assistance rendered to vessels in distress, even where that distress does not arise from the dangers of the sea, and where the assistance is not of a maritime kind; but the Court has

---

[218] *Governor Raffles (King)* (1815), 2 Dod. 14, 17.
[219] *Zephyr (Arrowsmith)* (1827), 2 Hag. 43, 46.
[220] *Joseph Harvey (Paddock)* (1799), 1 Rob. 306.
[221] *Aquila (Lunsden)* (1798), 1 Rob. 37, 46.
[222] *Branston (Wilson)* (1826), 2 Hag. 3.
[223] *Trelawney (Lake)* (1802), 4 Rob. 223, 227. Such a rescue from insurgent slaves was not proved in *Anne (Bicknell)* (1804), 5 Rob. 100, 101.

not been in the habit of considering such services, unless they have been very splendid and extraordinary, as entitling the parties to a salvage reward.[224]

Rescuing a derelict and bringing it to safety was, of course, a salvage act. Even where the master and crew of the derelict had exaggerated the danger and abandoned their ship too soon, the salvors merited a generous reward.[225] But where the vessel had been abandoned by the enemy captors of an English ship, Scott refused to apply the principle of derelict, since the owners of the derelict had not committed an act of abandonment. Treating this as a case of civil salvage, Scott awarded a small amount as salvage, not the large award ordinarily appropriate in a case of derelict.[226] Even though the owners had tried to recover their abandoned ship by sending out a party to rescue it, Scott in another case considered the ship derelict and made a generous award to the volunteer salvors who first found it.[227]

The ordinary rule, Scott insisted, was that a person not actually taking part in the salvage service was not entitled to a share in the salvage reward. But he made an important exception in favor of the owners of the ship rendering the service. Since the ship, in order to give assistance, often was diverted from its proper voyage and ran the risk of suffering some damage, the owners, though not present, were entitled to some compensation.[228]

Saving human life at sea, when not associated with preservation of the ship or cargo, could not receive a salvage award. Scott's statement on the subject manifested none of his accustomed hesitation when precedents were lacking and he was confronted with a novel question. Counsel for the salvors did not suggest that saving lives at sea merited a salvage award. Neither counsel nor Scott mentioned any precedents. Scott apparently was merely expressing the familiar expectation of the community of seamen: that they risked their lives to save the lives of others in peril from the sea without any hope of pecuniary award. Since Scott's words are still quoted as the basis of this

---

[224] *Francis and Eliza* (1816), 2 Dod. 115, 117–18.

[225] *Fortuna (Quest)* (1802), 4 Rob. 193, 194.

[226] *John and Jane (Askew)* (1802), 4 Rob. 216, 217.

[227] *L'Esperance (Stegman)* (1811), 1 Dod. 46, 48.

[228] *Vine (Jay)* (1825), 2 Hag. 1, 2; *Waterloo (Birch)* (1820), 2 Dod. 433, 443. In another case Scott gave an equal award to the members of the crew who actually boarded and saved a vessel in distress and to the remainder of the crew who were willing to board the vessel but were not selected for that service. *Baltimore (Baker)* (1817), 2 Dod. 132, 137.

seemingly perverse doctrine,[229] they merit repetition here:

> The mere preservation of life, it is true, this Court has no power of remunerating; it must be left to the bounty of the individuals; but if it can be connected with the preservation of property, whether by accident or not, then the Court can take notice of it, and It is always willing to join that to the *animus* displayed in the first instance.[230]

Since property had been saved in this case, Scott made an award (£611 or 10% of the value of the property) which apparently took into account the saving of life. Scott's statement should be regarded as encouraging life salvage, since apparently for the first time he held that the court could be more generous in its salvage award if the salvors had saved life at sea. He regarded the saving of property, however, as jurisdictional, perhaps because of the utter incongruity of a maritime lien on a person saved. Within the community of seamen, as Scott was aware, the willingness to risk one's own life to save another whose life was endangered at sea was usually enough to prompt heroic efforts. Every seaman hoped and expected that such heroic efforts might one day be exerted when his day of peril came.

Amount of the salvage award

The admiralty court in the eighteenth century had determined that the 'Allowance for Salvage is uncertain [and] will be left to the discretion of the court.'[231] The Simpson notebook stated that the amount of the award must be determined by the circumstances, the danger and hazard, the trouble and expense of the salvors.[232] The Simpson notebook also stated that the rule for measuring the award for saving derelicts was flexible and not a fixed percent of the value, 'only a reward for his trouble in preserving & taking care' of it.[233]

General average was well recognized in eighteenth-century

---

[229] S. F. Friedell, 'Compensation and reward for saving life at sea', *Michigan Law Rev.*, 77 (1979), 1218, 1226.

[230] *Aid (Teasdel)* (1822), 1 Hag. 83, 84. For the argument of counsel, see Arnold's Notebook, 1821–3, P.R.O. HCA 30/474.

[231] R.A., Simpson MS 225; see also 62, 167.

[232] *Ibid.*, fos. 345–7. In several cases in which Scott appeared as counsel, the court applied this rule, that the salvage award must be measured by the amount of risk and danger to the salvors. *Valk* (1791); *Sophia Magdalena* (1791); *Rufford* (1792), Arnold's Notebook, 1789–92, 54, 95, 101, P.R.O. HCA 30/474.

[233] R.A., Simpson MS 362. Sir George Lee in 1747 had also stated that salvors of derelicts merited only such an award as the court in its discretion decreed. H.S.P. Lee Admiralty Opinions.

admiralty practice. 'Owners of Ship & Cargo are respectively liable to contribute to charges of Salvage upon an averidge [*sic*] according to value of Ship & Goods.'[234]

Scott, when he became judge, insisted that the amount of the salvage award was within the discretion of the court. He rejected any fixed rule and consistently applied the measure of *quantum meruit*. Shortly after Scott became admiralty judge he heard a case involving a derelict found at sea. Counsel for the original salvors had argued that by the ancient practice of the admiralty court, derelicts were divided by moieties, half for the crown and half for the finders. Scott, as was often his practice when he had to decide a case without the help of precedent, carefully reviewed the authorities on admiralty practice, Jenkins, Selden, Loccenius, and Valin. He quoted from 'some manuscript notes, which I have of a very careful and experienced practiser in this profession, Sir E. Simpson', who had said that salvors of derelict property 'must be satisfied for their expence and trouble'.[235] Simpson, as we have seen, thus rejected the rigid rule that salvors of derelicts always merited one half the value. After reviewing recent precedents of the court and one case in which he acted as counsel and again quoting from the Simpson notebook, Scott concluded that salvors were not *de jure* entitled to a half. Applying the discretion of the court to the particular circumstances of the case, he awarded two-fifths of the value of the cargo saved.

The economic realities of maritime commerce, so familiar to Scott, had to be considered in making salvage awards. In considering the policy reasons for generous salvage awards, Scott looked to the broad interests of the shipping industry as well as the particular merits of the salvors. Where a ship of considerable value had been saved, Scott said:

The principles on which the Court of Admiralty proceeds, lead to a liberal remuneration in salvage cases; for they look not merely to the exact *quantum* of service performed in the case itself, but to the general interests of the navigation and commerce of the country, which are greatly protected by

[234] R.A., Simpson MS 253; see also 203, 395.
[235] *Aquila (Lunsden)* (1798), 1 Rob. 37, 38, 43–5. Scott quoted from the Simpson MS 255, 362. These passages from the Simpson MS are juxtaposed to Scott's quotation in the Appendix, p. 291 below. In an unpublished case of derelict Scott again insisted that the amount of remuneration due to the salvors was entirely in the discretion of the court. *Francis (Papmore)* (1809), Bod. Lib., 4 Monk Bretton Dep. 66. In the early seventeenth century, Welwood, *Sea-laws*, 53, seems to have thought that the English admiralty court awarded at least one half to the salvors of a derelict.

exertions of this nature. The fatigue, the anxiety, the determination to encounter danger, if necessary, the spirit of adventure, the skill and dexterity which are acquired by the exercise of that spirit, all require to be taken into consideration. What enhances the pretensions of salvors most, is the actual danger which they have incurred; the value of human life is that which is, and ought to be, principally considered in the preservation of other men's property: and if this is shewn to have been hazarded, it is most highly estimated.[236]

Scott's insistence on broad policy questions involving the shipping industry provided a meaningful rationale for following precedent. Salvage awards made sense only as a means of fostering the interests of maritime commerce by encouraging fearless efforts to save endangered property at sea.[237]

Where there were special[1] difficulties or great danger, Scott generously rewarded the salvors; in one case he awarded two-thirds of the value of the property saved.[238] The award for saving a derelict, however, could never exceed one half the value of the property saved.[239] Even in a case of derelict, if the salvage service was not accompanied with danger or difficulty, the award would be smaller.[240] If the value of the property saved was great, Scott tended to

[236] *William Beckford (Muirhead)* (1800 and 1801), 3 Rob. 355–6, 357, affirmed on appeal to the Court of Delegates (1801), *ibid.*, 360.

[237] In *Sarah* (1800), 1 Rob. 313, Scott had considered the interests of the shipping industry in making a salvage award. 'I do not think that the exact service performed is the only proper test for the *quantum* of reward in these cases. The general interest and security of navigation is a point to which the Court will likewise look in fixing the reward. It is for the general interest of commerce that a considerable reward should be held up; and as ships are made to pay largely for light-houses, even where no immediate use is derived from them, from the general convenience, that there should be permanent buildings of that sort, provided for all occasions, although this or that ship may derive no benefit from them on this or that particular occasion; so on the same principle it is expedient for the security of navigation, that persons of this description, ready on the water, and fearless of danger, should be encouraged to go out for the assistance of vessels in distress; and therefore that when they are to be paid at all, they should be paid liberally.'

[238] *Jonge Bastiaan (Steyting)* (1804), 5 Rob. 322, 324; *Elliotta* (1815), 2 Dod. 75, 77; *Baltimore (Baker)* (1817), 2 Dod. 132, 136. The highest merit was for risk of life *Elizabeth (Drew)* (1813), unpublished, Bod. Lib., 8 Monk Bretton Dep. A 17; *Triumpho* (1803), unpublished, Nicholl's Notebook, 1802–4, 142, P.R.O. HCA 30/465.

[239] *L'Esperance (Stegman)* (1811), 1 Dod. 46, 49. Scott was unable to find a precedent in a case of derelict for an award larger than one half and reluctantly limited the award to that amount. *Frances Mary (Kendal)* (1827), 2 Hag. 89, 90. Scott apparently in one case of derelict had suggested that the court could award more than a moiety. *Reliance (Wiley)* (1811), 2 Hag. 90.

[240] *Maria (Kilstrom)* (1809), Edw. 175, 176; *Caliban (Atkins)* (1813), unpublished, Bod. Lib., 7 Monk Bretton Dep. 207.

give a smaller percentage as a reward, whereas, if the property was of little value, he awarded a higher percentage.[241] Scott thought that a particularly generous reward was appropriate where the salvage service had been performed by a steam ship. He wanted to encourage these newly developed ships to take part in salvage operations because of 'the great power of vessels of this description'.[242]

Scott had no occasion to discuss the doctrine of general average, though he certainly was familiar with it.[243] Probably by Scott's day, average adjusters calculated these cases which were then settled without court involvement.

---

[241] *Blenden Hall (Barr)* (1814), 1 Dod. 414, 421; *Waterloo (Birch)* (1820), 2 Dod. 433, 442; *Mary Ann (Ferrier)* (1823), 1 Hag. 158, 160.

[242] *Raikes (Gardiner)* (1824), 1 Hag. 246.

[243] Scott discussed general average in the context of two prize cases: *Copenhagen (Mening)* (1799), 1 Rob. 289, 293; *Hoffnung (Hardrath)* (1807), 6 Rob. 383. He defined general average as '[T]hat loss to which contribution must be made by both ship and cargo; the loss, or expence which the loss creates, being incurred for the common benefit of both.' *Copenhagen*, 1 Rob. 294. A fuller contemporary discussion of general average can be found in Abbott, *Merchant ships*, 213–31.

4

PRIZE LAW: NATIONALITY –
A STUDY IN DETAIL

There can be no doubt that Sir William Scott, Lord Stowell, retains a small place in history primarily because of his application, interpretation and development of prize law. His instance judgments, significant for adding precision where there had been vague principles, are numbered in the dozens, whereas his prize judgments, far more significant as early pronouncements on the international law of war, are numbered in the hundreds. The wars which involved and nearly engulfed Great Britain for most of the years Scott sat as judge gave him a unique opportunity to achieve lasting fame as judge of the admiralty court.

Scott's profound grasp of the economic and social realities of the shipping industry, as we have seen, on occasion provided him with policy reasons for his instance judgments. His far more numerous prize judgments show his deep understanding of the much more complex realities of military strategy, shifting government policy and conflicting economic and social forces.

Scott was, after all, a thoroughly eighteenth-century man. He understood, though he did not always sympathize with, the political, economic and social developments going on around him. This historical matrix, so familiar to Scott, served as a basis for policy arguments, sometimes unspoken, in many of the significant cases he heard. A brief suggestion of some dimensions of the historical context of Scott's prize judgments, therefore, will make possible a better appreciation of his contribution.

BACKGROUND

One obvious policy consideration behind maritime warfare during the French wars and Napoleonic wars was military. Great Britain was at war with France and its allies from 1793 to 1802 and from 1803 till the final defeat of Bonaparte in 1815. France had virtually unlimited power on most of the Continent, especially after 1799 when Bonaparte made himself first consul and 1804 when he elevated himself to be Emperor of France. Britain had solid reason to fear that it too would be invaded by Bonaparte's seemingly unstoppable army. By 1805 Bonaparte had assembled enough vessels at the channel port of Boulogne to carry more than 150,000 men across the short span of water to Britain's southeastern coast.[1]

The British navy, divided into four squadrons, had a variety of responsibilities. It is most often remembered for a few great naval battles which had largely destroyed French naval power. The navy also had to try to prevent or intercept convoys of French troops or military supplies and especially to defend against an invasion of Britain. The navy likewise had the responsibility to disrupt and destroy the enemy's seaborne commerce. This included the task of severing the links between France and its overseas empire.[2] Ships and cargoes, therefore, were captured to reduce the threat of invasion and to weaken the enemy's military power. Britain, thus, had strong strategic motives to destroy or capture the enemy's navy, to cut off the flow of military supplies to the enemy, even to cut off the flow of goods and money between the enemy and its colonial empire and to seize the enemy's colonies. Each capture called for a prize adjudication in the High Court of Admiralty, or some vice-admiralty court.

The British–French wars between 1793 and 1815 were different in kind and intensity from the earlier eighteenth-century wars. The French fought with the determination of a crusade to bring the blessings of revolution to all the people of Europe. Most of the British, for their part, showed a like determination to root out the evil of revolution. Nationalism, partially the result of the crusading spirit of these wars, characterized these two decades of intense warfare.[3]

The maritime warfare with which Scott was so familiar, besides its

---

[1] R. Glover, *Britain at bay – defence against Bonaparte, 1803–14* (London, 1973), 14, 77–102.

[2] *Ibid.*, 55–60; I. R. Christie, *Wars and revolutions – Britain, 1760–1815* (Cambridge, Mass., 1982), 235–80, 306–26. There were, of course, still privateers (privately armed vessels specially commissioned to make captures). These privateers, however, played an insignificant role in naval warfare by the end of the eighteenth century.

[3] C. Emsley, *British society and the French wars, 1793–1815* (Totowa, N.J., 1979), 2–4.

obvious military rationale, also had significant economic justifications. The economic interests in Britain certainly were not in agreement on the desirability of the war or on the appropriate naval strategies. The old mercantilist, colonial and shipping interests approached the war with a totally different attitude than the newer manufacturing interests.

Since the sixteenth century nations had been engaged in maritime warfare not only as a means of weakening the enemy by striking at its import and export trade, but also as a source of self-enrichment. The prevailing mercantilist thought, not dead even in Scott's day, provided economic reasons for maritime warfare. Motivation clearly was mixed; some government leaders stressed the military justifications for maritime warfare while others emphasized the economic. Clearly some influential members of the cabinet believed Britain should employ its superior naval forces to weaken the enemy by destroying its sources of wealth, to impoverish its people and to cut off its commerce. Furthermore, Britain should foster its own commerce, open new markets for its products, assure access to raw materials and deprive neutrals of the opportunity to benefit from the war by increasing their share of international commerce. Henry Dundas, for instance, the Secretary of War in William Pitt's first administration, sought to persuade Pitt to manipulate the war for Britain's commercial advantage. Dundas was convinced that:

be the causes of the war what they may, the primary object ought to be, by what means we can most effectually increase those resources on which depend our naval superiority, and at the same time diminish or appropriate to ourselves those which might otherwise enable the enemy to contend with us in this respect ... I consider offensive operations against the colonial possessions of our enemies as the first object to be attended to in almost every war in which Great Britain can be engaged.[4]

Maritime warfare was, thus, economic warfare with the military and economic rationales intertwined. Security of Britain and security for British commerce often were synonymous. The economic advantages to be derived from maritime warfare were stressed by James Stephen in an influential pamphlet published in 1805. Stephen, a spokesman for the West Indian planters, saw the war as primarily an opportunity to foster British commercial advantage and to eliminate

---

[4] Quoted in A. D. Harvey, *Britain in the early nineteenth century* (London, 1978), 302; see *ibid.*, 301–6.

the maritime competition from neutrals like the Americans. Scott was thoroughly familiar with Stephen's view. Stephen, for instance, expressed this eighteenth-century attitude toward war when he wrote:

To impoverish our enemies used, in our former contests with France and Spain, to be a sure effect of our hostilities; and its extent was always proportionate to that of its grand instrument, our superiority at sea. We distressed their trade, we intercepted the produce of their colonies, and thus exhausted their treasuries, by cutting off their chief sources of revenue, as the philosopher proposed to dry up the sea, by draining the rivers that fed it. By the same means, their expenditure was immensely increased, and wasted in defensive purposes. They were obliged to maintain fleets in distant parts of the world, and to furnish strong convoys for the protection of their intercourse with their colonies, both on outward and homeward voyages. Again, the frequent capture of these convoys, while it enriched our seamen, and by the increase of import duties aided our revenue, obliged our enemies, at a fresh expence, to repair their loss of ships; and when a convoy outward-bound, was the subject of capture, compelled them either to dispatch duplicate supplies in the same season, at the risk of new disasters, or to leave their colonies in distress, and forfeit the benefit of their crops for the year.

In short, their transmarine possessions became expensive incumbrances, rather than sources of revenue; and through the iteration of such losses, more than by our naval victories, or colonial conquests, the house of·Bourbon was vanquished by the masters of the sea.[5]

The old-fashioned blue water policy of politicians like Dundas and lobbyists like Stephen probably influenced the British government far more than the current economic realities spawned by the Industrial Revolution. Britain was developing an export-driven economy, but the new manufacturers in the north had less of a voice in London than the London shippers and bankers and the West Indian interests. The industrial entrepreneurs probably suffered more in reduced profits due to the war than they gained in increased markets. Little wonder that the manufacturing interests generally sided with the loose-knit fellowship of anti-war liberals.[6]

[5] [J. Stephen], *War in disguise or the frauds of the neutral flags* (London, 1805), 7–8. Scott had reviewed the manuscript and advised Stephen to have it published to educate the public. B. Perkins, *The first rapprochement* (Berkeley, Cal., 1967), 180. See also P. C. Jessup and F. Deak, *Neutrality: its history, economics and law*, I: *Origins* (4 vols., New York, 1935–6), xii; G. Best, *Humanity in warfare* (New York, 1980), 99–108; Emsley, *British society*, 23.
[6] J. E. Cookson, *The friends of peace – anti-war liberalism in England, 1793–1815* (Cambridge, 1982), 1–83, 215–37; G. Hueckel, 'War and the British economy, 1793–1815 – a general equilibrium analysis', *Explorations in Economic History*, 10 (1973), 365–73, 393–5.

A total transformation, however, was taking place in British industry and trade, and eventually the new manufacturing interests joined the successful crusade to compel a change of government war policy.

By the end of the eighteenth century, the Industrial Revolution had radically changed the economy of Great Britain. A series of inventions had fundamentally altered the process of production and the structure of industry, especially in the textile industry. New innovations such as the use of machines, the use of steam power derived from coal, and the use of abundant sources of raw materials created an expanding industrial economy. This enormous increase in human productivity which developed primarily in England led not only to a higher standard of living there, but also to a greatly expanded foreign trade. Britain's maritime and commercial tradition made possible the opening of new markets around the world. Britain's economic strength lay in its ability to manufacture cheaply the precise types of goods for which there was the greatest demand overseas. By the end of the eighteenth century Britain had already become the world's dominant economic power. Export trade became ever more crucial to the economy.

The social structure of the country encouraged investment in the new mining and industrial activities. Trade remained respectable and there was a place in society for new men who had succeeded in manufacturing, commerce or banking. Scott's own rise from the son of a north country coal-fitter to a peer made him thoroughly aware of these changes which today we call the Industrial Revolution.[7]

In the later years of the war, Bonaparte, checkmated in his efforts to invade and conquer Britain, employed the economic weapons of the Continental System to achieve his goals. He issued decrees in 1806 and 1807 which, if they had been faithfully implemented, would have closed most of the Continent to British trade. He forbade the importation of British goods into those parts of Europe under his control. This self-blockade of the Continent to all British goods, which was both an offensive economic weapon and an extreme system of protection for local industries, posed a serious potential threat to the newly developed British manufacturers which were largely

[7] D. S. Landes, 'Technological change and development in Western Europe, 1750–1914', in *The Cambridge economic history of Europe* (7 vols., Cambridge, 1942–78), VI, 274–310.

dependent on commerce with Europe and the United States for raw materials and for the export of their products. But the British economy entered this economic struggle with significant advantages. Britain had achieved absolute ascendancy over the continental industries with the possible exception of silk. No continental industry could compete successfully with Britain's textile mills. The British economy rested secure on its well-developed base of technological progress, adaptability and capital organization. Its economy faced outward; its spirit of enterprise and profit-seeking looked to worldwide horizons.[8]

Britain did not weather Bonaparte's economic blockade without significant distress. The dam created by the Continental System remained porous, however, because when Bonaparte's attention was turned elsewhere, the unwatched French officials proved easily corruptible. The economic fluctuations, caused in part by the periods of success or failure of Bonaparte's policy, resulted in periods of boom and periods of severe depression which affected different industries at different times and with unequal severity. British merchants, accustomed to continued trade, by fair means or foul, with the Continent, expected the periods of flourishing trade to last throughout the war. When the Continental System was rigorously enforced, the British export trade to Europe was largely paralyzed.[9]

These economic realities played a significant role in the debates in Britain after 1807 over the Orders in Council that so drastically affected maritime warfare and the prize law Scott applied. The Orders in Council of 1807 and 1809 were the British government's answer to Bonaparte's Continental System. The British reponse to Bonaparte's boycott of British ships and cargoes was a proclamation of blockade of all the ports under Bonaparte's command. By these Orders the British government intended to compel neutrals trading with ports on the Continent to stop and pay duties on their cargoes at British ports.

The Orders in Council were defended by the Tory Government, by the gentry and by the rich, cultivated and respectable merchants of

---

[8] F. Crouzet, *L'Economie britannique et le blocus continental (1806–1813)* (2 vols., Paris, 1958), I, 203–4; F. Crouzet, 'Wars, blockade, and economic change in Europe, 1792–1815', *Journal of Economic History*, 24 (1964), 579.

[9] Crouzet, *L'Economie britannique*, I, 342–92; II, 419–81, 521–63, 606–14, 631–49. For the economic losses and gains on the Continent, see G. Ellis, *Napoleon's continental blockade: the case of Alsace* (Oxford, 1981), 1–25.

London and Liverpool, as well as by the ship owners. These were the traditional elements in the world of affairs, the eighteenth-century England of agricultural, commercial, mercantilist and colonial interests, especially the West Indian planters. These well-established interests had resented the competition from neutral carriers, especially from the Americans. They favored the Orders in Council which strangled any direct neutral commerce with the Continent.

The Orders in Council were opposed by nineteenth-century England, the Whig reforming politicians, the leaders of the new industrial and manufacturing centers, the commercial middle class and the working class. The northern manufacturers and merchants saw clearly that Britain's economy depended not on the old West Indian interests nor on the shipping interests, which derived profits from the re-export trade. Britain's economic future depended on the manufacturing made possible by the Industrial Revolution and the direct export of these inexpensive manufactured goods. These manufacturing interests, together with the religious and ideological anti-war liberals, viewed the war, and especially the Orders in Council, as contrary to principles of free trade and as the cause of enormous waste and misery. They especially opposed the risk of war with the Americans whom they regarded as among their best customers and as fellow believers in democracy and religious toleration. The debate was between those who benefited from protectionism and those who believed in economic liberty.[10]

Because of the severe industrial dislocations in Britain, especially in the cotton industry, and the collapse of the export trade in France, the two deadly enemies, Britain and France, made the necessary concessions in 1811 to establish mutual trade. Although the British government had for a long time provided British and neutral merchants with licences to engage in trade which would otherwise have been illegal, after 1811 this licence trade became enormous. British writers objected in vain to this subjection of the country's trade to the control of the government. Even though every licence was an anomaly, at variance with the nation's declaration of war as well as with the principle of free trade, thousands of licences were being granted which often permitted foreign vessels manned by French crews to trade to British ports. The system of licences encouraged fraud and bad faith, said these British writers. British licences could be bought in most ports of

[10] Crouzet, *L'Economie britannique*, II, 826–9; Cookson, *Friends of peace*, 215–37.

Europe.[11]

These brief suggestions of some of the strategic, economic, political and social dimensions of the long war years make possible a more accurate grasp of some of the arguments expressed or implied in Scott's numerous prize judgments. These prize cases, on occasion, forced Scott to consider broader policy questions. If he ever had to take sides between the two conflicting economic forces, one could expect that his personal philosophy would correspond closely with the eighteenth-century mercantilist, London-based shipping and colonial interests rather than with the new, reform-minded, manufacturing interests which favored economic freedom. But, as we shall see, it is far more likely that Scott's policy arguments would be most influenced by the British ministry's explanations of government policy based on military necessity and national defense against the perils of the French Revolution and the Napoleonic empire.

MID-EIGHTEENTH-CENTURY PRIZE LAW CONCERNING NATIONALITY

Suits in the prize court often involved questions of the nationality, or national commercial character, of the owners of the vessel or the cargo. Even though many of these cases involved British subjects, this question of nationality was not viewed as identical with the question of the bond of allegiance between king and subject, that is, subjectship, or, as we would say today, citizenship. In the eighteenth century the British authorities affirmed the well-established rule with regard to Britain's own subjects, once a subject always a subject.[12] But this citizenship discussion focused on the relationship between the subject and his own sovereign. The question of nationality, often litigated in prize cases, focused rather on whether merchants resident in various countries would be considered by the British prize court as nationals of the country where they resided and carried on trade or of some

[11] Anonymous [review of two pamphlets], *Quarterly Review*, 5 (1811), 457–71; Crouzet, *L'Economie britannique*, II, 676–82.
[12] J. H. Kettner, *The development of American citizenship, 1608–1870* (Chapel Hill, N.C., 1978), 44–61. C. Parry, in *British nationality* (London, 1951), discusses the common law concept of British nationality in the sense of permanent allegiance to the Crown, at 4–9. J. M. Jones, in *British nationality law and practice* (Oxford, 1947), also discussed this concept of subjectship or allegiance to the Crown in the context of *Calvin's Case*, at 28–73.

other country, often the country of their birth. This discussion of nationality, therefore, deals with the national character of interna-tional merchants.

Scott certainly was aware of the questions of British subjectship in the first sense, that is the permanent bond between the British Crown and its subjects. He had occasion to discuss the permanence of allegiance in the context of debates with American ministers over impressment (the forcible taking of seamen, at times from neutral ships, for service in the British navy).[13]

But in prize cases it was the question of the national character of merchants which frequently occupied his attention. This problem was inherent in the international commerce of the eighteenth and nineteenth centuries. By the later eighteenth century merchants, during wartime, took on a chameleon-like quality. Foreign merchants frequently maintained a residence or trading house in some other country or had agents resident there. The question the prize court had to determine was how a belligerent's courts would treat these foreign merchants and their property. They might be neutral subjects resident and doing business in a belligerent country, or they might be subjects of a belligerent nation resident in a neutral country. Scott and his predecessors in the admiralty court had to determine whether the property of such foreign merchants would be treated as enemy property, or neutral property, or British property.

This issue of national commercial character had often been dis-cussed by the civilians and the admiralty court in the eighteenth century. By the time Scott became judge a body of legal rules had been developed and applied, often with a certain woodenness. He had participated as counsel in the development of these rules. He at times showed a more realistic understanding than the court of the policies which should inspire these legal principles. When he became judge he could look back to this developed body of precedent in considering the new and unsettled questions which came before him.

Merchants born in neutral nations

During the American Revolution, Sir James Marriott, Scott's prede-cessor, decided a case involving the capture of a French ship and the

[13] Scott to Eldon, n.d., Encombe House Papers; Scott to Lord Harrowby, September 24, 1804, P.R.O. FO 83/2204, fo. 315; Liverpool to Scott, John Nicholl and Christopher Robinson, March 14, 1814, Brit. Lib., Add. MS 38,256, fo. 355.

property aboard it which belonged to two merchants who claimed to be natives of Prague in Bohemia and of Milan respectively. Neutral cargo aboard an enemy vessel was generally not liable to seizure. These two merchants had resided for two years in the French colony of St Domingo. Marriott, in a fully articulated opinion, rejected their claim to the property as neutrals. He noted that the maritime countries of Europe were 'full of renegadoes of all nations', and that 'the nationality of a character of a person taken in war, is with more peculiar propriety determined by the locality in the age we live in'. He concluded that

The principle of the law of nations is, that where the protection and power are, there is the subjection. If these persons had absolutely derelicted all inhabitancy in the colonies and territories of the King of France, and it had appeared that there was neither an intention, nor a possibility of their returning thither again ... [they would have been regarded as neutrals].[14]

Marriott was applying a crudely stated rule of commercial domicile to determine whether these merchants would be deemed neutrals or French belligerents.

In 1748 Sir George Lee, a prominent civilian, had expressed the same legal rule in an opinion he gave as counsel.

I am clearly of [the] opinion a Portuguese merchant resident in France & carrying on his Trade there is to be consider'd as a Frenchman [and] that such person has no right to claim a cargo belonging to him as neutral property but on the contrary that it ought to be condemn'd as the property of Enemys.[15]

Before a declaration of war, Lee said, merchants resident in a foreign country were not to be considered subjects of that country, but after a declaration of war 'all Persons residing in the Territorys or Dominions of an Enemy are to be consider'd as Enemys'.[16] When asked about a ship and cargo which belonged to merchants from Hamburg, Lee replied that the cargo should be condemned since it belonged to a Hamburg merchant who 'lived and carried on his Business' in France, but that the ship should be restored since the owners had been born and continued to live in Hamburg.[17]

---

[14] *Theodore* (1779), Hay & M. 261.
[15] *Nostra Seignora de Ares* (1748), H.S.P. Lee Opinions. This unbound collection of Lee's Opinions is not paginated or in any apparent order; thus it will be necessary to identify opinions only by the name of the vessel, the date and the name of the collection.
[16] No name (1745), H.S.P. Lee Opinions.
[17] *Post van Hamburgh (Paatz)* (1745), H.S.P. Lee Opinions.

Merchants who had been born in a neutral nation, therefore, but who resided in a belligerent country and continued to carry on business there were treated as having assumed the nationality of the belligerent country. This rule applied even if these neutral merchants were official representatives of their neutral homeland. In 1764 the Lords Commissioners for Prize Appeals considered the case of a Genoese ship which had taken on cargo at Marseilles belonging to the Genoese consul there. The vice-admiralty court had restored the cargo as neutral property. The Lords Commissioners reversed and pronounced the cargo belonging to the Genoese consul enemy property, as property of a merchant resident in France. There is a notation that Lord Mansfield, who sat as one of the Lords Commissioners, 'Offered to assign Mr. Attorney-General, Sir Fletcher Norton, a dáy to argue the question whether Lunoro, as consul, was by the Law of Nations entitled to privilege for the goods in question, but he declined accepting it.'[18] Apparently it was settled that the property of a neutral merchant resident in a belligerent country, even though he happened to be consul for a neutral country, was regarded as enemy property.

Merchants born in enemy nations

One would expect that if residence of a neutral in an enemy country made a merchant an enemy, conversely, residence of a merchant of enemy nationality in a neutral country would make the merchant a neutral. Sir Edward Simpson, a prominent civilian in the 1740s and 1750s, explicitly stated the opposite. A French merchant resident in Hamburg, but not a denizen there, was deemed an enemy because he was a natural born subject of France. His property was liable to condemnation in the British admiralty court.[19]

If Simpson's brief notes stated the law correctly for the middle of the eighteenth century, by 1779 the admiralty court had adopted the opposite position. In a case involving a vessel owned by neutrals carrying cargo belonging to a French merchant domiciled at Hamburg, the court restored the ship and cargo. The notetaker observed:

The ground of the decision was, that a native of Hamburg, resident in France, would have his property condemned by the law of nations as an adopted Frenchman, pro hac vice . . . and therefore the same equity operated the other way, that a Frenchman, resident at Hamburg, should be considered as a

[18] *Santo Crucifixo* (Lords, 1764), Burrell 161, 162.
[19] R.A., Simpson MS 123.

Hamburger, and have the advantage of protection, if he is the sole proprietor.[20]

Apparently this protection as a neutral included the right to bring suit in the British court for restoration of his property, despite the ordinary rule that an enemy had no right to commence or prosecute a suit in a British court.[21]

Merchants born as British nationals

Clearly it was unlawful for British subjects to carry on commerce by themselves or by agents with the enemy unless they had a licence from the government for such trade.[22] Despite this clear legal rule, Sir George Lee in 1747 had expressly given the opinion that British merchants could trade with the enemy as long as they did it in neutral ships. He wrote in answer to a client's inquiry:

[B]y General Law British subjects may be liable to Prosecution for Trading with a declar'd enemy but I suppose these goods going in a neutral ship to an enemy port if they are not in fact contraband are not confiscable or subject to be condemned as Prize and I am of Opinion they may safely claim any Goods on board this ship which are their own Property and would advise them so to do and in case their goods should be condemned I would advise them to appeal to the Lords.[23]

When this same case came before the admiralty court, Judge Henry Penrice rejected Lee's position. Lee continued to represent the British claimants. He rightly contended that the only question was whether the cargo belonging to British subjects on board a neutral ship going to Spain was liable to be condemned as prize for trading with the enemy. Penrice, however, rigidly insisted that the British could not aid the enemy in any respect. The king's declaration of war, Penrice con-

---

[20] *Postilion* (1779), Hay & M. 245.
[21] *Phoenix* (1745), H.S.P. Lee Opinions.
[22] R.A., Simpson MS 51, 118, 122, 124.
[23] *Deer Garden (Holmstrom)* (1747), H.S.P. Lee Opinions. See also *Jonge Printz Christian (Leeuw)* (1749), H.S.P. Lee Opinions, where Lee also gave the opinion that British goods on board a neutral ship going to or returning from an enemy port were not subject to condemnation as prize. Simpson apparently agreed with Lee on this point. He mentioned the case of British property captured aboard a Danish ship which, about the same time, had been condemned for trading with the enemy since 'being a subject of Britain [he] could not trade in Spain & his property liable to Condemn[atio]n'. Simpson, in an editorial comment, observed: 'This [is] a point of so great consequence to the trade of this Kingdom it ought to be reconsidered & I think the Sentence not well founded.' R.A., Simpson MS 216.

cluded, was a prohibition of trade with Spain. The goods claimed by these British merchants, therefore, were liable to condemnation as prize.[24] Thus it appears that in the late 1740s the admiralty court determined that British merchants could not engage in commerce with the enemy even if they shipped their goods aboard neutral ships. Their cargoes did not become neutral by being shipped on a neutral vessel. The court seems to have taken a narrow, legalistic approach. The extraordinarily favorable treatment Lee expected for his British clients perhaps reflected less the established law than the hopes of the British merchant community which had so much to gain by continuing to trade with the enemy in time of war.

In 1779 Judge Marriott restated the basic rule. He delivered a scathing rebuke to several British merchants who had used various artifices to conceal their trade with France during the American war. Such conduct was considered criminal in other British courts, Marriott said, but in the admiralty court the only penalty was confiscation of the property. He rejected the subtle distinctions of counsel who had argued that there had been no formal declaration of war. 'Metaphysical refinements about bellum justum, perfectum, legitimum are ridiculous', he said. If counsel insisted on quoting learned authorities, he observed, let them quote Bynkershoek who had a whole chapter on the subject. When the claimants argued that smuggling British goods through Ostend into France was 'greatly for the advantage of England, and as such to be tolerated, being like to the profits acquired by insuring the goods of the enemy, and the balance in favour of this kingdom', Marriott retorted that

[I]t is an aiding, abetting, and comforting of the King's enemies, a discovery of the national councils, and a prolonging of the war, to the oppression, taxation, and ruin of millions of subjects; and instead of a great balance of profit in favour of the whole community, it is a less balance turned into the narrow channel of the pockets of a few private men, who often, without

---

[24] *Deer Garden (Holmstrom)* (date given as March 16, 1747, which must mean 1747/8), H.S.P. Lee Cases.

Where a Dutch (neutral) ship had been captured with a cargo belonging to a merchant resident in Spain (enemy) but shipped by English merchants resident in Holland, Simpson arguing for the shippers contended that English subjects residing in Holland were to be considered as Dutch subjects. Therefore, he argued, they should be able to claim the privilege of the Anglo-Dutch Treaty of 1674 by which enemy cargo aboard a Dutch ship was free from seizure. Judge Henry Penrice, however, rejected this argument since the privilege of the treaty belonged to the Dutch ship and the ship owners had not claimed the privilege. The British shippers resident in Holland were not allowed to claim the privilege on behalf of the cargo owners. *Anna Maria (Noets)* (1745), H.S.P. Lee Cases.

property, prey and grow great upon the public vitals.[25]

Policy arguments, thus, carried little weight. Marriott distinguished these upstart merchants from 'true merchants . . . who are men of the greatest probity, and worthy of the confidence of Sovereigns, and of nations'.[26] The court obviously had little sympathy for the artifices used to foster trade. The property was condemned and the claimants ordered to pay freight and costs.

By the Treaty of Utrecht in 1713 subjects of one belligerent resident in the other belligerent country were given six months to remove their property after war was declared. A British subject, therefore, who had property in France and who had obtained a licence from the British government, could remove his property from France without fear of condemnation for trading with the enemy.[27] But if the British merchant continued to carry on trade as a merchant resident in the enemy country, he was regarded as an enemy merchant.[28] Certainly British merchants were not allowed to conceal the trade with the enemy by falsifying all the papers.[29]

If the British merchant resided in a neutral country, however, some thought that he could trade with the enemies of Britain as any neutral. In 1747 Lee responded to the inquiry of a client by stating:

I do not recollect one Instance during the Course of this War of the Effects of Englishmen residing in neutral Countrys being condemned on account of their trading with the Enemy but on the contrary the effects of such Englishmen have been restored in several cases and particularly the effects of Englishmen residing at Hamburg & belonging to the British Factory there[.][30]

Whether Lee was accurately stating the law in 1747, or merely saying what his clients wanted to hear is unclear. By the time of the American war, however, Judge Marriott approached the question with quite a different tone. He strictly applied the doctrine of permanent subjectship. The notetaker reported that the law should not be interpreted so as to assist

British merchants in aiding the enemies of their country; that no naturaliza-

[25] *Maria Magdalen* (1779), Hay & M. 247, 252–4.
[26] *Ibid.*, 256.
[27] *Duke of Kingston* (Lords, 1752), N.Y.P.L. Lee Prize Appeals. Cf. Treaty of Utrecht (1713) Art. 19.
[28] *Fort of Bordeaux* (Lords, 1747), N.Y.P.L. Lee Prize Appeals.
[29] *Juffrow Johanna* (Lords, 1749), N.Y.P.L. Lee Prize Appeals.
[30] *Commercium (Clavier)* (1747), H.S.P. Lee Opinions.

tion in a foreign state can absolve them of their allegiance, whenever their persons or their properties shall come within the vortex or reach of the power of British laws. That the Dutch have no privilege to carry the property of Englishmen to the enemies of England.[31]

British merchants resident in neutral countries frequently had to conceal their ownership of property from the enemy to prevent seizure. This practice, apparently common, was condoned by the British courts if the vessel was captured by a British ship.[32]

One final question, related to the treatment of British merchants by the prize court, dealt with the treatment of the property of allies of Britain. Lee was asked whether the property of a Hungarian subject, who had been trading with France, the common enemy of Britain and Hungary, should be condemned. Lee replied to this private inquiry: '[A]dmitting him to be an Hungarian subject I apprehend the English have no right to confiscate the property of their allie [*sic*] for trading with the common Enemy, and I am of opinion his goods ought to be restored to him.'[33]

This survey of some of the materials preserved by civilians concerning the nationality of merchants in time of war suggests that many significant issues had been discussed and settled in the context of individual prize cases. The admiralty court apparently tended to apply narrow legal principles strictly, with little serious reflection on the economic or social consequences of its decisions. Though the law does not have a final, definitive appearance, and some development in the law took place during the decades after 1740, there was a body of law which the civilians could cite and rely on and which provided some guidance for their clients as well as for the court. Within the small group of civilians at Doctors' Commons, a strong oral tradition of the law had clearly developed. The written notes merely helped preserve this body of law which 'the civilians discussed among themselves in court and in the Commons.

SCOTT AS COUNSEL – THE YEARS OF PREPARATION

Scott practiced before the admiralty court as a civilian advocate for

---

[31] *Naval Store Ships* (1779), Hay & M. 287, 288.
[32] *Grand Duke of Tuscany* (Lords, 1760), Burrell 188.
[33] *Jonge Pieter* (*Meyer*) (1747), H.S.P. Lee Opinions.

nearly twenty years before he was appointed judge of the court. Although during half of these years Britain was at peace, there were ample opportunities for him, both in his private practice and after 1788 as King's Advocate, to become thoroughly familiar with the legal disputes which arise in time of war concerning the nationality of merchants.

The notebooks of civilians for these years make clear that Scott, if not the leading civilian, certainly took part in the vast majority of the cases in the admiralty court and in the court of prize appeals. Even in those few cases in which he did not represent a party, he must have known the judgments and reasons of the admiralty court and of the Lords Commissioners. The small band of civilians preserved in their notebooks and in their mutual discussions every shred of learning concerning the courts where they practiced.

Three particularly important cases concerning nationality have been preserved in unusually full notes. These three cases provide a brief glimpse of the role of counsel before the admiralty court and the court of prize appeals as well as an insight into the care with which the notetakers recorded the observations from the bench.

The 'Jacobus Johannes' and the 'Harmonie'

In 1785 and 1786 the Lords Commissioners for Prize Appeals heard two cases, joined for argument, concerning the nationality of merchants. Since the cases were of obvious importance to civilians, John Nicholl, a young civilian, took full notes of the arguments of counsel and the speeches from the bench. His notes include the arguments of several prominent civilians as well as several of the barristers who customarily joined with civilians in preparing the printed cases and presenting oral argument in prize appeals.[34]

Two Dutch vessels, the *Jacobus Johannes* and the *Harmonie*, had been captured carrying cargo from St Eustatius, a Dutch colony, to Amsterdam. These two cases involved several merchants who had property at St Eustatius at the time when the Dutch became involved

---

[34] *Jacobus Johannes* (*Mille*) and *Harmonie* (*Rynders*) (Lords, 1786), P.R.O. HCA 45/ 12, fos. 10 and 28, and Nicholl's Notebook, 1781–92, No. 71, P.R.O. HCA 30/454. The notes from the trial of the *Harmonie* (1782) in the admiralty court are in Nicholl's Notebook, 1781–92, No. 16, P.R.O. HCA 30/464. Unless otherwise noted, the entire discussion of the arguments and the court's opinion has been derived from these notes by Nicholl. The role of barristers in prize appeals was discussed above, p. 28.

in the American war. Aboard the *Jacobus Johannes* was cargo claimed by two Danish merchants: Heysem, who had carried on trade in St Eustatius but who had returned to Denmark when war broke out, and Ernst, who had merely spent time in Amsterdam.

The *Harmonie* carried cargo claimed by Whithall, originally a British American, who upon the start of the American Revolution left America and returned to England. As a loyalist he clearly was a British subject. Subsequently he settled at St Eustatius where he had carried on trade, had taken an oath of loyalty and had become a burgher of the island. The *Harmonie* had sailed from St Eustatius before the island was captured by the British. It was not captured by a British ship, however, until after St Eustatius fell to the British. Whithall had left the island after its fall to the British, but before his cargo had been captured. Thus Whithall could claim as a British subject returning home at the time of the capture.

The cases of Heysem, Ernst and Whithall demonstrate the chameleon-like national character of international merchants. These three claims presented the Lords Commissioners with different dimensions of the issue of the nationality of merchants. Which of these three merchants had shipped cargo that could be condemned as enemy property: Heysem, originally a Dane who had operated as a merchant at St Eustatius; Ernst, a Dane who at least had visited Amsterdam and perhaps had carried on trade there, but whose property was shipped from St Eustatius; or Whithall, a British merchant who had traded from St Eustatius but shipped a cargo from the island after war was declared? Since a large number of other cases depended on the determination of these two, the court of prize appeals joined the two together and, after hearing full arguments of counsel, took the time to express the reasons for the court's judgment.

A full summary of the arguments and speeches from the bench in these two cases will greatly contribute to a grasp of the state of the law of nationality at this time. Policy reasons based on mercantilism pervaded the various arguments made for the parties. The mercantilist view held that Britain, or any colonial power, should use its navy to deprive the enemy of any profit or benefits from its colonies, to burden the enemy with the added cost of maintaining its colonies and to enrich Britain by opening new channels of commerce and by seizing enemy ships and cargoes. Implicit was the blue water foreign policy of naval development, colonial expansion and minimal involvement on the Continent.

William Wynne,[35] a civilian, stressed economic policy reasons in arguing for the captors that Heysem, originally a Dane, had become a Dutch subject by his residence and trade in a Dutch territory, St Eustatius. His commercial activity, therefore, enriched the Dutch. It was not the personal hostility of a resident in an enemy country that made his property subject to seizure, Wynne insisted, but his trade carried on there which enhanced the strength and wealth of the country and enabled the enemy to carry on the war. Wynne added appropriate references to Grotius, Bynkershoek, Vattel and Gaile, a pre-Grotian writer,[36] to establish that Heysem had ceased being a Danish national and had become a Dutch national since he resided in a Dutch territory, carried on trade there and paid duties there. Wynne reminded the court of its previous holding, without mentioning the case by name, that enemy merchants who took their property to a neutral country and carried on trade there would be considered neutrals and their property would be protected from seizure. The reverse must also be true.

The Attorney General, Richard Pepper Arden,[37] reminded the court that the economic consequences of restoring Heysem's property to him would be costly to Britain. No British ship would in the future risk the difficulties of capture and the possible court costs to seize such property. Merchants like Heysem could continue enriching the enemy merely by fraudulently claiming to be Danish, that is, neutral. Arden argued for the captors that even an English subject could be considered a foreign subject for certain purposes, though, of course, he could not surrender his allegiance to the British Crown. All persons domiciled in a foreign country, Arden said, were considered subject to reprisals by the enemies of that country. Heysem was a burgher of St Eustatius, his property was shipped on a Dutch ship from one Dutch port to another, with papers from the customhouse at St Eustatius.

---

[35] William Wynne, King's Advocate, 1778–88; admitted to practice as a civilian in 1757, G. D. Squibb, *Doctors' Commons* (Oxford, 1977), 193.

[36] H. Grotius, *De jure belli ac pacis libri tres*, B. 1, c. 5, s. 24; probably the reference should be B. 2, c. 5, s. 24, tr. F. W. Kelsey (Washington, 1925) is here used unless otherwise noted. 'Gaile' is mentioned in the notes, B. 2, obs: 56. The reference is to A. Gail, *Practicarum observationum* (Amsterdam, 1563), 395, but since this passage refers to a discussion of eminent domain, the reference is apparently incorrect. Wynne also referred to C. van Bynkershoek, *Quaestionum juris publici libri duo*, B. 2, c. 25, tr. T. Frank (Oxford, 1930), is used here, and E. de Vattel, *Le droit des gens*, [B. 1], c. 19, tr. C. G. Fenwick (Washington, 1916) is used here.

[37] Richard Pepper Arden, later Lord Alvanley, Chief Justice of Common Pleas 1801–4, *H.E.L.*, 12, 328–9.

James Mansfield,[38] another barrister, also stressed the economic consequences of the court's determination. Mansfield spoke for the Danish claimants. The only question, he insisted, was whether these claimants, Heysem and Ernst, were inhabitants within the meaning of the British proclamation authorizing seizure of Dutch property. This question should not be settled by quotations from the law of nations but by local laws, the Dutch laws determining which residents were subjects. The whole purpose of naval captures in war was to take the property of the enemy, not to harm neutral property. If this property should be condemned, Mansfield contended, the loss would fall on Denmark, a neutral, not on Holland, an enemy. Mere residence in the enemy country, he concluded, without a renunciation of one's original allegiance, would not suffice to make a person's property subject to reprisals. Mansfield's test to determine the national status of merchants would require renunciation of prior nationality. This went well beyond the earlier decisions which apparently had required only residence and continued commercial activity in the enemy country.

Scott's former teacher at Oxford, Dr Thomas Bever,[39] developed a different economic argument in his closing speech for the Danish claimants. He pointed out that St Eustatius, at the start of the Dutch war, was filled with subjects of all nations who had no notice of hostilities. He said that the court should distinguish those who immediately left the island from those who continued to reside there. It was the usual British practice to allow enemies a certain amount of time to leave British ports when war broke out. Any other policy would fall severely on British merchants resident abroad when hostilities commenced, since British trade was more extensive. British commerce, Bever implied, had far more to lose by considering Heysem Dutch, since, by the same rule, numerous British merchants abroad could be considered enemies to some warring nation. The claimants here, Bever concluded, were fair traders with no hostile intentions toward Great Britain.

Lord Grantley,[40] one of the Lords Commissioners, before the start of arguments on the claim of Whithall, intervened from the bench. He eliminated one issue which might have distinguished the two Danish

---

[38] James Mansfield, later Chief Justice of Common Pleas, 1804–14, *H.E.L.*, 12, 532–3.

[39] Thomas Bever, fellow of All Souls College, Oxford, admitted to practice as a civilian in 1758. Squibb, *Doctors' Commons*, 193.

[40] Sir Fletcher Norton, Baron Grantley, Attorney General, 1763–5, Speaker of the House of Commons, 1770–80, *H.E.L.*, 12, 560–1.

claimants from Whithall, the British claimant. He made clear that the same rule would apply to all three.

Scott opened the argument for the captors of the second vessel, the *Harmonie*, which involved the claim by Whithall, a British merchant. Scott appears from these notes as preeminent among the various counsel who appeared in both these cases. He sharply delineated the issues; he cited precedents which effectively drove home his precise points, and he turned easily to the various authorities on the law of nations to strengthen his contentions. Either his argument was the most elaborate of any of these two cases or the notetaker was more impressed with it.

Scott distinguished this case from the *Jacobus Johannes* with which it was joined. The *Harmonie* had sailed before St Eustatius was captured and was seized after the island fell. He cited a precedent of a similarly situated capture where the ship and cargo had been condemned.[41] He then focused sharply on the issues to be decided by stating two propositions supported 'by the practice of the admiralty & the Law of Nations. 1st that persons resident in Dutch territories for the purposes of trade are to be considered as Dutch subjects. 2nd That the rule extends to Englishmen.' In order to delineate who would be considered as Dutch inhabitants, he gave examples of those who were not: ambassadors or residents in a British trading station or factory abroad were not considered inhabitants of the country where they resided. Scott cited Fremeaux's case as a precedent.[42] He also quoted from Grotius, Barbeyrac, Gronovius and Cocceius, as well as Molloy, who, Scott observed, 'does not write merely his own opinion but what is the received Practice'.[43] Whithall's alleged latent intention to return home (*animus revertendi*) was immaterial since it was incapable of proof. Scott quoted from Sir Leoline Jenkins and again cited several

[41] *Negotie en Zeevart (Stechman)* (Lords, 1782), P.R.O. HCA 45/9, fo. 402.
[42] *Twee Frienden (Angel)* (Lords, 1784), see P.R.O. HCA 45/11, fo. 246. Scott had argued for Fremeaux, the claimant. Scott had contended that Fremeaux had traded at Smyrna under the protection of the Dutch consul there. Since there was no Dutch factory in Smyrna, however, Scott argued that Fremeaux should be considered an Ottoman subject, not a Dutch subject. Apparently his distinction was too subtle for the Lords Commissioners. They condemned the ship and cargo as Dutch property. Nicholl's Notebook, 1781–92, P.R.O. HCA 30/464.
[43] Grotius, *De jure belli*, B. 3, c. 2, s. 7 and c. 4, s. 8, and the comments of J. Barbeyrac, J. F. Gronovius and H. Cocceius on these passages of Grotius. The comments of Gronovius and Cocceius are in the Grotius, *De jure belli* (Lausanne, 1752). The comments of Barbeyrac are in the translation of Grotius by Barbeyrac (Basle, 1768). Scott also cited C. Molloy, *De jure maritimo et navali* (London, 1676), B. 1, c. 2, s. 16.

cases.[44] Perhaps suggesting that he questioned the correctness of these decisions, Scott said these cases were not quoted as authority but 'to show what is understood to be the Law'. He then stated the crucial test for deciding this case: nationality must be determined by the locality. The goods of Englishmen resident in France were therefore liable to confiscation. Again Scott cited cases.[45] Focusing finally on the economic policies underlying maritime warfare, Scott said that reprisals constituted a war against the wealth of a state. The property of the inhabitants made up the wealth of any state. The conclusion was obvious: Whithall's property should be liable to lawful capture by the British as any other Dutch property. Scott then turned to his second point and said that Lord Grantley's comment from the bench had made it unnecessary to argue that there was no distinction between Danish and English claimants. He concluded by reminding the court that Whithall had enjoyed the advantage of Dutch neutrality before the Dutch war began and must suffer the disadvantages once war commenced.

Scott's brother John, the future Lord Eldon,[46] continued the argument for the captors. He melodramatically told the court he would tremble for the interests of his clients if he felt it necessary to add anything to the arguments already made on their behalf. He presented the court with the economic policies in the form of a debate-style dilemma; either the claimant's property was Dutch and thus liable to condemnation by the British, or else it was British and must be liable to condemnation by the Dutch. But Whithall, if captured by the Dutch, could justly say that he had resided in Dutch territory and had brought it wealth for its sinews of war and that he was a burgher of a Dutch territory. Clearly the property should be considered Dutch. John Scott concluded by reminding the court of Aesop's fable of the bat. When the bat was captured by one weasel, an enemy of birds, he assured it he was a mouse, not a bird. But when he was captured by another weasel who disliked mice, the bat insisted he was not a mouse but a bird.

---

[44] Leoline Jenkins, judge of admiralty court, 1668–73, Squibb, *Doctors' Commons*, 180. Scott relied on the *Santo Crucifixo* (Lords, 1764), referred to above, fn. 18, *San Antonio* (Lords, 1764) and the *Theodore* (1779), referred to above, fn. 14.

[45] *Concordia* (*Thomas*) (Lords, 1782); *Maastron* (*Eeg*) (Lords, n.d.), *Juffrow Catharina* (*Groot*) (Lords, 1784), see P.R.O. HCA 45/9, fo. 118; 45/10, fo. 434; 45/11, fo. 29.

[46] John Scott, called to the bar of the Middle Temple, 1776, Chancellor, 1801–6, 1807–27, *H.E.L.*, 13, 615–38.

George Hardinge,[47] another barrister, spoke on behalf of Whithall's claim. He pointed out that Whithall had departed from St Eustatius before the capture of his cargo. He left his domicile there as soon as he could after the fall of the island to the British and swore (apparently after his property had been seized) that he had no intention of ever returning. The key to determine his nationality, Hardinge insisted, was the intention of staying or returning (*animus morandi* or *revertendi*). The British order of reprisals against Dutch property had been directed against the absolute inhabitants of Dutch territories, not against possessions detained by force, much less against those of inhabitants who had actually departed from the enemy's country. Disabilities, Hardinge said, should be strictly construed. Whithall's disability (his Dutch nationality) was removed when he took the first step toward removal of himself and his property from Dutch territory. Whithall was not resident in Dutch territory at the time of the capture of his property and had demonstrated his intention of absolutely quitting Dutch territory. Hardinge cited one prize case, Curtissos' case.[48]

A civilian, Dr William Compton,[49] apparently made only one point on behalf of Whithall: neutrals are permitted to trade from one port of the enemy to another. He cited a common law case and several commentators on the law of nations.[50] He was probably arguing that the mere fact that the vessel had sailed from a Dutch port and to a

---

[47] George Hardinge, called to the bar of the Middle Temple, nephew of Charles Pratt, Earl Camden, who was presiding in this case as President of the Council, *D.N.B.*

[48] Curtissos' case, *Snelle Zeylder* (*Leeuw*) (Lords, 1783), P.R.O. HCA 45/10, fo. 149. In this important prize appeal, in which Scott and his brother John represented the captors who were respondents, the claimant, Curtissos, was a British subject who had settled in Surinam in 1766 with his family. He continued there as a merchant until 1776 carrying on trade with Amsterdam. He possessed substantial property there and in Amsterdam and went to Amsterdam upon the outbreak of the American Revolution to settle accounts and to withdraw his property. He purchased a vessel to send his property home to Britain. Scott contended that the ship was the property of a Dutch subject who had for many years been domiciled with his family in a Dutch settlement carrying on extensive trade as a Dutch merchant. Although there is no notation of the determination by the Lords, it appears from the way the case is used in subsequent arguments that the Lords restored the property to Curtissos as a British subject who had already indicated his determination to return to Britain with his property.

[49] William Compton, fellow of Gonville and Caius College, Cambridge, admitted to practice as a civilian in 1763, Squibb, *Doctors' Commons*, 194.

[50] The citation given is merely Douglas 592, which must refer to *Le Caux v. Eden* (1781), 2 Dougl. 594. He also cited Grotius, *De jure belli*, B. 3, c. 6 (incomplete reference); Vattel, *Droit des gens*, B. 1, c. 1 (illegible), s. 272 (incorrect reference), and the Code, 10:39.

Dutch port did not make it liable to seizure.

The Solicitor General, Sir Archibald Macdonald,[51] continued the focus on the economic policies in his argument for Whithall's claim. He distinguished an English merchant from a neutral merchant. The English merchant trading abroad enriched England by bringing home his acquired wealth. Macdonald pointed out that the children of an English merchant born while he was residing abroad were considered natural-born English subjects.[52] Thus if Whithall had died at St Eustatius, his property would have been distributed by the laws of England, not Holland. After citing Curtissos' case as a precedent,[53] Macdonald concluded with a telling point: less evidence, he insisted, should be required to show an English subject's intention of returning to England than a neutral's intention of returning to his native land, since English subjects could never forfeit their allegiance.

Wynne spoke briefly in reply for the captors and again ploughed several of the already well-worked fields.

The Lords Commissioners took ten days to reflect and then spoke through Lord Camden, the Lord President of the Council,[54] in giving the judgment. Camden first discussed several preliminary questions. He saw no distinction between the two cases except that Whithall at the time of the ship's capture had returned to British territory. Camden viewed the issue as whether the claimants were inhabitants of Dutch territories within the meaning of the British proclamation of reprisals. The importance of these two cases, merely because of the large number of similar cases depending on this determination, Camden said, belied their difficulty. The defect here of a declaration of war, though it might have afforded the claimants an opportunity of leaving Dutch territory, could not be used as a plea by the claimants. Such a declaration was not required by the law of nations. Hardship necessarily exists at the commencement of a war. By the general practice of Europe, Camden insisted, every person was free to quit his native country and become an inhabitant of any other country. By

---

[51] Archibald Macdonald, Solicitor General, 1784–8, Chief Baron of the Exchequer, 1793–1813, *H.E.L.*, 13, 556–7.

[52] The notetaker actually stated: 'Children of Parents residing in foreign countries [are] naturalized.' Macdonald probably meant that these children would be treated as if born in England, not that a naturalization process was necessary.

[53] Curtissos' case, *Snelle Zeylder* (*Leeiw*) (Lords, 1783), P.R.O. HCA 45/10, above, fn. 48.

[54] Charles Pratt, Earl Camden, Chief Justice of Common Pleas, 1761–6, Chancellor, 1766–70, President of the Council, 1782–3, 1784–94, *H.E.L.*, 12, 304–8.

English law a person might become a subject of some other country though he continued to be an English subject.

In addressing the basic issue of these cases, Camden agreed with the point Scott had made, that not every form of residence would suffice to attach a second nationality. Residence merely for travel or for health reasons would not make one a subject of another country. The test to determine nationality for purposes of war, Camden said, was a settled and fixed residence, provided there was no proof that the residence was merely temporary. This effectively thrust the burden on the claimant to prove he intended to depart from Dutch territory. A residence for the purpose of trade most clearly satisfied this test and was the strongest proof of a settled residence. Camden relied on common experience to suggest that merchants called home any country where their trade would profit them most. The bare intention of returning home was insufficient, Camden said, again taking his cue from Scott's argument. Some concrete acts to manifest such an intention must be demanded. He concluded that the claimants had been found domiciled on St Eustatius and were certainly appropriate objects of British reprisals. Thus their property must be condemned.

Camden turned his attention specifically to Whithall's claim. It had been argued that since he had left St Eustatius before the capture of his property, his case should be distinguished from the other claims. Camden scoffed at the new doctrine espoused, that cargo could change its national character in the course of a voyage. The cargo, he said, was Dutch at the time of shipping and that was the decisive time to consider. The property was aboard a Dutch ship and under Dutch convoy. It certainly was liable to capture by the English. Turning to the point that Macdonald had made, Camden observed that the British law treating the children of English parents born in foreign countries as if natural-born English subjects was an act of benevolence, perhaps even of justice, to enable the children to inherit at common law. The act was not intended to encourage emigration among merchants. Camden continued that the policy of Europe to encourage the settlement of foreign merchants derived from the fact that a country benefited from its resident merchants.

With respect to Ernst's claim, Camden insisted that a distinction must be made. The two other claims involved merchants resident in Dutch territory. Ernst, however, never had a fixed residence at Amsterdam. His goods, therefore, must be restored. Camden concluded by considering two of the precedents relied on by counsel.[55] He showed that they were distinguishable on the facts.

Lord Nugent,[56] another of the Lords Commissioners, intervened at this point to note his dissent. He thought that Ernst's property ought to be condemned along with that of the other claimants. All goods coming from an enemy's country, he argued, should be confiscable without any consideration of the residence of the owners.

Lord Camden diplomatically agreed with Nugent's sentiment, but noted that unfortunately all the books and other authorities were directly contrary. Camden followed Scott's statement in summarizing the settled law: 'The character of the goods is taken from the character of the person[;] the character of the person is taken from the Place of his Inhabitancy.' Turning to the point made by Compton, Camden reminded Nugent that neutral property shipped from one enemy's port to another was not confiscable.

Lord Grantley concluded the court's judgment by stating that he fully concurred in Camden's opinion and that he was authorized to say that the Master of the Rolls[57] also entirely agreed. Ernst, Grantley said, was not an enemy but a Dane. He was not an inhabitant of Amsterdam but 'a mere passenger', apparently meaning that he was a transient.

Several observations on this lengthy summary of these two cases seem appropriate. In the first place, although several of the counsel mentioned commentators on the law of nations, it seems clear that the heart of the arguments and of the court's opinion rested on economic policy arguments and precedents of the admiralty court and the Lords Commissioners. The policy arguments focused on a mercantilist view of the desirability of enhancing the wealth of the nation and of destroying the wealth of the enemy. Secondly, counsel occasionally had to struggle in attempting to reconcile the concept of the permanent allegiance of British subjects with the concept of the acquired nationality of merchants who resided in enemy countries. Thirdly, the court clearly was not merely improvising in deciding the cases. The precedents cited by counsel were taken seriously by the court.

[55] *Concordia* (*Thomas*) (Lords, 1782), P.R.O. HCA 45/9, fo. 118; Curtissos' case, *Snelle Zeylder* (*Leeiw*) (Lords, 1783), P.R.O. HCA 45/9; 45/10, above, fn. 48.
[56] Robert Nugent, Earl Nugent, member of Parliament for borough of St Mawes, later for Bristol, President of the Board of Trade, 1766–88, *D.N.B.*
[57] Lloyd Kenyon, Master of the Rolls, 1784–8, Chief Justice of King's Bench, 1788–1802, *H.E.L.*, 12, 476–8.

Finally, Scott, even in 1786, appeared to be acknowledged as a leader of the civilian bar twelve years before he was appointed to be judge of the admiralty court.

The arguments in these two cases likewise bring out the inherent limitations of the commentators on the law of nations. Although several of the counsel referred to some of the standard sources on the law of nations, and some less familiar sources as well, the generality and abstractness of these commentators rendered them of little help in determining the specific questions presented by the claims of Heysem, Ernst and Whithall. In one of the passages cited, Grotius had discussed the capture of property from the enemy and the right of reprisal. In this context he raised the question of which individual's property could be seized. He wrote: 'By the law of nations all subjects of him who does the injury are liable to the furnishing of sureties, provided they are subjects from a permanent cause, whether native or immigrant, and not persons who are present anywhere for the purpose of travel or for a brief residence.'[58] Grotius, in thus distinguishing different residents in a territory, also excluded from capture the property of ambassadors. Gronovius, commenting on this passage, further excluded, but without specifying merchants, those who for any reason had spent some time in the territory of the ruler who caused the injury.[59] Cocceius, also discussing this passage, clarified Grotius' category of 'subjects from a permanent cause' by adding that these had permanently lived in the territory and thus had a fixed domicile there.[60]

Vattel, in a passage which was apparently referred to in argument before the Lords Commissioners, was specific enough to provide some guidance. He wrote:

Domicile is a fixed residence in a certain place with the intention of permanently remaining there. Hence a man does not establish a domicile in a place unless he has given sufficient signs, whether impliedly or by express declaration, of his intention to remain there. However, this declaration does not prevent him from changing his mind later on and transferring his domicile

---

[58] Grotius, *De jure belli*, B. 3, c. 2, s. 7.

[59] Gronovius, in *De jure belli*, in comments on Grotius, B. 3, c. 2, s. 7. '*Injuriam facientis* Ejus, qui jus non redidit, aut injuriam fecit, siquidem habitant in ejus territorio, non si itineris, aut peregrinationis, aliave de causa tempus aliquod dumtaxat ibi morati sunt.' The words in italics are the words from Grotius that Gronovius is commenting on.

[60] Cocceius, in *De jure belli*, in comments on Grotius B. 3, c. 2, s. 7. '*Qui tales sunt ex causa permanente* i.e. perpetuo in territorio commorantur, adeoque ibi domicilium constitutum habent.' The words in italics are from the text of Grotius.

elsewhere. In this sense a person who, because of his business, remains abroad even for a long time, has only a mere residence there, without *domicile*.[61]

Even this fairly specific passage from Vattel could not instruct the Lords Commissioners what constituted an implied declaration to remain nor define how long a merchant could reside and carry on trade abroad without implicitly making such a declaration. Traces of the distinctions made by Grotius and the Grotian commentators underlay some of the arguments made by counsel. But precedent and policy provided the solid foundation for counsel and the court.

Even though judges and lawyers had good reason to rely more on prior adjudicated cases than on the speculations of philosophers, these philosophical reflections which made up the law of nations were not mere moonshine. The commentators on the law of nations provided a great service to their own age and to the generations which followed by raising thoughtful questions, in a structured and systematic way, about the moral limits of international relations. But judges lack the luxury of raising questions; they must determine specific disputes. In the present case, they had to decide whether certain valuable property should be awarded to the captors or restored to Heysem, Ernst and Whithall. The civilians and the judges they appeared before knew the writers on the law of nations and took them seriously. But they understandably found more guidance in the precedents which had grown out of concrete, factually explicit disputes than in the inconsistent, *a priori* reasoning of philosophers.

It is hardly surprising that, after this case, the civilians would more readily refer to the words of Lord Camden from the bench rather than the abstract reflections of Vattel. Furthermore, the civilians surely knew that the writings of these commentators on the law of nations were no more free of national bias than English precedents. Expansive interpretations of neutral rights in maritime warfare were propounded by writers from nations which expected to benefit from neutrality.[62]

'Caroline'

John Nicholl preserved full notes of the 1794 argument of Scott and of

---

[61] Vattel, *Droit des gens*, B. 1, c. 19, s. 217. Italics in the original.
[62] Best, *Humanity in warfare*, 67–74, 100–8; F. Gilbert, *To the farewell address* (Princeton, 1961), 51–68.

the decision of the admiralty court in another case which raised the question of the nationality of merchants in time of war in a different factual context. The capture of the *Caroline* compelled the admiralty court to determine whether T. W. Griffith was an American, as he contended, and thus a neutral, or a British or French subject.[63] The court had to decide whether an American, who came to Europe to establish commercial relations, could travel between England and France, reside in both and carry on trade between both belligerent nations, and, all the while, remain a neutral, not a subject of either England or France.

Nicholl's notes focused almost entirely on the elaborate argument of Scott, as King's Advocate, and the fully stated reasons of the admiralty court in its judgment. Scott demonstrated a firm grasp of the economic policy reasons for refusing to treat Griffith as a neutral. The entire maritime commerce of the enemy could be protected from capture, Scott insisted, if merchants like Griffith could continue to trade as a neutral while residing in a belligerent country. Scott acknowledged that the court should approach policy arguments with diffidence. But where all the authorities disagreed on a point of law, he contended that policy should be presumed to provide a foundation for the rule of law. Here, Scott insisted, if Americans like Griffith could reside in Britain and trade as neutrals, their names would be used to protect British trade with the enemies. Other British trade would also fall into the hands of such resident neutrals, since it would be protected from enemy captures. Thus the lucrative commerce of British merchants would go to so-called neutrals like Griffith. Furthermore, the enemy could directly import British goods through such neutral merchants and avoid the added expense of indirect purchases through neutral ports.

This case again shows the developed state of the law of prize and the attitude of the bench and bar concerning precedent prior to the time Scott became judge. It also shows Scott's ability as a civilian, so essential a few years later when he became judge, to sift through the interrogatories, ship's papers and other documentary evidence and state the facts of the case accurately and clearly but in a way which highlighted those facts most helpful for his legal contentions.

Griffith, according to Scott's account, had been born and had

---

[63] Nicholl's Notebook, 1793–7, 178, 181–8, P.R.O. HCA 30/464. The entire discussion of the arguments and comments from the bench in this case have been derived from Nicholl's notes unless otherwise noted.

resided in America. He came to Europe to carry on trade between America and different European countries. Though a business establishment or counting house might not be essential for carrying on trade, Scott noted that Griffith had not claimed to have any establishment or partner in America. Griffith went to France to sell tobacco, but, Scott observed, he acted there only through agents. Apparently the French government considered Griffith as an American, and yet they imprisoned him for a time. He had an American passport, but nonetheless, Scott contended, another nationality might be imposed on him regardless of how the French regarded him. Griffith said he intended to return to Baltimore in America, his alleged home, but Scott pointed out he never indicated when or how long he planned to stay in Europe. While in England and France Griffith entered into new commercial transactions and carried on trade between America and Europe and between the countries in Europe.

Scott, after laying out the facts, focused on the issue confronting the court. Griffith contended that his trade was as an American, even though he resided in England and France. He did not carry on trade as an inhabitant of either England or France. Scott, as King's Advocate arguing on behalf of the captors, contended that Griffith could not continue to trade as an American.

Turning to the legal contentions, Scott insisted that it was not essential in determining the nationality of a merchant that he be naturalized or enjoy all the benefits of a native merchant. He cited the case of Ernst and Heysem, discussed above, indicating that the Lords Commissioners' judgment in that case had surprised the members of the bar. He obviously was questioning the Lords' judgment which had restored Ernst's property, considering him a Dane, even though Ernst had shipped it from a Dutch colony to Holland and had himself resided for a time in Amsterdam.[64] Though Ernst's trade had been completely Dutch, Scott said, yet as a Dane residing in Copenhagen he obtained restitution. The principle for which that precedent stood, Scott argued, was that the personal residence of the owner determined the national character to his property. Scott speculated that the decision in Ernst's case would not be affirmed if the Lords should again review the issue. Scott argued that the intention of a merchant like Ernst to settle permanently in a country certainly sufficed to impose on him that nationality, but the absence of that intention did

---

[64] *Jacobus Johannes* (*Mille*) (Lords, 1786), discussed above at pp. 130–41.

not prove the contrary. In other words the intention to settle was not a necessary requirement for determining the national character of a merchant. If that precedent stood, Scott argued, the whole of the enemy's trade could be carried on merely by a merchant's taking a residence in a neutral country.

In the earlier case of the *Ospray*, Scott pointed out, the admiralty court had departed from the authority of Ernst's case.[65] In the *Ospray*, Scott said, the property of a merchant resident in America had been condemned by this court as property of a French merchant. (This was true, but, as indicated in the footnote, the Lords Commissioners subsequently reversed this part of the admiralty court's judgment.) In the present case, Scott emphasized, Griffith was not only not resident in America, but had no house of trade in America nor any other connection with America.

Scott also distinguished Griffith's case from the earlier case of Curtissos. In Curtissos' case, Scott said, the property of an English merchant was captured while the merchant was on his way home to England, while he was merely detained at Amsterdam to collect his property.[66] Curtissos had not been engaging in any new business transactions, like Griffith, but was merely removing his property.

---

[65] *Ospray* (1793), Arnold's Notebook, 1793–4, P.R.O. HCA 30/471; Nicholl's Notebook, 1793–7, P.R.O. HCA 30/464; *Ospray* (Lords, 1795), Arnold's Notebook, 1795, P.R.O. HCA 30/468; Nicholl's Notes of Prize Appeals, 1794–1817, P.R.O. HCA 30/466. The *Ospray* involved a whale-fishing venture, engaged in by three Americans from Nantucket. Two of the Americans had residences in Dunkirk and sailed from there and returned there after the whaling trip. The third American had remained in Nantucket. Scott argued in the admiralty court that this commercial venture should be considered French. The court commented that this trade from France of Nantucket whalers was well understood. It had caused much injury in Boston and New York, the court said. The court, in condemning the ship and cargo as French property, observed that its judgment would be written in gold in Boston and New York. The court's test for determining nationality was the place of one's house of trade and the place he enriched by his trade.

On appeal to the Lords Commissioners, Scott argued that the Lords should take the opportunity to reconsider Ernst's case, *Jacobus Johannes*, discussed above at pp. 130–41. Scott was obviously thinking of the part of the cargo belonging to the American in Nantucket. The Lords reversed in part and restored the part of the cargo claimed by the Nantucket resident. Although this might seem to have affirmed Ernst's case, the Lords did not state the reasons for this partial reversal. Nicholl noted, however, that in a subsequent case it was stated, apparently by the Lords, that the property in the *Ospray* had been restored only because the 'transaction was wholly before Hostilities'. Perhaps the Lords had reservations about Ernst's case and were seeking to avoid reaffirming it.

[66] Curtissos' case, *Snelle Zeylder* (*Leeuw*) (Lords, 1783), P.R.O. HCA 45/10, discussed above at fn. 48.

Griffith, on the contrary, was indefinite as to his intention to return to America. He might stay in Europe carrying on trade till the end of the war.

Scott concluded by pointing out that in the previous war Parliament had passed an act allowing particular articles, necessary to British industry, to be imported from the enemy's country. This act, Scott said, showed that such importation was illegal without such a statute.

The notes include a brief outline of the argument of Arnold, who also argued for the captors.[67] Arnold returned to Ernst's case. He insisted that Ernst's property had been restored by the Lords Commissioners solely because there had been sufficient proof that he had a home, wife and family in Denmark. Ernst's residence in Amsterdam had been merely transitory. Griffith, on the contrary had no residence in America. Obviously the intention of a merchant was crucial to determine his nationality. But according to Arnold, an intention of remaining indefinitely in a country was not a prerequisite to establish nationality. The remote intention of returning home, however, Arnold argued, was insufficient to remove nationality once established.

The admiralty judge, James Marriott, spoke at length giving his reasons in full for rejecting Scott's argument and restoring Griffith's property. Marriott noted that he had sat as judge for many years and never had heard a case quite like the present. He insisted that this case must be determined according to the particular circumstances of this case rather than on general principle. The law of this court, Marriott stated, was the law of equity, reason and good sense. Cases must not be determined by precedents decided under different circumstances. (Marriott's blithe disregard of precedent must have infuriated Scott, whose whole argument depended on it.)

In his review of the facts, Marriott stressed that Griffith was born an American and came to Europe to establish commercial correspondence. Griffith had always acted through agents in England and France and was himself merely passing through (*in itinere*). The French government regarded him as an American. Griffith, Marriott said, was an itinerant American returning to America. The property clearly belonged to him and therefore its character must depend on his nationality.

[67] James Henry Arnold, admitted to practice as a civilian in 1787, Squibb, *Doctors' Commons*, 195.

Marriott turned to the precedents discussed by counsel. Curtissos had been present in court, Marriott pointed out, and therefore could provide full proof of his intention of returning home. Without explaining why, Marriott said that the case of Heysem and Ernst did not apply. He realized that that decision had not been satisfactory to the bar. The *Ospray* was distinguishable since there the Americans had a house of trade and a residence at Dunkirk.

Having disposed of the precedents, Marriott made some enlightening comments on policy. When commerce was simple, he said, domicile was a good principle, but now that merchants were so 'locomotive' it was no longer sufficient. Merchants, he insisted, must not be at peace while the government was at war. Marriott caught a brief glimpse of total warfare and rejected the idea. Whether trade, he said, was to be completely stopped and all intercourse cut off and war carried on with the utmost severity was a serious consideration. Policy, Marriott observed, cut both ways. A circuitous trade with the enemy was admitted to be advantageous to the British. The Dutch, he pointed out, had been allowed to act as middle men. Why not the Americans? This country would gain the advantage. Marriott's refreshing candor concerning the economic rationale for determining the precise outer limits of maritime warfare suggests the importance of such policy reasons in determining questions of neutral rights.

This was the first case where a merchant had no house of commerce, Marriott said. He could get no light from treaties or the instructions of the British government. Griffith, in Marriott's view, was forming a house of trade in Baltimore but had no settlement in England. He was on his way home and carried all his belongings to America 'on his back'. Griffith thus was to be considered as a transient. He had been imprisoned and ill-treated in France and had escaped from there. This last factual detail obviously impressed Marriott since he finished his speech with the rhetorical flourish that this court would not condemn the property even of a Frenchman leaving France with his plate. He decreed that the property should be restored to Griffith and that each party should be assessed its own costs. Although the *Caroline* seems to have been an important case, the records give no indication that it was ever appealed to the Lords Commissioners.

The reliance on policy and precedents again stands out in this case. The idea of total war, with the complete destruction of commerce, remained foreign to the thinking of Marriott and his contemporaries. The economic benefit to Britain of continued commerce had to be balanced carefully against the need to prevent enemies from receiving imported goods from Britain and elsewhere. There was no explicit discussion of neutral rights, only an implicit weighing of the advantages and disadvantages to Britain of allowing neutrals to continue carrying products, many of them British, to the enemy. Because of these policy reasons Marriott rejected Scott's point that continued residence of a merchant sufficed to establish the commercial residence of a merchant and thus his nationality. Marriott seemed to insist that a merchant have an established commercial establishment before he would be considered a national of a country. Perhaps Marriott was merely accepting the American merchant's claim that he was leaving his commercial residence in England and returning home to America.

It is well to remember that Scott's argument did not depend on determining whether Griffith should be treated as a French or an English national. In either case his property would be subject to seizure by the British. Only if he could continue to be treated as an American while he moved back and forth between France and England could his property remain neutral and free from condemnation. Scott could see more clearly than Marriott the door this indulgence would open for neutral merchants. When he became admiralty judge, he would have no hesitation condemning property of merchants who carried on trade from an enemy country, even though they did not have a commercial establishment there.

The use of precedents in the case of the *Caroline* is equally revealing. Prior cases were referred to in a familiary, shorthand manner, 'Ernst's case', 'Curtissos' case' and the reaction of the bar to the determination of the Lords Commissioners was noted both by Scott and Marriott. Clearly there was an accepted body of tradition which the civilians discussed and debated among themselves. This received tradition, shaped, nuanced and at times altered by judicial decisions, provided the framework for the practitioners before the admiralty court.

Other cases

The basic principle, that a neutral merchant could acquire the nationality of an enemy after long residence in the enemy country, seemed well settled.[68] Judge Marriott, in the same year he decided the case of the *Caroline* involving the property of Griffith, commented from the bench in another case that the Americans had a very mistaken opinion that they retained their American nationality even though they resided and were carrying on trade in another country.[69] Here Marriott did not seem to require an established house of trade as he had in the *Caroline*. But when Scott, arguing in another case before the Lords Commissioners, pressed the point to include neutral merchants who merely had agents in an enemy country, the Lords brushed aside his argument. The Master of the Rolls asked whether an American merchant with an agent in England would for that reason be considered an Englishman.[70] Of course, a mere transitory residence would not suffice to change a merchant's national character unless he had established a regular domicile.[71]

Merchants resident in a country when that country became a belligerent could settle their affairs there and move to a neutral country. Scott had relied on Curtissos' case when he represented just such claimants, two Dutch merchants who moved from Amsterdam to Emden and to Ostend, when Holland became involved in the American Revolution. These two merchants continued to carry on their trade in the accustomed channels from Amsterdam. Nonetheless, the admiralty court agreed with Scott that the claimants had left Amsterdam in good faith and had become domiciled in Prussia and in the Austrian Netherlands with the intent of remaining there. The claimant's property was restored.[72] A Frenchman by birth, however, who had been naturalized as an American but carried on trade from St Domingo and returned briefly to France, was treated as a Frenchman. The court held that despite the naturalization, when the merchant returned to his own native country, the court would presume that he

---

[68] *Perigrine* (*Webber*) (Lords, 1795), Nicholl's Notes of Prize Appeals, 570, P.R.O. HCA 30/466; 45/18. It is not clear whether Scott argued this case.

[69] *Molly* (1794), Nicholl's Notebook, 1793–7, 113, P.R.O. HCA 30/464.

[70] *Sally* (*Shayes*) (Lords, 1796), Nicholl's Notes of Prize Appeals, 17, P.R.O. HCA 30/466. Scott had made this same argument in *Bachus* (*Robins*) (Lords, 1796), Nicholl's Notes of Prize Appeals, 16, P.R.O. HCA 30/466.

[71] *Hooglandt* (1783), Nicholl's Notebook, 1781–92, No. 37, P.R.O. HCA 30/464.

[72] *Jacobus* (*Kras*) (1783), Nicholl's Notebook, 1781–92, No. 34, P.R.O. HCA 30/464. See also *Washington* (1797), Nicholl's Notebook, 1793–7, 97, P.R.O. HCA 30/464. In this latter case an American went to Brest, supposedly to settle his accounts in France, but continued for a year to carry on trade there. The admiralty court nonetheless considered him neutral and restored his property.

returned with the intention of remaining there.[73]

Trade with the far east raised novel questions for the court. A merchant had resided two miles from a Dutch settlement at Old Cochin on the coast of Malabar. He was under the jurisdiction of the Rajah, not the Dutch. The Lords Commissioners, nonetheless, treated him as a Dutch merchant since he had employed a Dutch pass and Dutch flag. This case appears particularly harsh since this merchant's property was seized while he was supplying the British army with provisions.[74]

The admiralty court and the court of prize appeals had likewise settled a number of questions concerning the nationality of British merchants. The Lords found it indisputable that any voyage from a British port to an enemy's port was illegal.[75] In another case Scott had argued that British merchants could not continue commercial intercourse with the enemy without a licence. He cited several precedents. The Lords Commissioners in that case had queried whether a British subject, immediately upon the outbreak of hostilities, could not without a licence in good faith withdraw his property from the enemy's country. But since the British merchant had continued the ordinary course of trade from the enemy country, his property was condemned.[76]

Where a British merchant had resided for some time at the Danish colony of St Thomas, Scott relied on Whithall's case to establish that the claimant should be treated as a neutral. The Lords Commissioners agreed. Lord Camden insisted that Whithall's case had been

---

[73] *Rebecca* (1795), Nicholl's Notebook, 1793–7, 223, P.R.O. HCA 30/464.

[74] *Rachel (Mobareck)* (Lords, 1792), Nicholl's Notebook, 1781–92, No. 101, P.R.O. HCA 30/464.

[75] *Bella Guidita (Lalli)* (Lords, 1785), Nicholl's Notebook, 1781–92, No. 94, P.R.O. HCA 30/464; 45/12, fo. 718. In another case Scott had referred back to the case of the *Deer Garden* (1747) (discussed above at fn. 24), for his contention that trading with the enemy was a ground for confiscation. The court, although apologizing for the inconvenience to the British merchants, refused to consider this a hardship case and condemned the property. Immediately after the commencement of hostilities, the court said, even without a declaration of war, all commercial correspondence with the enemy must cease. *Nancy* (1793), Arnold's Notebook, 1792–3, P.R.O. HCA 30/470; Nicholl's Notebook, 1793–7, 6, P.R.O. HCA 30/464.

[76] *Leon (Deering)* (Lords, 1796), Nicholl's Notes of Prize Appeals, 18, P.R.O. HCA 30/466; 45/19, fo. 188. A year earlier the Lords had declared that when war broke out all direct communication with the enemy was prohibited even for the purpose of withdrawing property from the enemy's country. *William (Leith)* (Lords, 1795), Nicholl's Notes of Prize Appeals, 14, P.R.O. HCA 30/466; 45/19, fo. 48. This position seems extreme and might merely reflect one Lord's expression of strong hostility to the facts of that case.

decided after great deliberation and must be the rule for all similar cases. That case had determined, Camden said, that domicile was to be based on a residence which was indeterminate as to time. He commented that it was not criminal for a British merchant to reside in a neutral country during war. It was, in fact, the constant practice. This merchant was, therefore, considered Danish for purposes of commerce.[77]

Although a British merchant could be considered a neutral if he had carried on trade for a long time in a neutral country, he lost that neutral character if he had remained at sea, away from the neutral country, for a considerable period (two years in this case). His British nationality reverted.[78] Neutral merchants resident in Britain, even an American consul, were regarded as British merchants and could not trade with the enemy any more than British subjects.[79]

A distinct but related question arose concerning the property of allies of the British. Could a merchant of an allied nation trade with the enemy? The British asserted the right to seize not only the property of British merchants trading with the enemy, but also the property of allies who engaged in such a trade. Scott had made that point in 1794 in a case involving the property of Hanse merchants. The Lords agreed that the Hanse town, as an ally, could not legally trade with the common enemy. Even though their own magistrates might wink at such trade, Britain was not bound by such connivance. Contrary to what Sir George Lee had intimated to a client a half century earlier, their property was condemned.[80]

These cases show the extent of Scott's experience in dealing with questions of nationality prior to the time he became admiralty judge. It certainly makes no sense in discussing his thirty years as admiralty judge to ignore the fact that they were preceded by nearly twenty years of practice as a civilian, half of these years spent with the significant responsibility of King's Advocate.

Far more importantly, these cases show the extent to which the law

[77] *Phoenix (March)* (Lords, 1785), Nicholl's Notebook, 1781–92, No. 93, P.R.O. HCA 30/464; 45/12, fo. 702. Whithall's case, *Harmonie (Rynders)* (Lords, 1786), was discussed above at pp. 130–41.
[78] *Cupid (Tatharing)* (Lords, 1796), Nicholl's Notes of Prize Appeals, 21, P.R.O. HCA 30/466. It is not clear whether Scott argued this case.
[79] *Pigou (Lewis)* (Lords, 1797), Nicholl's Notes of Prize Appeals, 26, P.R.O. HCA 30/466. It is not clear whether Scott argued this case.
[80] *Hercules (Jasper)* (Lords, 1794), Nicholl's Notes of Prize Appeals, 1, P.R.O. HCA 30/466; 45/17, fo. 17. For Lee's comments, see p. 129 above.

of nationality in prize cases had been influenced by British mercantilist commercial policy. There is no word in these cases suggesting that the military policies of winning a war had any impact at all. As previously mentioned, military policy and commercial policy in the eighteenth-century Anglo-French wars often became indistinguishable. Of course, as the commercial policy became fully absorbed into the court's decisions, it became less necessary for the civilians to discuss the policy reasons. They could rely on precedent since the court's prior judgments reflected the underlying policy of mercantilism.

An opinion as counsel

During the nearly twenty years Scott practiced as a civilian, he frequently gave written advice in answer to specific questions of his clients. He continued to give such advice during the years after 1788 when he was King's Advocate.[81]

Scott became familiar during these years with Rufus King, the American minister to England. The King papers contain many letters which they exchanged.[82] These papers include an opinion Scott gave as counsel in 1797, when he was King's Advocate, a year before he was appointed as admiralty judge.[83] Apparently Rufus King had asked whether persons born in England but settled in America, either before or after independence, were considered by Great Britain as American citizens, and secondly whether a vessel owned by such persons would be considered American when navigated with an American pass.

Scott replied that British subjects settled in America before independence were considered as Americans since the acknowledgment of independence operated as a release by the king of his subjects in America. Those British subjects who settled in America after the acknowledgment of independence, Scott said, remained British subjects and were not distinguishable from other British-born subjects residing in any other foreign country. They were not released from their allegiance. He added that

With respect to their ordinary Mercantile Character, they are considered as

[81] R.A., Stowell Notebook, contains many such opinions, mostly concerning ecclesiastical matters, in draft form for the years 1788–9, just at the time he became King's Advocate. See Appendix for a fuller description of this manuscript.
[82] N.Y.H.S., Rufus King Papers. Cf. Perkins, *First rapprochement*, 46, 85–91.
[83] N.Y.H.S., Rufus King Papers. Copy of an opinion of Scott, February 4, 1797.

entitled to the Privileges of the Merchants of that Country in which they reside; They can carry on their Trade generally in the same manner as those Merchants[,] can own Vessels sailing under Sea passes and Registers of that Country, and those Vessels will be considered here as the Vessels of that Country. A Vessel owned by such a Person residing in America and navigated under an American sea brief will be deemed American.[84]

Scott then turned in this opinion to a further question, whether a ship, with an American pass, owned by a British subject settled in America, could engage in trade to India and return with cargo to America. Scott replied that any British subjects who trade as American merchants remain bound by the British laws which protect the monopoly of the British East India Company. The laws prohibited 'any subject of the King' from trading in the East Indies. Scott concluded, however, that he was of the opinion 'that in the case of an Actual bona fide Resident in America acknowledged there as an American Citizen and navigating a Vessel under American sea briefs, so large and unfavourable a Construction of the Words would not be adopted'.[85]

This opinion, more than any of the prize cases in which Scott was involved as counsel, addressed the relationship between the two different meanings of nationality with which this section began. Nationality could refer to the permanent bond of allegiance which tied all British subjects to their king. It could also refer to the national character which the British courts would consider applicable to the property of merchants carrying on trade in different parts of the world. Scott in this opinion as counsel tried to reconcile these two meanings of nationality. Although he insisted on the permanence of British citizenship, he implied that a court would take a fairly broad view of this permanent bond and would consider a British subject who had become an American merchant as an American in interpreting the trade limitations of the East India Act.

SCOTT AS ADMIRALTY JUDGE

Scott, as the previous discussion indicates, was consciously part of a

[84] *Ibid.*
[85] *Ibid.* See also, J. H. Kettner, 'Subjects or citizens? A note on British views respecting the legal effects of American independence', *Virginia Law Rev.*, 62 (1976), 945, 959–61. The American attitude is thoroughly discussed in Kettner, *Development of American citizenship*, 213–47.

development of this body of law. He knew from intimate experience the law of nationality as it had been received from the mid-eighteenth century and participated in shaping it in the last two decades of the century. Though it was a complex, developed body of law, it was not frozen and immutable, and often it was expressed in offhand comments from the bench. The civilians gathered up these crumbs scattered by the court and preserved them for future use. Scott's genius, we shall see, lay more in clarifying this body of law than in creating it. His contribution to the law of nationality was in his accurate articulation of the received tradition and in his refinement of this tradition by applying it to new fact situations.

Neutral and enemy merchants

Continuity was the key to the first reported case Scott determined after being appointed judge. The ship *Vigilantia*, sailing under Prussian colors, had been captured in 1798 on a voyage from Amsterdam to Greenland.[86] It had been fitted out to engage in a Greenland fishing expedition. Peter Brower of Emden in Prussia claimed the vessel as neutral property. Scott, however, picked the factual record apart in order to show that the *Vigilantia* was really a Dutch ship, with a Dutch master and crew, engaged in its traditional Dutch venture of the Greenland trade. He concluded that the ship continued *de facto* as the property of the former Dutch owner and was therefore subject to condemnation. This, in itself, was a clarification of the law as it previously existed.

Although Scott could have stopped at this point, he instead stated the rule of law applicable to determine the nationality of a vessel sailing under neutral colors. The general rule, he said, was that a vessel 'navigating under the pass of a foreign country ... [was] considered as bearing the national character of that nation under whose pass she sails'. By this test, of course, the *Vigilantia* would be considered Prussian and thus neutral. But, on the other hand, he continued:

[86] *Vigilantia (Gerritz)* (1798), 1 Rob. 1, 4. The Lords Commissioners decided a similar case two years later and went further than Scott had in the *Vigilantia* in holding that even if the vessel had been transferred in good faith to a neutral, if that neutral engaged in the Greenland trade from, and returning to, Amsterdam, it would be considered as Dutch. *Emden (Meyer)* (Lords, 1800), Nicholl's Notes of Prize Appeals, 36, P.R.O. HCA 30/466. This appeal affirmed Scott's judgment in *Embden* [*sic*] *(Meyer)* (1798), 1 Rob. 16, 19.

,[I]f a vessel purchased in the enemy's country is, by constant and habitual occupation, continually employed in the trade of that country, commencing with the war, continuing during the war, and *evidently on account of the war*, on what ground is it to be asserted, that the vessel is not to be deemed a ship of the country from which she is so navigating; in the same manner as if she evidently belonged to the inhabitants of it?[87]

Scott's meticulous scrutiny of the record uncovered the dubious conveyance of the Dutch vessel to a neutral as insufficient to make the vessel neutral as long as it continued in its accustomed Dutch trade with a Dutch master and crew. Again and again we shall see that Scott's ability to pierce beneath the surface of the factual record (the ship's papers and the interrogatories submitted to the court) provided him with an occasion to restate, clarify and develop the legal norms applicable to the fact situation.

Scott, as judge, relied on the same mercantilist policy arguments he had developed in his arguments as counsel. If a neutral country, he said, offered to purchase and sail the ships of a belligerent, but fitted them out in the belligerent's ports and with masters from the belligerent country, such vessels could not be treated as neutral. These so-called neutrals would be contributing to the local industry of the belligerent and would support the manufacturing interests and revenues of the belligerent country.

Scott concluded with a careful discussion of the case of Ernst and Heysem and the case of the *Ospray*. He asserted that in the *Ospray* the Lords Commissioners had 'expressly laid down, that if a person entered into a house of trade in the enemy's country in time of war; he should not protect himself by mere residence in a neutral country'. He concluded that the Lords' decision in the *Ospray* established the doctrine '*that there is a traffic which stamps a national character* on the individual, independent of *that character*, which *mere personal residence* may give him'.[88]

Scott obviously relied on private notes of these two cases and was able to provide a more precise and relevant summary of the Lords

[87] *Vigilantia*, 1 Rob. 13. Italics in the original. In *Vrow Elizabeth (Probst)* (1803), 5 Rob. 2, 5, Scott stated the general rule in absolute terms: '[A] vessel, sailing under the colours and pass of a nation, is to be considered as clothed with the national character of that Country.' Apparently, as in the case of the *Vigilantia*, this rule was not as absolute as Scott stated it, if other factors led to the conclusion that the vessel must be considered enemy property.

[88] *Vigilantia*, 1 Rob. 15. Italics in the original. The case of Ernst and Heysem, *Jacobus Johannes (Mille)*, is discussed above at pp. 130–41. The *Ospray* is discussed at fn. 65 above.

Commissioners' holdings than that found in the notebook discussed above. Scott's analysis of these cases highlights the main problem of relying on privately compiled notes. They did not all necessarily say the same thing and ultimately the use of precedent became something of a game of finding the most helpful version of a prior case. One can readily understand why, with the publication of Scott's fully articulated judgments, the reliance on unpublished notes gradually vanished. Scott's statement of what the Lords had said, rather than what they actually said, took on a meaning of its own. Scott's first reported judgment thus marks a new beginning. Right from his first case he spoke decisively, with authority. This case brings out his ability to preserve and restate prior opinions in such a way as to provide the court and its practitioners with a more adequate summary of the law for future use.

In the *Endraught*, a Danish master, with a wife and family in Denmark, had for years engaged in Dutch commerce. He was treated by Scott as a Dutchman. Scott ignored a certificate of the master's domicile at Emden as a mere nominal residence since there was no proof that he had ever lived a day in Prussia. Scott's holding in this case closely followed the argument he had made as counsel which the court had rejected in the *Caroline*. Not satisfied with this factual determination which might have sufficed to decide the case, Scott laid down the court's requirement for domicile: 'The residence which the Court requires, must be taken up *honestly*, and a *bona fide* intention of making it the place of habitation: without such an actual residence, a certificate like this rather weakens than assists the case.'[89] Of course, a certificate of domicile in the master's native Denmark would have created a quite different response.

Scott certainly knew the difficulty of determining the domicile of a merchant. In deciding in another case the nationality of an American merchant, G. W. Murray, who had dwelt and carried on trade in France for four years, Scott commented on the 'active spirit of commerce now abroad in the world' which made such questions more difficult.[90] He addressed the commercial realities surrounding the trade of Americans with Europe. Since mercantilism had been woven into the fabric of the court's determination of questions of nationality, it is not surprising that Scott thought that freedom of commerce

---

[89] *Endraught (Bonker)* (1798), 1 Rob. 22, 24. Italics in the original. The *Caroline* was discussed above at pp. 141–7.

[90] *Harmony (Bool)* (1800), 2 Rob. 322.

raised delicate questions for the British prize court. Nonetheless, Scott said, the particular situation of America entitled American merchants to favorable treatment. Because of the distance American merchants lacked the same ready correspondence with merchants in Europe. Americans, thus in Scott's perceptive view, were more likely to have their commercial trusts abused and to have more frequent occasion personally to supervise their affairs in Europe. When they did cross the Atlantic, it is not surprising, Scott said, that they stayed longer in a country than European merchants who stepped lightly from one country to another.

In this case Scott observed that the one general rule he felt comfortable in laying down was that 'time is the grand ingredient in constituting domicil [*sic*]'.[91] If a merchant came to a belligerent country at the beginning of a war, it was reasonable not to impose too soon on him an acquired national character. He should be allowed time to disengage himself. But, on the other hand, if he continued to reside in the belligerent country for a considerable period and to contribute to the country by his taxes, he could no longer plead a special purpose, such as settling affairs, for his residence there. In this case an American trading house sent a partner to France with the intention of conducting the business of the house there. Scott concluded that if this American merchant had been 'resident in France, during the greater part of the war, conducting the business of his house, receiving cargoes, and disposing of cargoes, and giving accounts of the markets in France, and directing mercantile adventures there; it is, in my apprehension, impossible not to consider him as a resident trader of that country'.[92]

The surprising aspect of this last case is that neither counsel nor the court cited any precedents, even the case of the *Caroline*, in which the

[91] *Ibid.*, 324.
[92] *Ibid.*, 333. Scott also noted that G. W. Murray had been born a British subject and had migrated to America in 1784. Nonetheless, Scott did not hesitate to conclude that Murray 'was equitably entitled to the *American* character'. *Ibid.*, 326. Scott's treatment of Murray appears more generous to Murray's claim to be an American citizen than one would have expected from Scott's theoretical discussion of the issue in his 1797 opinion as counsel in response to questions of Rufus King. See above, pp. 151–2.
  Seven years later the Lords Commissioners had occasion to consider a different case involving G. W. Murray. This time the court of prize appeals reversed the admiralty court's condemnation of Murray's property and restored it to him since, prior to that transaction, he had returned to America. *Active* (*Statesbury*) (Lords, 1807), Nicholl's Notes of Prize Appeals, P.R.O. HCA 30/466. This is one of the few cases where Scott's judgment was reversed on appeal.

facts had been so similar.[93] Perhaps Scott was quite satisfied to forget that precedent in which the admiralty court had rejected his arguments. Of course, Scott knew that the precedent of the *Caroline* was distinguishable since in that case the American merchant had merely resided in France without setting up a house of trade and perhaps had convinced the court that he was returning to America. The arguments Scott had used in that case prevailed here: extended personal residence of a merchant in a belligerent country determined his nationality for commerce.

In another case involving an American who had shipped cargoes from France, Scott again distinguished two situations: a neutral merchant who engaged in transactions in an enemy country 'merely for the purpose of withdrawing his funds', who would be treated as a neutral, and secondly, a neutral merchant who engaged in 'a voluntary mercantile speculation in the enemy's trade'. The latter would be treated as an enemy merchant.[94] Scott did not suggest that establishment of a house of trade in the enemy country was a prerequisite to being treated as an enemy merchant. Scott's distinction in this case between the neutral merchant in a belligerent country who was there merely to wind up his affairs and the neutral merchant who voluntarily engaged in new business transactions is nearly identical to the argument he made, and which the court rejected, in the *Caroline*.[95]

The *Indian Chief* was a third case involving a claim by an American merchant.[96] The *Indian Chief* was an American ship with an American pass and documents. It had arrived in England with a Dutch East

[93] The *Caroline* is discussed above in the text at pp. 141–7. The arguments of counsel are included in *Harmony*, Nicholl's Notebook, 1799–1800, 210, P.R.O. HCA 30/464.
[94] *Dree Gebroeders* (*Vandyk*) (1802), 4 Rob. 232, 234.
[95] In the *Dree Gebroeders*, Scott had concluded that Mr Grant, the claimant, was no longer an American merchant. 'It now appears that Mr. Grant has disposed of his house, and has nothing left in *America* but his landed estate, which alone has never been held sufficient to constitute domicil, or fix the national character of the possessor, who is not personally resident upon it; except with regard to property which is going as the immediate produce of that landed estate. Mr. Grant does not even seem to have formed any definite *intention* of returning to *America* . . . Under this view of the circumstances in which Mr. Grant appears in this case, his mercantile connection with *America* if any, is held by a mere thread: This is a transaction not originating in any purpose of remitting his funds to *England*, and from thence to *America*, but in an independent mercantile speculation, from *Cherbourg* to *Seville*, or *Lisbon*.' 4 Rob. 235. As in the *Caroline*, Scott concluded that it made no difference whether the claimant's property was considered French or English. In either case, since it was not American, it would be condemned.
[96] *Indian Chief* (*Skinner*) (1800), 3 Rob. 12.

Indian cargo and orders to proceed to Hamburg, but apparently
sought instructions from its owner. The owner of the ship, Mr
Johnson, had engaged in trade in England for fourteen years, but, he
contended, as an American merchant. Counsel had discussed Curtissos' case[97] and the case of Ernst and Heysem[98] and several other cases
but not the *Caroline*. Scott concluded, without mentioning any
precedents, that during the time Johnson had resided in England and
carried on trade there, he was to be considered an English merchant.
'[F]or no position is more established than this', Scott said, 'that if a
person goes into another country, and engages in trade, and resides
there, he is, by the law of nations, to be considered as a merchant of
that country.'[99] In this case, however, Johnson had departed from
England a few weeks before his ship, the *Indian Chief*, arrived. Scott
concluded that Johnson had lost his English nationality and
reacquired his American nationality. He explicitly relied on Curtissos'
case. Johnson's English nationality had been based solely on his
residence. '[I]t must be held', Scott said,

that from the moment he turns his back on the country where he has resided,
on his way to his own country, he was in the act of resuming his original
character, and is to be considered as an American: The character that is
gained by residence ceases by residence: It is an adventitious character which
no longer adheres to him, from the moment that he puts himself in motion,
bona fide, to quit the country, *sine animo revertendi*.[100]

Scott therefore restored the ship as neutral property. Although this is
one possible basis for the court's holding in the *Caroline*, Scott did not
mention that case. It is clear from this case, as well as many others,
that, while he viewed the cases through British eyes, Scott applied the
principles enunciated by the court when they benefited the neutral
claimants and not only when they benefited the British captors.

It was legal, Scott said, for a neutral to purchase a vessel in France

---

[97] *Snelle Zeylder (Leeiw)* (Lords, 1783), discussed above at fn. 48.
[98] *Jacobus Johannes (Mille)* and *Harmonie (Rynders)* (Lords, 1786), discussed above
at pp. 130–41.
[99] *Indian Chief (Skinner)* (1800), 3 Rob. 12, 18.
[100] *Ibid.*, 20–1. Scott reiterated this principle, 'that the native character easily reverts',
in *Virginie (Coigneau)* (1804), 5 Rob. 98, 99.
    A few years later, in an unpublished opinion, Scott rejected the Americans'
pretension that they retain their American citizenship wherever they resided.
Whatever may be allowed in American domestic law, Scott said, other countries
(i.e. Great Britain) would not allow such a claim. *Alliance* (1807), Nicholl's
Notebook, 1807–8, P.R.O. HCA 30/465.

during the war.[101] Such a purchase, however, aroused suspicions; but if the neutral purchaser was a resident in France the suspicions were greatly increased. The court knew full well, Scott said, that France was in dire need of disguising its trade. He then laid down a legal rule, without citation of precedent, that '[W]herever it appears that the purchaser was in *France*, he must explain the circumstances of his residence there: the presumption arising from his residence is, that he is there *animo manendi*, and it lies on him to explain it.'[102] Probably Scott regarded such a rule as implicit in the prior practice of the prize court. Certainly the evidentiary rules of the admiralty court, as mentioned earlier, had for a long time countenanced suspicions and presumptions which increased or shifted the claimant's risk of non-persuasion.[103] Nevertheless it was Scott's capsule statement of these amorphous rules which would serve as a clear guide for future cases.

Merchants resident abroad when war began, as Scott had stated, would be permitted a reasonable time to leave the belligerent country with their property. He made this received rule much more precise by stating 'A mere intention to remove has never been held sufficient, without some overt act; being merely an intention, residing secretly and undistinguishably in the breast of the party, and liable to be revoked every hour.'[104]

Similarly Scott showed a healthy skepticism of a change of residence supported by a mere nominal adoption of another country. A Dutch merchant, born in Holland and living there till the sailing of the vessel and only then moving to Denmark, would be considered Dutch and therefore an enemy merchant. Scott displayed his usual grasp of the real world of merchants by observing that this merchant had merely gone through '[T]he slight formalities of obtaining a

---

[101] *Bernon (Dunn)* (1798), 1 Rob. 102.

[102] *Ibid.*, 104. See also *Adriana (Fitzpatrick)* (1799), 1 Rob. 313, 316, where Scott said: 'It is hardly necessary to observe, that the transactions of neutrals, resident in *France*, are, from the very nature of their situation, liable to great suspicions. They are exposed to great temptations from *French* merchants, who lying under an inability to export their own produce, will assail them with great inducements to cover and protect their trade ... It will be necessary, therefore, for the court to scrutinize all such claims with the minutest attention; and to expect, not, indeed, a mathematical demonstration, but a strong and fair moral probability, that the transaction is such as it is represented to be; otherwise, if this cannot be shewn, the presumption will lie very strong, on the other side, that it is a fraudulent case.'

[103] Brown, *A compendious view of the civil law, and of the law of the admiralty*, 2nd edn (2 vols., London, 1802), II, 451–2; Jessup and Deak, *Origins*, I, 224–46.

[104] *President (Welles)* (1804), 5 Rob. 277, 280.

burgher's brief – formalities, on which, it is said, great importance is attached in *Denmark*, but on which other countries, which have to consider its real nature and effect, certainly can attach but little, in the estimate of a real national character.'[105] Scott obviously considered such factual questions from a British point of view, but the vast understanding of the practices of the mercantile community which he brought to his position lent credence to his perception.

When Scott encountered the case of a native Dutch subject who had become a Prussian subject by maintaining a domicile there for seven years, he treated him as a Prussian, and therefore a neutral, even though he had purchased a Dutch vessel and was engaged in fishing off the Dutch coast.[106] Scott precisely delineated the line separating this case from others, where the neutral domicile was ignored. Here, he noted, the Dutch subject had not recently acquired the neutral domicile for reasons connected with the war. Thus as a neutral he could carry on his fishing trade even off the enemy coast.

Scott, of course, had to keep a steady eye on the impact of the ever expanding war on the Continent as he considered the claims of merchants to be treated as neutrals. Merchants from Holland or the Austrian Netherlands who sought to trade as neutrals had to move ever farther north and east. In one case a merchant who had been domiciled in Ostend, and had been a partner of a trading house there, moved to Hamburg when the French invaded Ostend. But the captors contended that he continued to be prominent in the Ostend firm and traded with Ostend. Scott demanded further proof from the merchant to unravel his trading affairs. On the one hand, if he was trading on his own from Hamburg, and therefore as a neutral, his property should be restored. But on the other hand, if he continued trade as partner of the Ostend firm, while claiming to be an emigrant and to have suffered for his opposition to the French, his property should be condemned as French. Scott's suspicions were again clearly expressed:

I think it is a circumstance open to just remark, that the tide of his commerce should have set so much that way, to the very place from which he had emigrated in apprehension and disgust: and I think it *does* raise a strong

---

[105] *Graaff Bernstorf (Belmer)* (1800), 3 Rob. 109, 115; see also *Juffrouw Elbrecht (Meintes)* (1799), 1 Rob. 127, 128, and *Phoenix (Susini)* (1800), 3 Rob. 186, 188.
[106] *Liesbet Van Den Toll (Heest)* (1804), 5 Rob. 283, 284.

suspicion, that he had yet an interest there [at Ostend], and that he had still a root left behind.[107]

A short business trip to England would not suffice to make a neutral merchant English. He could, therefore, continue to trade with the enemy from his trading house at Emden, but certainly not from London.[108]

Ordinarily the nationality of the shipper determined the nationality of the cargo. Scott, however, treated colonial cargoes differently. The produce of a plantation (for instance, sugar from a West Indian colony) was considered stamped with the character of the particular colony where it was grown, regardless of the residence of the owner.[109]

These numerous cases discussing aspects of the law of nationality as applied in the prize court were clearly built upon the foundations laid by the court prior to Scott's appointment as judge. He provided sharp distinctions where the lines had previously been blurred; he stated his reasons in well-thought-out, clearly expressed opinions, instead of the random comments of his predecessors from the bench. He looked to the same mercantilist policy arguments which he had used as counsel. But there are also some cases dealing with nationality in which Scott had to consider novel questions, where precedent offered little guide. Two examples should suffice to show how he dealt with such legal issues.

Scott recognized the peculiar difficulties of Swiss merchants in time of war and recognized that some accommodation to their trade was appropriate. They, and merchants from some interior parts of Germany, had no choice but to trade through foreign ports. But where a Swiss merchant traded in French cargo through French ports and appeared to be merely providing a neutral shield for enemy goods, Scott carefully scrutinized the proof, gave the merchant the opportunity to provide further proof, but ultimately condemned the cargo as French.[110] Scott's order to the registrar to search for precedents proved futile.

Scott had to determine the nationality of merchants from Louisiana at the time that Spanish colony had been ceded to France (prior to the

---

[107] *Portland (Farrie)* (1800), 3 Rob. 41, 49. Italics in the original. After considering the further proof offered by the merchant, Scott ultimately condemned one vessel and restored two. *Ibid.*, 50–2.

[108] *Herman (Schroeder)* (1802), 4 Rob. 228, 231.

[109] *Phoenix (Wildeboer)* (1803), 5 Rob. 20, 21.

[110] *Magnus (Sorensen)* (1798), 1 Rob. 31.

cession to the United States). More precisely he framed the issue as '[W]hether the Treaty did not in itself confer full sovereignty and right of dominion, and whether the inhabitants were not so ceded by that Treaty, as to become immediately *French* subjects.'[111] Without the help of any prize court precedents, Scott seemed to relish the opportunity to display his knowledge of Grotius, Pufendorf, Pothier and Barbeyrac. He also considered a revenue case which had recently been appealed to the Court of Delegates. Scott concluded 'on all the several grounds of reason or practice, and judicial recognition, until possession was actually taken, the inhabitants of *New Orleans* continued under the former sovereignty of *Spain*'.[112] After determining that there had been no delivery of possession to an authorized French agent, Scott held that the merchants in New Orleans must be considered Spanish subjects and therefore restored the property as neutral.

Finally, it is appropriate to include a rather lengthy quotation from one of Scott's decisions to recapture a bit of the flavor of his style and rhetoric. We will observe here the unrealistic way he viewed colonial relations in India. Probably most of his knowledge of India was from reading and hearing the tendentious statements of both sides during the trial of Warren Hastings. We also observe the classical quotation, here from Virgil, such as he occasionally dropped into his judgments in typical eighteenth-century style. Despite these distracting features, the passage shows well Scott's talent for precise and careful statement of the legal principles he applied. Even where there was ample precedent to support his judgment, Scott restated the norms, previously existing only in manuscript form, with such authority that his statement appeared definitively to settle the point.

This case involved the determination that an American consul resident at the British trading factory in Calcutta was to be treated as British, not as American (despite his consular character) nor indeed as Indian. Scott first dismissed the relevance of the consular character, since it had been fully established by precedent that a merchant is not protected by such a character. He turned then to the more difficult argument that the British king did not hold the British possessions in the East Indies in right of sovereignty, and therefore foreign merchants resident there did not become British merchants. Scott also rejected this argument.

---

[111] *Fama (Butler)* (1804), 5 Rob. 106, 113.
[112] *Ibid.*, 118.

But taking it that such a paramount sovereignty, on the part of the *Mogul* princes, really and solidly exists, and that *Great Britain* cannot be deemed to possess a sovereign right there; still it is to be remembered, that wherever even a mere factory is founded in the eastern parts of the world, *European* persons trading under the shelter and protection of those establishments, are conceived to take their national character from that association under which they live and carry on their commerce. It is a rule of the law of nations, applying peculiarly to those countries, and is different from what prevails ordinarily in *Europe* and the western parts of the world in which men take their present national character from the general character of the country in which they are resident; and this distinction arises from the nature and habit of the countries; In the western parts of the world alien merchants mix in the society of the natives; access and intermixture are permitted; and they become incorporated to almost the full extent. But in the East, from the oldest times, an immiscible character has been kept up; foreigners are not admitted into the general body and mass of the society of the nation; they continue strangers and sojourners as all their fathers were – *Doris amara suam non intermiscuit undam*; not acquiring any national character under the general sovereignty of the country, and not trading under any recognized authority of their own original country, they have been held to derive their present character from that of the association or factory, under whose protection they live and carry on their trade.[113]

Undoubtedly his policy reasons here are a bit confused. He would have been better advised to have discussed the mutual economic and commercial advantages derived from this association with the British trading station. His conclusion, however, certainly squares with the precedents and because of its clear and definitive ring, it would provide guidance for the future.

British merchants

Many of the legal norms already discussed concerning the nationality of enemy merchants or neutral merchants applied also to British merchants who had established a commercial domicile in some other country. Special legal considerations, however, came into play when British subjects were involved.

At the time of the war between Great Britain and the United States in 1812, Scott had to decide whether Smith, the owner and master of

---

[113] *Indian Chief (Skinner)* (1800), 3 Rob. 22, 28–9. In this judgment Scott cited, among other cases, the following cases which have been discussed above: *Concordia (Thomas)* (Lords, 1782), P.R.O. HCA 45/9, fo. 118; *Pigou (Lewis)* (Lords, 1797), Nicholl's Notes of Prize Appeals, P.R.O. HCA 30/466; *Twee Frienden (Angel)* (Lords, 1784), P.R.O. HCA 45/11, fo. 246, and *Rachel (Mobareck)* (Lords, 1792), Nicholl's Notebook, 1781–92, P.R.O. HCA 30/464.

the *Ann*, was British, and therefore under the protection of an Order in Council, or American and therefore an enemy.[114] This case presented Scott with the necessity to explain the relationship between British nationality, in the sense of a permanent subjectship, and the nationality of a British subject as a merchant. Although the *Ann*, taken in the river Thames, was under American colors, the Order in Council directed the admiralty court to restore vessels under the flag of the United States if the vessel was wholly the property of a British subject. (Sailing under false colors, of course, was common practice.) The owner had been born in Scotland and alleged that he and his wife and family lived in Scotland when he was not at sea or abroad. But Scott discovered in the record that Smith had spent much of his time abroad, principally at New York and Charleston. He had no house of trade in America, but he had made several voyages from America to Jamaica. Since he had not even visited his family in Scotland and since he had sailed constantly from American ports to the West Indies, Scott concluded that Smith could not be entitled to the protection of the Order in Council as a British subject. Scott, who often was not satisfied to determine a case purely on factual grounds, stated the legal principles to be applied to British subjects.

The question, therefore, comes to this, whether the claimant is, *quoad* this property, to be considered as a *British* subject. For some purposes he is undoubtedly so to be considered. He is born in this country, and is subject to all the obligations imposed upon him by his nativity. He cannot shake off his allegiance to his native country, or divest himself altogether of his *British* character by a voluntary transfer of himself to another country. For the mere purposes of trade he may, indeed, transfer himself to another state, and may acquire a new national character. An *English* subject, resident in a neutral state, is at liberty to trade with the enemy of this country in all articles, with the exception of those which are of a contraband nature.[115]

Scott held that Smith could not avail himself of the protection of the Order in Council, designed to protect British subjects, since the order 'applies only to those who are clearly and habitually *British* subjects, having no intermixture of foreign commercial character'.[116] British

[114] *Ann (Smith)* (1813), 1 Dod. 221.
[115] *Ibid.*, 223.
[116] *Ibid.* Apparently the Lords Commissioners would allow a British merchant, settled in good faith in a neutral country, to trade with the enemy, but they doubted whether a British seaman could personally trade with the enemy as master of a neutral vessel. The notes of this appeal are somewhat obscure. *Speedwell and Columbia* (1800), Nicholl's Notes of Prize Appeals, 35, P.R.O. HCA 30/466. A year

nationality, therefore, although indelible, could become attenuated if one engaged in commerce from a foreign base. Smith, apparently, could have been impressed into the British navy, but could not benefit from the protection of this Order in Council. Scott here obviously interpreted the Order in light of some unspoken policies which he found implicit in the law of nationality. British merchants should be allowed the benefit of trading as a neutral but when they regularly traded from an enemy port, they would be treated as enemies.

One would have thought that the prohibition against British nationals trading with the enemy in time of war was so clearly settled that it could have been assumed by the court. Yet shortly after Scott became admiralty judge he wrote an elaborate opinion, bristling with precedents and other authorities, merely to establish that '[A]ll trading with the public enemy, unless with the permission of the sovereign, is interdicted.'[117] In this case some merchants from Glasgow had imported raw materials for the textile industry (along with some gin and cheese) from Holland, then under the control of the French. The merchants had engaged in such trade for years, they said, and in the past had obtained licences from the Privy Council for these imports. Upon consulting the local customs officials, they had been told that licences were not necèssary. This was, as it turned out, fatally bad advice.

Nonetheless, Scott might have disposed of this case, which had some suggestion of misguided innocents, with the citation of a precedent and a statement of the clear rule of law, joined with a word of sincere regret that he had to apply such a harsh rule. Instead he seemed to be delivering a message to these merchants, and through them to all the powerful commercial interests which might not have known or followed the rules of the game. Trading with the enemy, no matter how profitable, was prohibited unless specifically permitted by the government. Scott began this lecture with a quotation from Bynkershoek and a reference to Valin. He showed that the prohibition of trade with the enemy was the law of Holland, France, Spain and of most of western Europe. He then discussed in detail thirteen cases, some from the 1740s and 1750s, which had been decided by the Lords

---

later the Lords Commissioners held that a British subject, settling in a neutral country after hostilities, might trade with the enemy from the neutral country, even personally. *Hope (Robinson)* (1801), Nicholl's Notes of Prize Appeals, 50, P.R.O. HCA 30/466.

[117] *Hoop (Cornelis)* (1799), 1 Rob. 196.

Commissioners for Prize Appeals, and one case decided by the admiralty court.[118] He gave the facts of these cases, quoted from the records, identified the Lords Commissioners who determined them and in one case quoted from the comments of the Lords in delivering their judgment. Not satisfied with this overwhelming, monolithic summary of precedent, Scott took the trouble to correct what he considered a careless comment of Lord Mansfield in a King's Bench case. Mansfield, Scott said, expressly laid down as the maritime law of England that subjects cannot trade with the enemy. It obviously troubled Scott that Mansfield had added 'but this does not extend to a neutral vessel'. Scott, recognizing the possibilities this loophole could give to merchants to ship their cargoes aboard neutral vessels and thus to continue their lucrative trade with the enemy, decisively eliminated the temptation of this course of trade. He suggested that Mansfield must have been misquoted, since Mansfield knew perfectly well that 'the neutral bottom gives, in no case, any sort of protection to a cargo that is otherwise liable to confiscation'.[119] This issue might have been debatable in the middle of the eighteenth century, as we have seen, but Scott had no doubt that British merchants could not trade with the enemy aboard neutral vessels.[120] Since this was not an issue in the case before him, it is clear that Scott was delivering a message, in giant capital letters, to British merchants inclined to continue the well-established trade with the nations of northern and western Europe. The Glasgow merchants in this case, and any other merchants who might care to listen, were clearly informed that without a licence they could not continue trading with the enemy. Economic justifications might in some cases sway Scott, but here the needs of the government

---

[118] Scott, among other cases, mentioned the *Deer Garden* (*Holmstrom*) (1747), H.S.P. Lee Cases discussed above at pp. 126–7 and the *Bella Guidita* (*Lalli*) (Lords, 1785), Nicholl's Notebook, 1781–92, No. 94, P.R.O. HCA 30/464, discussed above at fn. 75.

[119] *Hoop* (*Cornelis*) (1799), 1 Rob. 217. Scott referred to Lord Mansfield's opinion in *Gist v. Mason* (1786), 1 T.R. 88. The case involved an effort by an insurer to defend against a suit for recovery under an insurance policy on the ground that the policy was illegal since it allowed recovery for trading with the enemy. Mansfield at trial had directed a verdict for the plaintiff on the ground that the contract was not illegal on its face. Mansfield, on motion for a new trial, had commented that 'By the maritime law, trading with an enemy is cause of confiscation in a subject, provided he is taken in the act; but this does not extend to a neutral vessel', a comment with which Scott obviously strongly disagreed.

[120] See above, p. 129.

at war obviously prevailed. He clearly had little use for the merchants who would try to make a profit even at the price of assisting the enemy if the government had not granted a licence for such trade.

When Scott considered a case of a British merchant who had shipped a cargo from London to Emden, which was then neutral, for transshipment overland to Amsterdam, then in enemy hands, he again applied the principle that 'a subject cannot trade with the enemy, without the special licence of government'.[121] Scott here refused to consider questions of commercial policy which the claimants had raised. The merchant, Scott said, could not argue that such trade was convenient and therefore it was legal.

Of course, a British national resident abroad when war began was allowed some time to withdraw his property. But a British merchant, resident in Holland during the war who continued to export to Britain, took on the character of a Dutch merchant. Scott showed no favoritism to British merchants. 'An *Englishman* residing and trading in *Holland* is just as much a *Dutch* merchant as a *Swede* or a *Dane* would be.'[122] But if the British subject had remained in Holland only because detained by French force, his property would be restored as British.[123]

A merchant might have a dual nationality. 'A man may have mercantile concerns in two countries, and if he acts as a merchant of both, he must be liable to be considered as a subject of both, with regard to the transactions originating respectively in those countries.'[124] Although his predecessor had doubts on the point,

---

[121] *Jonge Pieter (Musterdt)* (1801), 4 Rob. 79. In a case heard by the Lords Commissioners, in which Scott sat as one of the appellate judges, the Lords Commissioners held that a British merchant had traded with the enemy even though he had unloaded the cargo he had carried onto lighters outside the enemy port for transshipment into the port. The Lords refused to take into account the policy reasons behind different forms of trading with the enemy. All trade with the enemy was illegal. *Chesterfield (Brooks)* (1804), Nicholl's Notes of Prize Appeals, 88, P.R.O. HCA 30/466.

[122] *Citto (Fehndrick)* (1800), 3 Rob. 38, 41. If the British merchant could corroborate his claim that he was returning to Britain, he would be treated as British. *Montreal (Gardiner)* (1808), unpublished, Bod. Lib., Monk Bretton Dep. 4.

[123] *Ocean (Harmsen)* (1804), 4 Rob. 90, 91. In *Doornhaag* (n.d.), 5 Rob. 91, 92, Scott gave advice to British merchants caught in such a situation: 'In such cases it would be adviseable for persons so situated, on their actual removal, to make application to government for a special pass, rather than to hazard valuable property, to the effect of a mere previous intention to remove, dubious as that intention may frequently appear under the circumstances that prevent it from being carried into execution.'

[124] *Jonge Klassina (Bol)* (1804), 5 Rob. 297, 302.

Scott explicitly stated that it was not necessary for a merchant to have a fixed commercial establishment in a country to make him a merchant of that nation. How much commercial business in this country is carried on in coffee houses, Scott asked. 'If he is there himself, and acts as a merchant of that place, it is sufficient.'[125]

Occasionally Scott relented a bit and found a basis for restoring the property of a British merchant trading from an enemy country. A British subject had been resident in Spain before war with that country began, though it was not clear that he was there as a merchant. Before the war he had purchased a quantity of wines to supply the British fleet. He left Spain when war broke out and three years later arranged the shipment of the wines. Although he had obtained no licence for this shipment, Scott said that the government would have been willing to grant one. 'The circumstances of this case may be taken as virtually amounting to a licence; inasmuch, as if a licence had been applied for, it must have been granted.'[126] A 'virtual' licence seems extraordinary when one considers Scott's accustomed interpretation of the licence requirements.

Generally Scott interpreted the licence requirement strictly. When a merchant, with a licence to import from Holland, also exported property to Holland, Scott condemned the cargo. 'If trade with the enemy is generally unlawful, it is not in the power of this Court to admit it, beyond the degree which is fairly described in the terms of the licence.'[127] No virtual licence here. A licence obtained to ship certain articles could not be used to ship others.[128] A licence for importation of a cargo aboard a neutral ship would not protect a cargo aboard a British ship.[129] A licence, of course, had to be granted by a proper authority, which did not include the lord lieutenant of Ireland.[130]

Where a licence had been obtained to import Spanish wool, Scott

---

[125] *Ibid.*, 303.

[126] *Madonna Delle Gracie (Copenzia)* (1802), 4 Rob. 195, 198. In *Juffrow Catharina (Hansen)* (1804), 5 Rob. 141, Scott allowed the importation of lace from France without a licence, because of the particular characteristics of the lace trade.

[127] *Jonge Klassina (Bol)* (1804), 5 Rob. 297, 301. The Lords Commissioners also interpreted licences strictly. They refused to give a licence a retroactive effect where the British merchants, without knowing their property had already been captured, obtained a licence to trade with the enemy. *Hoop (Bakken)* (1805), Nicholl's Notes of Prize Appeals, 93, P.R.O. HCA 30/466.

[128] *Vriendschap (Goverts)* (1801), 4 Rob. 96, 100.

[129] *Jonge Arend (Knowles)* (1803), 5 Rob. 14.

[130] *Charlotta (Dupleix)* (1814), 1 Dod. 387, 391.

felt confident that it had not been intended to permit the importation of Spanish wool still owned by Spaniards. To remove all doubt, Scott consulted with the Privy Council and was informed that the licence could not be interpreted 'to permit the trade in the unlimited manner contended for by the claimants'.[131] Scott's willingness to discuss with the Council a case he had under advisement gives a clear indication of his close relationship with the government and his deep commitment to follow its lead.

Where the Council had ordered that Spanish wool, consigned to British merchants, should be restored forthwith to the consignees, Scott interpreted the Order strictly. It had not been intended to protect a cargo of Spanish wool shipped to Emden, even though the claimants asserted that the ultimate, albeit circuitous, destination was Britain. 'It is my duty', Scott said, 'to consider only, whether the words of the order can be supposed to embrace such a case; and my opinion is, that they cannot.'[132]

Where a British ship had allegedly been sold to a neutral at Emden, but continued to sail, with its old master, between Guernsey and Amsterdam, Scott refused to treat it as a neutral ship. 'The Court has often had occasion to observe', Scott said, 'that where a ship, asserted to have been transferred, is continued under the former agency and in the former habits of trade, not all the swearing in the world will convince it that it is a genuine transaction.'[133] This rule, which he applied to enemy ships transferred to a neutral, he also applied here to British vessels.

Scott had occasion to discuss the effect of a surrender or capitulation of a colony on the property of the inhabitants who had surrendered. After the inhabitants of the Cape of Good Hope had surrendered to the British, some merchants claimed a ship which had

---

[131] *Beurse van Koningsberg (Shemills)* (1800), 2 Rob. 169, 173. Scott was referring to a letter from Lord Liverpool, dated March 6, 1800, from the Office of Trade, in which Liverpool conveyed the opinion of the entire Privy Council in response to Scott's inquiry. Liverpool wrote: 'We all agree, that the King's Licence was never meant to protect Enemies' Property; and that the sole Object of it, was to permit the Importation of Spanish Wool, brought into this Country, on British Account, in ships belonging to subjects in Amity with His Majesty; If the Wool had been Neutral Property, it wanted no such Protection. The Question was very much discussed . . . I beg you would believe that I never entertained an Idea, that you had any Disposition to embarrass the Commerce of this Country, in the Discharge of your official Duty. Brit. Lib., Add. MS 38,311, fo. 52b.

[132] *Flora (Klein)* (1804), 6 Rob. 3, 10.

[133] *Omnibus (Tennes)* (1805), 6 Rob. 71. See also *Odin (Hals)* (1799), 1 Rob. 248.

previously sailed while still Dutch property. The inhabitants, who, as a result of the capitulation, had become British subjects, claimed the ship as British property. Scott relied entirely on a precedent from the Lords Commissioners. 'I am of opinion that this is a decided case on the authority of the Supreme Court in *The Negotie en Zevaart*: I remember that case well, having been junior counsel in it, and having attended much to it; as there was much difference of opinion respecting it in the court below.'[134] Scott was bound, he said, by the *dictum* of Lord Camden in that case, that a Dutch ship could not change its national character in transit.[135] Since in the present case the ship was captured before it returned to the Cape, it continued to be Dutch property and was therefore lawful prize.

In a later case Scott greatly expanded this principle of no change of national character while property was in transit. Of course, Scott knew well that in time of peace merchants could freely transfer property while it was in transit and the transfer would be regarded as perfectly valid. The principle, which Scott derived from Lord Camden, applied in time of war. It would be a fraud on belligerent rights to allow merchants to change the property ownership, and therefore the nationality, of a ship or cargo while it was on the high seas. Scott restated this principle, clarified the policy reasons behind it and expanded it by applying it to a case of transfer of property in transit in contemplation of war.

Supposing the fact to be established, that it is a sale under an admitted necessity, arising from a certain expectation of war; that it is a sale of goods not in the possession of the seller, and in a state where they could not, during war, be legally transferred, on account of the fraud on Belligerent rights; – I cannot but think that the same fraud is committed against the Belligerent, not indeed as an actual Belligerent, but as one who was, in the clear expectation of both the contracting parties, likely to become a Belligerent, before the arrival of the property, which is made the subject of their agreement.[136]

Belligerent rights, of course, took on a particular meaning when viewed through British eyes.

Finally, in a somewhat related case, Scott applied what he con-

---

[134] *Danckebaar Africaan (Smit)* (1798), 1 Rob. 107, 111. The *Negotie en Zevaart (Stechman)* (Lords, 1782), P.R.O. HCA 45/9, fo. 402, is cited above at fn. 41.

[135] *Danckebaar Africaan (Smit)* (1798), 1 Rob. 112. See also *Herstelder (Koe)* (1799), 1 Rob. 114, and *Carl Walter (Schmidt)* (1802), 4 Rob. 207.

[136] *Jan Frederick (Bloedorne)* (1804), 5 Rob. 128, 133.

sidered settled legal principles in condemning the property of an ally which had been engaged in trading with the enemy. He relied on a precedent which he remembered well.

I think the law is perfectly clear; I have reason to remember the whole of that case; it was a case argued by myself, and one which went up to the Lords upon my advice. I had an opportunity of hearing the deliberation of the Lords upon it, and I know, that it was decided on the ground, that during a conjoint war, no subject of one belligerent can trade with the enemy, without being liable to a forfeiture of his property engaged in such a trade, in the Courts of the ally.[137]

Scott recalled that the Lords' rationale for condemning the property of an ally trading with the enemy was economic. '[I]t would place this country in a very disadvantageous situation indeed, if the subjects of an ally in war might trade with the enemy, whilst the property of *British* subjects so employed was subject to confiscation'.[138] British merchants obviously should not be forced to lose the profitable trade with the enemy only to see it fall into the hands of allied merchants.

Elsewhere, however, Scott gave a military justification for condemning the property of allies caught trading with the enemy.

Between [allies] it must be taken as an implied, if not an express contract, that one state shall not do any thing to defeat the general object. If one state admits its subjects to carry on an uninterrupted trade with the enemy, the consequence may be that it will supply that aid and *comfort* to the enemy . . . which may be very injurious to the prosecution of the common cause, and the interests of its Ally.[139]

Even though the allied nation gave its merchant a licence to trade with the enemy, such a licence could not protect the merchant's property from capture by the British if it were contraband.[140]

[137] *Nayade (Mertz)* (1802), 4 Rob. 251. Scott was referring to *Enigheid (Bogeberg)* (1795), P.R.O. HCA 45/28, fo. 272.
[138] *Nayade (Mertz)* (1802), 4 Rob. 251, 254.
[139] *Neptunus (Bachman)* (1807), 6 Rob. 403, 406. Italics in the original.
[140] *Mentor (Ligunberg)* (1806), unpublished, Arnold's Notebook, 1805–6, P.R.O. HCA 30/473.

5

PRIZE LAW – A SURVEY

The brevity of the treatment of the various important subjects in this chapter should not obscure the fact that the admiralty court dealt with each in at least as much detail as it dealt with the issues of nationality discussed in the last chapter.

NEUTRAL RIGHTS AND DUTIES – A GENERAL OVERVIEW

The high seas in time of war served two partially irreconcilable functions. As in peace, they served as the broad, free highways for the world's commerce. In wartime, however, the high seas became the preferred battle fields for the dominant naval power. Maritime warfare, therefore, became the flash point for claims of neutral rights. Neutrals asserted the right to carry on their commerce with the rest of the world, undisturbed by the warfare in which they were not parties and in which they sought to remain friendly to all belligerents.

Most of the law of maritime warfare after the time of Grotius was an attempt to balance the legitimate interests of the belligerent nations against the rights of non-belligerents or neutrals. Blockade, contraband and colonial trade are merely specific examples of this tension between neutral rights and neutral duties on the one hand, and the rights of the belligerents on the other. This law of maritime warfare had evolved within the context of the law of nations, which had not sharply distinguished between the law and the morality of international relations. Scott, who certainly knew the often vague and conflicting writings on the law of nations as well as anyone in England, had good reasons to look first to the settled precedents of the English prize courts for clearer guidance in deciding cases.[1]

---

[1] G. Best, *Humanity in warfare* (New York, 1980), 67–74, 100–8.

Background

Neutral rights

Belligerents could not commit acts of war within neutral territories. This proposition had gained wide acceptance throughout Europe by the end of the eighteenth century. In the context of maritime warfare this well-settled rule prevented the capture of enemy ships within the confines of neutral territorial waters. Territorial waters had come to mean those within the range of cannon-shot from the shore, which Scott, as counsel, contended meant one mile.[2] Although neutrals had an obligation to allow belligerents to use their ports for repairs or supplies, the warring nations could not enter these neutral waters to make captures. Upon complaint of the neutral whose waters had been violated, the offending nation had an obligation to punish the violators and declare the capture itself illegal. Scott, in an opinion as counsel, even contended that the English admiralty court did not have jurisdiction over a capture made within territorial waters. Scott's unusual argument that the violation of neutral waters created a jurisdictional limit, apparently had no solid basis. The Lords Commissioners for Prize Appeals in 1760 had assumed jurisdiction and restored a Dutch ship which would have been liable to seizure for engaging in French colonial trade. It was restored because it had been attacked and seized within a Spanish colonial port.[3]

The neutral nations had for centuries striven to assure the right to trade freely in time of war. Neutral ships carrying neutral cargo to neutral ports clearly were beyond the range of legitimate belligerent captures. Enemy ships with enemy cargo, on the other hand, could certainly be captured as lawful prize. The basic rule was clear: a nation could seize the property of its enemy but should respect the property of a neutral. The issues became far more unsettled when the neutral ships carried enemy cargo or enemy ships carried neutral

---

[2] In the case of the *Etrusco* (Lords, 1795), Scott had stated that the limits of a territory extended to the limits of cannon-shot, i.e. a mile from the coast. He was there discussing the territorial limits of an ally (Ostend) rather than of a neutral, but the limits should be the same. Scott did not indicate whether he meant a nautical mile or a statute mile. Nicholl's Notes of Prize Appeals, 3–4, P.R.O. HCA 30/466.

[3] P. C. Jessup and F. Deak, *Neutrality: its history, economics and law*, I: *Origins* (4 vols., New York, 1935–6), 249–56. See also *Fortuyn* (Lords, 1760), Burrell, 175. Perhaps jurisdiction was limited to the determination of the violation of neutral waters. R.A., Simpson MS 119.

cargo.

Although all writers were not in agreement on the point, English legal authorities in the eighteenth century stated the English understanding of the rule: enemy cargo could be taken as lawful prize, even though carried on a neutral ship, whereas noncontraband neutral cargo had to be restored to the owners, even if it was captured aboard an enemy ship. The English contended that these simple rules, long the subject of dispute during various European wars, could be modified only by treaty between two nations. Under such treaty agreements, if one of the signatory nations remained neutral while the other was at war, the neutral could carry enemy goods and the belligerent signatory could not lawfully make a prize of these enemy cargoes. Stated more concisely, the neutral rallying cry of 'free ships, free goods' was true, according to English authorities, only if a treaty between two parties had so provided.[4]

One can easily perceive the mercantilist rationale for the ordinary rule that enemy goods could be seized when carried on neutral vessels while neutral goods carried aboard enemy vessels were not subject to seizure. As long as the enemy could not export its own products, it would be economically weakened. Destruction of the enemy's export trade remained a primary objective of war in this mercantilist context.

---

[4] The English rule was stated with a decisive ring of authority in *Report of the law officers as to the action of Frederick II in withholding payment of interest on the Silesian loan* ... (1753): 'When two powers are at war, they have a right to make prizes of ships, goods, and effects of each other upon the high seas; whatever is the property of the enemy may be acquired by capture at sea; but the property of a friend cannot be taken, provided he observed his neutrality. Hence the law of nations has established: That the goods of an enemy on board the ship of a friend may be taken. That the lawful goods of a friend on board the ship of an enemy ought to be restored ... Though the law of nations be the general rule, yet it may, by mutual agreement between the two powers, be varied or departed from; and where there is an alteration or exception introduced by particular treaties, that is the law between the parties to the treaty; and the law of nations only governs so far as it is not derogated from by the treaty ... Particular treaties ... have inverted the rule of the law of nations, and by agreement declared the goods of a friend on board the ship of an enemy to be prize, and the goods of an enemy on board the ship of a friend to be free.' This *Report of the law officers* was composed primarily by Sir George Lee, King's Advocate, and Sir William Murray, later Lord Mansfield, then Solicitor General. It was also signed by Sir Dudley Ryder, Attorney General, and Dr George Paul, Admiralty Advocate. The *Report* is reprinted in *Documents relating to law and custom of the sea* (2 vols., n.p., 1915), ed. R. G. Marsden, II, 348–74. The passages quoted are from 350 to 354. See also Jessup and Deak, *Origins*, 124–52, and R.A., Simpson MS 118, 121, 123, 142, 213, 259–60, 327.

If the enemy, on the other hand, should be foolish enough to import more neutral goods than it could export of its own, this also, in the mercantilist theory, would lead to its ruin.[5]

Neutral duties

The admiralty court clearly took it for granted that a neutral vessel had the duty to submit to a visit and search by a belligerent. Only by this procedure could unnecessary use of force be avoided. In 1779 the admiralty court spoke of the correlative duties of captors and neutrals: 'It is as much the duty and interest of every party who stops a neutral ship, to demand a sight of a passport, as it is the duty and interest of a neutral to produce it whensoever and wheresoever duly required.'[6] Various seventeenth-century treaties to which England was a party had explicitly provided for this right of visit and search. The treaty provisions sought more to control the manner in which the right was exercised than to establish the right of visit and search, which was largely unquestioned. Neutrals generally acknowledged the legitimacy of this right of visit and search as long as the search was confined to a thorough perusal of the ship's papers.[7] If the arrested ship resisted or sought to flee or destroyed its papers, this defensive action created a presumption that the ship was a lawful prize.[8]

Belligerents certainly expected neutrals not to favor or assist their enemy by engaging in such fraudulent practices as concealing the true enemy ownership of a ship or cargo (coloring or covering enemy property, as it was called). Neutrals could continue to engage in maritime commerce as long as they could balance on this tightrope by not appearing to side with one belligerent. Unneutral conduct might lead to the condemnation of the ship or cargo, or at least to the admiralty court's decree that there was a just cause for the capture. Such a decree deprived the neutral of damages or costs due to the

---

[5] R. Pares, *Colonial blockade and neutral rights 1739–1763* (Oxford, 1938), 172.

[6] *Juffrow Gerarda* (1779), Hay & M. 269.

[7] Jessup and Deak, *Origins*, 159–70; C. Kulsrud, *Maritime neutrality to 1780* (Boston, 1936), 156–202. A manuscript, apparently drawn up in the seventeenth century, compiled the various treaty provisions to which England was a party concerning the right of visit and search. Brit. Lib., Sloane MS 2680, fos. 41–4.

[8] Jessup and Deak, *Origins*, 226–7. See also *Mentor* (1789), Arnold's Notebook, 1788–9, P.R.O. HCA 30/470. Scott appeared as counsel and argued that all ships were obliged to submit to search.

illegal capture.[9]

Scott, as King's Advocate, argued in 1795 that the purchase of an enemy ship in France during wartime by a neutral should be held invalid, and therefore the ship should be regarded as enemy property. Belligerents had good reason to fear fraudulent conveyances with the enemy retaining effective ownership. The French, Scott stated, held that a neutral could not validly purchase a ship from the enemy after hostilities had begun. The same rule should be applied by the English. The Lords Commissioners, following an earlier precedent, ordered the neutral purchaser to provide further proof that this had been a *bona fide* neutral purchase.[10] Thus the mere purchase of a vessel from the enemy was not in itself unneutral conduct.

Scott as judge

Neutral rights
Scott had ample opportunity to consider and apply the principle of a neutral's right to territorial integrity. The *Twee Gebroeders* involved the capture of four Dutch ships taken in the Western Eems, near Gronigen Watt, which was outside neutral territory. But the capture had been made by boats sent from an English naval vessel lying in the Eastern Eems within three miles of Prussian territory which was neutral. Although the British captors insisted that the naval vessel had committed no violence within the neutral territory and had merely sent its boats out of the neutral territory to make the capture, Scott thought otherwise.

But that is a doctrine that goes a great deal too far; I am of opinion, that no

---

[9] *Drie Gebroeders* (1746); *Goede Wind (Juriann)* (1748); *Goode Parl (Groot)* (1747), H.S.P. Lee Cases. Lee in 1749 compiled a list of twenty-one precedents concerning the award of costs and damages against the captors because there had been no just cause of seizure. H.S.P. Lee Cases. In *Jungfre Marie* (1779), Hay & M. 273, the court discussed the lenient practice of the British admiralty court which did not condemn neutral vessels for having false or defective papers, but merely decreed just cause of seizure in favor of the captors.

In *Polly (Smith)* (Lords, 1798), the Lords Commissioners, because of the fraudulent practices of the master, to which the neutral owner was not privy, restored the property but awarded costs against the neutral claimant. Nicholl's Notes of Prize Appeals, 34, P.R.O. HCA 30/466. The Lords also used the penalty of forfeiture of freight as a sanction for fraudulent practices by neutrals. *Sally (Griffith)* (1795), Nicholl's Notes of Prize Appeals, 13, P.R.O. HCA 30/466.

[10] *Handlesman* (1795), Nicholl's Notes of Prize Appeals, 7, P.R.O. HCA 30/466.

use, of a neutral territory, for the purposes of war, is to be permitted; I do not say *remote* uses, such as procuring provisions and refreshments, and acts of that nature which the law of nations universally tolerates; but that, no *proximate* acts of war are in any manner to be allowed to originate on neutral grounds; and I cannot but think, that such an act as this, that a ship should station herself on neutral territory, and send out her boats on hostile enterprizes, is an act of hostility much too immediate to be permitted.[11]

No act of war, Scott held, could commence within neutral territorial waters, even though it was completed on the high seas. Scott restored the enemy vessels to their owners and refused to allow the English captors costs or damages for bringing in enemy ships.[12] One dimension of Scott's office was to assure that the British naval vessels acted in accordance with the accepted rules of maritime warfare. The law of nations, as Scott understood it, overrode the interest of the British naval officers and crew who had captured the vessel.

Where another capture took place in these same waters, Scott had to determine two different issues, one largely factual and the other legal. First, he considered sea charts and the testimony of a buoy-keeper and concluded that the site of the capture was not part of Prussian (neutral) territory. Secondly, he relied on Grotius and Vattel to conclude that belligerent ships had a right of innocent passage through neutral waters and such a peaceful use of neutral waters did not vitiate a subsequent capture. '[T]he act of inoffensively passing over such portions of water, without any violence committed there, is not considered as any violation of territory belonging to a neutral state – permission is not usually required; such waters are considered as the common thoroughfare of nations.'[13]

When neutral territorial waters had been violated, Scott was clear as to the consequences. 'When the fact is established, it overrules every other consideration. The capture is done away; the property must be restored, notwithstanding that it may actually belong to the enemy; and if the captor should appear to have erred wilfully, and not merely through ignorance, he would be subject to farther punishment.'[14] Scott, as judge, never questioned the jurisdiction of the admiralty court to determine such issues.

The right of neutrals to have their territorial waters respected was the essential basis of sovereignty of any nation. Necessarily this right

---

[11] *Twee Gebroeders* (*Alberts*) (1800), 3 Rob. 162, 164. Italics in the original.
[12] *Ibid.*, 166.
[13] *Twee Gebroeders* (*Northolt*) (1801), 3 Rob. 336, 352.
[14] *Vrow Anna Catharina* (*Mahts*) (1803), 5 Rob. 15, 16.

of territorial integrity created an exception carved out of the general belligerent right to seize its enemy's property wherever found. In 1795, as already mentioned, Scott, as counsel, had interpreted the seaward territorial limits of a country to be the limits of cannon-shot, which he then interpreted as one mile from the shore. As judge, Scott went further, holding that 'The utmost extent which is given to this immunity, even in books, is confined to three *English* miles.'[15] This three mile limit Scott considered to be the recognized distance that a cannon could be fired from shore.[16] Scott's statement helped establish this three mile limit as the accepted standard for territorial waters for the next 150 years.

Other belligerents did not have the right to object to a capture on the ground that it had been made in neutral waters. Only the neutral had the right to challenge violence committed within its jurisdiction.[17] If the neutral did not see fit to vindicate its rights, the enemy, whose property was captured within the neutral's waters, was not competent to make the plea.[18]

The right of neutral territorial integrity in a quite different sense was involved in the case of the *Flad Oyen*.[19] In this case Scott demonstrated his commitment to follow the principles of the law of nations when these principles had been clearly stated. He held the French practice of trying prize cases before French consuls in neutral ports violated clear principles of the law of nations, even though Britain had also engaged in similar conduct. The *Flad Oyen* had originally been an English ship which the French had captured and sailed to a neutral port in Norway, where it had been condemned by the French consul there and sold at auction. Scott held that under the law of nations a sentence of condemnation, pronounced by the French consul within neutral territory, had no legal authority to transfer title to a *bona fide* purchaser. Claimant's counsel had argued that the English had taken prize vessels into neutral ports where they had been

[15] *Ibid.*, 17.
[16] *Anna (La Porte)* (1805), 5 Rob. 373, 385c. Thomas Jefferson, the American Secretary of State, had informed the British minister in 1793 that the United States intended to limit its claim to the adjacent sea to three miles. J. M. Raymond and B. J. Frischolz, 'Lawyers who established international law in the United States, 1776–1914', *American Journal of International Law*, 76 (1982), 802, 807.
[17] *Eliza Ann and others* (1813), 1 Dod. 244.
[18] *Purissima Conception (Ancres)* (1805), 6 Rob. 45, 47; *Jonge Josias (Jurgensen)* (1809), Edw. 128, 130; see also *Topaz* (Lords, 1811), Nicholl's Notes of Prize Appeals, 126, P.R.O. HCA 30/466.
[19] *Flad Oyen (Martenson)* (1799), 1 Rob. 135.

condemned, by the High Court of Admiralty in England it was true, but nonetheless irregularly, since the prize was not before the court in England. The prize court properly proceeded only *in rem*. Scott refused to allow the irregular and perhaps illegal practice of the English to justify an even more illegal practice of the French. The law of nations, he insisted, was not based on mere speculative general principles. To justify this novel practice '[I]t must be shewn that it is conformable to the usage and practice of nations.' Belligerents were bound to conform their practices to 'those modes which the common practice of mankind has employed, and to relinquish those which the same practice has not brought within the ordinary exercise of war'. Scott continued:

Now, it having been the constant usage, that the tribunals of the law of nations in these matters shall exercise their functions within the belligerent country; if it was proved to me in the clearest manner, that on mere general theory such a tribunal might act in the neutral country; I must take my stand on the ancient and universal practice of mankind; and say that as far as that practice has gone, I am willing to go; and where it has thought proper to stop, there I must stop likewise. . . Here a person, utterly naked of all authority except over the subjects of his own country, and possessing that merely by the indulgence of the country in which he resides, pretends to exercise a jurisdiction in a matter in which the subjects of many other States may be concerned. No such authority was ever conceded by any country to a foreign agent of any description residing within it: and least of all could such an authority be conceded in the matter of prize of war – a matter over which a neutral country has no cognizance whatever, except in the single case of an infringement of its own territory.[20]

If the ports of Norway were made seats of French prize courts, Scott concluded, the sea adjacent to Norway would become the theater of French hostilities. Few cases show more clearly that Scott did rely on the norms of the law of nations when they provided long-standing, consistently applied principles. His statement of the principles of the law of nations added clarity and precision. Scott's conclusion here, however, coincided with what he obviously perceived to be the best interest of Great Britain as a belligerent (British practice to the contrary notwithstanding).

Although the list is understandably short, Scott did consider other rights of neutrals. He insisted that neutrals had the right to have a prompt adjudication of any capture made of their property.[21]

[20] *Ibid.*, 140, 144.
[21] *Madonna del Burso* (*Antonopoli*) (1802), 4 Rob. 169, 171.

'Grievous would be the injury to neutral trade, and highly disgraceful to the honour of our country, if captors could bring in ships at their own fancy, and detain them any length of time, without bringing the matter to the cognizance of a Court of Justice.'[22] This adjudication should take place at a convenient British port; prizes should not be brought across the Atlantic without serious reason.[23]

One penalty for undue delay was an award of damages. Scott ordered the British government to pay damages, in the form of demurrage, for such a delay in bringing a capture to adjudication where the government, not the captors, was to blame for the delay.[24]

Neutrals also had a right, which the admiralty court would enforce, to have their crews protected from mistreatment at the hands of the captors. Only such restraint as was necessary could be employed by the captors. Thus, unnecessarily placing a captured neutral crew in irons called for an award of damages against the captors, to be distributed to the crew members who had been mistreated.[25]

Neutral duties

Scott had every reason to employ his best diplomatic tact in the case of the *Maria*.[26] Just at the time Scott was appointed admiralty judge in 1798, the Swedish and Danish governments, frustrated at the highhanded treatment of their merchant vessels by the British and to some extent the French navies, asserted that merchant ships under convoy were free from the belligerent right of visit and search. Commanders of the convoying frigates were ordered to assure any belligerent that the merchant ships carried no contraband. These neutrals insisted the commander's word should be accepted by a belligerent as conclusive evidence of the innocence of the cargo. The Swedish and Danish commanders had orders to resist visit and search with force if necessary.

This marked a turn of events which the British government could not accept. The right of visit and search, well established in European maritime practice, lay at the core of the British view of its own rights as a belligerent. In no other manner short of war against all neutral

---

[22] *St. Juan Baptista and La Purissima Conception* (1803), 5 Rob. 33, 38.
[23] *Anna (La Porte)* (1805), 5 Rob. 373, 384.
[24] *Zacheman (Kraeplien)* (1804), 5 Rob. 152, 154.
[25] *St. Juan Baptista and La Purissima Conception* (1803), 5 Rob. 33, 40.
[26] *Maria (Paulsen)* (1799), 1 Rob. 340. See also W. Phillips and A. Reede, *Neutrality: its history, economics and law*, II: *The Napoleonic period* (4 vols., New York, 1935–6), 94–106.

maritime nations could the British use its superior naval power to prevent the French from supplying its army and navy and to disrupt the French colonial trade and domestic economy. Mere assurances of a neutral commander would never satisfy the British that the self-interested neutral merchant vessels carried no contraband according to the British definitions of contraband.

In the case of the *Maria* a large number of Swedish merchant ships had sailed under convoy of a Swedish frigate with instructions to resist by force any attempt to visit or search the vessels. A British squadron, with overwhelming superior force, managed to bring in the vessels without actual hostilities, although it just barely prevented an imprudent resort to force by the Swedish commander. Sweden had indeed cast down a gauntlet which the British could hardly ignore. Basic military policies were at issue. Armed resistance to visit and search at sea would force Britain to choose between ever-widening hostilities or losing effective control of the enemy's maritime commerce.

Scott could not have expounded the policy of the British government more accurately if he had been writing as Foreign Secretary. The implicit policy of British naval warfare became the justification for the rule of the law of nations. Scott took pains to express his judgment in a fully documented and carefully reasoned opinion. He began the judgment in the case of the *Maria* with a stock diplomatic assurance, that the admiralty court sat as a court of the law of nations applying a supranational body of law even-handedly to belligerent and neutral alike.[27] After summarizing the facts he stated the legal principles and their *raison d'être* with definitive clarity. Once again, he followed the law and practice of nations, but clearly this practice furthered British naval interests. Scott here also implicitly rejected the neutrals' contention that neutral ships (free ships) should under the law of nations provide protection for enemy cargoes (make free goods). He followed the English doctrine that enemy goods aboard neutral ships, absent a treaty, were subject to capture. Scott's insistence on belligerent rights exactly suited the needs of a belligerent like Britain with a dominant naval force. He said:

[T]he right of visiting and searching merchant-ships upon the high seas,

---

[27] *Maria (Paulsen)* (1799), 1 Rob. 340, 350. For earlier assurances of this type, see Jessup and Deak, *Origins*, 210; J. Marriott, *The case of the Dutch ships considered*, 3rd edn (London, 1769), 43.

whatever be the ships, whatever be the cargoes, whatever be the destinations, is an incontestible right of the lawfully commissioned cruisers of a belligerent nation. I say, be the ships, the cargoes, and the destinations what they may, because, till they are visited and searched, it does not appear what the ships, or the cargoes, or the destinations are; and it is for the purpose of ascertaining these points that the necessity of this right of visitation and search exists. This right is so clear in principle, that no man can deny it who admits the legality of maritime capture; because if you are not at liberty to ascertain by sufficient inquiry whether there is property that can legally be captured, it is impossible to capture. Even those who contend for the inadmissible rule, that *free ships make free goods*, must admit the exercise of this right at least for the purpose of ascertaining whether the ships are free ships or not. The right is equally clear in practice; for practice is uniform and universal upon the subject. The many *European* treaties which refer to this right, refer to it as pre-existing, and merely regulate the exercise of it. All writers upon the law of nations unanimously acknowledge it, without the exception even of *Hubner* himself, the great champion of neutral privileges.[28]

Scott observed that this right of visitation at sea involved a lawful use of force, to be exercised with as little harshness as possible. But as lawful force it could not be lawfully resisted. As indicated above, Scott accurately stated the widely accepted practice of European nations. After reference to Vattel and the practice of other nations, Scott concluded that the penalty for forceful resistance to visitation was the confiscation of the property withheld from search.[29]

The Lords Commissioners affirmed Scott's judgment of condemnation, but dodged any diplomatic involvement by refusing to state their reasons.[30] Only Scott, of all the judges who considered the case, made the effort to justify the capture of the Swedish vessels as well as the policy behind visitation and search. Continuing the long tradition of civilians as diplomats, Scott at least tried to mollify the neutrals. The Swedish reaction, hardly mollified, can be gauged from a rambling and intemperate rejoinder in a pamphlet written by a Swedish civilian who flatly denied the legal right of belligerents to detain or capture merchant ships belonging to neutral states.[31]

When a second Swedish convoy was brought before the admiralty court for adjudication, Scott delayed hearing the case until the Lords

---

[28] *Maria (Paulsen)* (1799), 1 Rob. 340, 360. Italics in the original.

[29] *Ibid.*, 369. For the eighteenth-century understanding of the right of visit and search, see Jessup and Deak, *Origins*, 159–70, and Kulsrud, *Maritime neutrality*, 156–202.

[30] *Maria (Paulsen)* (Lords, 1802), Nicholl's Notes of Prize Appeals, 65, P.R.O. HCA 30/466.

[31] L. M. Philipson, *An examination of the judgment of the British High Court of Admiralty on the capture of a Swedish convoy* (Stockholm, 1800), 31.

Commissioners had affirmed the court's judgment in the case of the
Maria and until diplomatic negotiations were complete. Although the
Lords had given no reasons for their affirmance, Scott deduced that
they had agreed that the penalty for resistance to search was confiscation and that the defense of obeying orders of a sovereign afforded no
protection.[32] Scott repeatedly professed to apply the law of nations
where it was clear, but he never lost sight of the diplomatic realities
and the possible consequences of his judgments in important cases
involving sensitive neutral rights.

Clearly this right of visitation and search implied the right to bring
in ships on suspicion that they would be condemned as prize. If a
neutral master tried to rescue his property from capture by a belligerent, he would violate a duty imposed by the law of nations to submit to
a judicial inquiry as to the legality of the capture.[33] A ship which tried
to escape capture fell under a strong suspicion of being a legal prize.
As Scott said, in an unreported opinion, the ship trusted to her heels
rather than to the evidence.[34] The right of search also implied the
duty of a neutral master to turn over all his papers to the captors.[35]

This duty to submit to visitation and search was only a specific
example of the broader, more basic obligation of neutrals, not to assist
one belligerent at the expense of the other. Scott declared that the
'grand fundamental duty of neutrality' was 'not to relieve the distres-
ses of one belligerent, to the prejudice of another'.[36] Or, as Scott said
in another case where he found grossly fraudulent conduct on the part
of the neutrals, 'I wish neutrals to understand, that if they mean to
avail themselves of the rights of neutrals, they must conduct themselves as such.'[37] He said he could not shut his eyes to what happened
in the real world: as the war progressed neutrals could obtain ever
higher prices to conceal, with increasing ingenuity, the true ownership of property by the enemy.

---

[32] *Elsabe (Maas)* (1803), 4 Rob. 408, 412. In a subsequent case involving some of the
ships taken in this second convoy, Scott, after a full discussion of the constitutional
dimensions of prize law, determined that the Crown had the power to release
captured property to the owners prior to adjudication, notwithstanding the opposition of the captors. *Elsebe (sic) (Maas)* (1804), 5 Rob. 173.
[33] *Catharina Elizabeth (Le Grange)* (1804), 5 Rob. 232. See also *Topaz (Nicoll)*
(Lords, 1811), 2 Acton 21.
[34] *Ida (Pawson)* (1810), Bod. Lib., 5 Monk Bretton Dep., 169.
[35] *Concordia (Wise)* (1798), 1 Rob. 119.
[36] *Rendsborg (Nyberg)* (1802), 4 Rob. 121, 126. Scott used italics which have been
omitted here.
[37] *Rosalie and Betty (Gebhadt)* (1800), 2 Rob. 343, 359.

When Scott perceived in the prize ship's papers and the sworn interrogatories of its officers an intricate pattern of deceit, he did not hesitate to condemn the ship and cargo without allowing the neutral claimants to provide further proof of their ownership.

> The régular penalty of such a proceeding must be confiscation; for it is a rule of this Court, which I shall ever hold, till I am better instructed by the superior Court, that if a neutral will weave a web of fraud of this sort, this Court will not take the trouble of picking out the threads for him, in order to distinguish the sound from the unsound; if he is detected in fraud he will be involved *in toto*.[38]

Scott's ever-suspicious eye often detected fraud through many veils of neutral deceit. His suspicions were at times strongly confirmed, as when he read in a letter found aboard a neutral ship, 'In short, the most artful tricks that can be devised to elude the enquiries of the *English*, must be put in practice; for they must not discover the real destination to *Cayenne*.'[39]

If covering enemy property remained a continuing form of unneutral conduct, it was not the only example. Neutral ship owners risked condemnation if they transported enemy troops, even under duress.[40] A neutral vessel, therefore, could not lawfully transport French troops from a French colony to the mother country. 'Can it be allowed', Scott asked, 'that neutral vessels shall be at liberty to step in and make themselves a vehicle for the liberation of such person, whom the chance of war has made, in some measure, prisoners in a distant port of their own colonies?'[41]

If transportation of enemy troops was clearly unneutral conduct, a series of cases involving the carriage of foreign dispatches forced Scott to make important distinctions with little guidance from precedent or other authorities. When Scott for the first time had to determine whether neutrals could carry concealed enemy dispatches from the enemy colony, he took the time to discuss and distinguish five precedents. He concluded that a neutral vessel, seized while carrying enemy correspondence must be condemned as 'an aggravated case of active interposition in the service of the enemy'.[42] When the Lords

---

[38] *Eenrom (Fronier)* (1799), 2 Rob. 1, 9.
[39] *Calypso (Speck)* (1799), 2 Rob. 154.
[40] *Carolina (Nordquist)* (1802), 4 Rob. 256, 260.
[41] *Friendship (Collard)* (1807), 6 Rob. 420, 428.
[42] *Atalanta (Klein)* (1808), 6 Rob. 440, 460; see also *Rapid (Fleming)* (1810), Edw. 228.

Commissioners reviewed this judgment, they completely agreed with Scott's judgment and his statement of reasons, as well as his interpretation of the leading precedent.[43]

With no more than some general principles derived from Vattel, Scott held, on the other hand, that a neutral ship could legally carry dispatches from an enemy ambassador resident in a neutral country. This act of carrying messages from an enemy ambassador did not constitute unneutral conduct. Neutrals, Scott said, certainly had the right to receive ambassadors from belligerent states. Ambassadors were, after all, the objects of special protection under the law of nations. Neutrals had the right to preserve relations with all belligerents and one belligerent had no right to conclude that any communication between ambassadors resident in a neutral country and their home government would in any way imply hostility toward other belligerents.[44] Likewise there was no departure from neutrality when a neutral vessel carried dispatches the other way, from an enemy country to its representative in a neutral country.[45]

When the *Drummond* was brought before the court for condemnation, Scott had to decide a case involving both the carriage of enemy refugees, some of whom were apparently military, and the carriage of neutral government dispatches.[46] Since some of the passengers might have been part of the French military seeking passage to France from St Domingo, Scott had clear precedent to condemn the ship. But in the already tense atmosphere, just a year before war with America, Scott also had to determine whether an American merchant ship, carrying communications from the American president to the American minister in Paris, should be protected from capture. He found it strange that such public dispatches should be carried by a common merchant vessel. Furthermore, the dispatches were not produced and the American government had not intervened in the case. Scott first made a diplomatic feint. 'This country makes no pretension to any right of interrupting the communication of the *American* government with its minister; and I should certainly be extremely tender of interposing any difficulties in the way of such a correspondence.'[47] Ultimately, however, he sidestepped the difficult question whether a

[43] *Atalanta* (Lords, 1809), Nicholl's Notes of Prize Appeals, 110, P.R.O. HCA 30/466.
[44] *Caroline (Doah)* (1808), 6 Rob. 461, 467.
[45] *Madison (Frost)* (1810), Edw. 224, 226.
[46] *Drummond (Langdon)* (1811), 1 Dod. 103.
[47] *Ibid.*, 104.

neutral merchant ship, carrying neutral government dispatches, was for that reason protected from capture. He held that only the neutral government could raise such a claim and that the merchant vessel was not competent to set up such a ground for protection. The ship was condemned.[48]

CONTRABAND

Questions of contraband were determined more by reference to governmental policy than by reliance on the diverse and often inscrutable doctrines of the law of nations. A belligerent tended to define contraband as vaguely and broadly as it could without risking expanded hostilities with neutrals whose trade was thereby interrupted. Neutrals, of course, or those who expected to be neutral in future wars, sought definitions of contraband as narrow and definite as possible to assure continued lucrative contracts to carry goods during a war. With this power of defining contraband to suit the contingencies of war, a belligerent had a most effective weapon to combat any aid its enemy might receive from a neutral. Blockades would be unnecessary if contraband were defined broadly enough.

The many seventeenth-century treaties which purported to define contraband were often found to contain little true gold when tested in the cauldron of war. Only a specific and detailed list in a treaty of free goods would offer a neutral any protection when the other party to the treaty felt pressed by the necessities of war. Each nation sought its own perceived national interest in defining contraband in treaties. Its positions varied as the political exigencies, economic conditions and its status as neutral or belligerent changed.[49]

It was easy for Grotius and his successors to discuss contraband in terms of three categories: goods useful only in war, which were clearly prohibited; those of no use in war, which were clearly free, and the ambiguous goods which could have warlike or innocent uses.[50] Neutrals knew perfectly well that arms and ammunition could be

---

[48] *Ibid.*, 105.

[49] Jessup and Deak, *Origins*, 49–104; Kulsrud, *Maritime neutrality*, 261–94; Pares, *Colonial blockade*, 93–8, and H. J. Randall, 'History of contraband of war', *Law Quarterly Review*, 95 (1908), 316–27; 96 (1908), 449–64.

[50] H. Grotius, *De jure belli ac pacis libri tres*, tr. F. Kelsey (Washington, 1925), B. 3, c. 1, s. 5, p. 602.

carried to a belligerent only at the peril of the carrier. Neutral carriers were also fully aware that they could carry all the lace, hides or spices or other purely innocent goods they liked. From such trade they would make small profit indeed. Everyone knew that it was the elastic middle category, the conditional contraband, especially provisions and naval stores, over which belligerents and neutrals would battle. These ambiguous goods offered neutrals their greatest profits. Such goods, which might have a perfectly innocent purpose, but might also be used for military or naval purposes, were generally defined not according to philosophical principles or treaty terms but according to the policies of the belligerent governments.

Eighteenth century

General principles
In 1745 the admiralty court had to determine whether Swedish pitch and tar, aboard a Swedish vessel, could be condemned as contraband because bound to France.[51] Counsel for the Swedish claimants could point to a treaty between Britain and Sweden which did not mention pitch and tar among the contraband goods listed. He could also quote Sir Leoline Jenkins who had written in 1674 that pitch and tar aboard a Swedish vessel, but belonging to British subjects, then neutral, was protected from capture by the Spanish by the terms of the 1667 English–Spanish treaty.[52] Penrice, the admiralty judge, sidestepped the Swedish treaty and stated that pitch and tar were of a mixed nature; they could be used for civilian purposes or for fitting war ships. Even though the treaty declared that all articles not listed as contraband should be considered free, Penrice observed that this treaty had not in recent years been strictly observed. He surmised that there might be some other convention between the nations which the court did not know of. He continued, 'Sovereign Princes at War may declare such & such things to be contraband & after notice to his allies his subjects may certainly seize them.' Penrice discovered the mind of the sovereign, not in the treaty, but in the British government's instructions on captures at sea addressed to naval vessels and privateers. Penrice blinked at the facts in his convenient presumption

---

[51] *Med Gud's Hielp* (*Soderberg*) (1745), H.S.P. Lee Cases.
[52] W. Wynne, *Life of Sir Leoline Jenkins* (2 vols., London, 1724), II, 751.

that the British government usually notified neutrals of the current instructions on contraband goods.[53] On appeal, the Lords Commissioners diplomatically refused to announce their judgment until after the war. At that time they declared that pitch and tar were contraband according to the law of nations and the Swedish treaty.[54]

When a Prussian ship bound for France was captured with a cargo of timber suitable for ship building, Penrice again held it was contraband. He noted that there was no treaty between Prussia and Britain, as though that might have made a difference. He added with a surprising candor, 'Sovereigns have a right to declare what shall be deemed contraband & have always done so.' The king's instructions to British ships defining the limits of legal captures had declared naval stores to be contraband and Penrice presumed that the government had notified foreign courts of the terms of these instructions. Apparently nothing more was required.[55]

Elsewhere Penrice restored a cargo of Danzig timber because it was clearly not suitable for ship building. He again stated that '[T]he Crown may make a declaration what shall be contraband & then any contravener will be liable to confiscation.'[56]

Naval stores

Because of Britain's deep concern to maintain mastery of the seas, it insisted that supplies suitable for building or fitting out naval vessels were contraband when carried to an enemy's port. The underlying duty of neutrals not to aid one belligerent, already discussed, provided the British government with a rule of the law of nations on which to build an argument for condemning naval stores. The admiralty court was much more likely to condemn naval stores as contraband when they were shipped to a port where the enemy's fleet was being built or fitted out. As the court said in condemning a cargo of large timber suitable for ship building, '[This cargo] was going to Brest where Men of War only are built & fitted & timber carried there must be for fitting Men of War ... I think he is aiding our Enemys contrary to the Law of nations which prohibits a neuter from aiding

[53] Pares, *Colonial blockade*, 97–8.
[54] *Med Gud's Hielp (Soderberg)* (Lords, 1750), H.S.P. Lee Cases.
[55] *Twillinge (Kuht)* (1749), H.S.P. Lee Cases.
[56] *Fortune de la Mer (Jeshe)* (1745), H.S.P. Lee Cases. See also *Vergulte Sonn (Redder)* (1748), H.S.P. Lee Cases.

one state ag[ain]st another at War.'[57]

When the neutral's destination was not clearly a port where the enemy's fleet was being fitted out, the court might not condemn the cargo of naval stores, but rather restore on condition that the cargo be sold in England. This doctrine of preemption raised fewer outraged cries from neutrals and still kept the naval stores from the enemy. In the case of the *Providentia* the admiralty court found no mention in the treaty with Russia listing naval stores either as contraband or free. Nonetheless the court restored the ship and cargo to the Russian claimants who had to give security to sell the cargo in England. The court, however, ordered the claimants to pay the captors the costs of the capture and litigation since the captors had just cause to bring in the Russian vessel.[58] The Lords waited more than two years, until the war was over, to determine that the admiralty court had properly restored the ship and cargo, but reversed that part of the decree which required security for sale of the cargo in England and which ordered the Russian claimants to pay costs.[59] With the wartime pressures relieved, the Lords Commissioners could be generous to the neutrals. At that point in time, either the English naval yards had already benefited from the preempted cargo, or had no use for it.

During the American Revolution, the admiralty judge, James Marriott, reaffirmed this right of preemption. Despite the Dutch treaty of 1674 which did not list naval stores as contraband, and which, Marriott observed, the Dutch had used 'so often as almost to wear it out', Marriott ordered the cargo sold for the use of the British government. He relied on precedents and justified preemption as within the spirit of the treaty. 'By decreeing naval stores to be sold to the public', he said, 'and the freight and all incidental charges, as between merchant and merchant, made a part of the price, the carrier has the benefit of the treaty; the great object is his cabotage or carrying trade; give him that, the spirit of the treaty is fulfilled.' Not satisfied with this argument from policy, Marriott commented on the changed circumstances due to England's 'most extraordinary position, never

---

[57] *Juffrow Susanna* (1746), H.S.P. Lee Cases. This case was more fully argued than most, with many citations to precedents and other authorities. The court distinguished four of the precedents in its speech from the bench accompanying the judgment. In *Drie Gesusters (Gosses)* (1747), H.S.P. Lee Cases, the court likewise condemned ship timber because it was carried to an enemy ship building port. See also *Brigitta Catrina (Anderson)* (1748), H.S.P. Lee Cases.
[58] *Providentia (Boysen)* (1747), H.S.P. Lee Cases.
[59] *Providentia (Boysen)* (Lords, 1749), N.Y.P.L. Lee Prize Appeals.

possible in contemplation in the utmost range of the imagination of the contracting parties'.[60] The interests and unanticipated needs of the British government outweighed any rights of the neutral to carry cargo where it might choose, despite the language of the treaty. The law of contraband was largely law dictated by the needs of the strong.

The English admiralty court made one further small concession to neutral carriers of naval stores. Shortly after Scott began practice as a civilian he stated what apparently was the accepted law among civilians: preemption applied to naval stores shipped to an enemy port for fitting out the fleet, provided that the naval stores had been grown or produced in the country from which they had been shipped.[61] Neutrals should be allowed to ship their native products even to supply the enemy navy.

Provisions

The second source of running dispute between Great Britain and neutral carriers was the character of food supplies for the enemy. Sir George Lee, in an opinion as counsel, stated the mid-eighteenth-century British position that provisions carried to an enemy were contraband.

> [T]he doctrine laid down by Grotius ... has been exploded by later writers particularly by Bynkershoek ... and has not been regarded in the Admiralty Court in England. [I]n that Court both in the present & in former wars corn tho[ugh] not going to a besieged port has been condemned as Contraband in its own nature by the Laws of Nations and those Treatys which have expressly declared that corn shall not be deemed contraband seem to me to prove that it is so in its own nature for it would be fruitless to stipulate that a thing shall not be deemed contraband which would not have been so without such stipulation.[62]

Many admiralty court cases could be cited which condemned food supplies, such as wheat, wine, brandy, salt fish, salt and tallow, as contraband when carried to an enemy port.[63] Other provisions,

---

[60] *Vryheid* (1778), Hay & M. 188. See also *Vrow Antoinette* (1778), Hay & M. 142; *Sarah and Bernhardus* (1778), Hay & M. 174.

[61] *Port Franc* (1782), Nicholl's Notebook, 1781–92, No. 17, P.R.O. HCA 30/464.

[62] *Luisa Ulrica (Muller)* (1748), H.S.P. Lee Opinions. Lee cited Grotius, *De jure belli*, B. 3, c. 1, s. 5, and C. van Bynkershoek, *Quaestionum juris publici libri duo* (Amsterdam, 1747), B. 1, c. 10.

[63] *Jonge Frederick (Montagne)* (1746); *Vrow Anna Maria (Hurn)* (1747); *Elizabeth Catherina (Cornielzen)* (1747); *Junge Tobias (Setterboom)* (1747), and *Jonge Isaac (Bloom)* (1748), H.S.P. Lee Cases.

likewise shipped to an enemy port, had been restored.[64] The distinction lay not in subtle differences in the kinds of provisions, although it surely made a difference if the provisions were shipped to a port where the enemy army or fleet would probably benefit. The distinction can often be found in the political and diplomatic realities of the moment.

During the American Revolution a Swedish ship was seized by a British naval vessel and taken to Cadiz. It had been bound for Lisbon with a cargo of wheat. Apparently the enemy fleet was being fitted out at Lisbon. The ship and cargo had been restored by the admiralty court, but, since the perishable cargo had been sold at Cadiz, the Swedish claimants sought the amount the wheat would have brought if sold at Lisbon. Scott represented the captors. He contended that the Swedish shippers were entitled only to the fair market value, not the speculative price they could have received at Lisbon. The Lords Commissioners, however, decreed that the Swedish shippers should get the higher amount. A comment from the bench typifies the attitude of the admiralty court and the Lords toward questions of contraband. '[T]he necessity of the times made it necessary to determine questions of contraband more favourably to Neutrals.'[65] Undoubtedly the various writers on the law of nations would have nothing helpful to say on such a precise question as which market should be considered in determining fair market value. The Lords, however, here expressed what was implicit in other cases, the political nature of many decisions concerning contraband. Thus in this case, faced with the serious threat of an effective armed neutrality, the Lords in 1781 decided that neutrals should be treated more favorably.

Other issues

Apparently in the middle of the eighteenth century, if a neutral vessel was seized carrying some contraband cargo, the admiralty court at times held this was sufficient grounds for condemning all the cargo and the vessel. As Penrice said in 1746, '[G]oods illicit will taint what is not illicit.'[66] He condemned the Swedish ship and all its cargo. The following year, however, Penrice spoke with greater precision in restoring a neutral ship carrying contraband goods since the owners of the ship were not privy to the nature of the cargo. '[B]y the Text Law', Penrice said, 'the ship is not forfeited unless the owners had know-

---

[64] Cargo of lemons and oil, *St. Jacob* (Lords, 1759), Burrell, 160.
[65] *Case of a Swedish ship* (1781), Nicholl's Notebook, 1781–92, P.R.O. HCA 30/464.
[66] *Hewa*ʹ(*Oloffson*) (1746), H.S.P. Lee Cases.

ledge of the contraband goods being put on board.'[67]

During the American Revolution, in a case in which Scott appeared for the captors, Marriott seemed to think that earlier courts had condemned neutral ships carrying contraband goods. '[I]n former wars even the ships of Neutrals hav[in]g contraband were condemned. The Policy of this War has only confiscated the goods.'[68] Apparently the issue had not been clearly settled prior to Marriott's day or perhaps Marriott was merely trying to take credit for the court's generous policy toward neutrals.

Finally, the admiralty court and the Lords Commissioners had to determine whether a neutral vessel, carrying only innocent cargo, could be condemned because it had carried contraband on the outward voyage. The Lords Commissioners, in several carefully argued cases, held that a neutral ship or cargo could not be condemned merely because it had carried contraband on an earlier voyage. In 1752 the Lords Commissioners, in the case of the *Vreyheid* unanimously held that

[T]his appeared to be a Dutch ship & as the cargo on board at the time of the capture was lawful & going to Amsterdam, tho[ugh] the outward cargo was contraband & fictitious papers were made out for that voyage[,] they thought they could take no notice of any thing but what related to the present homeward voyage & could not punish the claimers for a past offence.[69]

This rule, that the neutral must be caught red-handed and could not be condemned for past contraband violations, was applied by the Lords right up to the time Scott became admiralty judge. As the notetaker wrote in one case in 1796, 'In the course of the hearing the Lords declared, that innocent goods in return for a Contraband cargo are clearly not liable to confiscation. [T]he contraband must be taken in the fact.'[70] The English court of prize appeals, therefore, explicitly held that an admiralty court could not trace the proceeds of the sale of contraband goods and condemn an innocent cargo because purchased

---

[67] *Fredericus II Koning von Prussian* (*Schulte*) (1747), H.S.P. Lee Cases.

[68] *Port Franc* (1782), Nicholl's Notebook, 1781–92, No. 17, P.R.O. HCA 30/464.

[69] *Vreyheid* (*Vos*) (Lords, 1752), N.Y.P.L. Lee Prize Appeals. See also *Fortune* (*Kandran*) (Lords, 1746), N.Y.P.L. Lee Prize Appeals.

[70] *Lady Walterstoff* (*Davis*) (Lords, 1796), Nicholl's Notes of Prize Appeals, 16, P.R.O. HCA 30/466. The next year Chief Justice Eyre, sitting with the Lords Commissioners, asked at argument: 'Can you establish that a person having an innocent cargo, is liable to have that return cargo condemned[?]' He was informed by counsel that there had been 'no such case since the usurpation'. *Solome* (*Wasson*) (Lords, 1797), Nicholl's Notes of Prize Appeals, 25, P.R.O. HCA 30/466.

with the money obtained from the sale of contraband. When the pressures of the war intensified, Scott and the Lords Commissioners, as we shall see, modified this position.

Scott as judge

While Scott was practicing as a civilian, perhaps about the time of the outbreak of war with France in 1793 when he was King's Advocate, he reviewed some old prize appeal cases dating from 1697 to 1758. He wrote a few lines summarizing the Lords Commissioners' determination for 136 cases, most of them dating from the period 1744 to 1748. Nearly a third of these notes of prize appeal cases concerned questions of contraband. His brief but careful analysis of these old cases certainly made him aware of the conflicting, at times, irreconcilable, precedents concerning contraband.[71] Although his notes seldom mentioned the possible distinguishing factors in each case, differences in treaties, in destination of vessel, in ownership of cargo and so forth, he must have used this effort at self-education to consider each case in as much depth as the source he relied on permitted.

Scott put this study and his years of practice to good use when he became admiralty judge. Because he was more precise and accurate in his analysis of each case than his predecessors, his judgments appear more principled, more protective of neutral rights and less swayed by the immediate pressing interests of the British government as tides of war ebbed and flowed. Scott was enough of a believer in the law of nations on occasion to interpret the rights of neutrals as imposing some limitation on the rights of his own country as a belligerent. There can be little doubt, however, that when national interests were pressing, Scott could develop new interpretations of the law of nations more favorable to Britain's needs as a belligerent.

General principles

In the case of the *Jonge Margaretha* Scott had to determine whether a Papenberg ship carrying Dutch cheese from Amsterdam to Brest was engaged in a lawful trade.[72] All Europe, he observed, knew that the French fleet was being readied at that moment at Brest for attack. He reviewed the precedents relied on by counsel and had to admit that 'the distinction appears nice' between butter which had been con-

[71] R.A., Stowell Notebook, 301–25. For a description of this notebook, see Appendix.
[72] *Jonge Margaretha (Klausen)* (1799), 1 Rob. 189.

demned as contraband and cheese which had been released as free. He conjectured that the cheese might not have been suitable for military use. He recalled that some continental philosophers, such as Christian Wolff and Vattel, favored the neutral position on provisions as contraband. The modern rule, Scott said, was that provisions were generally not contraband, but might become so 'under circumstances arising out of the particular situation of the war, or the condition of the parties engaged in it'. If he had stopped there, of course, no more elastic principle could have been stated. Scott summed up well-accepted principles of the admiralty court when he specified those circumstances which generally affected the status of cargo as contraband. In the first place, he said, if the cargo were the growth or product of the neutral exporter's country, this factor would incline the court to find the goods not contraband. Neutrals had a right to ship their own domestically produced goods. Secondly, articles 'in their native and unmanufactured state' would be treated more leniently than fabricated goods. 'Hemp is more favourably considered than cordage', wheat more favourably than bread. Most importantly, Scott continued, goods intended for non-military purposes would be treated more leniently than goods with a probable military destination. This distinction, not yet formulated in terms of combatant and non-combatant, underlay much of the discussion of contraband. If the destination of the cargo, therefore, was a general commercial port, the court would be inclined to conclude that it was shipped for the use of civilians. On the other hand, if the destination of the cargo was 'a port of naval military equipment', where the enemy fleet was being supplied and readied for war, the court would presume that the cargo had a military use and would condemn it as contraband. In this case, since the cheese was the kind used aboard French war ships, since it was produced in an enemy country and was not the native product of Papenberg, the neutral carrier's country, and since it was going to Brest, it would be condemned. Scott, however, did not condemn the neutral ship, even though the contraband cargo belonged to the ship owners. Although he stated these settled principles more clearly than his predecessors, they left ample room for maneuver by the court to meet the needs of the government at war.

Scott certainly was aware that the neutral nations had a different understanding of the scope of neutral rights concerning contraband. He was bound, he said, by the exposition of the law of nations 'authorized by the former decisions of this Court, founded on general

and disinterested views of the subject'.[73] That former decisions of the
admiralty court were disinterested, the neutrals rightly doubted.
Scott, however, worked within the framework of well-developed and
occasionally irreconcilable precedents. His role as expositor of this
judicially expressed and thoroughly British law of nations was to
appear as fair and independent as possible in its application. But, of
course, if the more politically attuned Lords Commissioners changed
the law, Scott felt bound to follow the new rule they stated.[74]

Native products

Even the principles which Scott stated were riddled with exceptions.
Scott, as we have just seen, acknowledged that a neutral's carriage of
the native goods of its own country was one factor which inclined the
court to treat the cargo as free.[75] Nonetheless, he had no trouble
finding precedent for condemning such cargo as contraband when he
knew that there would be no outcry by the neutral country. In the case
of the *Staadt Emden* he condemned a cargo of Russian masts and ship
timber, belonging to Russian shippers and bound to an enemy port,
Amsterdam, since at the time Russia, although not at war with
France, had been cooperating as a quasi-ally in blockading
Amsterdam.[76] In many other cases, Scott said, the admiralty court
had condemned as contraband native articles shipped to an enemy

[73] *Twee Juffrowen (Etjes)* (1802), 4 Rob. 242, 244.
[74] *Charlotte (Koltzenberg)* (1804), 5 Rob. 305, 313. In this case counsel for the Russian
claimants had been able to cite several clear precedents from the middle of the
eighteenth century which had held that a Russian cargo of masts, even though not in
Russian vessels, was protected from seizure by the treaty with Russia. Scott,
however, brushed aside these precedents because of a recently decided case on point
by the Lords Commissioners. He said: 'This case has been argued much at length on
the operation of the treaty, and on the authority of former practice; and it certainly
presents a question of considerable importance. But it will not be necessary or proper
for me to travel much into the argument, because, if there is a decision of the
Superior Court, so recent as 1803, on a similar point, it will be conclusive upon my
judgment, and I shall have only to follow the rule of law there laid down, and to act
under the authority of that decision.' *Ibid.*, 313. Masts, therefore, Scott held, were
contraband unless protected by treaty, regardless of whether they were shipped to an
ordinary commercial port of the enemy or to a port where the enemy's navy was being
fitted out. Scott relied on the recent precedent, *Graeffen van Gottland (Theel)*
(Lords, 1803), in which the Lords condemned the Russian masts because the treaty
with Russia 'did not apply to a Swedish ship'. Nicholl's Notes of Prize Appeals, 79,
P.R.O. HCA 30/466.
[75] See *Jonge Margaretha (Klausen)* (1799), 1 Rob. 189, discussed above, p. 193. See
also *Christina Maria (Kehnrock)* (1802), 4 Rob. 166, and *Evert (Everts)* (1803),
4 Rob. 354.
[76] *Staadt Emden (Jacobs)* (1798), 1 Rob. 26.

port by inhabitants of the country which produced them. He mentioned 'the famous case of the *Med Gud's Hielp* (*Soderberg*)' in which Swedish pitch and tar had been condemned because shipped to a French port. He added 'that condemnation was afterwards confirmed by a solemn judgment of the Lords, and the MS. note which I have of that case, expressly states it to have been condemned by the Lords of Appeal, on the ground of contraband'.[77] What Scott failed to mention in this decision, but what he probably recalled, since he had stated it in his notes of prize appeals, was that the Lords' judgment in this 1750 case was largely political.[78]

Infection of the vessel

Scott, like his precedessor, referred to the old rule that the ship carrying contraband cargo would be condemned along with its cargo. In modern times, he said, this point has been relaxed and '[T]he general rule now is, that the vessel does not become confiscable for that act.'[79] He carefully noted, however, the exceptions to this modern rule, 'Where a ship belongs to the owner of the cargo, or where the ship is going on such service, under a false destination or false papers', the neutral vessel would be condemned. But even though he had grave doubts in one case whether the ship and contraband cargo belonged to the same owners, he restored the ship while accusing himself of excessive leniency.[80]

As long as the neutral ship did not belong to the same parties as the contraband cargo, the only penalty for carrying contraband, Scott said in another case, was the loss of freight and expenses.[81] Even where Scott knew that one part owner of the ship had an interest in the contraband cargo, he only condemned this part interest in the vessel instead of the entire vessel, as he might have done. In this case, Scott stated the rule with greater refinement to avoid the harsher result of condemning the neutral vessel entirely. 'Where the owner of the cargo has any interest in the ship, the whole of his property will be involved in the same sentence of condemnation.'[82] This same basic rule applied

[77] *Ibid.*, 29. The *Med Gud's Hielp* (*Soderberg*) is discussed above at pp. 187–8.
[78] When Scott had earlier briefly described the *Med Gud's Hielp* in his personal notes, he had written '[S]aid to have been adjourned for political Reasons, but all the Lords [were] of opinion that [the cargo was] contraband.' R.A., Stowell Notebook, 311.
[79] *Neutralitet* (*Burning*) (1801), 3 Rob. 295, 296.
[80] *Sarah Christina* (*Gorgensen*) (1799), 1 Rob. 237, 242.
[81] *Ringende Jacob* (*Kreplien*) (1798), 1 Rob. 89, 90.
[82] *Jonge Tobias* (*Hilken*) (1799), 1 Rob. 329, 330.

likewise to the cargo. Even the innocent articles would be condemned along with the contraband if they belonged to the same owner.[83]

Destination

Two basic factors had to be considered in determining whether a cargo should be condemned as contraband: the nature and ownership of the cargo, already considered, and the destination of the cargo. The most clearly forbidden cargo would not be considered contraband unless shipped to an enemy port. Neutrals could trade with each other in any cargo they wished. As Scott stated, '[G]oods going to a neutral port, cannot come under the description of contraband, all goods going there being equally lawful.'[84] But, of course, since the opportunities for fraud were rife, the belligerents had the right to insist that the neutral destination be the true one. If the destination to a neutral port was false and a mere deception, Scott insisted that both the contraband cargo and the neutral vessel must be condemned.[85]

In a case where the neutral ship with contraband cargo had intended to touch at an enemy port, the Cape of Good Hope, on a voyage to an ultimate neutral port, Scott held that the ship and cargo should be restored because the Cape had fallen to the British before the ship arrived. Even though the ship owners might have had the design, or as Scott said, borrowing criminal law terminology, the *mens rea*, this evil intent had not been accompanied by the act of going to an enemy's port. Scott interpreted the law favorably to the neutral carrier in holding that '[T]here must be a *delictum* existing at the moment of seizure to sustain the penalty.'[86] This surely was an unsettled point in the law of contraband and Scott, had he been so inclined, might have condemned the contraband on the ground that the neutral carrier had the intent to bring the forbidden cargo to an enemy port and had attempted to do so. The neutral had been prevented from doing so only by the entirely fortuitous event of the fall of the Cape to the British. Certainly the captors had a point: the neutral carrier could legally touch at an enemy port with a cargo of contraband and then claim that he planned to carry the cargo to some ultimate neutral destination. Scott, nonetheless, held that '[F]rom

---

[83] *Staadt Emden (Jacobs)* (1798), 1 Rob. 26, 31. Scott quoted Bynkershoek as strongly supporting this principle, *Quaestionum juris publici*, B. 1, c. 12.

[84] *Imina (Vroom)* (1800), 3 Rob. 167.

[85] *Franklin (Segerbrath)* (1801), 3 Rob. 217, 224.

[86] *Trende Sostre (Missen)* (1807), 6 Rob. 390, 392.

the moment when the *Cape* became a *British* possession, the goods lost their nature of contraband.'

Preemption

Scott, of course, continued to follow the familiar practice of preemption. When a neutral ship was captured carrying contraband cargo, such as pitch and tar, which was a product of the country of the neutral shippers, the cargo would not be condemned, but rather restored on condition that it be sold in Great Britain. Condemnation of such a cargo, Scott explained, would be 'deemed a harsh exercise of a belligerent right to prohibit the carriage of these articles, which constitute so considerable a part of its native produce and ordinary commerce'.[87] This relaxation of the belligerent's right to seize contraband goods carried to an enemy port was a fair compromise, Scott insisted, between the belligerent's right of self-defense and the neutral's right to export his native goods. This entire milder doctrine, however, depended on perfect good faith on the part of the neutral carrier.

Scott certainly broke no new ground in applying this doctrine of preemption. He was not satisfied, however, with merely applying accepted principles. He went well beyond his predecessors in providing a full, contextual explanation of these principles.

The right of carrying pitch and tar has long been a subject of much contention, this country contending that they were to be considered as contraband, *Sweden*, on the contrary, maintaining, that they were not contraband when they were the produce of the exporting country. After long and passionate discussion on this subject, which has irritated the feelings of the two countries for two centuries, a sort of compromise was at length adopted, and the late treaty was formed as a kind of middle term, in which both parties abated something of their original pretensions. It was agreed that these articles should be considered not as absolutely contraband, nor yet as entirely free and innocent, but as liable to this exercise of the right of war, 'that they should be subject to seizure for *pre-emption*'.[88]

Innocent proceeds

Scott stated the well-settled rule concerning the innocent proceeds captured on a return voyage after carriage of contraband on the

---

[87] *Sarah Christina (Gorgensen)* (1799), 1 Rob. 237, 241. See also *Maria (Paulsen)* (1799), 1 Rob. 340, 373, and *Twee Juffrowen (Etjes)* (1802), 4 Rob. 242.

[88] *Neptunus (Bachman)* (1807), 6 Rob. 403, 405. In this case Scott held that preemption did not apply since Sweden at the time was an ally of Britain, not a neutral.

outward voyage. Contraband must be seized during the voyage to the enemy port. 'Under the present understanding of the law of nations, you cannot generally take the proceeds in the return voyage.'[89] No penalty attached to the carriage of contraband unless the vessel was taken red-handed, in the actual prosecution of the forbidden voyage.

Although Scott stated the principle so clearly, about five weeks earlier he had created a significant exception to it. The *Nancy*, decided in 1800, had been seized on a voyage from the Dutch East India settlement of Batavia to Copenhagen.[90] On the outward voyage the *Nancy* had carried a contraband cargo to Batavia, an enemy port, but the master had instructions to tell any British vessels he might encounter that the ship was going to Tranquebar or China, neutral destinations. Scott found other evidence of fraud in the venture, such as a possible Dutch interest in this purportedly Danish ship and cargo. The claimants had argued that the innocent return cargo should not be condemned because of the carriage of contraband on the outward voyage. Scott, without any precedent as authority, distinguished shorter voyages from longer ones. On short voyages, such as European ones, the return cargo was not tainted by the contraband carried on the outward voyage. On long voyages, however, such as to India, the entire voyage out and back must be regarded as a single venture. 'In such a transaction', he said, 'the different parts are not to be considered, as two voyages, but as one entire transaction, formed upon one original plan, conducted by the same persons, and under one set of instructions.' He held, therefore, that '[P]arties setting out on such an expedition with ill faith, and pursuing that measure of ill faith up to its consummation, in the delivery of the outward cargo, are implicated in the consequences of such a conduct, throughout the whole sequel of that transaction.'[91] Scott cited no precedent for this rule, undoubtedly because the Lords had decided several cases just a few years earlier which held that neutrals must be caught red-handed with the contraband cargo.

We have discussed the cases, prior to Scott's appointment to the admiralty court, in which the Lords Commissioners had refused to condemn the return cargo where the outward voyage had involved a concealed carriage of contraband to the enemy.[92] Scott, in the case of

[89] *Imina (Vroom)* (1800), 3 Rob. 167.
[90] *Nancy (Knudsen)* (1800), 3 Rob. 122.
[91] *Ibid.*, 126, 127.
[92] See above, p. 192.

the *Nancy*, cited no precedents for the modification of the settled doctrine which the Lords had stated. In creating a rule more favorable to Britain's needs as a belligerent, Scott probably was influenced by evidence of fraud and concealed Dutch participation in the entire venture. He tried to restrict the impact of this new rule. His distinction, however, between shorter voyages, in which the outward and return cargoes would be viewed independently, and long voyages which would be viewed as one whole, did not long survive the pressures of war. After this case the Lords Commissioners quickly followed, and indeed went well beyond, Scott's position. They condemned the return cargo even on short, European voyages.

Some time after Scott decided this case, the Lords Commissioners began condemning neutral ships and innocent cargoes because the ship had carried contraband on the outward voyage. After 1802 the fact that the seized cargo had been purchased from the proceeds of a contraband cargo, carried by deceit to an enemy port, was enough to condemn the innocent return cargo and sometimes the ship as well. No longer did the neutral have to be caught red-handed with the contraband cargo. As the Lords declared after a full argument on the point, '[T]he Returns of Contraband, carried to the Enemy under a false Destination, were confiscable.'[93] The Lords in this case maintained that they were relaxing a harsher ancient doctrine which allowed belligerents to condemn the proceeds of a contraband cargo on the outward voyage even when there had been no deception as to the destination. Nonetheless, the Lords had to concede that they could find no precedent. The Lords 'gave no Costs, because [there was] no express determination previously upon the Point'.

The Lords decided a number of similar cases after the recommencement of hostilities in 1803. They condemned an innocent cargo, and sometimes the ship also, because purchased from the

---

[93] *Elizabeth (Ropers)* (Lords, 1802), Nicholl's Notes of Prize Appeals, 63, P.R.O. HCA 30/466.

The political nature of some of the Lords Commissioners' decisions is well brought out in the case of the *Winst & Forlust* (Lords, 1800). A cargo of Portuguese provisions aboard a Swedish ship was condemned, despite the treaty with Sweden. But before determining the case, the Lords, who were divided on the issue of the effect of the Swedish treaty on the Portuguese cargo, asked the Foreign Secretary to certify that the Swedish treaty had been relaxed during the present war with respect to provisions, precisely the issue before the Lords. Nicholl's Notes of Prize Appeals, 46, P.R.O. HCA 30/466.

proceeds of a contraband cargo which on the outward voyage had been carried to the enemy despite a stated destination in the ship's papers to a neutral port. The Lords, for instance, determined in 1804 that the ship should be condemned because of the contraband cargo on the outward voyage. They said: '[The] ship having carried a cargo of contraband under a false destination [was] held to be confiscable on the return voyage, altho[ugh] the contraband Cargo did not belong to the owner [of] the ship[,] the owner of the ship by himself or [the] Master being a Party to the falsehood of the destination.'[94] It is important to note in this case that the entire voyage was quite short, only along the coast of France, certainly a European voyage. Once again we see that the interests of the belligerents, rather than any theoretical law of nations, defined the ever-malleable term, contraband. It is perhaps somewhat to his credit that Scott had only bent the well-settled rule, whereas the Lords Commissioners, under pressure of wartime necessity, shattered it. Apparently Scott did not have occasion to decide any other cases on this issue.

BLOCKADE

Unlike the other areas of prize law, Scott wrote the law of blockade on a virtually clean slate. There had been no significant development of this body of law by the admiralty court or the court of prize appeals prior to the time Scott became judge of the admiralty court. We sense in these cases, where Scott worked without the usual framework of decided cases, that he often manifested a sensitivity to neutral rights, at least until the clear determination of the British government had expressed a contrary policy.

[94] *Success (Babcock)* (Lords, 1804), Nicholl's Notes of Prize Appeals, 84, P.R.O. HCA 30/466. See also *Catharina Maria (Randalls)* (Lords, 1805); *Merchant (Meyer)* (Lords, 1809); *Curaco (Maria)* (Lords, 1811), Nicholl's Notes of Prize Appeals, 93, 106, 131, P.R.O. HCA 30/466. In the case of the *Mary Ann (Anthony)* (Lords, 1809), the Lords Commissioners affirmed the condemnation of the cargo of an American ship which was returning from the short voyage to St Thomas and Puerto Rico with an innocent cargo. On the outward voyage it had carried, as part of its cargo, a few spars, small in size and value. This meager contraband cargo was held sufficient to condemn the return cargo. Bod. Lib., 4 Monk Bretton Dep., 50; Nicholl's Notes of Prize Appeals, 104, P.R.O. HCA 30/466. See also *Margaret (Heard)* (Lords, 1810), 1 Acton 333, 335, and *Baltic (Donaldson)* (Lords, 1809), 1 Acton 25, 33, in which Scott, as one of the Lords Commissioners, gave the judgment for the Lords.

Eighteenth century

The essential idea of blockade had developed in the seventeenth century. It found expression in treaties at that time which assured the parties to the treaty that, if one of them should be involved in war, the other could freely trade as a neutral to the ports of the other party's enemy provided it carried no contraband cargo and provided that the port was not besieged. Treaty language on the point became fairly standardized, permitting the other signatory to trade in non-contraband goods even to enemy ports 'sauf aux Villes & Places assiegées, blocquées ou investies'.[95] By the eighteenth century some treaties indicated that the blockade must be effective to be legal. Blockade by mere proclamation would not suffice. Apparently breach of a blockaded port did not constitute an independent basis for condemnation. If the vessel violating the blockade was seized (and often it was merely warned off), the seizure would often be justified on the ground of contraband rather than blockade.[96]

Bynkershoek had expressed his view of the law of nations on blockade more fully than other treatise writers. Since some of Scott's later judgments appear to follow distinctions set forth in Bynkershoek, his ideas merit a brief summary. Bynkershoek wrote:

For it is reasonable, and in accord with international usage, that when cities are besieged nothing should be permitted to be carried in or out ... [I]n a blockade it is lawful to intercept even the ships of friendly nations. And this holds true if the ships are taken before the voyage is complete, and while employed in illicit trade; and the voyage is not considered complete until the vessels have reached their own or a friendly port.[97]

Blockade here was treated as equivalent to a land-based siege; vessels could be taken for blockade violations at any time during that illicit voyage until the vessel returned to its home port. Neutral vessels, Bynkershoek stated elsewhere, could be seized and condemned not only for entering or leaving a blockaded port, but also for hovering so

[95] Jessup and Deak, *Origins*, 113, 105–23; Kulsrud, *Maritime neutrality*, 238–42.
[96] Jessup and Deak, *Origins*, 116–21.
[97] Bynkershoek, *Quaestionum juris publici*, tr. T. Frank, B. 1, c. 4, pp. 34–5. E. Vattel, in *Le droit des gens*, tr. C. Fenwick (Washington, 1916), merely stated: 'All trade with a besieged town is absolutely forbidden. When I am besieging a town, or merely blockading it, I have the right to prevent any one from entering it, and to treat as an enemy whoever attempts to enter it, or to carry anything into it, without my permission; for such a person would be opposing my undertaking, and might contribute thereby to its defeat and thus bring upon me all the evils of an unsuccessful war.' B. 3, c. 7, s. 117, p. 173.

near a blockaded port that their intention to enter was clear. If the suspect vessel alleged necessity in entering a blockaded port, only extreme and completely proven necessity could offer a justification. If a vessel were seized a distance from a blockaded port, but its papers showed that its destination was that port, it could be condemned.[98] We shall see that Scott incorporated some of these details into the British law of nations.

The dearth of blockade cases before the British admiralty court becomes apparent from a study of the notes of prize cases compiled by Sir George Lee. He has left notes of more than 250 prize cases, mostly from the years 1740 to 1750. Of these more than thirty dealt with issues of contraband, but only one even remotely discussed blockade. In that case the court condemned the prize, but not on the ground that it had violated a blockade. Even though the court noted that it was 'notorious that in Dec[embe]r and Jan[uar]y last the King's ships were cruizing to intercept ships going into or coming out of Dunkirk to prevent the Invasion', the court concluded that Dunkirk 'was not blocked or besieged'.[99] The admiralty court apparently required more before it would find an effective blockade even where the British navy was doing its best to blockade the port.

In a later case where the admiralty court did find that Dunkirk had been blockaded, it condemned the cargo but on the ground that it had become contraband because of the violation of the blockade. Even here the Lords Commissioners refused to take judicial notice of the fact that Dunkirk was blockaded and decided the case on other grounds.[100]

Right up to the time Scott became admiralty judge, the Lords Commissioners often refused to condemn vessels for breach of a blockade. They repeatedly found insufficient proof of an effective blockade. For instance, in one case Scott had argued as King's Advocate that it was just as illegal to bring a cargo out of a blockaded port as it was to carry supplies to the port. The Lords 'gave no opinion

---

[98] Bynkershoek, *Quaestionum juris publici*, B. 1, c. 11, pp. 74–7.
[99] *Drie Gebroeders* (1746), H.S.P. Lee Cases.
[100] *Vier Gebroeders (Martynnes)* (Lords, 1760), P.R.O. HCA 45/2. In the *Alexander the Great (Van Staaden)* (Lords, 1750), the British commander who made the capture alleged that he had 'all the Reason Imaginable to think he should soon become Master' of Martinique because of his naval blockade which had cut off all supplies. Nevertheless, the Lords Commissioners held that the only evidence of the blockade came from interested parties (the captors) and was inadmissible. The ship and cargo were restored. N.Y.P.L. Lee Prize Appeals.

on the law as [there was] no proof of the fact of blockade'.[101]

Perhaps few blockade cases remain in the records because the English courts treated blockade violations as examples of contraband since the cargoes became contraband by their destination to a besieged port. Or perhaps the captors faced insurmountable evidentiary obstacles in proving a blockade because of a technical interpretation of the rule which barred evidence from interested parties. More likely, the scarcity of blockade cases resulted from the extreme difficulty of maintaining an effective naval blockade for a long period. Surely in the seventeenth and early eighteenth centuries, when nations still relied heavily on privateers as a partial substitute for a navy, blockade would not have been feasible. Even when blockades had been created in the eighteenth century, the naval objective was not so much the interruption of commerce as the neutralization of the enemy's fleet.[102] Whatever the explanation, it is abundantly clear that the British courts had not developed a body of principles governing blockade cases.

Scott as judge

General principles

The lack of precedents in blockade cases becomes apparent from a careful reading of Scott's many judgments dealing with the issue. Only twice did he even hint at a precedent in his more than sixty reported blockade decisions. He acknowledged that he had little authority to refer to and therefore he had to 'collect the law of nations from such sources, as reason, supported in some slight degree by the practice of nations'.[103] He further acknowledged the novelty of the

---

[101] *Dove (Burke)* (Lords, 1796), Nicholl's Notes of Prize Appeals, 18, P.R.O. HCA 30/466. See also *Columbia (Boiner)* (Lords, 1796) and *Hannah (Brown)* (Lords, 1798), *ibid.*, fos. 17 and 32.

[102] A. T. Mahan, *The influence of sea power upon history 1660–1783* (New York, 1890), 187, 261–2, 469–71; W. M. James, *The British navy in adversity – a study of the war of American independence* (New York, 1926), 81–3, 415–28, and S. W. Roskill, *The strategy of sea power – its development and application* (Westport, Conn., 1962), 46–52, 77.

[103] *Adonis (Gottschalk)* (1804), 5 Rob. 256, 259. Scott referred to a precedent, without mentioning the name or date, involving a case '[D]etermined by the Supreme Court during the present war. The *West India* islands were declared under blockade by Admiral *Jarvis*; but the Lords held, that as the fact did not support the declaration, a blockade could not be deemed legally to exist.' *Mercurius (Gerdes)* (1798), 1 Rob. 80, 83. See also *Betsey (Murphy)* (1798), 1 Rob. 93a, 95.

law of blockade. '[T]he law of blockade', he wrote, 'is a thing rather out of the common course of mercantile experience; it is new to merchants, and not very familiar to lawyers themselves.'[104] Scott never doubted, however, that the law of nations supported the imposition of a blockade. Although he understood that blockades fell harshly on neutrals, he was certain that the law of nations from the earliest times, as well as the practice of nations, justified belligerents in employing this weapon. He insisted '[T]here is no one principle of the law of nations better established, than that a belligerent has a right to impose a blockade on the ports of his enemy.'[105] The penalty of confiscation for breach of a blockade was equally certain. Scott claimed it could be found in all law books and treatises, and that it was universally acknowledged by all governments.[106] Possibly Scott's uneasiness about the lack of precedents made him protest too much about the clarity of the non-judicial authorities. His claim of certainty about the law clashed with the confessed novelty of the application of the law.

Scott revealed his insecurity in sailing these uncharted waters. He said he thought he should press the neutrals as lightly as possible, but he pleaded with the court of prize appeals to provide him with some guidance. 'It is extremely desirable that questions of this nature should find their way to the ultimate judgment of the Court of Appeals; and that the principles which this Court has thought itself warranted, under occasions of peculiar difficulty, to lay down may be corrected or affirmed.'[107] Despite the uncertainty, however, Scott felt obliged to carry out his unpleasant duty in enforcing the necessarily harsh rules of blockade.[108]

Scott, with his usual precision, stated the factors which raised the legal question of blockade. The captors had to prove, '1st, The existence of an actual blockade; 2dly, The knowledge of the party; and 3dly, Some act of violation, either by going in, or by coming out with a cargo laden after the commencement of blockade.'[109]

[104] *Neptunus (Kuyp)* (1800), 3 Rob. 173–6. In an unreported case Scott again pointed out that there were few authorities or precedents in blockade cases. He said he had to 'decide on principles'. *Goode Hoop (Dyk)* (1799), Nicholl's Notebook, 1799–1800; Arnold's Notebook, 1799, P.R.O. HCA 30/464; HCA 30/472.
[105] *Juno (Beard)* (1799), 2 Rob. 116, 118.
[106] *Columbia (Weeks)* (1799), 1 Rob. 154.
[107] *Lisette (Steg)* (1807), 6 Rob. 387, 393.
[108] *Arthur (Rathburn)* (1810), Edw. 202, 203.
[109] *Betsey (Murphy)* (1798), 1 Rob. 93a; see also *Mercurius (Gerdes)* (1798), 1 Rob. 80, 82, and *Frederick Molke (Boysen)* (1798), 1 Rob. 86.

Elsewhere Scott added a fourth essential trait of a blockade: that it was established by a competent authority.[110] Once these points had been proven, the burden of proof shifted to the claimant whose property had been captured to show that there had been some particular circumstances which would exempt this ship from the legal penalty for violating a blockade.[111]

The purpose of a belligerent in setting up a blockade had to be military. Blockades were created not only to prevent the importation of supplies, but to prevent exportation as well. They were meant 'to cut off all communication of commerce with the blockaded place'.[112] Although blockades necessarily had an economic impact, they were, as Scott insisted in 1812, economic warfare justified only as a means of achieving military advantage over the enemy. Commercial advantage for British manufacturers or shippers would never suffice as the basis for imposing a blockade. British subjects, therefore, could not trade to blockaded ports. At a time when the military and economic needs of Britain were at their greatest, Scott stated with considerable emphasis:

> The measure which has been resorted to, being in the nature of a blockade, must operate to the entire exclusion of *British* as well as of neutral ships; for it would be a gross violation of neutral rights, to prohibit their trade, and to permit the subjects of this country to carry on an unrestricted commerce at the very same ports from which neutrals are excluded. It would be a shameful abuse of a belligerent right, thus to convert the blockade into a mere instrument of commercial monopoly.[113]

Scott, beyond any doubt, knew the economic situation in Britain in 1811 and 1812: unemployment, bank failures, food riots, fear of uprisings, industrial sabotage, and all caused in large part by the stagnation of commerce.[114] He refused, nonetheless, to allow commercial advantages, the urgent need to increase exports, to outweigh his sense of fairness to neutrals who had to face the harsh consequences of blockades.

---

[110] *Rolla (Coffin)* (1807), 6 Rob. 364, 365.
[111] *Ibid.*
[112] *Frederick Molke (Boysen)* (1798), 1 Rob. 86, 87.
[113] *Success (Smith)* (1812), 1 Dod. 131, 134.
[114] F. Crouzet, *L'Economie britannique et le blocus continental (1806–1813)* (2 vols., Paris, 1958), II, 645–808; A. D. Harvey, *Britain in the early nineteenth century* (London, 1978), 285–99.

Actual blockade

Scott, in the early years of the war, adamantly insisted that a blockading force must actually impede entry to or exit from a port before a blockade would have legal effect. He accepted the test suggested by a neutral that a state of blockade existed 'when it is dangerous to attempt to enter'.[115] Evidence of the existence of an effective blockading force had to be clear and decisive. A mere proclamation by the naval force that the French islands were in a state of complete blockade would not suffice to constitute a legal blockade.[116] A few vessels might suffice to constitute a blockading force, at least where there had been official notification of the blockade given to neutral nations. This notification, accompanied by some small, actual blockading force, created a presumption that the blockade continued in force.[117]

Of course, a temporary absence of the blockading force, as when it was blown off station by an adverse wind, did not suspend the blockade.[118] But if the blockading ships had been driven away by a superior enemy force, the blockade no longer existed unless it could be proven that an actual blockade had been reinstated. The neutrals need not presume the continuance of the blockade.[119] A mere 'fluctuating and vacillating' blockade was thus treated as no blockade at all.[120]

The case of the *Juffrow Maria Schroeder* demonstrates most clearly Scott's insistence on an actual blockade.[121] This ship had been taken leaving Le Havre which had been declared in a state of blockade. In spite of the proclamation of a blockade 'of a most serious kind', the neutral ship here was stopped, questioned and allowed to enter Le Havre. Although the Lords Commissioners of the Admiralty sent a letter to Scott certifying the existence of a blockade of Le Havre, Scott ignored their statement and held that the *Juffrow Maria Schroeder*

[115] *Mercurius (Gerdes)* (1798), 1 Rob. 80, 84.
[116] *Betsey (Murphy)* (1798), 1 Rob. 93a, 95.
[117] *Neptunus (Kuyp)* (1799), 1 Rob. 170, 172.
[118] *Frederick Molke (Boysen)* (1798), 1 Rob. 86, 87.
[119] *Triheten (Wallen)* (1805), 6 Rob. 65, 67; *Hoffnung (Schmidt)* (1805), 6 Rob. 112, 116, 120. The Lords Commissioners had no difficulty in condemning a neutral vessel in very similar circumstances. *Hare (Chew)* (Lords, 1810), 1 Acton 252, 261.
[120] *Christina Margaretha (Helgesen)* (1805), 6 Rob. 62, 64. The Lords Commissioners agreed that no actual blockade of a port existed where most of the blockading vessels had sailed to a different island. *Nancy (Hurd)* (Lords, 1809), Nicholl's Notes of Prize Appeals, 108, P.R.O. HCA 30/466, 1 Acton 57.
[121] *Juffrow Maria Schroeder (Greenwold)* (1800), 3 Rob. 147.

must be restored. With noticeable frustration he said:

> If the ships stationed on the spot to keep up the blockade will not use their
> force for that purpose, it is impossible for a court of justice to say, there was a
> blockade actually existing at that time, so as to bind this vessel . . . It is in vain
> for governments to impose blockades, if those employed on that service, will
> not enforce them: The inconvenience is very great, and spreads far beyond
> the individual case; reports are eagerly circulated, that the blockade is raised;
> foreigners take advantage of the information; the property of innocent
> persons is ensnared, and the honour of our own country is involved in the
> mistake.[122]

Scott's rejection of mere paper blockades, blockades by proclamation
but not supported by an actual blockading force, could not have been
more clearly stated. The Lords Commissioners, however, showed
fewer scruples in condemning vessels on the ground of breaching an
equally porous blockade.[123]

   In the interest of neutrals' rights, Scott thus clearly tried to impose
some restrictions on Britain's right of blockade. Unfortunately, as we
shall see, he had to swallow these settled principles late in the war
when the British government declared blockades of most of the coast
of Europe by the Orders in Council.

Notification

Since violation of a blockade was similar to a criminal act, a *scienter*
element must be found; the vessel entering or leaving a blockaded
port had to have actual or constructive knowledge of the existence of a
blockade. The notice to other nations of a blockade might be by
formal, public notification, or to a neutral ship by actual notice given
by the blockading vessels. Scott pinpointed the requirements in
stating:

> It is certainly necessary that a blockade should be intimated to neutral
> merchants in some way or other. I may be notified in a public and solemn

---

[122] *Ibid.*, 156–8.

[123] A few years after Scott determined the *Juffrow Maria Schroeder*, the Lords
Commissioners ignored the strenuous argument of the neutral's counsel that the
blockading force at Cadiz had allowed vessels to enter and leave the port, and,
therefore, that no actual blockade existed. The Lords condemned the ships, they
stated, because a *de facto* blockade existed at the time and the neutrals had been
warned of the blockade. *Savannah* (Lords, 1804), Nicholl's Notes of Prize
Appeals, 85, P.R.O. HCA 30/466. As late as 1809 the Lords Commissioners,
however, insisted on an actual blockade, with a force 'sufficient to enforce the
blockade'. *Nancy (Hurd)* (Lords, 1809), 1 Acton 57, 59. One ship at times was a
sufficient force. *Nancy (Woodbury)* (Lords, 1809), 1 Acton 63.

manner, by declaration to foreign governments; and this mode would always be most desirable, although it is sometimes omitted in practice: but it may commence also *de facto*, by a blockading force giving notice on the spot to those who come from a distance, and who may therefore be ignorant of the fact.[124]

Formal notice was neither necessary nor sufficient. A blockade, therefore, could exist without formal notice to neutral governments, and, on the other hand, formal notice without an actual blockading force did not create a legal blockade.[125] If the master of the vessel actually knew that the port was blockaded, this knowledge sufficed.[126]

A blockade created without formal notification ceased when no blockading force remained on station (unless temporarily driven off by the winds). But the court would presume, until the contrary had been proven, that a blockade with formal notice continued to exist until the belligerent gave notice of its cessation. The belligerent, of course, had a duty promptly to notify neutrals that the blockade had been lifted.[127]

Notice must be timely; Scott demanded that the neutral nation must have received notice of the blockade in time to warn this particular vessel of the fact.[128] Scott, perhaps sensitive to the strained diplomatic relations with America at this time, stretched this requirement quite far to assure that American merchants had received notice in sufficient time to countermand orders already given to agents abroad. Where a general agent in Amsterdam had followed an earlier order to ship goods on the account of an American merchant, the court had to consider whether the American merchant would have changed the order had he known that Amsterdam lay under naval siege. Scott applied a principle of 'reasonable equity' to assure fairness to American merchants. '[I]n cases of agency of persons in an enemy's country, during a blockade, something more than the mere strict principle of law is necessary in order to bind employers by their acts.

---

[124] *Vrouw Judith (Volkerts)* (1799), 1 Rob. 150, 152.

[125] *Mercurius (Gerdes)* (1798), 1 Rob. 80, 83.

[126] *Columbia (Weeks)* (1799), 1 Rob. 154, 156, and *Tutela (Reintrock)* (1805), 6 Rob. 177, 181.

[127] *Neptunus (Kuyp)* (1799), 1 Rob. 170, 172, and *Vrow Johanna (Okhen)* (1799), 2 Rob. 109.

[128] *Ringende Jacob (Kreplien)* (1798), 1 Rob. 89, 91. Scott held one week's notice was not sufficient, *Jonge Petronella (Kens)* (1799), 2 Rob. 131, and that even twenty-three days were not sufficient notice to reach a master in a foreign port. *Vrow Margaretha*, unreported (1808), Bod. Lib., 4 Monk Bretton Dep. Constructive notice sufficed. *Calypso (Schultz)* (1799), 2 Rob. 298.

There must be time to give the principal an opportunity of countermanding.'[129]

Furthermore, notice must be specific; the navy's warning to a ship must clearly identify the ports actually blockaded and not merely warn vessels to stay away from any Dutch port. Scott insisted that the British navy abide by the limits he declared to apply to blockades. 'A declaration of blockade is a high act of sovereignty; and a commander of a king's ship is not to extend it.'[130] Similarly formal notice must correctly specify the place blockaded. Scott again used his judicial authority to restrain the impact of blockades. Notice that the ports of Holland were blockaded, he insisted, did not include the neighboring Flemish town of Antwerp, even though the river Scheldt which formed the boundary might have been declared blockaded.[131]

Once timely notice had been given to the neutral countries, the neutral master could not aver ignorance of the blockade. If official notice had been given, the mere act of sailing with a destination to a blockaded port was sufficient ground to condemn a neutral vessel. Until notice that the blockade had been lifted, 'the port is to be considered as closed up, and from the moment of quitting port to sail on such a destination, the offence of violating the blockade is complete'.[132] But if the neutral master was mistakenly told by a British naval commander that such a port was not blockaded, the neutral was free to sail to that port.[133] Scott would not tolerate the appearance of entrapment.

Violation of a naval blockade

As already indicated, a ship could violate a blockade either by entering the blockaded port, or by taking on cargo and leaving the port after the

[129] *Adelaide (Bose)* (1801), 3 Rob. 281, 284. Scott had apparently read the diplomatic situation correctly. Later that year he was informed by the Foreign Secretary that in cases involving American vessels, where the master was in fact ignorant of the blockade, the government desired to release all rights in the captured property, thereby effectively dismissing the prize suit. Lord Hawkesbury to the King's Advocate, November 27, 1801, Arnold's Notebook, 1801, P.R.O. HCA 30/473.
[130] *Henrick and Maria (Baar)* (1799), 1 Rob. 146, 148.
[131] *Frau Ilsabe (Pieper)* (1801), 4 Rob. 63, 64.
[132] *Neptunus (Hempel)* (1799), 2 Rob. 110, 114. The Lords Commissioners insisted on the same rule. *Patrioten (Wolff)* (Lords, 1807); *Jacob (Zacharias)* (Lords, 1807), and *Posten (Kyll)* (Lords, 1807), Nicholl's Notes of Prize Appeals, 96–7, P.R.O. HCA 30/466.
[133] *Neptunus (Hempel)* (1799), 2 Rob. 110, 115. Erroneous information from the Swedish consul, however, did not excuse. *Maria (Hagquist)* (Lords, 1807), Nicholl's Notes of Prize Appeals, 99, P.R.O. HCA 30/466.

blockade had been imposed. Scott often thought of these breaches of blockade in criminal law terms. The British common law of crimes, therefore, had some impact on the development of the law of blockade.

Scott looked, for example, to the developing rules of the law of criminal attempts. In order to convict a party of an attempt to violate a blockade, the court had to find both elements of a criminal attempt: the *mens rea* (the intention to evade the blockade), and an overt act.[134] The mere act of sailing, with a destination to the blockaded port, was enough of an overt act.[135] But, of course, if the master, on hearing of the blockade, altered his course to avoid the blockaded port, the attempted breach had been abandoned.[136] The deviation from the original course had to be voluntary. Where the change of course had been compelled by a privateer, Scott found no change of heart and therefore held that the attempted breach continued.[137] Whether or not the master had indeed altered his course was a factual question for a determination of which Scott might turn to the nautical expertise of Trinity Masters.[138] Finally, even where the attempt was complete because of the intent to sail to a blockaded port and the overt act, Scott found no criminal act if the blockade had in fact been lifted. As Scott expressed it, again borrowing criminal law terminology, there was no *corpus delicti* still existing.[139] In another case he concluded, 'But the ship was not *taken in delicto*, and I have not had any case pointed out to me, in which the Court has pronounced an unfavourable judgment on a ship seized for the breach of a *by-gone* blockade.'[140] Although Scott did not use the modern terminology of impossible attempt to describe this case, he surely was thinking of the same issue.

Scott, in the many cases of attempted entry of a blockaded port,

---

[134] *Columbia* (Weeks) (1799), 1 Rob. 154, 156. The fundamental idea of attempt crimes is discussed, without using the word attempt, in W. Eden, *Principles of penal law* (London, 1771), 76. For a sketchy discussion of the development of the law of criminal attempts at common law, see J. Stephen, *A history of the criminal law of England* (3 vols., London, 1883), II, 221–7, and *H.E.L.*, 2, 452; 3, 373; 5, 201; and 8, 433–4.

[135] *Vrow Johanna* (*Okhen*) (1799), 2 Rob. 109, and *Neptunus* (*Hempel*) (1799), 2 Rob. 110, 113.

[136] *Imina* (*Vroom*) (1800), 3 Rob. 167, 170; *James Cook* (*Jougain*) (1810), Edw. 261, 264.

[137] *Minerva* (*Andaulle*) (1801), 3 Rob. 229, 231.

[138] *Mentor* (*Williams*) (1810), Edw. 207.

[139] *Conferenzrath* (*Baur*) (1806), 6 Rob. 362, 363.

[140] *Lisette* (*Steg*) (1807), 6 Rob. 387, 395. Italics in the original.

established rigorous standards to preserve the integrity of the British right to maintain a blockade. Slipping past a blockading force in the dark or foggy weather, or with adverse winds keeping the blockaders a safe distance at sea, was all too simple and fairly risk-free for the neutral. Scott, therefore, created legal rules which plugged some of the leaks in otherwise porous blockades. As Bynkershoek had indicated much earlier, merely hovering near a blockaded port constituted a breach of the blockade.[141] Scott, for instance, held that a neutral merchant could not send his vessel to the entrance of a blockaded port to inquire there whether the blockade continued in force. 'Who does not at once perceive the frauds to which such a rule would be introductory?' Scott asked. 'The true rule is, that after the knowledge of an existing blockade, you are not to go to the very station of blockade under pretence of enquiry.'[142] Such inquiry, right at the mouth of the port, constituted an attempted violation of the blockade. Because of the great distance involved, Scott had conceded that American merchants could send their vessels with a contingent destination to blockaded ports, with instructions to inquire whether the blockade continued in force. He insisted, however, that the inquiry must be made at some port away from the blockaded area and certainly not at the mouth of the blockaded river.[143] As the intensity of the war increased, Scott tightened this rule to remove the possibility of fraud by the neutrals. He insisted that American ships, sailing with contingent destinations, must inquire at some British channel port whether the blockade continued.[144]

Scott had little hesitation in finding an attempted breach of a blockade where a neutral master alleged he was sailing near the

---

[141] See fn. 98 above.
[142] *Spes (Cornelis)* and *Irene (Lubben)* (1804), 5 Rob. 76, 80, affirmed (Lords, 1807), Nicholl's Notes of Prize Appeals, 99, P.R.O. HCA 30/466. The neutral likewise was not allowed to wait, after warning, near a blockaded port to make up his mind where he would go as an alternative destination. *Apollo (Karsdadt)* (1804), 5 Rob. 286, 289.

The Lords also condemned a neutral vessel for hovering near a blockaded port after a warning. *Aeolus (Tubecke)* (Lords, 1809). But in the *Little William (Brown)* (Lords, 1810), the Lords Commissioners reversed an unreported judgment by Scott. The Lords held, after allowing further proof, that the neutral had not intended to make an inquiry of the blockading ships. Nicholl's Notes of Prize Appeals, 98, 109, 111, P.R.O. HCA 30/466, 1 Acton 141, 162.
[143] *Betsey (Goodhue)* (1799), 1 Rob. 332, 334, and *Dispatch* (1807), unreported, Nicholl's Notebook, 1807–8, P.R.O. HCA 30/465.
[144] *Shepherdess (Miller)* (1804), 5 Rob. 262, 264.

blockade to become better acquainted with the French coast;[145] or
where a neutral vessel anchored near the blockaded port;[146] or where a
neutral vessel approached a blockaded port allegedly to obtain a pilot
to enter another port.[147] As the military necessity for an effective
blockade increased, Scott's tolerance for such excuses decreased. By
shifting the burden of proof more to the neutral claimants, he
repeatedly plugged the loopholes in order to make the blockades
effective. As he explained:

If the Belligerent Country has a right to impose a blockade [*sic*], it must be
justified in the necessary means of enforcing that right; and if a vessel could;
under the pretence of going farther, approach, *cy pres*, close up to the
blockaded port, so as to be enabled to slip in without obstruction, it would be
impossible that any blockade could be maintained. It would, I think, be no
unfair rule of evidence, to hold as a presumption *de jure*, that she goes there
with an intention of breaking the blockade.[148]

Scott, perhaps even more strenuously than Bynkershoek before
him, insisted on a plea of clear and extreme necessity, an imperative
compulsion, as a justification for attempting to enter a blockaded
port.[149] '[N]othing but an absolute and unavoidable necessity will
justify the attempt to enter a blockaded port.'[150] Scott remained
unmoved by a plea of exhaustion of the crew, loss of the mate, distress
of the vessel and loss of the compass.[151] But where the ship in distress
struggled into the blockaded port to receive necessary repairs, Scott
allowed the Trinity Masters to determine that fact that the deviation
was necessary and that the blockaded port was a preferable place to go
for repairs due to the wind conditions.[152] Scott found sufficient

[145] *Adonis (Gottschalk)* (1804), 5 Rob. 256, 258, affirmed (Lords, 1807), Nicholl's Notes of Prize Appeals, 99, P.R.O. HCA 30/466.
[146] *Neutralitet (Zeverver)* (1805), 6 Rob. 30, 35, and *Gute Erwartung (Gay)* (1805), 6 Rob. 182, 184.
[147] *Charlotte Christine (Petersen)* (1805), 6 Rob. 101, 103, and *Arthur (Rathburn)* (1810), Edw. 202, 206, affirmed (Lords, 1811), Nicholl's Notes of Prize Appeals, 125, P.R.O. HCA 30/466.
[148] *Neutralitet (Zeverver)* (1805), 6 Rob. 30, 35.
[149] See fn. 98 above.
[150] *Hurtige Hane (Dahl)* (1799), 2 Rob. 124, 127; *Fortuna (Rhode)* (1803), 5 Rob. 27. Nothing in the case papers for these two cases calls in question the masters' pleas of necessity. Scott obviously looked for extreme necessity. P.R.O. HCA 32/677/187 and 32/1423/1805. The Lords Commissioners likewise insisted on extreme necessity. *Neptunus (Exvast)* (Lords, 1807), and *Charles (Watts)* (Lords, 1809), Nicholl's Notes of Prize Appeals, 99, 109, P.R.O. HCA 30/466.
[151] *Elizabeth (Nowell)* (1810), Edw. 198, 202.
[152] *Charlotta (Elliot)* (1810), Edw. 252, 253.

justification and the ship and cargo were restored. This case was surely an exception to his usual deep suspicion of such excuses.

Although often unwilling to put much faith in the creative stories of neutral masters, Scott persisted in trying to restrain the belligerent's blockade rights within some bounds. If a port was blockaded by sea, therefore, as was invariably the case with British blockades, Scott refused to extend the blockade to internal movement of commerce from the same port city. Where Amsterdam had been blockaded from the sea, Scott restored to the neutral claimants cargoes which had come from Amsterdam by way of canal or overland and were shipped from Rotterdam.[153] 'This Court cannot ... take upon itself to say', Scott insisted in another case of inland movement of goods from Amsterdam, 'that a legal blockade exists, where no actual blockade can be applied.'[154]

Sailing out of a blockaded port, in general, constituted a breach just as sailing to such a port. As always, Scott carefully refined this overly broad statement. True, 'the act of egress was just as culpable as the act of ingress'.[155] Furthermore, this violation, as Bynkershoek had indicated, continued to the end of the voyage, when the escaping vessel had reached its home port.[156] Or, as Scott said more graphically, '[T]he offence is not purged away till the end of the voyage.'[157] But, to define the limits of this offense more precisely, Scott added that ships could depart from a blockaded port in ballast or with cargo taken on before the imposition of the blockade.[158] The neutral violated a blockade by leaving the port when he had made any purchase in that port after the commencement of the blockade.[159] Of course, the purchase of a ship in the blockaded port, after the imposition of a blockade, was also an illegal act.[160]

---

[153] *Ocean (Parker)* (1801), 3 Rob. 297, 298, affirmed (Lords, 1807), Nicholl's Notes of Prize Appeals, 97, P.R.O. HCA 30/466, and *Jonge Pieter (Musterdt)* (1801), 4 Rob. 79, 83.
[154] *Stert (Johnson)* (1801), 4 Rob. 65, 66. The Lords appeared stricter in condemning for breach of a blockade where the cargo had been shipped by an inland route and then loaded aboard a vessel at an open port. *Sophia (Elizabeth) and others* (Lords, 1809), Nicholl's Notes of Prize Appeals, 108, P.R.O. HCA 30/466, 1 Acton 45.
[155] *Frederick Molke (Boysen)* (1798), 1 Rob. 86, 88.
[156] *Welvaart van Pillaw (Botter)* (1799), 2 Rob. 128, 130. For Bynkershoek, see fn. 97 above.
[157] *Maria Schroeder (Greenwold)* (1800), 3 Rob. 147, 154.
[158] *Vrouw Judith (Volkerts)* (1799), 1 Rob. 150, 152; *Neptunus (Kuyp)* (1799), 1 Rob. 170, 171, and *Potsdam (Gerts)* (1801), 4 Rob. 89.
[159] *Betsey (Murphy)* (1798), 1 Rob. 93a, 94.
[160] *General Hamilton (Flinn)* (1805), 6 Rob. 61, 62.

Orders in Council

It will be recalled that Bonaparte, by 1807, had gained control of the whole of northern Europe, including virtually all the ports through which British commerce had continued to enter the Continent. Bonaparte, finally realizing after Trafalgar that his dream of an invasion of Britain must remain unfulfilled, decided to strike at the British economy by prohibiting the importation into the vast portions of Europe under his domination of all goods made in or shipped from Great Britain. This Continental System, first imposed by the Berlin Decree of November 1806, and later tightened by the Fontainebleau and Milan Decrees of 1807, sought to checkmate the predominant sea power of Britain by the French military superiority on land. Bonaparte tried in vain to dam the stream of commerce but the force of the stream burst through each weak spot.[161]

In January 1807 the Grenville administration proclaimed the right to retaliate against the Berlin Decree by prohibiting all trading between ports under French control.[162] The Portland ministry, when it assumed power, criticized these restrictions as ineffective. In November 1807, therefore, it once again eloquently proclaimed the right in international law to retaliate against Bonaparte's Continental System. The two Orders issued on November 11 declared that all ports of France and its satellites, which Bonaparte had closed to British ships and British merchandise, would be considered in a state of blockade. Neutrals (and this clearly meant primarily the United States) could trade to French ports only if their ships had paid duties at some British port. Further unclearly drafted clauses qualified these principal provisions, but the main thrust of the British Orders in Council was to compel neutral vessels to break their voyages and pay duties at British ports.[163] As Spencer Perceval, Chancellor of the Exchequer, accurately summarized these Orders: 'If you [France] will not have *our* trade, as far as we can help it [you] shall have *none*. And as to so much of any trade as you can carry on yourselves, or others carry on with you through us, if you admit it you shall pay [us] for it.'[164]

---

[161] F. Markham, 'The Napoleonic adventure', in *The new Cambridge modern history*, ed. C. Crawley (14 vols., Cambridge, 1950–74), IX, 326–8.

[162] January 7, 1807, P.R.O. PC 2/172, fo. 17. See also *Key to the Orders in Council* (London, 1812).

[163] P.R.O. PC 2/174, fos. 479 and 481.

[164] Quoted in B. Perkins, *Prologue to war, England and the United States 1805–1812* (Berkeley, Cal., 1963), 201. Italics in the original.

The flagrant discrimination against neutral shipping in favor of British commerce was neither unintended nor unnoticed. The West Indian commercial interests in London had campaigned long and effectively to have Britain close American ships and cargoes out of the colonial trade to assure a commercial monopoly for British interests, or, as they stated it, to assure British maritime rights.[165]

In April 1809 the Portland administration, seriously wounded by other problems, modified the 1807 Orders by an Order in Council which more clearly defined the geographical limits of the blockade of French territories. The whole coast of Europe from the river Ems on the north to Pesaro and Orbitello in Italy was declared under blockade.[166] This Order slightly mitigated the harshness of the 1807 Orders by allowing neutrals, primarily Americans, to trade with the ports of the Weser and the Elbe and the ports of Denmark and Prussia.

The British government certainly did not intend by these Orders in Council to deprive British merchants entirely of their lucrative markets in northern Europe. The British ministries issued licences, at first in small numbers and eventually in enormous quantities, primarily to British ships, to trade to the ports supposedly closed up by the Orders in Council. As long as Bonaparte winked at or eventually cooperated with this licence trade, or his officers accepted bribes, British goods could find their way into Europe. Clearly discriminatory in effect, and probably in purpose, these licences convinced many neutrals that Britain merely sought commercial gain for itself by driving neutral commerce from western Europe.[167]

In 1810 Napoleon, through the Duke of Cadore, shrewdly informed the American minister in France that, under certain conditions, the Berlin and Milan Decrees would not have any effect after November 1. The conditions, unlikely of realization, were that prior to November 1 the Orders in Council should have been repealed or the United States should have prohibited commerce with Britain. The American president, James Madison, naively accepted the

[165] Perkins, *Prologue to war*, 196–204; J. Stagg, *Mr. Madison's war – politics, diplomacy, and warfare in the early American republic, 1783–1830* (Princeton, 1983), 18–39. The influential pamphlets by [J. Stephen], *War in disguise or the frauds of the neutral flags* (London, 1805), and [J. Marryat], *Concessions to America the bane of Britain* (London, 1807), were published with the blessing of the British ministry and the West Indian commercial interests.
[166] April 26, 1809, P.R.O. PC 2/180, fo. 519.
[167] Perkins, *Prologue to war*, 304–15, 330–1.

Cadore Letter at face value and declared that the Berlin and Milan
Decrees had been terminated. The British, he thought, no longer
could claim that their Orders in Council were purely retaliatory in
purpose. Madison unrealistically hoped that the British ministry
would lift the blockade imposed by the Orders.[168]

This is surely not the place to sort out the shifting political tides, the
swirls and eddies, which bafflingly marked the British government
during the first decade and a half of the nineteenth century.[169] There
can be no doubt that some politicians were influenced by the West
Indian interest group and the British ship owners. These interests
favored the Orders in Council of 1807 and 1809 because of the
commercial advantages they gave to British merchants. The navy,
they thought, should be used to strangle American shipping. Other
politicians, however, argued that these Orders were a necessary
military response, an act of military retaliation against Bonaparte's
Continental System proclaimed in the Berlin and Milan Decrees.

The northern manufacturers, along with the disparate group of
anti-war liberals, protested against the Orders in Council. Long-
standing political grievances had pitted the provincial cities against
the powerful interests in London and the religious and ideological
opponents of the war against those who sought eternal war until the
French Revolution was crushed. These groups were joined after 1807
by the northern manufacturing cities which saw the nation's most
important commerce, the imports of raw materials and exports of
manufactured goods, imperiled by the government policies expressed
in the Orders in Council. When the Orders were finally repealed in
1812, this new coalition received much of the credit for a great victory.
A reform-minded coalition, which would become a dominant force in
British politics in the following decades, celebrated its first victory.[170]

It is Scott's views, however, which concern this study. The paper
blockades created by British Orders in Council violated the essential
characteristic of a legal blockade, as the commentators on the law of
nations had expressed it and as Scott had repeatedly required. By

[168] *Ibid.*, 245–60.
[169] J. Watson, *The reign of George III, 1760–1815* (Oxford, 1960), 378–462, 476–502,
and Harvey, *Britain in the early nineteenth century*, 115–299, and I. R. Christie,
Wars and revolutions – Britain, 1760–1815 (Cambridge, Mass., 1982), 281–326.
[170] Perkins, *Prologue to war*, 147–9, 257–8, 275–8, 300–41; Crouzet, *L'Economie
britannique*, I, 200–5, 342–56, 382–405; II, 563–641, 809–29, and J. E. Cookson,
The friends of peace – anti-war liberalism in England, 1793–1815 (Cambridge,
1982), 215–37.

these Orders Britain could enforce its blockade of most of Europe from anywhere on the high seas, rather than from naval vessels stationed at a blockaded port. Only an effective blockade, Scott had stated, which actually deterred entrance to or exit from a port would be recognized as a legally binding blockade. Anything less, he had implied, would be a fraud on neutral rights.[171] His reaction to the Orders in Council, therefore, provides a unique insight into Scott's judicial character.

Even as the first cases involving captures under the Orders in Council were coming before the admiralty court, Scott expressed his views on their legality in Parliament. In 1807 and 1808 there had been extensive debate in Parliament on the 1807 Orders. Some opposition members questioned not only their wisdom but their legality under the law of nations. Near the end of the debate which had continued off and on for months, Scott delighted the government by speaking in support of the Orders in Council. He discussed the law of nations as conventional and binding only when its rules were observed by all parties concerned. When one party departed from the rules, Scott proclaimed, '[T]he other was left to the guidance of natural justice; and by the laws of natural justice, retaliation was authorised as an essential part of self-defence.'[172] Scott elaborated on this right of retaliation, the heart of the ministry's justification of the Orders. If an enemy, he said, abided by the restrictions of the law of nations, then the other belligerent was obliged to fight under the same restrictions. But if one belligerent 'resorted to unusual modes of warfare, then it was competent for his adversary to pursue him even to neutral ground'. Proceeding from these general principles, Scott turned to the situation created by the Berlin Decree. France had intended to cut off Britain from all commerce with the Continent. Even if France had tolerated exceptions to its Decree, this merely proved again that France remained 'fluctuating and capricious'. Carrying his argument to a patriotic extreme, Scott told Parliament that even if France had

---

[171] See above, pp. 207–8.

[172] Hansard, 1st ser. X, 1066–7 (March 10, 1808). Spencer Perceval, Chancellor of the Exchequer, wrote to the king on March 12, 1808 to inform him that the government's bill for carrying into execution the Orders in Council had passed the House. Perceval said that Scott began the debate on the third reading and made a most able and powerful argument on the legality of the Orders. Scott was followed in presenting the government's position by James Stephen, author of *War in disguise* and principal spokesman for the West Indian planters. *The later correspondence of George III*, ed. A. Aspinall (5 vols., Cambridge, 1966–70), 3620. See 48 Geo. III, c. 26; 48 Geo. III, c. 37.

not actually enforced its Decree, 'it was nevertheless an injury, because it was an insult to the country'. Scott thus completely supported the position of the Portland ministry by endorsing the legality of the Orders in Council as justifiable retaliation. He concluded: 'Upon the morality of the measure, therefore, there was no doubt. The question of its policy was more complex.'[173] Even though standards change over the centuries, it is hard to imagine a clearer appearance of impropriety than for a judge to express such views on highly controversial topics in advance of the many cases which would surely come before him raising the same issue. Certainly neutrals had good reason to remain skeptical of Scott's protestations of the fair, supranational character of the law he applied.

In the first cases which came before him for breach of the 1807 Orders in Council, Scott treated this new form of blockade as any other blockade. He did not even mention that the blockades enforceable from the high seas differed from the actual blockades he had earlier considered the norm.[174] He expressed his regrets that blockades caused inconvenience to neutrals, but this sort of soothing remark applied to all blockades. Any permission the American president gave for ships to sail, Scott observed, applied only to exemptions from the American embargo. Scott felt confident that no neutral government would assume it had the power of relaxing a belligerent's blockade. It could hardly be expected, he said, 'that the belligerent country should trust the preservation of its rights to the vigilance of others'.[175]

Scott at times construed the Orders in Council narrowly. 'It is extremely necessary', he insisted, 'not to carry the rule one inch beyond the purpose for which it was adopted.'[176] Elsewhere he stated: '[C]ertainly it is not within the power of this Court to extend the operation of the blockade beyond the limits which the Public Authority has assigned to it.'[177] Nonetheless, he applied the Orders in Council to a case involving carriage of passengers for hire, even

[173] Hansard, 1st ser. X, 1066–7.
[174] *Christiansberg (Vanderweyde)* (1807), 6 Rob. 376; *Exchange (Ledet)* (1808), Edw. 39; *Speculation (Koht)* (1810), Edw. 184; *Elizabeth (Nowell)* (1810), Edw. 198. The Lords likewise treated these cases as ordinary blockade cases. *Ann (Howland)* (Lords, 1810), Nicholl's Notes of Prize Appeals, 113, P.R.O. HCA 30/466.
[175] *Comet (Mix)* (1808), Edw. 32, 34, affirmed (Lords, 1810), Nicholl's Notes of Prize Appeals, 114, P.R.O. HCA 30/466.
[176] *Lucy (Taylor)* (1809), Edw. 122, and *Johan (Abraham)* (1810), Edw. 275, 276.
[177] *Luna (Southworth)* (1810), Edw. 190, 191.

though the Orders might have been interpreted to apply only to the carriage of cargo for freight.[178] Scott even enforced the Orders where a British commander near the blockaded port gave the American vessel permission to proceed. Earlier he had refused to condemn a neutral vessel under such circumstances which could be perceived as entrapment,[179] but now his tone had changed.

So long as these Orders in Council exist, they are to be expounded and applied by this Court; and if they press with any unnecessary severity on the commerce of other countries, they may be matter very proper for the consideration of His Majesty's Government; but this Court must proceed upon general Rules of interpretation.[180]

In the case of the American ship, the *Fox*, Scott for the first time seriously addressed the question of the legality of the Orders in Council.[181] The group of vessels considered together in this case had sailed from America in the belief, encouraged by President Madison, that the Cadore Letter would eliminate the British need to retaliate and that Britain would therefore repeal the Orders in Council. The British government stayed proceedings in these cases to buy time in the hope that America would on its own acknowledge its error of putting any credence in the Cadore Letter. When the American position became clearer, however, the government put aside whatever misgivings it had about the legality of the Orders and allowed the cases to proceed in the admiralty court.[182]

Scott began his *Fox* judgment with what all must have perceived as a rhetorical question: 'What would be the duty of the Court under Orders in Council that were repugnant to the law of nations?'[183] Since the answer was so obvious, especially after Scott had publicly endorsed in Parliament the government's explanation of a purely retaliatory purpose, his lengthy judgment has more of the flavor of a

---

[178] *Rose in Bloom* (*Olcott*) (1811), 1 Dod. 57, 58. Perhaps Scott was relying implicitly on the *Peggy* (*Destonet*) (Lords, 1810), in which the Lords stated that breach of the Orders in Council to discharge passengers was no excuse. Nicholl's Notes of Prize Appeals, 115, P.R.O. HCA 30/466.

[179] *Neptunus* (*Hempel*) (1799), 2 Rob. 110, 115, and *Juffrow Maria Schroeder* (*Greenwold*) (1800), 3 Rob. 147, 156–8, discussed above, pp. 207–8.

[180] *Courier* (*Erick*) (1810), Edw. 249.

[181] *Fox and others* (1811), Edw. 311.

[182] Perkins, *Prologue to war*, 277–8, 312–13.

[183] *Fox and others* (1811), Edw. 312.

government White Paper than of a judicial opinion.

In answer to this question Scott did at least hint that the law of nations placed some outer limits on the power of the British government in its Orders. The court, he said, was obliged to administer the law of nations on the one hand, but on the other hand, he acknowledged that the King in Council had legislative power over the admiralty court. Any contradiction between these seemingly opposed duties disappeared, however, since the government's Orders were presumed to be consistent with the law of nations. With this effectively irrebuttable presumption as a premise, Scott's conclusion ineluctably followed. He drew an inapt analogy from the relationship between acts of Parliament and the common law, which the common law courts presumed to be in accord. His analogy was inapt since the Orders in Council had their primary impact, not on British subjects, but on neutrals, beyond the legitimate reach of the Council or Parliament. Scott went as far as he needed to go in justifying the Orders in Council, as he had in his speech before Parliament. 'I have no hesitation in saying, that [the Orders in Council] would cease to be just if they ceased to be retaliatory; and they would cease to be retaliatory, from the moment the enemy retracts in a sincere manner those measures of his which they were intended to retaliate.'[184] By presuming no conflict between the law of nations as stated by the admiralty court and the Orders in Council, Scott left no room for doubt about the legality of the Orders.

Scott insisted that even the Americans could not have expected the admiralty court to annul the Orders by interpretation. Only an official revocation of the Orders would justify the court in not applying them. Surely the court would not presume the government had revoked

---

[184] *Ibid.*, 314. Scott spelled out the retaliatory nature of the Orders in stating: 'When the State, in consequence of gross outrages upon the law of nations committed by Its adversary, was compelled by a necessity which It laments, to resort to measures which It otherwise condemns, It pledged Itself to the revocation of those measures as soon as the necessity ceases. – And till the State revokes them, this Court is bound to presume that the necessity continues to exist. It cannot, without extreme indecency, suppose that they would continue a moment longer than the necessity which produced them, or that the Notification that such measures were revoked, would be less public and formal than their first establishment. Their establishment was doubtless a great and signal departure from the ordinary administration of justice in the ordinary state of the exercise of public hostility, but was justified by the extraordinary deviation from the common exercise of hostility in the conduct of the enemy.' *Ibid.*, 314–15.

them. Furthermore, the supposed French withdrawal of its Decrees involved no public edict or declaration of repeal. Scott could not contain his contempt for the Cadore Letter. 'The declaration of the person stiling himself Duke de *Cadore* imports no revocation; for that declaration imports only a conditional retractation, and this upon conditions known to be impossible to be complied with.'[185] The American government's willingness to accept the Cadore Letter as official could not be binding on a British court, Scott insisted. Since the British government had not revoked its Orders, and since there was a total failure of evidence that France had revoked its Decrees, Scott concluded that he must pronounce 'that the Orders in Council subsist in perfect justice as well as in complete authority'.[186]

Scott just as easily brushed aside the objection that the Orders in Council existed merely to ensure a favorable trading position for British merchants and that the numerous licences demonstrated the discriminatory commercial purpose of the Orders. He conceded 'that a blockade, imposed for the purpose of obtaining a commercial monopoly for the private advantage of the State which lays on such blockade, is illegal and void on the very principle upon which it is founded'.[187] Scott asserted, however, that more licences had been granted to neutral than to British vessels to trade with France. He did not state his authority for this unproven proposition. But regardless of the question of discrimination, the Orders were justified, he said, as retaliatory measures. France had attempted to stop neutrals from trading with Britain, so Britain was justified in stopping neutrals from trading with France. All too facilely Scott answered this well-founded objection that the Orders contained more than a suggestion of commercial chauvinism.

Although Scott gave the American claimants time to bring in further proof that the French Decrees had in fact been revoked, in the end they could only produce 'the letter of the person styling himself *Duc de Cadore*'. Scott held that the French Decrees had not been revoked and therefore condemned the American vessels for breach of the Orders in Council.[188]

---

[185] *Fox and others* (1811), Edw. 319.
[186] *Ibid.*, 320.
[187] *Ibid.*
[188] *Ibid.*, 324–6.

Scott elaborated his views on the Cadore Letter and other alleged evidence of a revocation of the French Decrees in the extraordinarily lengthy opinion involving the *Snipe* and other American vessels.[189] America's declaration of war on Britain was perhaps already known in London before Scott issued this justification of Britain's Orders in Council (which had by that time been repealed). The tone and repetitious care for detail, the attachment of documents as appendices and the uncompromising demand for the highest level of proof of French revocation all suggest that Scott prepared the *Snipe* opinion more as an exercise in diplomacy than of judicial decision-making. Any foreign office would have been proud to have issued to the world such a forceful justification of the nation's policies.

If the cases of the *Fox* and the *Snipe* exhibit Scott as more a functionary of the British government than a fair, unbiased judge administering even-handedly to all nations a supranational body of law, as he had professed to be, one can reasonably ask whether any judge from any nation has responded differently to such circumstances. Judicial heroism in time of war is seldom observed. *Silent leges inter arma*, as Cicero had observed centuries earlier.

Scott had interpreted, often with no precedents to guide him, the legal norms for blockades. He framed this body of law in a manner which did restrict some excesses of the British navy and provide some protection for neutral rights. But when the British government established a new policy, opposed to prior legal norms on the law of blockade, Scott marched to the drum of his government without flinching. Only the utterly naive neutral could have expected him to do otherwise. It would surely be unthinkable for the judge of the admiralty court to hold the Orders in Council invalid because they had conflicted with the loosely stated, conflicting norms of the law of nations or with the self-generated precedents of that court, and merely to enable neutral merchants to reap windfall profits made possible by the war.

---

[189] *Snipe and others* (1812), Edw. 381. America declared war on Britain on June 17, 1812. On June 23, the Orders in Council were repealed. On July 14, Lord Castlereagh, the Foreign Secretary, assured Parliament that information concerning the repeal of the Berlin and Milan Decrees had been forwarded to the admiralty court. Scott issued the decision in *Snipe* on July 30. Apparently America's declaration of war became known in London on July 31. Perkins, *Prologue to war*, 336–8, 406–19; Hansard, 1st ser. XXIII, 1044 (July 14, 1812).

COLONIAL TRADE

Eighteenth century

This section will focus on two important doctrines of prize law, the Rule of War of 1756 and the doctrine of Continuous Voyage. This discussion will be greatly facilitated by a detailed and reliable history of these doctrines for the middle decades of the eighteenth century.[190] These two rules, largely the creation of British legal authorities, had the effect of imposing a partial blockade on the enemy's colonial ports. But, because of these rules, the British avoided the expense of maintaining a naval force on station and the health-risks of hovering in the disease-ridden, semi-tropical seas. Even without these costs the enemy's colonies could be weakened, rendered useless to their mother country and perhaps reduced to submission by the capture anywhere on the high seas of many of the neutral vessels trading there.

The colonial warfare of the eighteenth century, which focused primarily on the West Indian colonies, can be best understood within the mercantilist context of that era. Colonies were founded and fostered to enrich the mother country, to assure a steady supply of otherwise unavailable or costly raw materials and also to provide a closed market for the mother country's products. In peacetime the colonial trade was generally limited exclusively to nationals of the mother country. Those nations which had been tardy in establishing colonies viewed times of war as golden opportunities to establish trading routes to the colonies of a belligerent nation. Britain, of course, with its naval superiority could adequately maintain its own colonies with no help from meddling neutrals. It resented the intrusion of the greedy neutrals, who had few if any colonies of their own, into the lucrative and essential trade of its enemy's colonies. Colonies, in the mercantilist view, were considered as crucially important to enhance the wealth, power and prestige of the mother country. During war, however, colonies could become costly encumbrances unless the mother country could maintain the flow of commerce in its own or in neutral ships. Each belligerent sought to cut off from the enemy the trade with its colonies in order to reduce the national wealth which supported armies and fleets. The belligerent with the

[190] Pares, *Colonial blockade*, 180–225, 261–4, 286–8.

most powerful naval force could often sever the commercial ties between the enemy and its colonies so that the isolated colony might become an easy prey for the naval force.[191]

Rule of '56

The British traditionally applied the rule that enemy cargo aboard a neutral ship was subject to capture.[192] According to this view of the law of nations, neutrals in time of war could not carry cargo belonging to a belligerent. Britain in the late seventeenth century, hoping to be a neutral carrier in future wars, had insisted on reversing this ordinary rule in its treaty with the Dutch. Under the Anglo-Dutch Treaty of 1674, when either party was at war, the other party's ships could carry enemy cargo without fear of capture. Free ships, under this treaty provision, made the cargo free. Unfortunately for the British, however, the Dutch derived the benefits from this treaty since the Dutch became the most significant neutral carrier in the eighteenth-century wars while Britain was invariably a belligerent.[193]

The people and the government of Great Britain, during the wars of the 1740s and 1750s, found it difficult to accept the consequences of the Dutch Treaty of 1674. By the terms of that treaty, the Dutch, because neutral, claimed the right to carry cargo freely to or from the French or Spanish colonies in the West Indies, which France and Spain had been forced by the war to open to neutral trade. Britain's naval prowess remained partly foiled as long as the French or Spanish could continue normal commerce with their colonies in Dutch vessels. While Britain fought wars to expand its own commerce, it had to watch the Dutch profit from the British war-effort. A German who became a great financier in London, Nicholas Magens, expressed the British indignation at the ability of neutrals to undermine the mercantilist dogma:

Might not those who fought the battles ask, what signifies our being masters at sea, if we shall not have liberty to stop ships from serving our enemy? And when we examine to the bottom of the thing, it appears very evident, that sea battles are fought not so much to kill people, as to be masters of trade,

---

[191] Kulsrud, *Maritime neutrality*, 61–74.
[192] See, for instance, *Report of the law officers*, in Marsden, *Law of the sea*, II, 350. The various positions on neutral commerce are discussed in Best, *Humanity in warfare*, 68–74.
[193] Pares, *Colonial blockade*, 175–80. Other treaties with other nations were also involved, but the Dutch Treaty will serve as the most difficult and clearest example.

whereby people live; and by stopping their supplies, to compel our enemies in the end to live in friendship with us.[194]

British lawyers searched for arguments which would annul the effect of the Anglo-Dutch Treaty. Trading *with* the enemy, they contended, was fair neutral trade, but trading *for* the enemy was an illegal, unneutral act. Trading *with* the enemy came to mean pursuing established trade routes, while trading *for* the enemy meant engaging in newly created avenues. In other words, the Dutch trade should not be worse off because of the war but it certainly should not be in a better position because Britain was at war. When the French or Spanish, because of the pressure of the British fleet, threw open to neutrals the formerly exclusive trade with their colonies, the neutral who took advantage of this new trade was trading *for* the enemy. The argument was also made that the Anglo-Dutch Treaty of 1674 did not apply to the American colonies, since the Dutch had no trade there when the treaty was made. Treaties, after all, remained binding only as long as the circumstances had not changed, *rebus sic stantibus*. Finally, the British contended, if a Dutch ship, by the authorization to trade with a Spanish colony, became an adopted Spanish ship, it could no longer claim the protection of the Dutch Treaty.[195]

William Murray, the future Lord Mansfield, led the way in this creative reinterpretation of the Dutch Treaty both as counsel arguing before the Lords Commissioners for Prize Appeals and later as the leading force on this semi-judicial and semi-political body. He later stated the essence of the Rule of '56 in a case argued before King's Bench. 'The rule is, that if a neutral ship trades to a French colony, with all the privileges of a French ship, and is thus adopted and naturalized, it must be looked upon as a French ship, and is liable to be taken.'[196]

Britain, therefore, had no need to annul the Dutch Treaty of 1674; the Rule of '56 had rendered it irrelevant. If any neutral in time of war was allowed to trade with an enemy's colony which had been closed to that neutral in peacetime, by that act the neutral was considered by

[194] Quoted in Pares, *Colonial blockade*, 181.
[195] *Ibid.*, 181–204. The evolution of the Rule of '56, so fully documented by Pares, can also be seen in sources he did not consider, such as: R.A., Simpson MS 94, 110–11, 124, 142–3, 196–7, 260, 328; Unnamed (1746), Lee Opinions, and *Eendraught (Graaf)* (1747), H.S.P. Lee Cases. Most of the legal arguments for the Rule of '56 were expressed in a partisan and murky pamphlet, J. Marriott, *The case of the Dutch ships considered*, first published in 1759.
[196] *Barens v Rucker* (1760), 1 Black. W. 313, 314.

the British admiralty court as an adopted enemy ship liable to capture. The Rule of '56 applied to several different situations. Most clearly neutrals could not carry cargo between the French colonies and France; such trade in peacetime most certainly had been the monopoly of French ships. The Rule could also be applied to carriage of cargo by a neutral from a French colony to some neutral port, for instance, to Holland. Since the French colonies had been closed in peacetime to such trade, the Dutch could not engage in it once the pressures of war compelled the French to open their colonial ports to neutral ships. But, as we shall see, the British government could relax the Rule of '56 and tolerate this trade if it suited its interests. Finally, the Rule of '56 could be applied to the cabotage or coastal trade of the enemy. If in time of peace Dutch ships could not carry cargo from one French port to another, they could not engage in such a trade in war.[197]

A generation after this doctrine had been developed, during the years Scott practiced as a civilian, the Rule of '56 continued as a binding principle of British prize law. This can be shown most clearly by an analysis of the case of the *Sally*, decided by the Lords Commissioners in 1796.[198] This case also highlights the fact that the British government applied or did not apply the Rule depending on the diplomatic pressures of the moment. The British government could tighten its grip to harm the enemy until the cries of injured neutrals forced it to relax its hold.

The American vessel *Sally* had been captured with a cargo shipped from one of the French islands. The admiralty court had restored the ship and cargo to the American owners but had refused to allow costs and damages to the American claimants. On appeal to the Lords Commissioners, counsel representing the American claimants contended that the Rule of '56 did not affect this capture since the Rule had not been applied during the American Revolution. The capture, therefore, was illegal and the American owners should receive damages and costs for this interruption of neutral commerce. Scott, the King's Advocate, accurately restated the Rule of '56 on behalf of the captors. He briefly restated the mercantilist policies behind the Rule, policies which much earlier had been incorporated into the

[197] Several cases in which the Lords Commissioners applied or discussed the Rule of '56 are published in Burrell's *Reports. America* (Lords, 1759); *Resolutie* (Lords, 1760); *Anna* (Lords, 1760); *Good Christian* (Lords, 1760); and *Johanna Margretta* (Lords, 1761), Burrell, 210, 213, 214, 216, 218.
[198] *Sally* (*Choates*) (Lords, 1796), Arnold's Notebook, 1795–6, P.R.O. HCA 30/468, and Nicholl's Notes of Prize Appeals, 17, P.R.O. HCA 30/466.

prize judgments of the Lords Commissioners and the admiralty court. When a neutral interposed in the distressed commerce of the enemy, Scott said, the neutral engaged in commerce in which it could not have traded in peacetime. Neutrals had a right to continue to carry on their usual commerce, undisturbed by the outbreak of war. But when neutrals devised a new trade growing out of the necessities of war and thereby snatched the enemy from the distress to which the British fleet had reduced its colonial trade, any neutral claim, Scott insisted, exceeded the bounds of justice. The neutral, excluded from such trade in peacetime, must not interpose to aid the enemy to carry on its warfare more effectively. Scott distinguished the situation during the American Revolution. Then the French had declared that their colonies were open to neutral trade. Although dubious of France's sincerity, the British courts, Scott maintained, had treated this as a permanent relaxation of the French colonial ports to most non-French commerce. After the French Revolution, Scott noted, the control of the mother country remained weak over the French colonies and some governors in the West Indies did tolerate many irregularities in allowing non-French trade. These unlawful practices, Scott implied, did not demonstrate that the French colonies had been opened to non-French vessels, and therefore the Rule of '56 must be applied. Furthermore, the British Privy Council by its instructions to naval commanders of 1793 had applied the Rule of '56. British ships had been instructed to bring in for adjudication any ships carrying the produce of the French colonies. Even though the captors had not known of these instructions, they had acted properly, Scott concluded, in bringing in the *Sally* for a determination by the court. The Lord President of the Council, the Earl of Mansfield, in his speech for the Lords, completely accepted Scott's argument.[199]

[199] Scott made these same basic arguments in his correspondence as King's Advocate with Lord Grenville, August 2 and 4, 1794 and January 14, 1796, P.R.O. FO 83/2204, fos. 27, 33, 73. Scott had also argued before the admiralty court that the Rule of '56 should be applied in *Active (Blair)* (1794), but to no avail. Nicholl's Notebook, 1793–7, 99, P.R.O. HCA 30/464.

The Lords Commissioners, by a general order of July 9, 1796, had directed that French products from the French islands, which had become American property and were being carried to America in an American vessel, would be restored to the American owners. The captors were warned that they would not have a just cause to bring in such captures for adjudication and would thus be exposed to liability for costs and damages. Nicholl's Notes of Prize Appeals, 21, P.R.O. HCA 30/466. Shortly after the general order of July 9, 1796, Scott argued before the Lords Commissioners that the relaxation of the Rule of '56, in favor of Americans trading between the French islands and America, should not be applied to a Danish vessel.

Continuous Voyage

The Rule of '56 went far to solve the British problem of cutting off the trade to the French of Spanish colonies when it was at war with France or Spain. But this Rule only applied to direct trade to or from an enemy colony. The Dutch could neatly circumvent this Rule by trading with their own West Indian colonies, St Eustatius and Curaçao. Of course, everyone knew that the cargoes shipped at St Eustatius often had come from one of the French islands. In many cases the French cargo had not even been unloaded onto the shore of St Eustatius, but was transshipped in the port from one vessel to a Dutch vessel. Without a close blockade of the French islands, the British found it impossible to stop all trade between those islands and St Eustatius.

British legal authorities solved this problem by applying a presumption that products of the French islands remained French and therefore enemy property, even though transshipped at St Eustatius. Because the Dutch Treaty permitted the carriage of enemy cargo, this presumption by itself would not suffice to stop Dutch ships from carrying French colonial cargoes shipped from St Eustatius. The shipment of the cargo, however, was treated as one continuous voyage from the French colony, and therefore the Rule of '56 applied to the cargo which could be condemned. Since the first part of the voyage, from the French islands to some neutral port, was prohibited under the Rule of '56, the mere transfer of the goods from one ship to a neutral ship would not sufficiently interrupt the voyage. In other words, the entire voyage would be regarded as one, from start at the French islands, to finish at some French port, and thus fall within the Rule of '56. The convenient use of a neutral port to reload the cargo aboard a neutral vessel would not create a second, legal voyage. If the British courts found that the original destination was to a French port and that the cargo remained French property, then the voyage would be regarded as one continuous voyage. Because of this doctrine of Continuous Voyage, the Rule of '56 applied to each segment of the voyage.[200]

The Lords Commissioners, however, restored the property. Nicholl observed in his notes that the Lords 'thereby admitted that in the present war all neutrals may legally trade to the French Islands'. *Unity (Verdit)* (Lords, 1796), Nicholl's Notes of Prize Appeals, 20, P.R.O. HCA 30/466. ˜

[200] Pares, *Colonial blockade*, 204–24.

.These two doctrines, intertwined as they were, deprived the French of virtually all benefit from their colonies. Neutrals, without British leave, could not directly import or export any cargo to or from the French colonies without risk of capture by the British. The Rule of '56 barred such trade. Furthermore, neutrals could not even carry French products from a neutral port unless they could overcome the presumption that the cargo remained French and that the continued voyage was part of the original intention to ship the cargo from the French colony to France.

The records from the years Scott practiced as a civilian do not discuss many cases in which the doctrine of Continuous Voyage was applied. Scott certainly knew of the doctrine from these years. For instance, an American ship, the *Harriet and Eliza* had sailed under protection of a French convoy apparently from some American port to the French islands.[201] Clearly it could have been captured under the Rule of '56 as an adopted French ship. But it had been separated from the convoy and put into a different American port. The owners alleged that the cargo had been sold in America and therefore should no longer be treated as French property. The British court, however, doubted that the sale had truly been effected since the cargo had been captured in the same vessel in which it had first been shipped. The Lords Commissioners held that the proof of the sale of the cargo was insufficient, undoubtedly because they questioned whether it had ever been unloaded from the vessel. Although not discussed explicitly, this case apparently applied the doctrine of Continuous Voyage.

Scott as judge

The Rule of '56
Scott, in his character as judge, summed up, reformulated and clarified the settled and thoroughly British principles of the Rule of '56 and the mercantilist policies which had long been absorbed into prize precedents. The government could apply the Rule more or less rigorously and Scott followed the government's policies.

For instance, in the case of the *Immanuel* he reiterated, in a more elaborate form, the rationale for the Rule of '56 which he had

---

[201] *Harriet and Eliza (Shuman)* (Lords, 1797), Nicholl's Notes of Prize Appeals, 28, P.R.O. HCA 30/466.

presented as counsel in the case of the *Sally*.[202] The *Immanuel*, a Hamburg ship, had sailed from Hamburg on a voyage to St Domingo, a French colony in a state of rebellion by the slave population. The *Immanuel* had made a stop at Bordeaux to discharge and pick up cargo. Counsel for the Hamburg owners acknowledged that the system of colonial monopolies once had provided the justification for the Rule of '56. But, the counsel for the neutrals argued, that mercantilist system during the American Revolution and the current war with France had been so riddled with exceptions by French and British relaxations of exclusive trading rights that the Rule of '56 should not be applied. Neutral merchants, because of these many exceptions, rightly presumed that they were at liberty to trade with the colonies of a belligerent with impunity. The Rule of '56 rested on the mercantilist system of exclusive trade which once had prevailed. Only if the court should find a trade wholly and exclusively confined to the enemy, counsel contended, and only if the colonial ports had been opened to neutrals solely because of the pressures of war, should the Rule of '56 be applied.[203]

Scott began his judgment in the case of the *Immanuel* by brushing aside the suggestion that St Domingo no longer remained within the French colonial system because of a slave rebellion. The court could not for obvious reasons, he sniffed, accept the authority of common newspapers.[204] Scott then distinguished those cargo items which had been originally shipped from Hamburg from those loaded at Bordeaux. Since former decisions had established the legality of direct trade between Hamburg and St Domingo, the cargo shipped from Hamburg was restored.[205]

Turning to the far more difficult question, Scott addressed the issue whether the Rule of '56 applied to the rest of the cargo. When war broke out, Scott said as he had in the *Sally*, neutrals have the right to continue as fully as possible their accustomed trade, with the exception of contraband and blockade. But trade to which the neutral

---

[202] *Immanuel (Eysenberg)* (1799), 2 Rob. 186. The *Sally* was discussed above at pp. 227–8.

[203] *Immanuel (Eysenberg)* (1799), 2 Rob. 186, 189–94, argument of Drs Arnold and Sewell.

[204] *Ibid.*, 194. When the British government, although not recognizing the rebels, showed a favorable disposition to them because of their hostility to the French, Scott no longer considered all of St Domingo a French colony. *Manilla (Barret)* (1808), Edw. 1.

[205] *Immanuel (Eysenberg)* (1799), 2 Rob. 186, 197.

had no right or title in peacetime, which became available to the neutral only because the British had succeeded in disrupting its enemy's colonial trade, was not open to neutrals. A belligerent, Scott insisted, had the right to capture its enemy's colonies and no neutral had a right to intervene to prevent the fall of these colonies. Scott restated the Rule of '56 with its familiar rationale:

> Upon these grounds, it cannot be contended to be a *right* of neutrals, to intrude into a commerce which had been uniformly shut against them, and which is now forced open merely by the pressure of war; for when the enemy, under an entire inability to supply his colonies and to export their products, affects to open them to neutrals, it is not his will but his necessity that changes his system; that change is the direct and unavoidable consequence of the compulsion of war, it is a measure not of *French* councils, but of *British* force.[206]

Scott acknowledged, as counsel for the Hamburg claimants had argued, that the British had at various times relaxed the Rule of '56 by instructions to the captors. No instructions, however, had ever allowed direct trade between the mother country and its colony. Scott rejected the argument that these various relaxations of the Rule of '56 had undermined the Rule itself. Scott fully supported the government's authority to manipulate the Rule of '56 and would go no further in allowing exceptions than the language of the government's instructions to naval commanders: '[W]hat is not found therein permitted, is understood to be prohibited, upon this plain principle, that the colony trade is generally prohibited, and that whatever is not specially relaxed continues in a state of interdiction.'[207] Scott attempted to distinguish other changes in its accustomed policy which a nation at war commonly made, such as opening free ports and admitting foreigners into its armed services. To distinguish these from the colonial trade, thrown open to neutrals in time of war, Scott pointed out that the difference lay in the motive. Free ports or use of foreign troops, Scott conceded, arose out of the state of war, but opening the colonial monopoly to neutral trade were 'acts of distress, signals of defeat and depression . . . partial surrenders to the force of the enemy'.[208] With this somewhat shaky distinction, Scott tried to provide a policy basis for the government's manipulation of the Rule of '56. Scott, therefore, condemned the cargo shipped from Bordeaux

---

[206] *Ibid.*, 200. Italics in the original.
[207] *Ibid.*, 202.
[208] *Ibid.*, 205.

Prize law – a survey

233

but, because of the neutral's understandable mistake about the Rule, Scott restored the neutral vessel.

Scott consistently marched to the beat of the government's drum. In the case of the *Providentia* he discussed the various, conflicting instructions to naval commanders which the government had issued during the war of 1793.[209] The *Providentia* had been captured on a voyage from Vera Cruz, Mexico, to Hamburg with a special licence to trade at this ordinarily restricted Spanish port. Scott pointed out that the government's instructions of 1793 had directed the British ships to seize all vessels trading with the enemy. In 1794 the government's instructions had directed British vessels to capture any ship with a cargo of West Indian produce coming directly from the West Indies to any port of Europe. Clearly the government in these instructions was tolerating commerce between the West Indies and America. In 1798 the government directed the capture of ships with the produce of French or Spanish colonies which were coming from the West Indies to some port of Europe other than the ports of the country to which the vessel belonged. By these 1798 instructions the government allowed trade with the West Indies to some neutral country of Europe as long as the neutral vessel belonged to that country.[210] A Hamburg vessel, therefore, like the *Providentia*, could carry Spanish produce to Hamburg, whereas an American vessel could not. Scott, after tracing the history of the Rule of '56, merely followed the applicable instructions of the British government. 'I shall look principally to the King's instructions to his cruizers as the safest guide for this Court to follow', he said.[211] When the government, for diplomatic reasons, relaxed the Rule of '56, Scott readily allowed neutrals to enjoy the benefit of the less rigorous instructions. He, therefore, rejected the captor's argument that the Spanish licence had special significance as showing that the Hamburg vessel had become an adopted Spanish ship. He treated the instructions as a statute and found nothing in them which limited the trade with Spanish colonies if a Spanish licence had been granted.[212] He therefore restored the *Providentia* and its cargo to the Hamburg owners. It bothered Scott not at all that the *Providentia* would have been a lawful prize under the broad terms of the Rule of

---

[209] *Providentia* (*Hinch*) (1799), 2 Rob. 142.
[210] *Ibid.*, 151. These instructions are reproduced in the Appendix to Robinson's second volume of *Reports*, 2 Rob. App. 1–2.
[211] *Providentia* (*Hinch*) (1799), 2 Rob. 142, 151.
[212] *Ibid.*, 152.

'56, or under the government's instructions of 1793 or 1794. If ever there was a Spanish port closed to non-Spanish trade, it was Vera Cruz, as was shown by the special licence the Spanish required. Scott certainly realized that Vera Cruz had been opened solely because of the pressures of war. But when the British government relaxed the Rule of '56, Scott followed its lead.[213]

Scott had many occasions to restate and apply the Rule of '56.[214] Despite the argument that the Rule had been abandoned by the British during the American Revolution, he applied it to neutrals carrying cargo from one enemy port to another, the coasting trade of France or Spain.[215] But he distinguished the case of neutral trade from a port in one enemy country (France) to a port in another enemy country (Holland) because such traffic was open in time of peace.[216] Where an American vessel carried cargo from a Spanish colony to Spain only because it had been captured by the French and taken to Spain, Scott restored the ship and cargo. The deviation to Spain was not voluntary and therefore the ship did not come within the Rule of '56.[217] Scott also applied the Rule to neutral trade from the Dutch East Indian settlements when he was convinced that non-Dutch Europeans were not ordinarily permitted to trade at the settlement in time of peace.[218] But since Americans had been permitted to trade before the war with the Dutch colonies in the East, he ordered restitution of the American property unless the captors could prove that Holland had excluded American vessels from the East Indian settlements in time of peace.[219] Similarly, once Scott concluded that Senegal, a French settlement in Africa, had ordinarily permitted non-French trade in peacetime, he refused to apply the Rule of '56.[220]

The Lords Commissioners reinforced Scott's interpretation of the Rule of '56. A year after Scott, in the case of the *Immanuel*, had traced

[213] Scott followed the terms of the government's instructions also in *Rosalie and Betty* (*Gebhadt*) (1800), 2 Rob. 343. In *Conferenzrath* (*Baur*) (1806), 6 Rob. 362, 363, Scott stretched the letter of the instructions of 1803 to allow a return of a Danish ship from Altona to the adjacent, but foreign, port of Hamburg. He viewed the ports of Altona and Hamburg as in reality one commercial port.

[214] *Rebecca* (*Moore*) (1799), 2 Rob. 101; *Nancy* (*Joy*) (1800), 3 Rob. 82; *Phoenix* (*Susini*) (1800), 3 Rob. 186, and *Star* (1801), 3 Rob. 193n.

[215] *Emmanuel* (*Soderstrom*) (1799), 1 Rob. 296; *Convenientia* (*Peterson*) (1802), 4 Rob. 201, and *Johanna Tholen* (*Osterlo*) (1805), 6 Rob. 72.

[216] *Wilhelmina* (*Carlson*) (1799), 2 Rob. 101n.

[217] *Minerva* (*Andualle*) (1801), 3 Rob. 229.

[218] *Rendsborg* (*Nyberg*) (1808), 4 Rob. 121.

[219] *Missouri* (*Read*) (1808), unreported, Bod. Lib., 4 Monk Bretton Dep.

[220] *Juliana* (*Carstens*) (1803), 4 Rob. 328, 341.

the history of the Rule of '56 and explained away its apparent abandonment by the British during the American Revolution, his brother, Lord Eldon, provided the same reasoning for the Lords Commissioners.[221] Eldon restated the Rule in another case in which he asserted that it was derived from the law of nations.[222] There is some indication that the Lords applied the Rule of '56 more strictly than Scott, since they condemned the neutral ship along with the cargo and they went beyond the letter of the instructions and based the condemnation of neutral property upon their interpretation of the principle of reason.[223]

Continuous Voyage
The various changes in the instructions to captors which the British government issued from time to time reflected the different pressures on the government. As the war developed it became more evident that the security of British commerce and the security of Britain were the same. One aim of some members of the ministry upon entering the war in 1793 had been to expand British commerce and to use its naval superiority to take French possessions in the West Indies. On the other hand the government had to pay some attention to the complaints of neutrals who objected to the capture of their vessels engaged in trade with the French colonies and to other highhanded conduct of the British navy.[224] The Americans especially complained that the Rule of '56 had no justification in any of the authorities on the law of nations and that the British government had manipulated it to gain commercial advantage.[225] British commercial interests vigorously complained that the government had been far too lenient in applying

---

[221] *Mary (Starr)* (Lords, 1800), Nicholl's Notes of Prize Appeals, 39, P.R.O. HCA 30/466. The *Immanuel* was discussed above at pp. 230–2.
[222] *Wilhelmina (Otto)* (Lords, 1801). The Lords also discussed the Rule of '56 and the various relaxations in the government's instructions in: *Frederica (Asmus)* (Lords, 1801); *Anne (Lord)* (Lords, 1801); *Charlotte (Coffin)* (Lords, 1803); and *Jerusha (Giles)* (Lords, 1803), Nicholl's Notes of Prize Appeals, 49, 54, 57, 74, P.R.O. HCA 30/466.
[223] *Jonge Thomas* (Lords, 1801), 3 Rob. 233n; *Lucy (Glover)* (Lords, 1802); and *Nancy (Benjamin)* (Lords, 1802), Nicoll's Notes of Prize Appeals, 63, 70, P.R.O. HCA 30/466.
[224] Harvey, *Britain in the early nineteenth century*, 301–6; Phillips and Reede, *Napoleonic period*, 27–49.
[225] The most elaborate discussion was in the lengthy and scholarly pamphlet written by James Madison, the American Secretary of State in 1805 and published anonymously: *Examination of the British doctrine, which subjects to capture a neutral trade, not open in time of peace* (n.p., n.d.).

the Rule of '56 and that enterprising American adventurers were exploiting British generosity to take over the trade of the French West Indies. Since the instructions of 1794 and 1798 left the Americans free to trade directly between the French islands and America, this opened up a vast indirect trade between the French islands and Europe. All that the American merchants needed to do was import the French colonial cargoes into America and reship them to ports of Europe. This relaxation of the Rule of '56 angered and frustrated the British commercial interests.[226] As James Stephen wrote in his influential pamphlet, *War in disguise*, 'Of course, the cargoes [the Americans] received there, as well as those they delivered, were all declared by their papers to be neutral property . . . It was evident, that the flag of the United States was, for the most part, used to protect the property of the French planter, not of the American merchant.'[227]

Stephen's call for enforcement of the Rule of '56 in its pristine form – no neutral trade with the enemy's colonies – was widely viewed as an official policy statement of the British government. Stephen graphically described how the Americans profited from the circuitous trade between the French or Spanish islands and Europe, with a token stop at an American port. The American merchants merely went through the motions of unloading the cargo in America and obtaining a certificate from an accommodating customs official that the duties had been paid. If some duty had been paid, the merchants often received a rebate. Then they could re-export these French cargoes as American property. The harm to British shipping was obvious, Stephen pointed out, since the neutrals could obtain lower insurance rates when shipping this purportedly neutral cargo. The French continued to carry on their colonial commerce under the American flag cheaply and safely, competing successfully with British colonies and merchants. British seamen were tempted to desert to the American merchant service. There can be little doubt that Stephen described American merchant practices all too accurately. Americans had no qualms about such commercial practices which they justified as fair neutral trade. In part because of the British instructions of 1794 and 1798 American merchants had in general prospered. By 1805 a large oversupply of West Indian produce overhung the world market, depressing the

---

[226] [Stephen], *War in disguise*, 7–35.
[227] *Ibid.*, 20.

British West Indian export trade.[228]

The legal issues concerning this circuitous trade between the French islands and Europe had been briefly discussed, as we have seen, but had not called forth a full and detailed judicial discussion before Scott became judge of the admiralty court. In 1800 Scott decided the case of the *Polly*, the first case in which some clear legal standards for the doctrine of Continuous Voyage were set forth.[229] The *Polly*, with a cargo of fish, sugar and cocoa, had been captured on a voyage from Marblehead, Massachusetts, to Bilbao, Spain. The sugar and cocoa had been imported into America from Havana, a Spanish colony. Scott had no hesitation in restoring the ship and the fish, since the fish was a normal American export to southern Europe. The captors contended, however, that the sugar and cocoa had not really been imported into America. Surely a direct trade between Havana and Spain in such products would have led to condemnation under the Rule of '56. If American merchants could not legally carry on such trade directly, neither should they be allowed to do so circuitously. Scott, showing again his fairness to neutrals, rejected this argument. 'An *American*', he said, 'has undoubtedly, a right to import the produce of the *Spanish* colonies for his own use; and after it is imported *bona fide* into his own country, he would be at liberty to carry them on to the general commerce of *Europe*.'[230] But what constituted importation into America? Scott replied, blinking at the reality of this type of American trade:

It is not my business to say what is universally the test of a *bona fide* importation: it is argued, that it would not be sufficient, that the duties should be paid, and that the cargo should be landed. If these criteria are not to be resorted to, I should be at a loss to know what should be the test; and I am strongly disposed to hold, that it would be sufficient, that the goods should be landed and the duties paid.[231]

The *Polly* was one of the cases which drove the West Indian interests in London into a frenzy and led to Stephen's assault on this form of American trade.[232] When the Lords Commissioners first addressed the issues raised by the *Polly*, they indicated no disagreement. They

[228] *Ibid.*, 58–172. See also Perkins, *Prologue to war*, 21–31, 77–9, and Stagg, *Mr. Madison's war*, 16–20.
[229] *Polly (Lasky)* (1800), 2 Rob. 361.
[230] *Ibid.*, 368.
[231] *Ibid.*, 369.
[232] Perkins, *Prologue to war*, 77–8.

condemned a Danish ship which had taken on cargo at Amsterdam and sailed to the Dutch colony of Surinam, but with a brief stop at the Prussian port of Emden. The Lords, however, indicated that the cargo would have been restored if there had been proof that it had been in good faith shipped from Emden.[233] This seemed to affirm the test Scott had applied in the *Polly*. In another case the Lords held that where a cargo had been landed and warehoused, duties had been paid and the goods offered for sale, this same cargo, when reshipped, was not liable to capture. The continuity of the voyage, the Lords said, had been broken.[234] The Lords made the test of the *Polly* considerably more demanding.

The Americans had come to rely on Scott's decision in the *Polly* as assuring immunity from capture of their circuitous trade between the French or Spanish islands and Europe provided they went through the motions of unloading the cargo in America and paying duties. This, they thought, sufficed to neutralize the enemy cargo and circumvent the Rule of '56. The American re-export trade increased after the *Polly* from $40 million in 1800 to $60 million in 1805.[235]

In 1805 the Lords Commissioners decided the case of the *Essex*, which set a new tone on Continuous Voyage. The *Essex* had taken on its cargo in Barcelona, Spain, and sailed for Salem, Massachusetts, where the cargo was landed and duties were paid. The cargo was then shipped to Havana and the *Essex* was captured on this part of the voyage. The Lords Commissioners viewed the evidence as showing a clear intention of the owner's agent in Spain to ship the cargo to Havana, clearly a violation of the Rule of '56. The formalities of landing the goods in Salem and paying duties did not suffice to interrupt this voyage once the Lords became convinced that the original intent had been to carry the cargo from Spain to one of its colonies.[236] Scott, who apparently had severe reservations about the doctrine as stated in the *Essex*,[237] expressed his understanding of the Lords' judgment in a way which appeared to reconcile it with the *Polly*. Describing the *Essex* test, he said:

[233] *Jonge Thomas* (*Laurens*) (Lords, 1801), Nicholl's Notes of Prize Appeals, 56, P.R.O. HCA 30/466.
[234] *Eagle* (*Weeks*) (Lords, 1803), Nicholl's Notes of Prize Appeals, 75, P.R.O. HCA 30/466.
[235] Perkins, *Prologue to war*, 79–80.
[236] *Essex* (*Orne*) (Lords, 1805), Nicholl's Notes of Prize Appeals, 78, 91, P.R.O. HCA 30/466.
[237] Perkins, *Prologue to war*, 81n.

[I]t is an inherent and settled principle in all cases in which the same question can have come under discussion, that the mere *touching* at any port without importing the cargo into the common stock of the country, will not alter the nature of the voyage, which continues the same in all respects, and must be considered as a voyage to the country, to which the vessel is actually going for the purpose of delivering her cargo at the ultimate port.[238]

In the *Maria* Scott distinguished the *Essex*, and carefully avoided the results of that case.[239] The *Maria* had taken on cargo at Havana and sailed to New Providence, in America. The cargo was landed and most of the cargo was reloaded and shipped to Amsterdam. The captors, relying on the *Essex*, argued that the ship and cargo should be condemned. Scott, however, restored the ship and cargo. He pointed out that the *Maria* had not engaged in a regular course of trade between Havana and Spain, that the destination here was not to the mother country at all but to Amsterdam, and that some of the cargo had apparently been sold in America. He, therefore, did not find an original intention to ship the cargo from Havana to Amsterdam. His more lenient attitude toward the neutrals came out when he said: 'There is room to let in the supposition that there might be an intention of selling in *America*, and that in consequence of the failure of that prospect only, the design was taken up of sending on these goods to the *European* market.'[240] This case, quite consistent with the *Polly*, implicitly imposed upon the captors the burden of proving that there had been an intention to carry on trade between the mother country and its colony, or, in other words, that there had been no *bona fide* importation into America sufficient to break the voyage.[241]

The Lords Commissioners put an end to Scott's excessive leniency in the case of the *William*.[242] The *William* had taken on a cargo of cocoa at La Guayra in South America and carried it to Marblehead, Massachusetts. The cargo of some 30 tons of cocoa was unloaded and

---

[238] Scott discussed the *Essex* in some detail in *Maria (Jackson)* (1805); 5 Rob. 365, 368. Italics in the original.

[239] *Maria (Jackson)* (1805), 5 Rob. 365.

[240] *Ibid.*, 372.

[241] Scott discussed some precedents of the admiralty court in which the intention to carry on commerce between the mother country and its colony appeared in the ship papers or the interrogatories, the proofs on which the captor's case depended. *Ibid.*, 370–1.

[242] *William (Trefry)* (Lords, 1806), 5 Rob. 385. The intended importance of this case is apparent from the elaborate decision by Sir William Grant, Master of the Rolls, and by the publication of Grant's judgment by Robinson.

the cargo owners posted a bond to pay $1,239 in duties. The insurance had just covered the voyage from Marblehead to the West Indies and back. The bulk cargo was put in casks and bags, the crew of the *William* was discharged and thus the owners claimed the voyage was terminated. The owners found that they could not sell the cargo in America and therefore reshipped most of it aboard the *William* to Bilbao, Spain. Under American law, the owners received a drawback or rebate of most of the import duties when the cargo was cleared for re-export. The *William* was captured by a British naval vessel and taken to Halifax, where it was condemned. Under the tests Scott had applied in the *Polly* and the *Maria*, the *William* should have been released, since the captors could not prove an intention to carry the cargo from La Guayra to Bilbao nor could they prove that the importation into America lacked good faith.

In the *William* Sir William Grant began his thorough judgment for the Lords Commissioners with the assertion that under the British understanding of the law, the only right the Americans had to trade with the colonies of the French derived from the king's instructions to captors. In other words, neutrals had no right to trade at all with the colonies of the enemy unless granted as a concession by the British. The British instructions had surely allowed no direct trade between the enemy's colonies and the mother country. Grant considered the factors which constituted a direct voyage. Certainly a slight deviation from the shortest route would not render it indirect. Grant rejected any fictions as a basis for determining the voyage was indirect. 'If the voyage from the place of lading be not really ended, it matters not', Grant asserted, 'by what acts the party may have evinced his desire of making it appear to have been ended.'[243] The Lords held that, to break the continuity of the voyage, it was necessary for the shippers to land the cargo and pay duties in America. Mere fictitious landing and payment of duties would not show *bona fide* importation. Grant pointed out the reshipment of the cargo in this case and the reimbursement of the duties. The landing thus had little appearance of an actual importation. Even if the owners had once intended to import the cargo into America for sale there, that intention did not constitute importation. Grant perceived the true intent of the importation and payment of a trifling amount of duties: the American owners thought it was expedient to have some pretence which the British court might

---

[243] *William* (*Trefry*) (Lords, 1806), 5 Rob. 385, 396.

consider importation. Grant then considered several precedents, especially the *Essex*, which he claimed had come as a surprise to American merchants. He concluded by stating that the payment of a slight duty would not suffice to show *bona fide* importation into America, and therefore the *William* was subject to capture. Grant made explicit what had been implicit in the *Essex*: the burden of proof had shifted from the captors (to prove that the importation had not been in good faith) to the owners (to prove that the importation had been in good faith). Lord Auckland, who had attended the Lords Commissioners' session to hear the judgment in the *William*, reported to Lord Grenville, who headed the ministry:

> The tendency of that Judgment is to set aside the Pretensions of the Americans to legalize their cargoes by a fictitious landing & reshipping, & by a pretended payment of duties, &c. The Judgment was given with great ability; but will create a *very strong* sensation. That whole subject calls for an immediate & very solemn Consideration.[244]

Since the year after the Lords decided the *William* the British ministry adopted the Orders in Council closing most of the ports of Europe to any trade, the *William* judgment became largely irrelevant. American vessels trading with the Continent, unless they paid duties in Britain, could be condemned under the Orders in Council regardless of the origin of the cargo. Scott appears to have had no opportunities of applying the *William*. In his subsequent reported judgments concerning Continuous Voyage, Scott dealt with less controversial issues. He had no difficulty determining that a voyage from Bordeaux to Antwerp, two enemy ports, with a short stop in the Prussian port of Emden, constituted a continuous voyage. He concluded, as the Lords Commissioners had in the *Essex*, from the original intention to sail from Bordeaux to Antwerp.[245] Similarly Scott had no problem seeing through a mere transshipment of a cargo in a Portuguese port. The cargo had not been imported or exported at this neutral port, but merely transferred from one vessel to another. Certainly the voyage was continuous.[246] But the British navy went too far when it brought in a Bremen ship, sailing with a cargo of brandy from Bordeaux to Bremen. The ship had instructions to stop at a British port to get a licence to carry on this trade and was trying to carry out these

---

[244] Auckland to Grenville, May 14, 1806, quoted in Perkins, *Prologue to war*, 84. Italics in the original.

[245] *Ebenezer* (*Christensen*) (1806), 6 Rob. 250, 256.

[246] *Thomyris* (*Russel*) (1808), Edw. 17, 19.

instructions. Scott pointed out that a stop at a British port for such a purpose surely broke the continuity of the voyage.[247]

Although Scott had tried to apply the Rule of '56 and the doctrine of Continuous Voyage in a manner least destructive to legitimate neutral rights, there can be little doubt that he would have followed the Lords Commissioners' determination in the *William* if occasion had arisen.

[247] *Mercurius (Harmens)* (1808), Edw. 53, 54.

SCOTT'S JUDICIAL PHILOSOPHY

SOURCES

Precedent

Sir William Scott, Lord Stowell, was appointed as admiralty judge in 1798 and continued to serve through the years of the French wars and the Napoleonic wars until he retired in 1828 at the age of eighty-two. Earlier biographies of his work as judge have created the impression that he wrote on a clean slate. The only serious study this century of his admiralty judgments appeared at the time of the First World War. E. S. Roscoe, the registrar of the admiralty court, published a book analyzing Scott's influence on the development of prize law. Roscoe, of course, because of his position as registrar, knew that for more than half a century prior to Scott's years as judge the judgments of the admiralty court had been preserved in manuscript form. He maintained, however, that '[T]hese judgments and decisions were no more than formal expressions of the results of the hearing in the first instance and in others of an appeal, and did not, except in a few rare instances, contain the reasoning on which a decision was based.'[1] Roscoe highlighted this point by insisting that, prior to Scott, no judicial precedents existed in any systematic compilations. 'Nothing, in fact', he wrote, 'in the nature of a series of judicial precedents having the validity of a legal code was to be found – there was a chaotic collection of law, the usefulness of which was slight.'[2] In order that no one could misunderstand him, Roscoe concluded that at the time when Scott became admiralty judge, 'no body of jurisprudence by which judges and advocates could be guided, or by which an

---

[1] E. S. Roscoe, *Lord Stowell – his life and the development of English prize law* (Boston, 1916), 33.
[2] *Ibid.*, 35.

Administration could be assisted in dealing with foreign Powers, was to be found.'[3]

Holdsworth has perpetuated this impression of the legal void which preceded Scott. The scarcity of judicial authority, Holdsworth said, gave Scott's genius a freer play than if a body of precedents had existed. Holdsworth gave credence to an earlier biographer of Scott by quoting his assertion that 'For a generation [Scott] was rather a law giver than a judge in the ordinary sense of the term.'[4]

The detailed study of Scott's instance and prize judgments in the previous chapters dispels any notion that Scott wrote on a clean slate. The admiralty court and the court of prize appeals had developed a body of unpublished precedents which the small closely knit group of civilians, like high priests of an occult religion, knew and treasured in their personal notebooks. For these civilians, as well as for the admiralty judges selected from among them, this body of law, both procedural and substantive, provided guidance for advocates arguing and for judges deciding future cases. The civilians cherished and cultivated in their notebooks and mutual conversations this otherwise unavailable body of law. This common learning of the civilians contained clear legal norms for most of the instance and prize issues which came before the court.

Unpublished law, of course, suffered greatly from the offhand, unpolished nature of the comments from the bench and from the variety of versions of these comments due to the carelessness, inattention or inaccuracy of the various notetakers. These speeches from the bench, however, as we have seen, often discussed the reasons for the decision, the precedents which were relied on or distinguished, the policies underlying the judgment and occasionally the writings of various commentators on the law of nations, as well as the relevant treaties, statutes and instructions of the government. Besides these comments from the bench, the notetakers paid equal attention to the arguments of counsel in each case, thus assuring an accurate and detailed record of the factual and legal issues before the court. Clearly when Scott became admiralty judge he did not hover like the Spirit of the Creator over a primordial void.

In prize appeal cases the Lords Commissioners for Prize Appeals frequently gave the reasons for their judgments. Even when reasons

---

[3] *Ibid.*, 36.
[4] *H.E.L.*, 12, 678–9. Holdsworth quoted from Lord Summer's sketch of Scott's career in the *D.N.B.*

were not expressed the civilians had accurate records of the issues before the court and the arguments of counsel, not only from their notes of the oral arguments, but also from the printed 'cases' which had to be filed. These 'cases' contained a detailed summary of the facts and lower court proceedings as well as a concise statement of the reasons for affirmance or reversal. Furthermore, these printed 'cases' often contained marginal notes of civilians as comments on the oral arguments made before the court.[5]

Appeals in instance cases were taken to the High Court of Delegates which apparently never gave reasons for its judgments. In these appeals the civilians carefully recorded the arguments made by counsel on either side along with the formal judgment of the Delegates so that they could surmise the reasons for the judgment.[6]

Another source for preserving the common learning of the civilians can be seen in the opinions which these civilians had written as counsel in answer to formal legal questions submitted for their consideration. In the Simpson notebook, which was a draft abridgment of the law and practice of the admiralty court, Simpson derived much of his materials from opinions of counsel, opinions he or some other civilian had given to clients. Simpson recorded these opinions of counsel alongside the opinions of judges expressed from the bench as equally valuable sources for determining the traditions of the civilians.[7]

Scott certainly never thought of himself, as Holdsworth implied, as a law-giver. He left no doubt that he considered himself bound to follow the common wisdom of the civilians, especially the judicial precedents for which he repeatedly searched and which he summarized in his own notebook.[8] In the detailed analysis of Scott's instance and prize judgments in the previous chapters, we have examined his care to be faithful to precedent as well as the changes, often quite subtle, he made in the established trajectory of the law. Scott did not leave his policy of following decided cases to be

---

[5] Numerous folio volumes of these printed cases are preserved in the P.R.O. in the series HCA 45.

[6] G. I. O. Duncan, *The High Court of Delegates* (Cambridge, 1971), 173–4; see also *Merry v. Jamison & Co.* (1764, 1774), Burrell, 1, 118; *Scorsby v. Hutchinson* (1768), Burrell, 86; *Clift and Myrylees v. Davis* (1770), Burrell, 99.

[7] The Simpson notebook is described in detail in the Appendix. Many opinions of counsel from the mid-eighteenth century have been preserved in the collection labeled Sir George Lee Opinions, H.S.P.

[8] Scott's practice notebook is described in the Appendix.

deciphered from such analysis; he repeatedly insisted that he was bound by the principle of *stare decisis*. In an instance case, for example, Scott indicated that he was inclined to decide for one party until he unexpectedly discovered a case which, he said, was 'determined by my predecessor, which comes so very near to the circumstances of this case, that I can find no distinction between them ... As long as that case stands uncorrected by the superior Court', he continued, he was bound to follow it.[9] Similarly in a prize case Scott insisted:

> The Court must necessarily be governed by the principle which it has laid down and acted upon in other cases ... In what light the matter may be viewed in the superior Court, it is not for me to conjecture; but it stands as a decided rule in this Court, and must be adhered to, till it shall be reversed by the decision of a higher tribunal.[10]

Scott, of course, as any well-trained lawyer, found occasion to distinguish precedents when they did not quite fit the facts of the immediate case.[11]

Since, prior to Scott's appointment as judge, no admiralty judgments had been published, earlier cases had to be cited from memory or from some unpublished notes. Scott occasionally referred to earlier cases which he recalled,[12] especially those in which he had acted as counsel.[13] He occasionally cited cases which he had discovered in manuscript notes he had in his possession.[14] In some judgments Scott confidently referred to the practice of the court without taking the trouble to cite any specific cases.[15]

The unpublished judgments of the court of prize appeals, the Lords Commissioners, provided Scott with the most binding precedents for the numerous prize cases he determined. Even if he were tempted to question the correctness of a judgment of the Lords Commissioners, he said, he certainly would never disapprove of it

[9] *Martha (Martin)* (1801), 3 Rob. 106, 107.

[10] *Vrow Deborah (Luyk)* (1812), 1 Dod. 160, 167.

[11] *Manly (Hansen)* (1813), 1 Dod. 257, 262; *Union (Olmsted)* (1813), 1 Dod. 346, 351.

[12] *Indian Chief (Skinner)* (1801), 3 Rob. 12, 31; *Fortuna (Tadsen)* (1802), 4 Rob. 278, 281.

[13] *Gratitudine (Mazzola)* (1801), 3 Rob. 240, 270.

[14] *Staadt Emden (Jacobs)* (1798), 1 Rob. 26, 30; *Aquila (Lunsden)* (1798), 1 Rob. 37, 43; *Santa Cruz (Picoa)* (1798), 1 Rob. 50, 63; *Gloire and Three Others* (1810), Edw. 280.

[15] *War Onskan (Biedumpel)* (1799), 2 Rob. 299; *Henrick and Maria (Baar)* (1799), 4 Rob. 43, 58.

'because the decisions of that Court bind authoritatively the judicial conscience of this'.[16] Scott likewise felt obliged to follow the determinations of the High Court of Delegates in instance cases.[17] Where the appellate court had effectively overruled an earlier precedent, that precedent no longer bound the admiralty court.[18] Until the superior court spoke, however, Scott considered himself bound by prior practice even though he doubted the correctness of the precedent.[19]

Stare decisis thus marked the narrow channel through which Scott charted his course. When the Lords Commissioners had affirmed a judgment of the admiralty court, though without giving reasons, Scott took the occasion to reflect on the importance of adhering to the authority of prior decided cases. '[T]he solemn judgment of the Court upon general principles *must* be an authority to the Court itself; inasmuch as instability of principle would be one of the greatest mischiefs, that could arise in the administration of any system of jurisprudence.' He suggested the remote possibility of departing from an admiralty court precedent. 'A case may occur, indeed, in which it may be the duty of a Court of Justice to break through the restraint of former authority imposed by itself; but I confess no such feeling attends this case.'[20]

Where lingering doubts remained or where the case involved diplomatically sensitive issues, Scott frequently invited the parties to seek review of his judgments in the superior court. As he stated in one case: 'If there is any doubt upon the rectitude of that principle, it will be a great satisfaction to my mind to see it corrected by the decision of the Superior Court.'[21] In another case he disarmingly stated: 'The opinion which I have formed, may be incorrect; but I fear it is invincible, and must be left to be corrected by the decision of the Superior Court, who will have the means of forming a more exact judgment, on the interpretation which is to be given to the instruments, on which this question depends.'[22]

[16] *Fortuna (Verissimo)* (1811), 1 Dod. 81, 86.
[17] *Fabius (Cowper)* (1800), 2 Rob. 245, 250.
[18] *Carlotta (Pasqual)* (1803), 5 Rob. 54, 59.
[19] *Anna Dorothea* (1801), 3 Rob. 233.
[20] *Elsabe (Maas)* (1803), 4 Rob. 408, 410. Italics in the original.
[21] *Johanna Tholen (Osterlo)* (1805), 6 Rob. 72, 78; see also *Vriendschap (Goverts)* (1801), 4 Rob. 96, 99; *Jonge Johannes (Parlerliet)* (1802), 4 Rob. 263, 268.
[22] *Nostra Signora del Carmen* (1806), 6 Rob. 302, 304.

The suggestion by Roscoe and Holdsworth, therefore, that Scott found no existing body of law when he became judge simply does not square with Scott's perception of his role as judge, nor with the numerous examples of his reliance on precedents. When Scott referred to prior decided cases, as he frequently did, it was to a complex, developed, though disjointed, body of unpublished legal opinions, known and preserved by the civilians. When he prodded parties to appeal to the superior court, he certainly was not thinking of himself as a law-giver, but rather as the judge of a court of first instance commissioned to apply the legal norms passed on by precedent and by the traditional wisdom of the civilians until altered by the superior court.

Of course, as the years passed, Scott relied more frequently on his own prior decisions. Perhaps we should somewhat discount his insistence that such precedents were binding since one's own prior opinions appear peculiarly compelling. Furthermore, when we read Scott's many statements on the binding nature of the judgments of the Lords Commissioners, we should recall that Scott was also a member of that exclusive group. Scott frequently sat as one of the Lords Commissioners for Prize Appeals, not only to review the numerous prize appeals from the colonial vice-admiralty courts, but even to review many prize judgments he himself had rendered as admiralty judge.[23] Because of his acknowledged background and expertise, he must have had significant influence with the other Lords Commissioners. Although there are cases in which the Lords reversed Scott's admiralty court judgments, it appears that they never reversed his judgments when he took part in the appeal.[24]

[23] For instance, Scott participated in reviewing and affirming his own judgments in the following cases: *Nancy (Joy)* (1802), P.R.O. HCA 45/38, fo. 175; *Susa (Hussey)* (1803), P.R.O. HCA 45/39, fo. 222; *Diligence (McGhie)* (1803), P.R.O. HCA 45/39, fo. 325; *Nancy (Knudsen)* (1803), P.R.O. HCA 45/42, fo. 458; *Neptunus (Kuyp)* (1804), P.R.O. HCA 45/47, fo. 1; *Sally (Williams)* (1808), P.R.O. HCA 45/54, fo. 98; *Dispatch (Smith)* (1809), P.R.O. HCA 45/54, fo. 344; *Santo Thomas (Castillo)* (1811), P.R.O. HCA 45/63, fo. 156.

Just in passing, it is well to note that Scott occasionally continued to argue cases before the Lords Commissioners for some years after he was appointed judge of the admiralty court. Apparently these were cases in which he had been retained as counsel before his appointment as judge. See, for example, *Neptunus (Dannberg)* (1803), P.R.O. HCA 45/38, fo. 378. In this case his brother John, then Lord Chancellor, joined him as counsel.

[24] Scott was reversed in the following cases: *Little William (Brown)* (Lords, 1810), 1 Acton 141, 162; *Jungfer Charlotta (Otma)* (Lords, 1809), 1 Acton 172, 178; *Manchester (Reynolds)* (Lords, 1811), 2 Acton, 60, 651.

Scott, therefore, found a significant body of law preserved in the memories and notebooks of the civilians, and in the precedents of the admiralty court and superior courts. One contribution he made to admiralty law was to gather these loose stones of all shapes and sizes and to start reshaping and fitting them together to build a coherent body of law. What had been generally familiar to the esoteric group of civilians, Scott made clear, accurate and intelligible to all who were interested in the law and practice of the admiralty court. He was undoubtedly aided in this effort by the high quality of the reporters who published volume after volume of his admiralty court judgments. His published instance and prize judgments constitute a clearly articulated restatement of the prior unpublished tradition and a new, more solid beginning for future development. Because Scott added precision and precise, insightful reasons to the prior collective wisdom of the civilians, subsequent civilians, text writers and judges turned to his judgments as a prime source of instance and prize law.

Scott, of course, did not always enjoy the comforting constraints of applicable precedents. The entire body of the law of blockade and much of the law of Continuous Voyage, as we have seen, were indeed created by Scott writing on a slate containing only dim outlines. He had some general principles derived especially from Bynkershoek, but no helpful precedents existed to guide him.

Because of the volume of prize cases he had to decide, there occasionally were completely new questions in other areas of prize law which he had to determine. His definition of territorial waters in terms of a three mile limit, for instance, appears to be redefinition rather than a simple reliance on precedent. In the instance cases, likewise, Scott from time to time was confronted with new issues, as we have seen, and stated new legal rules, such as that salvors can be granted no award merely for the saving of life at sea. But the overwhelming impression one derives from studying what Scott said and what he did as judge is that wherever possible he looked first to the prior decided cases of the admiralty court and the superior courts. The conservative mind of the future Lord Stowell weighed the immediate facts of each new case in the balance fashioned by precedents.

Scott's handling of common law cases which occasionally were raised before the admiralty court contrasts sharply with his insistence on the principle of *stare decisis* for admiralty precedents. Scott treated these common law cases, which were only rarely cited in the admiralty court, not as binding precedents but merely as sources of legal principles of persuasive value. Where the law of the admiralty court was unsettled, Scott might seek guidance from well-settled principles of the common law.[25] He might feel obliged to reach the same result as the Chancery Court, but not because its decisions bound the admiralty court.[26] Where common law cases confirmed the practice of the admiralty court, Scott occasionally discussed them as additional support for his decision.[27] But where common law cases had been cited in argument, Scott felt free to dismiss them as inapplicable,[28] or as founded in factual error or as mere *dictum*,[29] or as distinguishable because of factual differences between the cases.[30]

At the end of his career as admiralty judge Scott, then Lord Stowell, discussed his attitude toward common law precedents, and precedents in general, in a letter to the American Supreme Court Justice, Joseph Story. His comments on common law precedents confirm that he did not regard them as binding in the admiralty court. His other comments on courts being too fond of cases hardly squares with his own constant search for guidance in prior decided admiralty cases. He wrote:

I have ventured to differ sometimes in the interpretation of the law as given by our Judges, and have incurred censure on that account, as straying from an authority that ought to bind me. I have rather thought, that in the jurisdiction of the Admiralty, I am to look to the real justice of the case, and not to what has been pronounced in a somewhat similar case by the decision of a single Judge of the Common Law. I rather think we are too fond of cases; when a matter is to be argued, we look immediately for the cases, and by them we are determined more than perhaps by the real justice that belongs to the question; this may enforce the uniformity of the law, which is certainly a very desirable purpose, but is by no means the first purpose that ought to be considered; for if the judgment be erroneous, it is but an indifferent exposition of the law.[31]

Scott did not always ignore common law cases. Where the common law court had granted a prohibition to prevent the admiralty court from proceeding with a case, Scott regarded the common law order as binding on the admiralty court. '[S]ince it appears by the cases cited',

---

[25] *Foltina (Julins)* (1814), 1 Dod. 450, 451.

[26] *Vreede (Hoffker)* (1811), 1 Dod. 1, 7. Scott showed great deference to the Court of Exchequer in *Swift (Begbie)* (1813), 1 Dod. 320, 343.

[27] *Pomona (M'Naught)* (1811), 1 Dod. 25; *Nostra Signora del Carmen* (1806), 6 Rob. 302, 306; *St. Ivan (Wacklin)* (1811), Edw. 376, 377.

[28] *Friends (Creighton)* (1810), Edw. 246, 247.

[29] *Elsebe (Maas)* (1804), 5 Rob. 173, 187–8.

[30] *Hiram (Still)* (1800), 3 Rob. 180, 184–5.

[31] Stowell to Story, May 17, 1828, W. W. Story, *Life and letters of Joseph Story* (2 vols., London, 1851), I, 554, 556.

Scott said in one case, 'that the courts of common law have determined otherwise, and have granted a prohibition on this point; the petition must be reformed according to those determinations.'[32] Scott, on the other hand, found it worth noting that the common law courts had refused to grant a prohibition.[33] Common law prohibitions, which apparently never were directed to him, were merely a fact of life for Scott. They had in the past, he knew, effectively drawn the boundaries of the admiralty court's jurisdiction. We have already noted in many cases that Scott did not seek to expand the jurisdiction of the admiralty court nor to continue the long-lost jurisdictional battles with the courts of common law. Some writers have suggested that Scott's scrupulous regard for jurisdictional limits derived from his intense fear of being prohibited.[34] His brand of conservativism, we have seen, derived in large part from his fear of any change. Paranoia would certainly be understandable for any civilian. It seems more likely, however, that Scott had developed a much better working relationship with the members of the bench and bar of the common law than previous admiralty judges had enjoyed. Respect for the common law rather than fear explains his willingness to leave unchallenged the existing balance between the courts. Scott expressed his less bellicose attitude toward the rival but clearly dominant jurisdictions when he stated: 'Upon the whole, I am of opinion that I must keep within the known limits; and no sense of judicial duties, which I have ever entertained, has led me to suppose that *ampliare jurisdictionem* by private authority be one of those duties.'[35] Common law prohibitions in the past had marked the boundaries of admiralty jurisdiction and Scott had no inclination to move the markers.

Since the law of nations had to be derived from many diverse sources, if Scott found that a principle of the common law had been borrowed from the law of nations, he had sound reason to follow it.[36] Similarly he followed the doctrine of the common law where it

---

[32] *Favourite (Nicholas de Jersey)* (1799), 2 Rob. 232, 238.

[33] *Gratitudine (Mazzola)* (1801), 3 Rob. 240, 268.

[34] One of Scott's successors, Dr Lushington, spoke of Scott's 'awe of a prohibition', in *Milford (Morgan)* (1858), Swab. 362, 366, and a recent legal historian wrote that Scott had an 'intense fear of prohibition'. F. L. Wiswall, *The development of admiralty jurisdiction and practice since 1800* (Cambridge, 1970), 33.

[35] *Apollo (Tennant)* (1824), 1 Hag. 306, 315; see also *Atlas (Clark)* (1827), 2 Hag. 48, 62.

[36] *Nostra Senora de los Dolores (Morales)* (1809), Edw. 60, 62.

coincided with 'the general expression of the mercantile law on the subject'.[37] The contrast, however, seems obvious between Scott's frequent insistence that the admiralty court precedents bound the court, and his occasional reference to common law cases merely to confirm principles he derived from other sources or to mark the limits of the admiralty court's jurisdiction.

Statutes and treaties

Although precedents constituted by far the most frequent source of legal norms Scott relied on, he occasionally had to consider the applicability of written norms spelled out in statutes or treaties. He clearly viewed statutes or treaties, when applicable, as the controlling legal sources, but first he looked closely at these written norms dictated by Parliament or the government to determine whether they applied at all. In a number of cases he interpreted statutes and treaties in a manner which imposed restrictions on British parties and protected the property rights of foreign parties.

Scott repeatedly insisted that the admiralty court, when hearing prize cases, was a court of the law of nations which belonged to other nations as well as to Great Britain, under whose authority it sat. British statutes, therefore, like the Navigation Acts, could appropriately be applied to British subjects settled or doing business abroad, but not to subjects of other nations. Foreigners, he insisted, 'have a right to demand . . . the administration of the *law of nations*, simply, and exclusively of the introduction of principles borrowed from our own municipal jurisprudence, to which, it is well known, they have at all times expressed no inconsiderable repugnance'.[38] Scott's willingness to follow the policies dictated by the government, especially in the Orders in Council, will be discussed more fully below. For the present it is enough to observe that Scott refused to apply British statutes to foreign parties insisting it would be unjust; but it was no injustice to apply these legal norms to British subjects.

Even where only the rights of British subjects were in dispute, Scott held that acts of Parliament departing from the law of nations must be narrowly construed. The disposition of British property recaptured from the enemy was regulated by statute. Under the law of nations,

---

[37] *Constantia (Henricksen)* (1807), 6 Rob. 321, 325.
[38] *Recovery (Webb)* (1807), 6 Rob. 341, 348–9; see also *Walsingham Packet (Bell)* (1799), 2 Rob. 77, 82; *Fortuna (Verissimo)* (1811), 1 Dod. 81, 84.

Scott said, the ship captured by the enemy and condemned as prize, if recaptured, became the property of the recaptors. Britain, however, as a commercial country, departed from the law of nations 'and has made a new and peculiar law for itself, in favour of merchant property recaptured'. This new policy differed from the practice of other nations and even from Britain's older practice. 'A rule of policy so introduced', Scott insisted, 'must still be considered as an exception from the general law, and is to be interpreted, where any doubt arises, with a leaning to that general law which is no farther to be departed from than is expressed.'[39] If Scott concluded that a case did not come within the precise terms of an act of Parliament, he still had to 'consider it to come under the old rule of the law of nations'.[40] Of course, if the prize act merely declared the same norms which the law of nations required, Scott had no difficulty applying the statute.[41] Parliament could properly define the rights and obligations of British captors, since by the law of nations all captured property belonged to the Crown. 'Prize is altogether a Creature of the Crown', Scott stated. 'No man has, or can have, any interest but what he takes as the mere gift of the Crown.' Therefore, whatever interest captors might have in a prize 'rests wholly on the Order of Council, the Proclamation, and the Prize Act'.[42]

Scott never forgot the lesson of centuries of struggle with the common law courts, that 'the Courts of Common Law are the most effectual expositors of Acts of Parliament'. But he also knew that 'particular acts of parliament are not always modelled and drawn up by persons sufficiently acquainted with, or attentive to, the state of the general law to which the new regulations are to apply'.[43] The admiralty court, Scott insisted, should not 'pass light observations on Acts of Parliament'.[44] But Scott had spent enough years as a member of Parliament to feel free in deriving the intention of Parliament from his personal recollections. 'I perfectly well recollect', Scott said in one case, 'that it was the intention of those who brought this bill into

---

[39] *Actif (Lorrial)* (1810), Edw. 185, 186–7. A narrow interpretation of Parliament's prize act, 'nearer to the terms of the Act', was also appropriate. *Vryheid (de Winter)* (1799), 2 Rob. 16, 22.
[40] *Ceylon (Mulac)* (1811), 1 Dod. 105, 111; see also *Charlotta (Dupleix)* (1814), 1 Dod. 387, 391.
[41] *Mariamne (Morel)* (1803), 5 Rob. 9, 10.
[42] *Elsebe (Maas)* (1804), 5 Rob. 173, 181.
[43] *Hoffnung (Berens)* (1799), 2 Rob. 162, 168, 176.
[44] *Ibid.*, 165.

Parliament that privateers should not be allowed to make depreda-
tions upon the coasts of the enemy for the purpose of plundering
individuals.'[45] By applying British statutes only to British subjects,
Scott sought to avoid conflicts with the law of nations applied to
foreign parties.[46] Neutrals should enjoy the protection afforded by
the law of nations.

Treaties likewise had to be interpreted with reference to the law of
nations. When he was called upon to interpret the written norms
embodied in treaties, Scott usually applied a contract theory. Nations
who were not parties to the treaty could not seek protection from its
stipulations. Furthermore, the construction of a treaty must correspond with the intentions of the parties.

> [A]lthough the Court might be disposed to put a favourable interpretation
> upon the articles of the treaty, it is bound to construe them according to their
> natural and fair meaning, and not to impose upon the contracting parties
> stipulations, which were never in their contemplation. The business of the
> Court is to expound and explain, not to frame original treaties.[47]

Scott frequently found in treaties a basis for protecting neutral
property.[48] But he certainly would not accept an exaggerated and
implausible meaning of the treaty terms. When it was contended that
the treaty with Morocco overrode the basic right of a belligerent to
visit and search a vessel, Scott rejected that construction.

> It is not hastily to be admitted that in these times a treaty (and this is a very
> modern treaty) would be made with so improvident a meaning, that it might
> be applied to protect the whole trade of the enemy from the rights of *British*
> cruizers: I cannot conceive that the purpose of it was more than to protect the
> ordinary commerce of each nation.[49]

[45] *Thorshaven and its dependencies* (1809), Edw. 102, 113; see also *Helen (Marshall)*
(1801), 3 Rob. 224, 227; *Apollo (Veal)* (1801), 3 Rob. 308, 309; *Alerte (Demay)*
(1806), 6 Rob. 238, 291.
[46] *Nostra Signora de los Dolores (Morales)* (1813), 1 Dod. 290, 297.
[47] *Jonge Josias (Jurgensen)* (1809), Edw. 128, 131.
[48] For instance, when the captors pointed to the language in a treaty between England
and Sweden which forbade subjects of either signatory 'to sell or lend their ships for
the use and advantage of the enemies of the other', Scott refused to interpret the word
'lend' to include allowing a ship to carry freight to the ports of the enemy. 'Lend',
Scott observed meant that the signatories to the treaty could not 'give up the use and
management of their ships directly to the enemy, or put them under his absolute
power and direction'. *Ringende Jacob (Kreplien)* (1798), 1 Rob. 89, 90. See also
Nossa Senhora da Adjuda (Araujo) (1803), 5 Rob. 52, 53, and *Marianna (Posadillo)*
(1805), 6 Rob. 24, 29.
[49] *Annemur (Sarrey)* (1800), 3 Rob. 71, 74.

Treaties and statutes provided Scott with clearly stated legal norms which he had to apply. He applied them, however, with the broader principles of the law of nations constantly in the background. An unthinking, wooden application of the terms of a statute or treaty offended Scott's sense of his judicial role. But he had no hesitation in applying these written norms in ways which often restricted British captors and protected neutral rights.

Policy

It would be easy to conclude from a broad reading of Scott's judgments that he seldom referred to policy questions and only did so when he had no precedents to follow. This, of course, is accurate enough but overlooks the fact that the policies had already been incorporated into the received body of decided cases. When Scott did rely on questions of policy to determine an unsettled legal question, he did not introduce new policy interests, but generally found the policies implicit in the prior decided cases. Scott restrained his policy arguments within the trajectory of the case law determined by prior admiralty judges.

Scott, we have seen, assumed a paternalistic role as protector of ordinary seamen because of their relatively helpless and uneducated position.[50] Perhaps he showed greater concern than his predecessors for the welfare of seamen. The essential role of the admiralty court as a guardian of seamen, however, certainly predated Scott and can be found implicitly in prior judgments. Furthermore, Scott never lost sight of the economic realities of the shipping industry nor was he willing to sacrifice the ship owners in order to assure greater recovery for the seamen. Scott's contribution may well have been a more sophisticated grasp of the policies to be weighed, but he found the same policies in less developed form implied or expressed in the judgments of his predecessors.

Scott's thorough grasp of the operations of the shipping industry gave him a realistic assessment of the legal issues which came before the court in cases involving bottomry bonds or salvage or possession of ships. But the policies which lay behind Scott's judgments, and which he from time to time made explicit, were the same policies which had long been weighed by the English admiralty court in similar cases.[51]

[50] See above, pp. 78–9.
[51] See above, pp. 80–96, 103–14.

When Scott found no precedents to follow, he frequently took the trouble to state explicitly the policies which guided him in deciding the case.[52] It is surely unrealistic to think that policy questions played no role in determining instance cases.

Even more clearly we can see the public policies which had long been woven into the fabric of prize law. Scott surely did not create the mercantilist theory which best explains the British interpretation of various doctrines of the law of nations. As already discussed, it made good mercantilist sense to legitimate the capture of enemy cargoes aboard neutral ships while allowing neutral cargoes on enemy ships to remain free from capture.[53] Scott likewise applied a mercantilist theory, both as counsel and as judge, in weighing the factors to be considered in determining the national status of merchants.[54] And as we have seen, mercantilist theory had been woven into the Rule of '56 long before Scott accepted the same policies in determining similar cases of colonial warfare. Because of his extraordinarily clear and detailed grasp of the policies behind the law applied in the admiralty court, Scott did not often discuss questions of policy. The lengthy analysis of his instance and prize judgments in the earlier chapters has shown that he weighed the policies of the law, sometimes explicitly, when he found insufficient guidance in precedents.

Scott's conservative mind would, of course, gravitate to the well-accepted, long-established policy justifications for admiralty judgments. While Scott was still at Oxford, Adam Smith had published *The wealth of nations*. Its message was antithetical to the mercantilist doctrines which had dominated British economic thought in most of the eighteenth century. By the time Scott became judge of the admiralty court, Smith's new free trade ideas had influenced the governmental policies of leaders such as William Pitt and Lord Grenville. Smith's views on the economic consequences of war influenced the leaders of the anti-war movement. The reform-minded arguments of the new industrialists, as we have seen, eventually carried weight with the government in repealing the Orders in Council in 1812.[55] But any pebble cast in the sea had greater

[52] See above, pp. 94–5, where Scott stated the policies behind his evaluation of interest rates on bottomry bonds.
[53] See above, pp. 174–5.
[54] See above, pp. 134–5, 142–7, 154–61.
[55] A. D. Harvey, *Britain in the early nineteenth century* (London, 1978), 311–21; J. E. Cookson, *The friends of peace – anti-war liberalism in England, 1793–1815* (Cambridge, 1982), 55, 215–37.

international impact than the new economic theories had on Scott's admiralty judgments. Scott's conservative, Tory outlook on the world remained set in its eighteenth-century mold. When he turned to policy arguments, it was to those policies with a proper pedigree assured by the accepted wisdom of prior admiralty practice.

Commentators on the law of nations

From his years of study at Oxford, Scott had become imbued with a knowledge and appreciation of the law of nations. Throughout his life it remained for him a legal framework binding on nations.[56] In his long years as admiralty judge he frequently had to look to the law of nations as one source for deciding cases. Since he had read the various commentators on the law of nations so thoroughly, he had few illusions about the vast areas of disagreement among these commentators. Nonetheless, the law of nations never appeared to him as mere wooly-minded speculation. The unshakeable bedrock of his legal philosophy consisted of his belief in natural law founded on reason and in the law of nations founded on reason and the practice of nations. Despite the lack of uniformity of practice and the disagreements over the dictates of reason, of which Scott was more aware than most contemporaries, the law of nations continued to have a powerful influence on his judicial decision-making.

In one case Scott had the opportunity to make explicit his understanding of the legal principles derived from the law of nations.[57] This case of the recapture of a British ship raised the question whether the ship had become enemy property, and was thus a lawful prize for the captors, or had retained its character as a British vessel and therefore should be restored by the captors to the original British owners upon the payment of a suitable award as salvage. Scott inquired whether condemnation in the court of a belligerent was required by the law of nations to transfer ownership of the ship to the enemy captors. He pointed out that in British law a sentence of condemnation was necessary, but that some claimed this conflicted with the practice of other nations which allowed transfer of ownership when the ship had been held as prize for twenty-four hours or had been brought to a place of safety (*infra presidia*). Scott disagreed with these views, which rested on various authorities on the law of nations. He con-

[56] See above, pp. 34–8, 57–8.
[57] *Flad Oyen (Martenson)* (1799), 1 Rob. 135.

cluded that by the general practice of European nations a sentence of condemnation in a belligerent court was required to transfer ownership. He continued with an analysis of the respective roles of reason and the practice of nations as a basis for the law of nations. '[I]n my opinion, if it could be shewn, that regarding mere speculative general principles, such a condemnation ought to be deemed sufficient; that would not be enough; more must be proved; it must be shewn that it is conformable to the usage and practice of nations.' He clarified this general statement by adding:

A great part of the law of nations stands on no other foundation: it is introduced, indeed, by general principles; but it travels with those general principles only to a certain extent: and, if it stops there, you are not at liberty to go further, and to say, that mere general speculations would bear you out in a further progress: thus, for instance, on mere general principles it is lawful to destroy your enemy; and mere general principles make no great difference as to the manner by which this is to be effected; but the conventional law of mankind, which is evidenced in their practice, does make a distinction, and allows some, and prohibits other, modes of destruction; and a beligerent [sic] is bound to confine himself to those modes which the common practice of mankind has employed, and to relinquish those which the same practice has not brought within the ordinary exercise of war, however sanctioned by its principles and purposes.[58]

Scott, therefore, based his prize decisions 'on all the several grounds of reason or practice, and judicial recognition'.[59] If the court had no precedents to rely on, Scott had to 'collect the law of nations from such sources, as reason, supported in some slight degree by the practice of nations'.[60] Scott's natural law training led him to describe the law of nations as 'a law made up of a good deal of complex reasoning, though derived from very simple rules, and altogether composing a pretty artificial system'.[61]

Reason, of course, has never spoken with a single voice. Scott knew the conflicting conclusions, all purportedly derived from reason, expressed by various writers on the law of nations. But he also knew that some basic propositions were widely accepted. When he discussed the law of blockade, for instance, where he found little guidance in precedent, Scott indicated the sources he had consulted on the law of nations. Possibly his insistence here on uniformity is intended to mask the fact that he was developing a largely

[58] *Ibid.*, 139–40.
[59] *Fama (Butler)* (1804), 5 Rob. 106, 118.
[60] *Adonis (Gotschalk)* (1804), 5 Rob. 156, 159–60.
[61] *Hurtige Hane (Dahl)* (1801), 3 Rob. 324, 326.

undeveloped area of law. He certainly was correct, however, in stressing that at least the outlines of the law of blockade had been stated, especially by Bynkershoek.[62] He said:

Among all the contradictory positions that have been advanced on the law of nations, this principle [breach of a blockade subjects the ship to confiscation] has never been disputed: it is to be found in all books of law, it is universally acknowledged by all governments who possess any degree of civil knowledge.[63]

Although the law of nations might ultimately rest on principles of reason, Scott had no illusions about building the system entirely on such a foundation. The law of nations, he knew, could not find its support solely in abstract principles of reason. Wherever the 'use and practice of nations have intervened', Scott insisted, the law of nations no longer derived from reason alone. Scott considered the expression of Grotius, *placuit gentibus* to be 'perfectly correct, [in] intimating, that there is a use and practice of nations, to which we are now expected to conform'.[64]

This practice of nations was not as broad a base for the law of nations as it might seem. Scott differentiated 'the law of nations as understood' and practised amongst the civilized states of *Europe*', from the law and practice of the Barbary states.[65] Thus the '*European* law of nations is not to be applied in its full rigour to the transactions of persons' in Morocco,[66] the East Indies[67] or the Ottoman Porte.[68] Even within Europe Scott could not always find unanimous agreement on the principles of the law of nations.[69] The practice of European nations might change with time if the older rules of the law of nations no longer suited changed circumstances. Scott, in such a

---

[62] See above, pp. 202–3, 213–14.
[63] *Columbia* (*Weeks*) (1799), 1 Rob. 154. Scott, in applying the principles derived from natural reason, often used other terms, such as: 'the soundest maxims of justice and humanity', *Dispatch (Addison)* (1801), 3 Rob. 278, 279; 'general principles', *Daifjie (Soaring)* (1800), 3 Rob. 139, 141; 'equity', *Narcissus (Moulton)* (1802), 4 Rob. 17, 23; 'the nature of things', *Rebecca (Maddick)* (1804), 5 Rob. 102, 105; or 'the substantial justice of the case', *Alexander (Tate)* (1812), 1 Dod. 278, 280.
[64] *Henrick and Maria (Baar)* (1799), 4 Rob. 43, 54. Elsewhere Scott spoke of 'all the principles on which the public affairs of *Europe* have hitherto been managed', *Daifjie (Soaring)* (1800), 3 Rob. 139, 146.
[65] *Fortune (Smith)* (1799), 2 Rob. 92, 99; *Kinders Kinder (Haysen)* (1799), 2 Rob. 88.
[66] *Hurtige Hane (Dahl)* (1801), 3 Rob. 324, 326.
[67] *Indian Chief (Skinner)* (1801), 3 Rob. 12, 29.
[68] *Madonna del Burso (Antonopoli)* (1802), 4 Rob. 169, 172.
[69] *Twee Juffrowen (Etjes)* (1802), 4 Rob. 242, 294.

case, felt obliged to follow the 'later usage of States', that is, 'the practice now prevailing'.[70] As we have seen throughout the chapters on prize law, Scott often cited the various writers on the law of nations, especially when he could find no precedent or when he dealt with sensitive issues which affected neutral rights. He relied on Bynkershoek more frequently than other writers, undoubtedly because Bynkershoek had discussed many prize issues more precisely and in greater detail and with the greater authority of his long judicial experience.[71] Scott, for instance, argued in one case from reason and practice and 'almost all the elementary writers on the law of nations', with an appropriate quotation from Bynkershoek.[72] In another case Scott stated the rule to be applied and indicated that it was derived from the 'rule of practice' laid down in an earlier admiralty case, that it was 'conformable to the text law, and the opinion of eminent Jurists', again quoting Bynkershoek.[73] Of course, Scott's repertory of apt cites was not limited to Bynkershoek. He turned to the authority of Vattel, for instance, with the comment: 'I stand with confidence upon all fair principles of reason, – upon the distinct authority of Vattel, – upon the Institutes of other great maritime countries, as well as those of our own country.'[74] As has been noted elsewhere, Scott felt comfortable referring to an extremely wide range of commentators on the law of nations. The individual writers on the law of nations, however, merely provided evidence of the law of nations, but the law of nations itself in Scott's view derived ultimately from reason and the practice of European nations.

[70] *Eliza Ann and others* (1813), 1 Dod. 244, 248.

[71] C. van Bynkershoek, *Quaestionum juris publici libri duo*, tr. T. Frank (Oxford, 1930), is used here. Scott cited Bynkershoek, for instance, in *Staadt Emden (Jacobs)* (1798), 1 Rob. 26, 31; *Hoop (Cornelis)* (1799), 1 Rob. 196, 198; *Franklin (Segerbath)* (1801), 3 Rob. 217, 221. Scott showed his discernment in never citing R. Lee, *Treatise of captures in war* (London, 1759). Lee, a rough translation of Bynkershoek's first book verging on plagiarism, was cited more frequently by American lawyers during the American Revolution than any other authority on prize law. H. Bourguignon, *The first federal court – the federal appellate prize court of the American Revolution, 1775–1787* (Philadelphia, 1977), 214, 244, 246–7, 263, 279–81, 293, 295. Obviously Scott could understand Bynkershoek's difficult Latin better than most American lawyers of the day.

[72] *Cosmopolite (Mathison)* (1801), 4 Rob. 8, 10. This quotation occurs in a footnote which apparently was by Scott. When the reporter added footnotes he seems to have felt obliged so to indicate. See 2 Rob. 174; 5 Rob. 385g, and 6 Rob. 293.

[73] *Fortuna (Tadsen)* (1802), 4 Rob. 278, 281.

[74] *Maria (Paulsen)* (1799), 1 Rob. 340, 369. E. de Vattel, *Le droit des gens*, tr. C. G. Fenwick (Washington, 1916), is used here.

In deciding instance cases Scott likewise looked frequently to a supranational body of law. In a case involving the significance of a bill of sale as proof of ownership of a vessel, Scott rejected some common law opinions which had been suggested in argument. A different legal norm must be applied in the admiralty court. Scott said:

The opinions of gentlemen at that [common law] bar must undoubtedly be entitled to entire respect on a question of Municipal Law: But this is a question of a more general nature, arising out of a system of more general law – out of the universal maritime law, which constitutes a part of the professional learning of this Court and its Practicers. According to the ideas which I have always entertained on this question, a bill of sale is the proper title to which the Maritime Courts of all Countries would look. It is the universal instrument of transfer of ships in the usage of all maritime countries; and in no degree a peculiar title deed or conveyance known only to the law of *England*: It is what the Maritime Law expects, what the Court of Admiralty would in its ordinary practice always require, and what the Legislature of this country has now made absolutely necessary, with regard to *British* subjects, by the regulations of the Statute Law.[75]

In an area long troubled by prohibitions from the common law courts, Scott here spoke with full confidence of the authority of general maritime law. Perhaps his convictions, derived from a lifetime of studying the common learning of civilians, were reinforced by the English statute which incorporated for British subjects the principles of the universal maritime law.[76]

This maritime law rested on the basis of the universal commercial practices of Europe.[77] Scott distinguished this 'practice of merchants, in the ordinary course of commerce', which constituted the law merchant, from the law of nations applicable in prize cases.[78] As we have seen repeatedly, Scott could cite a broad range of authorities on

[75] *Sisters* (1804), 5 Rob. 155, 159.
[76] Scott was apparently referring to Lord Liverpool's Acts, 26 Geo. III, c. 60; 30 Geo. III, c. 68. Scott elsewhere stated that Lord Liverpool's Act applied only to British subjects. 'But I am yet to learn that this rule of law is applicable to Foreigners, who are not bound by the municipal regulations of this country. This is a question of the law of nations: and the party complainant, being a foreigner, comes to a court which has to administer that law.' *Nostra Signora de los Dolores (Morales)* (1813), 1 Dod. 290, 298. Scott had discussed these acts with his brother, Lord Eldon, who replied that 'There are not two worse drawn Acts in the Statute Book.' See Chapter 3, n. 112 above.
[77] *Vrow Mina (Behrends)* (1813), 1 Dod. 234, 235; *Alexander (Tate)* (1812), 1 Dod. 278, 280.
[78] *Haabet (Vette)* (1800), 2 Rob. 174, 180–1.

the law merchant, just as he was thoroughly familiar with the authorities on the law of nations.

Reconciliation

Scott, therefore, spoke frequently of the supranational body of law applied by the admiralty court, the law of nations relied on in prize cases and the law merchant applied in instance cases. But it is overwhelmingly apparent from reading his many judgments, published and unpublished, that he referred far more frequently to precedent as his source than to all other sources taken together. These precedents of the High Court of Admiralty clearly incorporated many British policies. How would Scott have reconciled this apparent conflict as to the source of the law applied? The supranational body of law which he asserted as the basis of his judgments had acquired a distinctly English accent as it had been applied by the admiralty court over the decades.

If Scott had ever been confronted with this question, which probably bothered him not at all, he might well have replied as the common lawyers of his day replied to the question of the relationship between the common law, as the immemorial customs or usage of the land, and the precedents of the common law courts. Precedents of the common law courts merely declared the common law, the common lawyers claimed; the judicial decisions certainly did not create or constitute the common law. As Sir Matthew Hale had stated in the seventeenth century: 'This Common Law, though the Usage, Practice and Decisions of the King's Courts of Justice may expound and evidence it, and be of great Use of illustrate and explain it; yet it cannot be authoritatively altered or changed but by Act of Parliament.'[79]

Perhaps Scott, if asked, would have recalled the lecture which Blackstone had given on the precedents of the common law courts as declaratory of the common law. Blackstone had said:

But here a very natural, and very material, question arises: how are these customs or maxims to be known, and by whom is their validity to be

[79] M. Hale, *The history of the common law of England*, ed. C. M. Gray (Chicago, 1971), 18. See also R. N. Cross, *Precedent in English law*, 3rd edn (Oxford, 1977), 26–7.

determined? The answer is, by the judges in the several courts of justice. They are the depositaries of the laws; the living oracles, who must decide in all cases of doubt, and who are bound by an oath to decide according to the law of the land. Their knowledge of that law is derived from experience and study; ... and from being long personally accustomed to the judicial decisions of their predecessors. And indeed these judicial decisions are the principal and most authoritative evidence, that can be given, of the existence of such a custom as shall form a part of the common law.[80]

Scott undoubtedly saw no conflict at all between these different sources of the law: on the one hand there was his consistent reliance on precedent, whenever available, and his repeated suggestion that the party dissatisfied with his judgment should appeal to the more politically attuned Lords Commissioners of the British Privy Council; on the other hand there were his many statements that the prize court sat as a court of the law of nations to apply principles derived from reason and from the practice of nations to resolve the disputes of the parties, often foreign, before him. The law of nations in prize cases, or the law merchant in instance cases, existed independent of any national court. The precedents of the British admiralty court, apparently in Scott's way of thinking, had expressed these supranational legal principles more accurately and reliably than any of the philosophical commentators. This reconciliation strains the credulity of today's legal scholars. But Scott, a thoroughly eighteenth-century British subject, probably never bothered probing the question and if he had, would have felt comfortable replying that the precedents of the British admiralty court merely declared the truest principles of the customary international practices of nations, the law of nations, and of the customary practices of merchants, the law merchant. The law of nations for Scott, as the common law for Blackstone, consisted of principles of reason expressed in common

[80] Bl. *Comm.*, I, 69. Blackstone, in this same lecture, answered the question: what should happen if a former determination of the common law courts should be clearly contrary to reason? He replied in words which Scott probably would have felt comfortable applying to the law of nations. Blackstone asserted: 'But even in such cases the subsequent judges do not pretend to make a new law, but to vindicate the old one from misrepresentation. For if it be found that the former decision is manifestly absurd or unjust, it is declared, not that such a sentence was *bad law*, but that it was *not law*; that is, that it is not the established custom of the realm, as has been erroneously determined. And hence it is that our lawyers are with justice so copious in their encomiums on the reason of the common law; that they tell us, that the law is the perfection of reason, that it always intends to conform thereto, and that what is not reason is not law.' Bl. *Comm.*, I, 70. Italics in the original.

usage. Precedents had merely discovered and applied these principles
to the concrete facts of individual cases. Most likely Scott was
suggesting this relationship between precedent and the law of nations
when he stated in one case that the law of nations was the court's
'unwritten law evidenced in the course of [the court's] decisions, and
collected from the common usage of civilized states'.[81]

JUDICIAL INDEPENDENCE

Scott claimed for himself a level of independence of his own government which neither he, nor probably any judge, could achieve, at least
in time of war. His claim was two-fold, both that the law he applied
was truly a supranational, not a British, body of law, and secondly,
that he interpreted and applied it as a fair and neutral judge above any
partiality to his own nation's interests. There is much truth, of course,
in his claim. But, although it is unfortunate that he held up an
unattainable ideal for himself, he certainly must be measured by the
yardstick he himself devised.

Early in his career as admiralty judge, in 1798, he had eloquently
proclaimed both the supranational source of the law he applied in
prize cases and his even-handed application of this law to all parties.
The case of the *Maria*, discussed above, involved the right of a
belligerent to visit and search neutral merchant ships on the high seas
sailing under convoy with instructions to resist visit and search.[82]
Scott, obviously aware of the serious impact the condemnation of
these Swedish vessels would have on Britain's relations with neutral
nations, repeated the diplomatically soothing, stock assertion of his
predecessors, that his duty as admiralty judge required him

[T]o consider myself as stationed here, not to deliver occasional and shifting
opinions to serve present purposes of particular national interest, but to
administer with indifference that justice which the law of nations holds out,
without distinction to independent states, some happening to be neutral and
some to be belligerent. The seat of judicial authority is, indeed locally *here*, in
the belligerent country, according to the known law and practice of nations:
but the law itself has no locality. – It is the duty of the person who sits here to

[81] *Fox* (1811), Edw. 311, 312.
[82] See above, pp. 180–2.

determine this question exactly as he would determine the same question if sitting at *Stockholm*; – to assert no pretensions on the part of *Great Britain* which he would not allow to *Sweden* in the same circumstances, and to impose no duties on *Sweden*, as a neutral country, which he would not admit to belong to *Great Britain* in the same character.[83]

Scott was neither naive nor hypocritical in claiming to apply, even-handedly, a supranational body of legal principles to all parties before his court. He applied these legal principles in many cases even when British interests were adversely affected. The law of nations remained the unshakeable bedrock of his legal convictions, as he demonstrated in his private correspondence with his brother when discussing the troubling problem of disposing of the defeated Bonaparte in accordance with the dictates of the law of nations.[84] He believed in the rationally ordered universe of the natural law philosophers and the rationally ordered dealings between nations outlined by the commentators on the law of nations.[85]

He certainly applied the law of nations in many cases, as we have seen, as a limit on the British captors and a protection of neutral rights. We have considered his insistence, for example, that British warships must not prey on enemy shipping from the safe haven of neutral territorial waters, and his insistence that British merchants must not be permitted to gain commercial advantage by ignoring the blockades which so severely impaired the rights of neutral merchants.[86] We have also seen how he initially applied the doctrine of Continuous Voyage more favorably to neutrals than the Lords Commissioners ultimately did.[87] He developed, with no precedent to

---

[83] *Maria (Paulsen)* (1799), 1 Rob. 340, 350. An earlier admiralty judge, Sir Charles Hedges, had given the same assurances in 1689. *Documents relating to law and custom of the sea*, ed. R. G. Marsden (2 vols., n.p., 1915), II, 131. See also P. Jessup and F. Deak, *Neutrality: its history, economics and law*, I: *Origins* (4 vols., New York, 1935–6), 210, and J. Marriott, *The case of the Dutch ships considered*, 3rd edn (London, 1769), 43.

[84] Discussed above at pp. 57–8.

[85] Scott stated in Parliament '[T]hat the courts of Admiralty are not restricted within the narrow limits of municipal institution: the law of nature, and of nations, is the foundation on which they build; all the subjects of foreign states, on the general principles of justice and humanity, have a right to redress for injuries received upon the high seas, and look for protection to these establishments.' Hansard, 1st ser. IV, 62 (1805).

[86] See above, pp. 176–7, 206.

[87] Discussed above, pp. 237–41.

guide him, the rule that neutral vessels had a right to carry dispatches from enemy ambassadors.[88] Furthermore, no precedent or clear doctrine of the law of nations required him to release a neutral ship which had been captured attempting to breach a blockade that, without the knowledge of the neutral, no longer existed because the port had fallen to British arms.[89] The neutrals in this case clearly had the intention to enter the blockaded port and did everything in their power to do so. They could hardly have complained if Scott had held their property was liable to condemnation for the attempted breach. Yet Scott applied the law of blockade, which he knew fell severely on neutrals, in a way which mitigated some of the harshness.

In the vast majority of the cases which came before him, Scott was able to strive for the ideal of judicial independence from the government which he proclaimed as the proper standard for his court. When Scott felt compelled to enforce British belligerent rights in a manner highly objectionable to neutrals, however, he often wrote elaborate, lengthy decisions in which he attempted to demonstrate that the law of nations, not British policy, supported his position. Diplomatic tact marked these sensitive judgments.

Many precedents on which Scott relied, as we have repeatedly seen, had incorporated policies favorable to British interests long before Scott became judge. British policy considerations had thus been woven into the texture of the rule of law he applied. The law of nations was not quite the supranational body of law which Scott claimed. But, as we have already pointed out, Scott had no qualms about following precedent which had acquired an English accent. Scott probably considered these precedents as declaratory of the law of nations or the law merchant.

The cases most directly in conflict with Scott's asserted fair application of a supranational body of legal principles to belligerents and neutrals alike are those involving the Orders in Council of 1807 and 1809. These Orders in Council led Scott to become exactly what he had told the world he was not, a minor functionary of the British government dutifully carrying out the commands of his superiors.

Scott, of course, knew exactly what Orders in Council were in the political world of his day. He was thoroughly immersed in the political

---

[88] See above, pp. 184–5.
[89] See above, p. 211.

realities of his day and understood the workings of the government and the authority of the Orders in Council.[90] The Privy Council, by Scott's day, was still spoken of as the king's principal council even though the number of privy councillors had been indefinitely increased.[91] In reality, as Scott knew well, the Privy Council retained only formal and ceremonial functions. The small select body consisting of the heads of the governmental departments, the efficient cabinet, actually conducted the business of the government.[92] By the end of the eighteenth century, therefore, the king's prerogative powers, such as the power of conducting foreign affairs and making war and peace, were in practice exercised by the cabinet rather than the Privy Council which merely registered the cabinet's decisions.[93] Orders in Council, therefore, were official directives of the cabinet rather than actual policy expressions of the king in his Privy Council.

Scott also knew that numerous Orders in Council had been issued over the decades. Long before the controversial Orders in Council of 1807 and 1809, the government had issued many Orders which affected the practice of the admiralty court. During the seventeenth

[90] There is a revealing letter from Scott to Lord Melville, dated October 1, 1809, in which Scott apologized for his abrupt departure from Melville's home in Scotland. Scott had heard some news of the political situation in London and felt obliged to rush there immediately. Perhaps he had just heard of the duel between Robert Castlereagh and George Canning, which had taken place on September 21, or more likely he had received word that his friend and future son-in-law, Viscount Sidmouth, would receive no position in the new Perceval ministry. Scott's overreaction to the news gives an extraordinary insight into his exaggerated sense of his own role on the political stage. He wrote to Melville: 'The shock which the surprise of intelligence so unexpected & so painful gave me, aggravated by the circumstances of having been at such a distance at the time that the misfortune occurred extinguished every Idea but that of getting to the House of Mourning with all possible dispatch.' Scottish Record Office, GD/51/1/147. It appears from the rest of the letter that Parliament was the house of mourning.

[91] Bl. *Comm.*, I, 229–30.

[92] T. Williams, 'The cabinet in the eighteenth century', *History*, 22 (1937), 240–52; A. Aspinall, 'The cabinet council, 1783–1835', *Proceedings of the British Academy*, 38 (1952), 145–51. Although Scott was a member of the Privy Council after 1798, he seldom was noted in the register as present. One of his infrequent appearances was noted when he signed the Order in Council granting general reprisals against France on May 16, 1803, the day before Britain's declaration of war on France. Perhaps the cabinet wanted to spread the responsibility for the act, since thirty-one privy councillors signed the order. P.R.O. PC 2/162.

[93] *H.E.L.*, 10, 464–87. Blackstone discussed the king's prerogative in conducting foreign affairs, Bl. *Comm.*, I, 253–61. R. Pares discussed the unsettled and erratic role of the king in determining government policy, in *King George III and the Politicians* (Oxford, 1953).

and eighteenth centuries the admiralty judges had struggled, often in vain, to maintain independence of the government in deciding cases. The government interference could take the form of directions how to proceed in a particular case or of declarations of legal norms, especially definitions of contraband, which the judge was expected to follow.[94] Scott undoubtedly had some inkling that admiralty judges had not always been free from governmental orders. His instincts as an admiralty judge, however, must have inclined him to accept at face value the statement of the law officers in 1753 which had clearly asserted the contrary. In the report of that year on the Prussian reprisals, the law officers had swept aside much prize court history in contending that '[I]n England the crown never interferes with the courts of justice. No order or intimation is ever given to any judge.'[95]

Scott was likewise familiar with the more recent Orders in Council. During the French wars, years before the Orders of 1807 and 1809, the government had issued Orders in Council which affected the law and practice of the admiralty court. These Orders had authorized, for instance, the capture of ships of certain nations, defined contraband and imposed or lifted blockades or embargoes.[96] More specifically, instructions were issued ordering the admiralty court to release from capture cargoes of certain goods belonging to British merchants trading with the non-blockaded enemy ports;[97] and to release neutral vessels bringing grain to Great Britain even if the neutral had sailed from a blockaded port.[98] In particular cases the admiralty court was ordered to release two Russian vessels,[99] and to condemn a Turkish

---

[94] R. Pares, *Colonial blockade and neutral rights 1739–1763* (Oxford, 1938), 84–101.
[95] *Documents relating to law of the sea*, II, 348, 364. A few examples of intervention of the crown in prize matters can be seen in *ibid.*, II, 55–6, 131–4, 203–4, 210, 212, 289. This assertion of no interference with the admiralty judges might be accurate in the narrow sense that the government avoided intervention in any matter once it was properly before the court. Even this narrow area of independence was not always secure. In the notes of the case of the *Dorothea Maria (Bender)* (1748), H.S.P. Lee Cases, Sir George Lee noted, after giving the court's determination of the case: 'N.B. The Lords Justices by Letter to the Judge order'd the ship & cargo to be restored without any expences to the Claimers.' The Lords Justices' letter did correspond with the previously noted determination by the judge, but it is hardly clear which came first.
[96] For example, P.R.O. PC 2/141, fo. 7; 2/142, fo. 83; 2/144, fo. 184; 2/147, fo. 35; 2/151, fo. 465; 2/157, fo. 82; 2/158, fo. 218; 2/162, fo. 397; 2/166, fo. 390.
[97] P.R.O. PC 2/167, fo. 528.
[98] P.R.O. PC 2/156, fo. 255.
[99] P.R.O. PC 2/175, fo. 46.

vessel.[100] But the government seemed reluctant to interfere in a particular case which was actually being heard by the admiralty court.[101]

The background to the Orders in Council of 1807 and 1809 has already been discussed in detail.[102] In the case of the *Fox*, discussed at length above,[103] Scott displayed his awareness of the wholly unprecedented rule of law the Orders compelled him to apply. Although he and his predecessors had found nothing amiss in conforming their judgments to the many Orders in Council which had previously been issued, Scott grasped the unique significance of these new Orders which altered the established rule of the law of blockade. He showed his awareness of the different character of these recent Orders when he raised the ultimate question in his decision in the *Fox*: 'What would be the duty of the Court under Orders in Council that were repugnant to the law of nations?'[104] But he immediately surrendered to the government with a virtually irrebuttable presumption that the Orders were in conformity with the law of nations. Furthermore, Scott contended that the Privy Council possessed legislative power over the admiralty court similar to the legislative power of Parliament over the courts of common law.[105]

---

[100] P.R.O. PC 2/179, fo. 33. In this case although commissions had not yet issued authorizing admiralty courts to condemn Turkish ships and cargoes, the Council ordered the admiralty court to 'take cognizance of and judicially proceed upon the said Turkish ship of War Badere Jaffer, and shall hear and determine the same according to the Course of Admiralty and the Law of Nations and upon due proof that the said ship was a Ship of War bearing the Flag of the Ottoman Empire shall adjudge and condemn the same as good and Lawful prize to His Majesty'.

[101] P.R.O. PC 2/163, fos. 358, 381, 582.

[102] See above, pp. 215–19.

[103] Discussed above, pp. 220–2.

[104] *Fox* (1811), Edw. 311, 312.

[105] *Ibid.*, 313. During the First World War the Judicial Committee of the House of Lords explicitly rejected this dictum of Scott's *Fox* judgment. The Lords stated that '[T]here was no power in the Crown, by Order in Council, to prescribe or alter the law which Prize Courts have to administer.' *Zamora* (1916), Appeal Cases 1916, vol. II, 77, 96. In the same year as the *Zamora* decision, H. R. Pyke, a British writer on international law, took a more positivistic view of Scott's basic position. He wrote that Scott's broad dictum about administering a supranational body of law made no sense. Pyke stated: '[T]he law of nations has *per se* no authority over the national courts, which are bound to follow and administer only such rules and regulations as are prescribed by their own sovereign government.' 'The law of the prize court', *Law Quarterly Review*, 126 (1916), 144, 151. Pyke, of course, disagreed with the Judicial Committee's decision in the *Zamora*. Pyke insisted that the Judicial Committee had 'not allowed sufficient weight to the peculiar prerogative of the Crown in international affairs under the British constitution'. *Ibid.*, 167.

Thus ended Scott's claim to administer, as a fair and neutral arbiter, a supranational body of law. As he often did when deciding a diplomatically sensitive case, in his *Fox* decision he repeated this claim of even-handed treatment of neutrals under the law of nations. Here he protested too much in insisting that

[T]his Court is bound to administer the Law of Nations to the subjects of other countries in the different relations in which they may be placed towards this country and its government. This is what other countries have a right to demand for their subjects, and to complain if they receive it not. This is Its unwritten law evidenced in the course of Its decisions, and collected from the common usage of civilized states.[106]

Measured by the standard he himself had insisted on, Scott failed here to show he was truly independent of his own government. If we apply the standard he repeatedly proclaimed, he appears in cases like the *Fox* more as a lesser official, articulating a defense for the government's policy, than as an independent judge commissioned to evaluate and apply the law of nations fairly to all parties.

A contemporary British writer strongly criticized Scott's decision in the *Fox* case. This anonymous writer contrasted the Scott of 1798 with the Scott of 1811. In 1798, as we have seen, Scott had stated in the *Maria* that he even-handedly administered a supranational body of law for neutrals and belligerents alike. Twelve years later in the *Fox* Scott nodded his assent when the British government changed the law of nations. This author rhetorically asked:

How then can the Court be said to administer the unwritten law of nations between contending states, if it allows that one government, within whose territories it 'locally has its seat', to make alterations on that law at any moment of time? And by what stretch of ingenuity can we reconcile the position, that the Court treats the English government and foreign claimants alike, determining the cause exactly as it would if sitting in the claimant's country, with the new position, that the English government possesses legislative powers over the Court, and that its orders are in the law of nations what statutes are in the body of municipal law?[107]

Scott's judicial independence certainly does not appear at its high

---

[106] *Fox* (1811), Edw. 311, 312.
[107] Anonymous, 'Disputes with America', *Edinburgh Review*, 19 (1811–12), 290, 315. This review of a pamphlet entitled *The crisis of the dispute with America* undoubtedly was part of the campaign to repeal the Orders in Council.

point in his *Fox* judgment or in the subsequent judgment in the case of the *Snipe*.[108] It would be absurd, however, to expect Scott, or any judge, to be able in time of war to rise above all claims of national interest. In the first place, the law of nations already spoke with a British accent. The law of nations which Scott applied had been thoroughly permeated with policies based on national interest. The more politically attuned Lords Commissioners for Prize Appeals, who sat as the supreme court for prize cases, had frequently based their determinations on policies which favored British interests.[109] The rules which the Lords Commissioners pronounced, Scott felt bound to apply. The law of nations which Scott applied, therefore, was hardly a pure body of supranational legal norms.

Furthermore, Scott's claim of applying this body of law even-handedly, with no hint of tilting the balance in favor of his own nation, raised expectations of god-like fairness which no mere human judge can always satisfy. Scott could view a question only through British eyes. His British character penetrated to the core of his being. He craved, as we have seen, for the recognition of a peerage which the government, apparently, had dangled before him.[110] Before he became admiralty judge, Scott, as King's Advocate, had for ten years represented the government's interests and argued the government's cases.[111] Probably Scott was made admiralty judge precisely because he had effectively and convincingly spoken for the government as King's Advocate. Mere donning of judicial robes could not alter his willingness to accept the cogency of the government's policies. And Scott, even after he became judge, continued to support the government as a member of Parliament. He even justified the government's controversial Orders in Council in a speech in Parliament. Before he decided the case of the *Fox*, he had told Parliament that the Orders were justified under the principle of retaliation of the law of nations.[112] Not surprisingly, he used this same government argument in his *Fox* decision. Ultimately, and far more significantly in skewing his purported even-handedness, Scott was a loyal, conservative

---

[108] See above, p. 223.
[109] See above, pp. 199–201.
[110] See above, pp. 53–4.
[111] See above, pp. 129–51. No one is surprised when a former prosecutor, elevated to the bench, is peculiarly impressed with the veracity of the police and the arguments of the prosecutors that society must be rid of criminals.
[112] See above, pp. 218–19.

Sir William Scott

British subject, thoroughly convinced of the rightness of the British cause and fervently opposed to France and the diabolical French Revolution.

It is only because Scott had proclaimed his independence of the government that we have taken the trouble to discuss the issue. Scott did exactly what one would expect a judge to do in his situation, and did it with great competence and learning. He consistently made an honest effort at remaining even-handed. But Scott, even without an Olympian vantage point above all national interest, still had to balance, in the context of individual cases, the interests of the parties before the court. And the neutrals in this judicial balance could lay claim to no compelling moral position. Neutral merchants merely sought to make vast profits from carrying cargoes to and from the belligerents who were too distracted by the war to carry on their own trade. Neutral ship owners and masters engaged in every conceivable ruse and subterfuge to evade legitimate capture by the belligerents. The neutral rights Scott ordinarily had to balance did not involve basic human rights of the type familiar in twentieth-century warfare, such as widespread killing of civilians, confinement or deportation of refugees and destruction of villages. No judge in Scott's position, balancing the rights of his own country vigorously to pursue its war policies against the rights of neutrals to profit from the war, would have found the weight of neutral rights always overwhelming. Only if there were truth in those recurring charges against the British government that the Orders in Council were indeed merely an effort to monopolize trade can one object to the weight which Scott gave to the national interest.[113]

Scott, as a judge, did not engage in this sort of balancing in a vacuum. He viewed the rights of neutrals and belligerents in the concrete. He approached each case with extraordinary insight into the political, military, social and economic realities involved. As admiralty judge, he was compelled to determine the facts of each case as well as the legal principles to be applied. Many cases turned solely on questions of fact. Scott's careful, shrewd and perceptive sifting of the written evidence is obvious from his opinions. He often employed his ferret-like ability to discover in the ship's papers and the inter-

---

[113] Such charges were made, for instance, in Anonymous, 'Disputes with America', 290, 307, where the author stated: 'The principle, then of the new system – new at least in *our* Prize courts, and repugnant to the rules laid down by our most eminent Judges heretofore, is profit and monopoly, and not retaliation or self-defence.'

rogatories of the master and mate enough slips, inadvertent admissions and contradictions to warrant condemnation of the ship or cargo. When one consults the mountain of ship papers and depositions in the numerous individual case files which Scott had once pored over, one sometimes finds small marks and notations in the margins, most likely by Scott himself, highlighting the facts which swayed his judgment.[114]

Scott's balancing of British rights against the rights of neutrals, therefore, was done within the structured framework of vague international principles as filtered through the decisions of his predecessors and within the concrete, detailed factual situations of each individual case. Scott's genius as a judge lay largely in his persistent effort, in a generally unbiased manner, to consider and weigh all the relevant legal and factual questions in determining each case. Judged by such a realistic standard Scott's judicial record appears impressive indeed.

JUDICIAL ADMINISTRATION

A judge should be responsible, not only for deciding the many cases which come before him, but also, to some extent, for the conduct of all the officials and practitioners who are associated with the court. Holdsworth, for instance, after praising the judicial career of the Earl of Hardwicke as Lord Chancellor, disapproved of Hardwicke's failure to correct the abuses in the Chancery Court of his day. Hardwicke, according to Holdsworth, failed to exercise adequate supervision of the many Chancery Court officials. After enumerating some of the administrative problems in the Chancery Court in the eighteenth century, Holdsworth criticized Hardwicke for taking no effective steps to cure these defects.[115]

For nearly thirty years Scott sat as admiralty judge. His record as a supervisor of the personnel connected with the court must be briefly discussed. Although Scott did at times exercise vigorous control over various officers of the admiralty court, he was extremely thin-skinned

---

[114] See, for instance, the case files in *Two Brothers* (*M'Clousky*) (1799), 1 Rob. 131, P.R.O. HCA 32/868/109; *Rising Sun* (*Wilkye*) (1799), 2 Rob. 104, P.R.O. HCA 32/823/51; *Neptunus* (*Moswold*) (1800), 3 Rob. 80, P.R.O. HCA 32/774/120; and *William and Mary* (*Dickson*) (1803), 4 Rob. 381, P.R.O. HCA 32/911/82. Scott's role as fact-finder was crucial in each of these cases.

[115] *H.E.L.*, 12, 285–97.

about any hint of interference in the administration of the court from the outside.

On several occasions while Scott was admiralty judge, some members of Parliament called for investigations into perceived abuses of various personnel of the admiralty court. The proponents of these investigations generally represented the interests of the naval officers and seamen who wanted quick and inexpensive determinations of prize cases and prompt delivery of the proceeds from their captures. They objected to the long delays involved in getting their hands on the prize money from the captures they had made; they objected to the exclusive representation of their interests by the King's Proctor whose partner in practice had at times represented the interests of the adverse party claiming restitution; they objected to the large legal fees deducted from the prize money; and they objected to the practice of the registrar of the admiralty court who kept the money from the sale of prizes pending litigation on deposit in his own name and drew interest on these funds. These, of course, were significant allegations of abuses in the admiralty court calling for correction.[116]

Scott's repeated response in Parliament was to oppose any efforts at investigation or reform of the admiralty court, or, if possible, to dilute any proposed bills. He reminded the members that the admiralty court sat not only to deliver prize money to the British captors, 'but likewise to protect foreign and British merchants; to restore property which had been improperly seized, and to do justice to all parties'.[117] He denied that the abuses existed, but even if they did, Scott insisted:

[T]here was a respect due to a court of justice, which ought not to be forgotten. The noble lord [Cochrane] would recollect, that it was the province of that court to maintain the maritime rights of this country, and that this could not be done without exciting a good deal of irritation in neutrals. But if these imputations were perpetually thrown out against it, neutral nations would not submit with any degree of patience ... [And] such imputations as these might produce dangerous impressions in the lower orders [of the navy], for he could not suppose that the officers could be misled by them. What would be their feelings if they were really to believe that there was a general conspiracy in the admiralty court against them?[118]

Scott here demonstrated that anti-change conservatism which we

---

[116] Hansard, 1st ser. IV, 61–5; V, 132–9, 174–5; XV, 12–15, 469–79; XIX, 476–9; XX, 985–1001; XXIII, 626–9; XXVI, 246. The leading proponents of reforming the admiralty court were Thomas Cochrane, Earl of Dundonald, and Sir Charles Pole. Both were closely identified with the interests of the navy.
[117] Hansard, 1st ser. XIX, 477.
[118] Hansard, 1st ser. XV, 14.

have observed elsewhere. Any intrusions by Parliament into his domain would be deeply resented and vigorously opposed. In his own supervision of the internal workings of the admiralty court, however, Scott acted like the lord of a manor, occasionally correcting abuses and censuring the offending subordinates. But he certainly could not be called a vigorous judicial reformer. For Scott, the standard of conduct for the officers of the court was the long-established usage within such offices; traditional practice defined the limits of present conduct.

Scott's control of the officers of the court appeared most clearly in the cases involving the marshal of the court. The marshal's primary responsibility was service of the process of the admiralty court. Since process was ordinarily *in rem*, the marshal's duties included custody of the ships and cargoes arrested by the court. The character traits required for the office of marshal are suggested in a letter written by Scott in 1811. He indicated that he had been called to appear before the king who asked if Scott had any objection to the appointment of a certain Robert Thornton to be marshal. The only traits mentioned were that Thornton had been good to the royal family and that he had been unfortunate in his mercantile affairs. Scott, of course, expressed no objection.[119] If the marshal's office was regularly filled by impecunious royal friends, there can be little surprise that abuses occurred.

In the case of the *Rendsberg*, decided six years before Thornton was nominated for the marshal's office, Scott abruptly put a stop to the outrageous fees and commissions which had been charged by the marshal at that time.[120] The *Rendsberg* had been seized at St Helena and sent by the governor to Falmouth. When the seizure came before the court, Scott directed the marshal to have the ship moved to London and appraised. Eventually the marshal submitted his bill for the various services he had performed. This bill was challenged before the court. The marshal had not only asked for £475 as a charge for having the ship moved from Falmouth to London, but also a commission of ½% of the value of the cargo for unloading the vessel, another ½% for delivery of the cargo to the claimant and a commission for the marshal and broker of 3½% for the sale of the ship. Scott, in restrained tones, expressed his outrage at these charges of more than £1,400.

[119] Scott to Charles Yorke, n.d., but clearly in 1811, Brit. Lib., Add. MS 45,044, fo. 140.
[120] *Rendsberg* (*Nyberg*) (1805), 6 Rob. 142.

I must confess that such a general statement is at least awakening. I know nothing like it in any other office of the same description . . . [These charges arise] from the mere execution of the ordinary processes of the Court, in which the party is an officer . . . [The office of marshal] is an office requiring the valuable qualifications of common prudence, common integrity, and common civility in the holder; but well satisfied by these endowments, and demanding no peculiar elevation of talents, no laborious preparations of study, and personal accomplishments, and imposing no particular obligations of splendor and expence.[121]

Scott, in a meticulous thirty-page judgment, totally deflated the ballooned charges the marshal had submitted. Scott insisted that the marshal must be limited to the fees sanctioned by traditional fee schedules or by unwritten usage. Occasionally, he admitted, fees might be based on an equitable claim for work performed. But Scott completely rejected any charges based on a percentage commission, supposedly based on an analogy with merchant's commissions. Scott would have none of this. 'I do most entirely repudiate all analogy between mercantile profits and official charges. The merchant charges his commission because he is a merchant. The Marshal has not a right to charge it, because he is not a merchant. He has not the education of a merchant, nor the functions of a merchant.'[122]

Several years after trimming the sails of the marshal, Scott wrote a letter insisting that there was no need for parliamentary regulation of the fees of marshal, since he had taken care of the problem himself. 'When I was appointed Judge I found the Marshal charged pretty much ad libitum, and particularly had established a claim to a charge of a percentage commission on all property. I felt it to be my duty to resist & overthrow that claim and to reduce his charges to the old standard.'[123]

Shortly after becoming judge, Scott had rejected a suit by the marshal as recaptor of a British ship. Scott found that the seizure by the marshal was so irregular that it was utterly invalid. Because it was not the accepted practice, Scott refused to decree any award to the marshal as military salvage.[124] In another case Scott ordered the

---

[121] *Ibid.*, 147.
[122] *Ibid.*, 163–4.
[123] Scott to [addressee unknown], August 31, 1811, Brit. Lib., Add. MS 45,044, fo. 138.
[124] *Minerva (Molowny)* (1800), unreported, Nicholl's Notebook, 1799–1800, P.R.O. HCA 30/464.

marshal to pay for the loss of a long boat and bower cable from a ship while in his custody.[125] Although Scott clearly was ready to listen to any statement that the marshal had exercised due care in maintaining custody of this property, the marshal simply refused to put in an appearance before the court.

Scott occasionally acted as judge to correct other abuses, especially when Parliament had called attention to the abuse. The King's Proctor had been criticized in Parliament for conflict of interest. It was alleged that the Proctor, who alone was authorized to represent the naval captors, had partners who had represented claimants, the other parties in prize suits. Scott insisted in a private letter that this abuse no longer existed. He told his correspondent he had spoken with the King's Proctor and had received a solemn promise that he and his partner would immediately give up all representation of claimants and represent only captors. Scott assured his correspondent that all other complaints against the King's Proctor were frivolous and unfounded.[126]

Scott likewise oversaw the office of the registrar. But in this oversight of the registrar's office, Scott hardly showed himself to be a vigorous reformer. He objected to the registrar's delay in paying out the proceeds of a capture once the court had issued its decree. One party, apparently, had warned the registrar not to deliver the funds to the other party, and the registrar delayed because of this warning. Scott insisted that parties had no right to interfere in the registrar's duties unless they came before the court and stated their objections. Since this had become a regular practice, Scott suggested that a rule might be appropriate to end the practice. 'I cannot think that it is correct practice', he said, 'for the individuals to stop the payment, absolutely, and as long as he pleases, without the authority of this Court.'[127]

When the deputy registrar of a colonial vice-admiralty court had transferred prize funds to a business establishment in England which soon failed, Scott had to consider whether the colonial registrar and his deputy should be held strictly liable for the loss of the funds.[128] Scott merely held these officers to a standard of due care for the funds and found no negligence on their part. The registrar and deputy had

[125] *Hoop (Morrel)* (1801), 4 Rob. 145.
[126] Scott to [addressee illegible], dated only June 13, H.S.P.
[127] *Fortuna (Tadsen)* (1802), 4 Rob. 278, 279.
[128] *Prima Vera (Vodonick)* (1808), Edw. 23, 31.

done all they could to transfer the funds to England for ultimate deposit in the Bank of England. He refused to compel them to make good the loss, especially since the captors had been guilty of some inactivity which, Scott thought, had occasioned the loss.

Scott also applied this standard of due care to the captors of two ships who, under order of the court, had unloaded the cargoes and stored them in a warehouse pending determination of the validity of the capture. The goods disappeared from the warehouse when it was broken into. Scott here let the loss fall on the warehouseman and the neutral owners of the goods, since the captors had exercised due care in storing the goods in a safe place. '[N]othing has been advanced to shew that these warehouses were not proper places, and sufficiently secure.'[129]

Scott did not even impose liability on an individual who had been appointed as one of the commissioners to appraise and sell two Spanish vessels.[130] This commissioner had taken possession of the bullion on these vessels and had apparently invested it and collected the interest. Although the court had ordered the commission to be returned in six weeks, no return was made for sixteen months. Scott insisted that commissioners of appraisement were merely ministerial officers of the court and that they were not entitled to make sixpence above the percentage allowed them under their commission. But Scott found no precedent for an award of interest even in this case. Traditional practice served as his norm. He, therefore, sought to correct the abuse for the future by insisting on prompt return of such commissions. Since such delays, Scott discovered, had been all too frequent, he refused to punish one individual for following a common practice. Scott expressed his hesitant attitude toward reform of the court when he said:

However disposed I may be to censure this practice and correct it in future, it would seem too hard to lay down, that here was special delinquency that called for penalties; it is a bad sort of reformation, which begins by an act of vindictive justice, on a person, who has been acting only as every other person has been permitted to act, under such circumstances.[131]

---

[129] *Maria (Jortz)* and *Vrow Johanna* (1803), 4 Rob. 348, 352.

[130] *Princessa (Zavala)* and *Reine Elizabeth* (1799), 2 Rob. 31.

[131] *Ibid.*, 44–5. In another case Scott corrected an abuse by making a rule for future conduct. In the *Frau Maria (Jansen)* (1799), 2 Rob. 292, 293, the marshal had refused to execute a commission for appraisement since neither party had paid his expenses. Scott ordered that in the future the captors should pay such expenses pending final adjudication of the validity of the capture.

Even though restitution of the interest does not seem to be a radical suggestion, Scott insisted that the reform should be prospective only. He published an order of the court to correct this abuse for the future.[132] He ordered the commissioners and the marshal henceforth to make returns on the day stated in their commissions or else to come before the court and request an extension of time. Furthermore, the commissioners were ordered promptly to deliver the proceeds from any partial sale into the court and not to wait until all the proceeds were ready to be delivered. If this order was observed, it would have done much to correct the abuse of allowing a commissioner to derive interest for a long period of time from his possession of the proceeds of a prize sale.

Scott would surely have been horrified to be called a judicial reformer. But, although he used what little influence he had in Parliament to prevent statutory reforms of the admiralty court, he did use his authority as judge to root out some of the worst abuses by officers of the court. Scott's thoroughly conservative nature is highlighted in this analysis of his administration of the admiralty court.

[132] Order of the Court, July 3, 1799, 1 Rob. 187.

SCOTT'S INFLUENCE

For nearly a century after Sir William Scott, Lord Stowell, had completed his lengthy tenure on the admiralty court, his numerous decisions were read and respected by judges and commentators who considered questions of admiralty law and international law. Scott's younger contemporaries appeared overawed by his work. Francis Holt, in an elaborate dedication to Scott of his work on shipping law, asserted that he knew of no instance in which the common law courts had questioned any of Scott's decisions when they had occasion to consider them.[1] Arthur Browne, professor of civil law at the University of Dublin, also dedicated his work on the civil law to Scott, pointing to Scott's 'superior knowledge and unrivalled administration of the civil law, and of the law of nations'.[2]

Throughout the nineteenth century, Scott's prize judgments continued to influence British writers on international law. William Hall and T. J. Lawrence, for instance, repeatedly cited Scott's judgments as a leading, often as the only, authority for various doctrines of international law.[3] During the First World War, Scott's biographer,

[1] F. L. Holt, *A system of the shipping and navigation laws of Great Britain* (2 vols., London, 1824), I, vi. Holt, in this dedication, continued with effusive praise: 'In learning, in eloquence, in the condensation of strong sense in language exact and apposite, without quaintness and obscurity; in knowledge of the practices of life and character, in divesting subjects of all that is merely formal, technical, and artificial, and grounding them upon their proper and natural principles, and their due strength in right reason – your judgments, my Lord, have done for your own country, what the writings of Grotius, Vinnius, and Montesquieu, have done for France, Holland, and Germany. And it will no longer be said, that England has not contributed her share both to the practical illustration of the law of nations, and to that general maritime law which, under the name of the Law Merchant, is no less the law of single countries, than the public mercantile code of Europe.' *Ibid.*, vii.
[2] A. Browne, *A compendious view of the civil law, and of the law of the admiralty*, 2nd edn (2 vols., London, 1802).
[3] W. E. Hall, *A treatise on international law*, 7th edn (Oxford, 1917), and T. J. Lawrence, *The principles of international law* (Boston, 1895).

the uncritically laudatory registrar of the admiralty court, E. S. Roscoe, could still refer to Scott's prize judgments as the 'corner-stone of one branch of British jurisprudence'.[4]

It would have been surprising if Scott's enormous contribution to admiralty law and international law had not been well received in Britain. A far better index of Scott's influence comes from an assessment of the American legal writers who could approach his work with no suspicion of chauvinism.

James Kent was widely respected in the United States throughout the nineteenth century, both as a legal scholar and as Chancellor of New York. Kent devoted 200 pages of his four-volume work, *Commentaries on American law*, to the law of nations. Kent cited Scott's decisions some 140 times in these 200 pages. In discussing the sources of international law Kent contrasted the legal precision of judicial decisions from Great Britain and the United States with the looser discussions by continental philosophical writers. With his usual accurate insight, Kent offered this assessment of Scott's judgments:

In the investigation of the rules of the modern law of nations, particularly with regard to the extensive field of maritime capture, reference is generally and freely made to the decisions of the English courts. They are in the habit of taking accurate and comprehensive views of general jurisprudence, and they have been deservedly followed by the courts of the United States, on all the leading points of national law. We have a series of judicial decisions in England, and in this country, in which the usages and the duties of nations are explained and declared with that depth of research, and that liberal and enlarged inquiry, which strengthens and embellishes the conclusions of reason. They contain more intrinsic argument, more full and precise details, more accurate illustrations, and are of more authority, than the loose *dicta* of elementary writers. When those courts in this country, which are charged with the administration of international law, have differed from the English adjudications, we must take the law from domestic sources; but such an alternative is rarely to be met with, and there is scarcely a decision in the English prize courts at Westminster [*sic*], on any general question of public right, that has not received the express approbation and sanction of our national courts ... The great value of a series of judicial decisions, in prize cases, and on other questions depending on the law of nations, is, that they liquidate, and render certain and stable the loose general principles of that law, and show their application, and how they are understood in the country where the tribunals are sitting. They are, therefore, deservedly received with very great respect, and as presumptive, though not conclusive, evidence of the law in the given case. This was the language of the Supreme Court of the

---

[4] E. S. Roscoe, *Lord Stowell – his life and the development of English prize law* (Boston, 1916), 91.

United States, so late as 1815, and the decisions of the English High Court of Admiralty, especially since the year 1798 [the year Scott became admiralty judge], have been consulted and uniformly respected by that court, as enlightened commentaries on the law of nations, and affording a vast variety of instructive precedents for the application of the principles of that law.[5]

Justice Joseph Story of the United States Supreme Court also looked to Scott's judgments for guidance in his scholarly writing and in his judicial decisions. Story corresponded with Scott in Scott's later years and they exchanged comments on judicial decisions and political affairs. Story had sent to Scott some volumes of reports containing some of his own decisions. Scott replied expressing a sense of pride that his judgments had been followed in the United States.[6] Story wrote back that he appreciated Scott's comments especially since he had tried to follow the principles expressed in Scott's judgments. Story wrote:

I return you also my sincere thanks for the favorable manner in which you have been pleased to speak of the former volumes, the decisions in which, whatever may be their merits in other respects, were made under an anxious desire to administer the law of Prize upon the principles which had been so luminously pointed out by yourself.[7]

In a later letter addressed to Scott as Lord Stowell in 1828, his last year on the bench, Story hinted at the enormous admiration he felt for Scott's admiralty decisions.

I have had occasion to know that your judgment [in the *Slave Grace*] has been extensively read in America, (where questions of this nature are not of unfrequent discussion,) and I never have heard any other opinion but that of approbation of it expressed among the profession of the Law. I cannot but think that, upon questions of this sort, as well as of general maritime law, it were well if the common lawyers had studied a little more extensively the

---

[5] J. Kent, *Commentaries on American law* (4 vols., New York, 1832), I, 69–70. The 1815 Supreme Court decision Kent referred to was *Thirty Hogsheads of Sugar* (1815), 9 Cranch 189, 198. Chief Justice Marshall, in that decision, was somewhat less emphatic about the authority of British prize cases in the United States than Kent was in his *Commentaries*.

[6] Scott had written: 'It makes me proud, indeed, that any labors of mine are approved by gentlemen of a country upon which they may sometimes have operated with apparent harshness, but who are so well capable of estimating fairly, and upon reflection, their real conformity to the law, which it was my duty to administer.' Scott to Story, July 2, 1818, reproduced in W. W. Story, *Life and letters of Joseph Story* (2 vols., London, 1851), I, 307.

[7] Story to Scott, January 14, 1819, *ibid.*, 318.

principles of public and civil Law . . . I am free to say that in every case, in which you have been called to review any of the Common Law doctrines on maritime subjects, and have differed from them, I have constantly been persuaded that your judgment was correct.[8]

Testimonials from Kent and Story, two American legal heavy-weights of the early nineteenth century, might seem sufficient to show Scott's influence in the United States. Far more convincing, however, is the opinion of Story's protégé, Henry Wheaton, the international legal scholar and Supreme Court reporter.[9] Wheaton, who is today largely forgotten, wrote three books on aspects of international law: *A digest of the law of maritime captures and prizes*, published in 1815 at the end of the British–American War of 1812; his classic *Elements of international law*, first published in 1836 and frequently republished and translated into French, Italian, Chinese, Japanese and Spanish throughout the nineteenth century, and his *History of the law of nations in Europe and America from the earliest times to the Treaty of Washington, 1842*, which was first published in French in 1841 as an essay for a competition and subsequently enlarged and published in English in 1845.

No American, not even Joseph Story, was more knowledgeable about the history and current state of international law than Henry Wheaton. Furthermore, Wheaton certainly approached Scott's judgments with a critical eye. When he had visited England in 1806, Wheaton expressed the frustration of many neutrals in a letter to his father: 'The Prize Courts continue in their decrees to manifest a disposition not to recede from those doctrines upon the faith of which they have confiscated so much of our neutral property.'[10] In the preface to his *Digest of the law of maritime captures*, Wheaton

---

[8] Story to Lord Stowell, September 22, 1828, *ibid.*, 558–9. Story's reliance in his legal scholarship on Scott's judgments is briefly discussed in R. K. Newmyer, *Supreme Court Justice Joseph Story – statesman of the Old Republic* (Chapel Hill, N.C., 1985), 97, 121, 285.

On December 20, 1826 Story had expressed his admiration of Scott's work in his letter addressed to Lord Stowell: 'I can scarcely conceive of any situation more enviable than that of an octogenarian, who can look back upon a long career of usefulness with the consciousness of an unfaltering performance of duty, & the feeling, that his own glory is essentially to be mixed up with that of his country through all future time.' Beinecke Library, Yale University, Osborne File.

[9] Wheaton's scholarship and his close personal and scholarly relationship with Joseph Story in Wheaton's younger years are discussed in detail in C. Joyce, 'The rise of the Supreme Court reporter: an institutional perspective on Marshall Court ascendancy', *Michigan Law Review*, 83 (1985), 1291, 1312–86.

[10] Quoted in E. F. Baker, *Henry Wheaton 1785–1848* (Philadelphia, 1937), 15.

expressed precisely his ambivalent attitude toward Scott's prize judgments. He could not help admiring them, yet he strongly objected to Scott's subservience to his government. Wheaton wrote:

The decisions of the present judge of the high court of admiralty in England are entitled to great respect and attention, and being the adjudications of a court of the law of nations, are of binding authority in that law, except upon those questions in regard to which certain peculiar doctrines have been maintained by the British government. Whatever reason our country may have to complain of the injurious application of those doctrines to us as a neutral nation, it must in candour be admitted that on every other head the decisions of Sir William Scott merit the highest consideration, on account of their intrinsic value and the judicial eloquence by which they are adorned[.] I have therefore made a liberal, though cautious use of them, in the compilation of this digest. Had that great man followed the example of his illustrious countryman, Sir James Mackintosh, in refusing to be bound by the instructions and rescripts of his government, where they infringed the law of nations and abridged the rights of neutrals, the authority of his adjudications would have been entitled to still more respect with foreign nations and with future ages.[11]

Such a cautious critic can best attest to the influence of Scott's work as admiralty judge. Wheaton's actions spoke more eloquently than his words; he cited Scott's judgments about 225 times in the *Digest*. It is clear that for many doctrines in this book on prize law, Wheaton relied exclusively or primarily on Scott's judgments.

Wheaton's enormous debt to Scott can best be assessed, not by counting citations, but by evaluating them. In Wheaton's most mature work of scholarship, his *Elements of international law*, he cited more than 150 different decisions which Scott had rendered. Many of them he cited repeatedly. On many questions of international law, Scott's opinions were clearly the most significant authority for Wheaton. For instance, Wheaton relied primarily on Scott's judgments in discussing such issues as: the limits of territorial waters, the effect of an embargo prior to the declaration of war, the principle of reciprocity in dealing with enemy property within a belligerent's territory at the outbreak of a war, the rule against trading with the enemy, the definition of domicile for merchants in time of war, the illegality of captures made within neutral waters, the illegality of neutral ships carrying enemy military personnel or dispatches, the

[11] H. Wheaton, *A digest of the law of maritime captures and prizes* (New York, 1815), vi.

legality of neutral ships carrying enemy diplomatic messages and the definition of blockade.[12] Though occasionally Wheaton disagreed with Scott, on some issues he explicitly stated that the rule of the British prize court should also be the rule adopted in the United States.[13] Wheaton's repeated use of Scott's decisions provides the most effective testimony to Scott's enduring influence.

Finally, it should be noted that the enormously influential Chief Justice of the United States, John Marshall, also felt obliged to acknowledge that he often followed the judgments Scott had rendered. Marshall, certainly not a legal scholar like Story or Wheaton, paid tribute to Scott while at the same time tempering his praise: 'I respect Sir William Scott, as I do every truely great man; and I respect his decisions; nor should I depart from them on light grounds; but it is impossible to consider them attentively without perceiving that his mind leans strongly in favor of the captors.'[14]

Marshall clearly followed Scott's decisions in many of his own opinions, often, as was his practice, without any citation.[15] Marshall's reliance on the authority of Scott's judgments, like that of Wheaton, is particularly impressive since he was so clear in expressing his reservations.

Up to the time of the First World War, the law of naval warfare bore the imprint of Scott's many prize judgments.[16] With the late nineteenth-century rise of legal positivism and the twentieth-century reality of total warfare, Scott's world and his influence had largely vanished. Throughout his long professional life Scott believed in a rationally ordered universe, with a binding rule of reason and international custom to restrict governmental action. He could not have accepted the concept of total war. The vision of a law of nations which so influenced him at least furnished him with a goal to strive for. If he at times failed to achieve this goal, his work was certainly the richer for his striving.

---

[12] H. Wheaton, *Elements of international law*, ed. G. G. Wilson (Oxford, 1936), sections 177, 293, 301, 309–10, 322–6, 428, 502–4.
[13] *Ibid.*, sections 380, 507.
[14] *Venus (Rae)* (1814), 8 Cranch 253, 299.
[15] B. M. Ziegler, *The international law of John Marshall* (Chapel Hill, N.C., 1939), 18.
[16] C. J. Colombos, *The international law of the sea*, 5th edn (New York, 1962), 11.

APPENDIX: THE STOWELL NOTEBOOKS

In the office of the Registrar of the Admiralty at the courts of justice in London are two notebooks ascribed to Sir William Scott, Lord Stowell.[1] Since both are significant for the study of Scott's admiralty judgments, both merit a separate study.

One volume, which for reasons explained below will be referred to as the Simpson Manuscript, is a 7½- by 9½-inch bound notebook with the following words on the spine, 'Copies Important Memorandums Stowell'. It contains 400 hand-numbered pages which are nearly all used, as well as some blank, unnumbered pages in the front and at the back. Since, as will be argued, this volume provides the most complete picture available anywhere of mid-eighteenth-century admiralty law, its significance is obvious regardless of who its author was. This full and complex manuscript will be described in detail and its author identified, but first a brief description of the much simpler second volume will be given, since a few words will suffice.

Throughout this book the second manuscript will be referred to as the Stowell Notebook, since that is the way it can be identified in the office of the Registrar. It is the same size as the first volume and has the following notation on the spine, 'Original Important Memorandums Stowell'. It contains over 300 pages, but only pages 1 to 172 and 300 to 329 have been used, plus 8 unnumbered pages at the rear which have topics for an index. The rest of the pages are blank.

On the first numbered page of this Stowell Notebook is the notation, 'Presented to me by Lord Stowell Judge of the Admy Wm Rothery'. William Rothery, 1775 to 1864, was King's Proctor and thus closely associated with the admiralty court. His son, Henry Cadogan Rothery, 1817 to 1888, was Registrar of the Admiralty after 1853, which explains how the two notebooks found their way into the Registrar's office. Practically the whole notebook appears to be in Scott's handwriting. The first 172 pages can best be described as a practice notebook which Scott kept during the years 1788 and 1789. There are many notations which include dates, such as 'Michaelmas 1788' at the top of page 1. Scott summarized the opinions he provided as counsel, the arguments he attended in various civilian courts, a few judgments he gave as

---

[1] I am greatly indebted to Mr J. Rochford, Registrar of the Admiralty, who was extremely helpful in making these two manuscript notebooks available for my research.

judge of the consistory court and the judgments from other courts. Most of the material deals with ecclesiastical questions. There are a few professional letters which Scott included and one list of law cases he compiled, apparently in preparation for argument of a case. Pages 173 to 299 are blank, but on page 300 there begin twenty-nine pages captioned, 'Adm Prize Appeals' also in Scott's hand. There is no way of determining when Scott prepared these brief, one or two sentence, summaries of prize appeal cases. Perhaps in the early 1790s, with the outbreak of war with France, Scott felt the need to analyze these old cases, dating mostly from the 1740s and 1750s, in order to use them as King's Advocate in prize litigation. At the back of the book Scott started to make an index to the volume by alphabetically listing topics dealing mostly with ecclesiastical law. He never completed the project by entering the page references. On page 167 is the notation in Scott's hand, 'So much business came on that I have been under a necessity of desisting for 3 months or more.' The notetaking stopped shortly thereafter and a few pages were later added, perhaps in a different hand.

The other notebook, which will be referred to as the Simpson Manuscript, merits a more detailed evaluation, especially since it is virtually certain that it was not Scott's own work and was never in his own hand. At the top of the first page that was used, page 8, is the notation, 'Wm. Rothery This Contains a Copy taken from an Original Book, lent to me by Lord Stowell for that purpose, all in his own handwriting'. The book clearly is a copy of some other manuscript, but the reasons for doubting that it was ever in Scott's hand will appear as the Manuscript is analyzed. Though probably not written or copied by Scott, it must have belonged to him, thus leading Rothery to reach the wrong conclusion about the handwriting. It will be possible to draw a fairly strong conclusion that the original of this notebook was by Sir Edward Simpson, a civilian from the mid-eighteenth century. Its importance for a study of Scott's work as admiralty judge will appear when its contents, date and authorship have been discussed.

Since this notebook contains no explicit signposts to indicate its purpose or structure, only a close study of the contents can reveal the compiler's intention. The first part of the book, pages 8 to 71, appears to be a roughly prepared commonplace book for the admiralty court. There are topical headings in alphabetical order starting with 'Admiralty' and running to 'Witness'. Nearly 100 topics apparently were initially entered in these pages and subsequently the appropriate legal notes were added from time to time under the proper topic. In some instances the space left after an entry did not suffice, so the passages are continued on what must have been available blank pages, usually with cross-references. A few entries were added out of alphabetical sequence. The original thus seems to have been compiled over a period of time, with the compiler trying to arrange the material in a way that would remain available and useful for later work. The topics touch many aspects of admiralty law (instance and prize) and admiralty procedure and practice.

Throughout this first section there are about seventy references to cases, most of them clearly admiralty cases, but others perhaps common law cases. Case captions are given, such as *'Eagle Galley'*, *'Sandhill con Stevens'*, *'Rex con Blyth & Hurst', 'The Olive Branch', 'Rye con the Greyhound', 'Weir agt Houghton'*, but no published common law reports are mentioned. A good number of the citations include dates, which are all between 1704 and 1743, a point which will be brought up again when the date of the original book is discussed. Occasionally the court which gave the judgment is mentioned, such as 'Lds Privy Council', 'Adm' or 'Lds of Appeal'. After most of the case citations is a page or folio number followed by the letter 'A'. This A source will be discussed later.

After page 71 the compiler began what can best be described as a draft abridgment of admiralty law, or at least, a great expansion of the initial commonplace book. For the rest of the book, between pages 72 and 400, the compiler has listed topics no longer in alphabetical order and has left much larger amounts of blank space to make entries under each topic, two, four or six pages. Two topics beginning with the same letter are often joined. When these blank pages were filled, the compiler continued the discussion of the topic or topics on the next available blank pages. Thus the topic 'Wages' is treated on pages 76 to 79, 218 to 219, 246 to 247, 250 to 251, 278 to 285, 292 to 297, 336 to 339, 356 to 359 and 372 to 377. The two topics 'Appeal & Agent' are discussed on pages 90 to 93, 126 to 129, and the topic heading is changed to 'Appeal & Average' on pages 208 to 211; all three topics are then continued at pages 228 to 233. The compiler's intention to have all the scattered sections on a particular topic viewed as part of a single discussion is clear from the cross-references he included at the beginning and end of each section, indicating the page from which the discussion is continuing and the page to which one should turn for a continuation. Often the end of a sentence can be found only by turning to the continuation some fifty or a hundred pages later. The hop-scotch arrangement of this largest part of the volume makes it apparent that the compiler worked over a long period of time. He fitted bits of legal information into the topic headings he had listed and then, when he filled the pages he had allowed for that topic, he started a new section for further entries wherever blank pages could be found. About 150 topics are discussed in this part of the book, some briefly, some at considerable length, many of them overlapping the topics in the first part of the book and often with cross-references in one part of the book to the place where the topic is discussed in the other part. Throughout the entire volume there are page references under one topic to places in the book where a particular aspect of that topic is discussed under a different topical heading. Practically every aspect of admiralty law, instance and prize, substantive and procedural, is discussed. As already mentioned, no comparably full treatment of admiralty law from the mid-eighteenth century exists, a sad commentary on the state of admiralty law.

The most notable change in the second part of the compilation, besides the much fuller treatment of many of the topics, is the nearly total lack of any case citations. Only two admiralty cases are mentioned by name in the final 320 pages of the book. The second part does contain scattered citations to common law cases, with exact references to the reports of Strange, Lord Raymond and Peere-Williams. There is one reference to each of the following sources: Molloy's *De Jure Maritimo et Navali*, Roccus' *De Navibus et Naulo*, the *Laws of Oleron*, and Hale's *Pleas of the Crown*. There is also a single reference to the *Institutes* and to the *Digest*.

Throughout the entire volume there are hundreds of references to a source merely noted as 'A', usually followed by a page or folio number. In spite of repeated efforts to find this A source in the various archives and libraries, it could not be located. Apparently the A source was a practitioner's notebook containing notes of admiralty cases and opinions prepared as counsel. Probably the compiler of this notebook, Simpson, was also the compiler of the A source, but it is possible that he relied on the notebook of some other practitioner. Throughout this notebook there are about 375 citations to the A source. There are citations to every page of the first thirty-seven pages of the A source, then no citations to any page of the A source between 38 and 62. Perhaps the A source contained non-admiralty materials on these pages. There are then citations in the Simpson Manuscript to pages 63 to 106 of the A source, with the exception of pages 90 and 105. The order of the references in the Simpson Manuscript to the pages of the A source do not at all correspond with the order in that source. For instance, A source, page 8 is referred to on pages 26, 65, 87, 88, 89, 98, 106, 118, 124, 126, 134 and 150 of the Simpson Manuscript. It is also obvious that each page of the A source often contained discussions of several different topics. For instance, references to page 4 of the A source are given for such disparate topics as the admiral's share of a prize, joint capture, time for appeal and construction of the Anglo-Dutch Treaty of 1674.

An important point to note concerning the A source is the type of material it contained. Many of the citations to that source concern specific admiralty cases in which the parties and ship names are given by letters or vague names. But often there are clear indications that the A source was not discussing a litigated case, but a dispute in which some civilian had provided advice as counsel. The material derived from the A source, for instance, uses such language as: '[T]here may be some doubt to what Court they appeal from [the Admiralty of Ireland] ... I incline to think it must be to [the] High Court of Admiralty here',[2] or 'However as this seems to be a new method of proceeding in [a] case of this nature if he can avoid being arrested he may by opinion of Court [obtain a commission to take bail at Liverpool] by appointing Proctor to Appear for him to give bail for appearance and to pray Com[missio]n',[3] or 'For if the Warr[an]t be legal as I presume the Court of Admiralty will pronounce it to be ...'.[4] There are a good number of these statements which must have been made originally in an opinion of counsel. Much of the material is ambiguous and could have been derived from a speech of the admiralty judge in giving judgment, from a civilian's notebook summary of a case or from an opinion of counsel. There are also editorial comments by the compiler of the A source or of the Manuscript itself, such as: 'This [is] a point of so great consequence to the trade of this Kindome it ought to be reconsidered and I think the sentence not well founded.'[5] All is blended together often indistinguishably. When we look closely at what has been

[2] R.A., Simpson MS, 262. [3] *Ibid*., fo. 286.
[4] *Ibid*., fo. 287. [5] *Ibid*., fo. 216.

described above as the Stowell Notebook, a practitioner's working notebook, it is not at all implausible to postulate such a compilation of diverse materials in the A source, though, of course, a far more complete compilation focusing mostly on the admiralty court.

The Simpson Manuscript, besides the numerous references to this A source, also contains occasional references to statutes and proclamations, treaties and, as already mentioned, a small number of published sources such as common law reports. The largest single source for the second part of the Manuscript, however, was the A source.

Rothery had stated in the initial notation that the Manuscript, in its present form, was a copy of an original. Apparently Rothery or someone else handed the original, borrowed from Scott, to a group of clerks and instructed them to copy it. The first 150 pages of the Manuscript were copied by several different hands, each person copying one page. Even if this page ended in the middle of a sentence, one clerk stopped at the bottom of the page and another started at the top of the next. They were probably under instructions to copy the original, page for page, in order to preserve the system of internal cross-references. After page 154 the Manuscript is copied entirely by one hand and is therefore more legibly and accurately copied. The copyists made many mistakes, indicating that they often did not understand what they were copying. 'Rusticum judicium', for instance, was copied as 'Rusheum judicium'.[6] 'Embezzlement' was copied as 'Imbecility',[7] perhaps suggesting what the copyist thought of the whole project. It is clear that much of the difficulty in understanding the Manuscript in its present form results from the incompetence and carelessness of the copyists.

The notation by Rothery, that this Manuscript was copied from an 'Original Book, lent to me by Lord Stowell for that purpose, all in his own handwriting', could be interpreted to mean that Scott had personally copied some previously compiled notebook. But clearly, no competent civilian in his right mind would have copied this notebook in the same order as this original. The topical arrangement cries out to be rearranged with all the scattered discussions of each topic brought together, since this is clearly how the volume was meant to be used. Only the hack copyists who made the present copy would have preserved the order of the original, since it made as much sense to them one way as the other.

The obvious question remaining, then, is whether Scott had prepared the original compilation himself. Although this is possible, it is very unlikely, since all the internal evidence points to the compilation of the original about the middle of the eighteenth century, when Scott was about five years old. It has already been mentioned that all the dates given for admiralty cases cited were earlier than 1750. The few published books cited had all appeared by 1756 at the latest. With the exception of the Treaty of Utrecht, all the treaties discussed were from the seventeenth century. No statutes were referred to later than the two of 13 and 17 George II from the 1740s. In one place the statute passed in 1740 is referred to as 'the late Act 13 Geo[rg]e 2'.[8] There is also a reference to a judgment by Sir Charles Hedges 'about 30 years ago'.[9]

[6] *Ibid.*, fo. 61.   [7] *Ibid.*, fo. 261.
[8] *Ibid.*, fo. 156.   [9] *Ibid.*, fo. 377.

Hedges was admiralty judge from 1689 to 1714. It is hard to imagine Scott a generation later preparing this compilation and limiting his sources to those from the 1750s or earlier or calling a forty-year-old statute 'the late Act'. Scott might have relied on the A source even knowing it to be dated. But surely a civilian in the late 1770s or 1780s would have included more recent citations and discussions of more recent topics such as the Rule of '56. Although Rothery knew that the volume he had copied belonged to Scott, he must have been mistaken in concluding that it was in Scott's handwriting.

If Scott did not compile the original of this Manuscript, who did? It seems quite certain that the original Manuscript was compiled by Sir Edward Simpson, who became a civilian in 1736 and was appointed King's Advocate in 1756. He died in 1764.[10] In three of Scott's published judgments he quoted from a manuscript in his possession which, he said, had been prepared by Simpson. The three quotations from Scott's judgments will be placed, side by side, with closely parallel passages from the Simpson Manuscript found today in the office of the Registrar of the Admiralty. By comparing these three passages it becomes clear that Scott was referring to the original of this Manuscript which Rothery had copied and which has been preserved in the office of the Registrar.

Shortly after becoming admiralty judge Scott quoted from 'some manuscript notes, which I have of a very careful and experienced practiser in this profession, Sir E. Simpson'.[11] The passage Scott said he derived from his Simpson notes will be placed to the left of two passages from the Simpson Manuscript in its present form.

By Marine Law the Lord High *Admiral* had the custody of the derelicts found at sea: if no owner appears they become perquisites of Admiralty: the finder can have no property in them; only a reward for his trouble, in preserving them; if no owner appears, or if the claimant cannot prove his property, the salvors have not acquired any right in the thing found, but they must be satisfied for their expence and trouble from a sale of the ship and cargo.[12]	Derelicts] by Marine Law has [*sic*] Admiral has custody of Derelicts found on Sea in same manner as Lords of Manor have of Warps & Strays – If owner does not claim the[y] become perquisites of Adm[iral]ty – the Finder can have no Property in them only a reward for his trouble in preserving & taking care of them.[13] If no Owner appear or they should not be able to prove Property, Salvors would have no right to Ship or Cargo but it would become *perquisite of Adm[iral]ty* & Salvors must be satisfied expense & trouble, from Sale of Ship.[14]

[10] G. D. Squibb, *Doctors' Commons* (Oxford, 1977), 190.

[11] *Aquila (Lunsden)* (1798), 1 Rob. 37, 43.

[12] *Ibid.* Scott again referred to the Simpson MS in this case, relying on the same passage he had previously quoted. He said: 'The notes of Sir *E. Simpson*, which I have before cited, prove that he knew of no such rule; for after saying, "In such a case it becomes a perquisite of Admiralty;" had there been such a rule, he would naturally have added: not, as the words now stand, "*The salvors must be satisfied for their expence and trouble*;" but the salvors shall "take a moiety:" he therefore had no knowledge of such a rule.' *Ibid.*, 45. Italics in the original.

[13] R.A., Simpson MS, 362, under topic 'Derelicts'.

[14] *Ibid.*, fo. 255, under topic 'Salvage'.

Although the officially reported version of Scott's judgment in the left column gives the impression that Scott quoted from one passage in the Simpson Manuscript, the notes of a practitioner who was present when Scott gave his judgment in this case state explicitly that Scott had quoted from two passages.[15]

The second passage which Scott quoted from the Simpson Manuscript does not have as close a parallel in the present version of the Simpson Manuscript. Again the two passages will be placed side by side for comparison, with Scott's published judgment on the left.

The rule is: that *England* restores, on salvage, to its allies; but if instances can be given of *British* property retaken by them and condemned as prize, the Court of Admiralty will determine their cases according to their own rule.[16]

But Recaptor is only entitled to *Salvage* which the Statute has settled as to British Ships – yet in regard to to [sic] those of our Allies will be left to discretion of C[our]t upon a quantum Meruit from hazard & trouble . . . according to circumstances of Recapture because by Treaty subjects of each Nation are to aid & assist each other[.] But if instances can be given of English Ships retaken in same manner being condemned as Prize at Ostend the C[our]t of Adm[iral]ty here will determine according to their own rules.[17]

In the third reference by Scott to the Simpson Manuscript, Scott quoted from 'A manuscript book of great accuracy, which I possess by the kindness of the late Sir *William Wynne*, composed by Sir *Edward Simpson*, a distinguished practitioner, and Judge in these Courts.'[18] The passages will again be placed side by side, with the version quoted by Scott on the left and the version from the present form of the Simpson Manuscript on the right.

[T]hough there are words in the act of the 2 Geo. 2., binding and conclusive to the contract described in that same act of Parliament, yet the Court of Admiralty, being a Court of Equity, will consider how far these engagements are reasonable or not.[19]

Contract] Stat of 2 Geo 2 for regulating Seamen directs that Contract signed by the Mariner shall be conclusive & binding to all parties & that Master on coming from beyond Sea is to pay sailors within 30 days . . . Yet Adm[iral]ty being a Court of Equity may judge of the reasonableness of the Coven[an]t & allow or disallow the same Tender to be made with Costs if any due by Law which will bring the point before the Court & it may

[15] Nicholl's Notebook, 1797–9, 161, P.R.O. HCA 30/464. In his notes of Scott's argument in the case of the *Aquila*, John Nicholl made this summary: 'Salvor only right to reward. Manuscript of Sir E. Simpson. Derelicts by Marine Law if no owner appear belong to the Admiralty Salvor only a r[igh]t to reward. [A]nother passage to same effect – expressly that salvors have adq[uire]d no r[igh]t to the Property.'

[16] *Santa Cruz (Picoa)* (1798), 1 Rob. 49, 63.

[17] R.A., Simpson MS, 182, under topic 'Recapture'.

[18] *Minerva (Bell)* (1825), 1 Hag. 347, 357.

[19] *Ibid.*

be doubted whether this is a reasonable Coven[an]t.[20]

These three passages strongly suggest that the notebook which is now in the office of the Registrar of the Admiralty, which is here called the Simpson Manuscript, is indeed a copy of the manuscript notes of Sir Edward Simpson which Scott had in his possession and which Scott referred to and loaned to Rothery to be copied. Scott's rather loose quotation or paraphrase of the passages in the Simpson Manuscript does not seem surprising, since his purpose was merely to indicate the state of the admiralty law at the time of Simpson.

There is a fourth passage in which Scott referred to the Simpson Manuscript, not while he was admiralty judge, but in 1795 while he was arguing a case as King's Advocate before the Lords of Prize Appeals. According to the contemporary notes of another civilian, John Nicholl, Scott referred to the following proposition of prize law which he explicitly derived from the Simpson Manuscript: 'Neutrals cannot trade from one enemy's port to another.'[21] No close parallel to his statement can be located in the Simpson Manuscript as it now exists in the office of the Registrar. Perhaps it is there but concealed under some improbable topic heading, or perhaps the copyist failed to include the proposition in the present copy, or perhaps the notetaker, Nicholl, gave an abbreviated summary of what Scott had said. It is also possible that Scott was loosely paraphrasing two statements which are in the present Simpson Manuscript concerning neutrals engaging in the coasting trade of a belligerent. These two statements both say that such trade by a neutral between two ports of an enemy is legal if allowed by treaty.[22] Scott, using the Simpson Manuscript as a source for his proposition, might have been drawing the negative inference from these two statements and applying them to the situation where there was not a treaty giving neutrals the right to engage in such coastwise trade of a belligerent.

Whether or not one is satisfied with the suggestion that the original of the notebook in the office of the Registrar of the Admiralty is a copy of the Simpson Manuscript which Scott possessed and used, it at least seems clear that the Manuscript which exists today is a copy of some manuscript which Scott possessed and which was originally compiled in the mid-eighteenth century. Since the hypothesis that it is a copy of the Simpson Manuscript from which Scott repeatedly quoted seems quite probable, it will be referred to by that name.

Regardless of the actual authorship, however, it clearly is an extremely valuable source for analyzing Scott's work as admiralty judge. It discusses in far greater detail than any other known source the state of admiralty law a half century before Scott was appointed to the admiralty court.

[20] R.A., Simpson MS, 367, under topic 'Contracts'.

[21] *Mercurius*, Nicholl's Notes of Prize Appeals, 1794–1817, 5, P.R.O. HCA 30/466.

[22] R.A., Simpson MS, 121, under heading 'Prize', states: 'Frenchman residing in Spain may trade on his own Acc[oun]t from one port in Spain to another by 17 Art of Utrecht in French or Neutral Ships.' This is restated at page 125 under the topic 'Trading' as follows: 'A French man trading in Spain may (*sic*) when we are not at war with France may trade on his own acc[oun]t From one port in Spain to another by 17 Article of treaty of Utrecht.'

BIBLIOGRAPHY OF PRIMARY SOURCES

PAPERS AND CORRESPONDENCE OF SIR WILLIAM SCOTT, LORD
STOWELL
Beinecke Library, Yale University, Osborne File
Bodleian Library, Oxford, Dep. Bland Burges; MS Eng. Letters
British Library, London, Add. MS; Add. Egerton
Brown University Library
Clements Library, University of Michigan
Encombe House, Corfe Castle, Dorset, Eldon Papers
Harvard Law Library
Historical Society of Pennsylvania
Humanities Research Center, University of Texas
Huntington Library, San Marino, California
Inner Temple Library, Opinions as Counsel, Mitford Legal MS
Lambeth Palace Library, Opinions as Counsel, Fulham Papers; S.P.G.
    Papers; MS 1542
New York Historical Society, Rufus King Papers
Northumberland Record Office
Office of the Registrar of the Admiralty, Stowell Notebook (described in
    Appendix)
Old Ashmolean, Oxford, Student Notebook, Univ. Coll.
Public Record Office, will of Lord Stowell, Prob. 11/1859/190
Scottish Record Office, Edinburgh
Warwickshire Record Office, Newdegate Papers

OTHER MANUSCRIPTS
Act Books, Lambeth Palace Library
Admiralty Court, Assignation Books, Instance, Public Record Office, HCA
    6/ –7/
    Assignation Books, Prize, Public Record Office, HCA 8/ –11/
    Criminal Sessions, Public Record Office, HCA 1/
    Minute Books, Prize, Public Record Office, HCA 28/ –30/
Appeal Cases in Prize Causes, Law Library of Congress, Washington, D.C.
Arnold, J. Notebooks of Admiralty Cases, Public Record Office, HCA 30/
    468–74
Bever, T. 'A course of lectures on jurisprudence and civil law read in the
    Vinerian Law School', Codrington Library, All Souls College, Oxford
    'A history of the legal polity of the Roman state, and of the rise, progress

and extent of the Roman Law', Codrington Library, All Souls College, Oxford

Black book of the admiralty, transcript, with notes by W. Scott, Inner Temple Library

Cases on Appeals in Prize Causes, Public Record Office, HCA 45/

Collection of cases from delegates, arches, prerogative, admiralty courts, Lincoln's Inn Library, Misc. MS 147

Consistory Court Sentences of Sir W. Scott, Inner Temple Library, Misc. MS 101

Correspondence of Lord Eldon, Encombe House, Corfe Castle, Dorset

[Croke, A.] 'A digest of the law of the British courts of admiralty', Bodleian Library, Oxford, MS Add. C. 156–8

[Dodson, J.] Notebooks of Admiralty Cases, Bodleian Library, Oxford, Monk Bretton Dep.

'In what cases the King's Courts of Common Pleas may grant prohibitions', Lincoln's Inn Library

Lee, G. Admiralty Opinions, Historical Society of Pennsylvania, Philadelphia

Great Britain, Prize Causes, New York Public Library

Prize Cases, Historical Society of Pennsylvania, Philadelphia

Nicholl, J. Notebooks of Admiralty Cases, Public Record Office, HCA 30/464–7

Precedent book concerning admiralty court 1640–70, Lambeth Palace Library

Privy Council Orders, Public Record Office, PC 2/

[Simpson, E., 'Draft digest of the law of the admiralty court'], office of the Registrar of the Admiralty (described in Appendix)

Treasurers' book of Doctors' Commons, Lambeth Palace Library

'Treatise of prohibitions with the arguments pro et contra', Lincoln's Inn Library, Misc. 581

PRINTED SOURCES

Abbott, C. *A treatise of the law relative to merchant ships and seamen* (London, 1802)

Abreu, F. d'. *Tratado juridico-politico, sobre pressas de mar, y calidades, que deben concurrin para hacerse legitamamente el corso* (Cadiz, 1746)

Accounts relating to salaries and allowances of admiralty court, R. Com. Rep., 1833 (230), XXXI

Acts and ordinances of the Interregnum, eds. C. Firth and T. Rait (3 vols., London, 1911)

Annual Register (195 vols., London, 1758–1953)

Atkyns, J. *Reports, Court of Chancery* (3 vols., London, 1765–8)

Beawes, W. *Lex mercatoria rediviva* (London, 1752)

A bill to amend and render more effectual the laws relating to spiritual persons (London, 1803)

Black book of the admiralty, ed. T. Twiss (4 vols., London, 1871–6)

Blackstone, W. *Commentaries on the laws of England*, 9th edn (4 vols., London, 1783)

Boswell's life of Johnson, ed. G. Hill, rev. L. Powell (6 vols., Oxford, 1934–50)

Browne, A. *A compendious view of the civil law, and of the law of the admiralty*, 2nd edn (2 vols., London, 1802)

Bulstrode, E. *Reports in King's Bench* (London, 1657–9)

Burlamaqui, J. *Principles of natural and politic law* (London, 1752)

Burrell, W. *Reports of cases determined by the High Court of Admiralty*, ed. R. Marsden (London, 1885)

Bynkershoek, C. van. *Quaestionum juris publici libri duo*, tr. T. Frank (Oxford, 1930)

Clerke, F. *Praxis supremae curiae admiralitatis*, 4th edn (London, 1743)

Coke, E. *The fourth part of the institutes of the laws of England* (London, 1797)

Collection of all such statutes ... as any way relate to the admiralty, navy and ships of war (London, 1755)

Collection of the statutes relating to the admiralty, navy, ships of war, and incidental matters, to the eighth year of King George the Third (London, 1768)

C[onset], H. *The practice of the spiritual or ecclesiastical courts*, 3rd edn (London, 1708)

[Coote, C.] *Sketches of the lives and characters of eminent English civilians* (London, 1804)

The correspondence of Edmund Burke, eds. R. McDowell and J. Woods (10 vols., Chicago, 1958–78)

Courts of justice the report of the select committee appointed by the House of Commons to enquire into the establishment of the courts of justice ... (London, 1799)

Decisions in the High Court of Admiralty during the time of Sir George Hay and of Sir James Marriott (London, 1801)

Digges-Latouche, J. *Collections of cases, memorials, addresses and proceedings in Parliament relating to ... admiralty-courts* (London, 1757)

Documents relating to law and custom of the sea, ed. R. Marsden (2 vols., n.p., 1915)

Dodson, J. *Reports of cases argued and determined in the High Court of Admiralty* (2 vols., London, 1815–28)

Eden, R. *Jurisprudentia philologica sive elementa juris civilis* (Oxford, 1744)

Eden, W. *Principles of penal law* (London, 1771)

Edwards, T. *Reports of cases determined in the High Court of Admiralty* (London, 1812)

English privateering voyages to the West Indies, 1588–1595, ed. R. Andrews (Cambridge, 1959)

Exton, J. *The maritime dicaeologie, or sea jurisdiction of England* (London, 1664)

Gail, A. *Practicarum observationum* (Amsterdam, 1563)

Gibbon, E. *Memoirs of my life*, ed. G. Bonnard (New York, 1966)

Gilbert, G. *Law of Evidence* (Dublin, 1754)

Godolphin, J. *A view of the admiral iurisdiction* (London, 1661)

Grotius, H. *De jure belli ac pacis libri tres*, tr. F. Kelsey (Washington, 1925)

De jure belli ac pacis with comments of J. Gronovius, J. Barbeyrac, H. Cocceius and S. Cocceius (4 vols., Lausanne, 1752)

Le droit de guerre et de la paix, with notes by J. Barbeyrac (2 vols., Basle, 1758)

Haggard, J. *Reports of cases argued and determined in the High Court of Admiralty* (3 vols., London, 1825–40)

Reports of cases ... in the Consistory Court of London (2 vols., London, 1822)

Hale, M. *The history of the common law of England*, ed. C. Gray (Chicago, 1971)

Heineccius, J. *Elementa juris naturae et gentium* (Halle, 1746)

Holt, F. *A system of the shipping and navigation laws of Great Britain*, 2nd edn (2 vols., London, 1824)

Huber, U. *Praelectionum juris civilis* (Louvain, 1766)

Keble, J. *Reports, King's Bench* (3 vols., London, 1685)

Kent, J. *Commentaries on American law* (4.vols., New York, 1832)

Key to the Orders in Council (London, 1812)

The late will and testament of the Doctors' Commons (n.p., 1641)

The later correspondence of George III, ed. A. Aspinall (5 vols., Cambridge, 1966–70)

Law and politics in Jacobean England: the tracts of Lord Chancellor Ellesmere, ed. L. Knafla (Cambridge, 1977)

Law officers' opinions to the Foreign Office, ed. C. Parry (97 vols., Westmead, England, 1970–3)

Laws, ordinances, and institutions of the admiralty of Great Britain, civil and military (2 vols., London, 1746)

Lee, R. *Treatise of captures in war* (London, 1759)

A letter to Sir William Scott upon his curate's bill (London, 1803)

Letters of William Scott father of Lords Stowell and Eldon (Newcastle, 1848)

Life and letters of Joseph Story, ed. W. Story (2 vols., London, 1851)

[Madison, J.] *Examination of the British doctrine, which subjects to capture a neutral trade, not open in time of peace* (n.p., n.d.)

Magens, N. *An essay on insurances* (2 vols., London, 1755)

Marriott, J. *The case of the Dutch ships considered*, 3rd edn (London, 1769)

Formulare instrumentorum: or, a formulary of authentic instruments, writs, and standing orders, used in the High Courts of Admiralty of Great Britain, of prize and instance (London, 1802)

[Marryat, J.] *Concessions to America the bane of Britain* (London, 1807)

Molloy, C. *De jure maritimo et navali* (London, 1676)

Observations on the course of proceedings in admiralty courts in prize causes (London, 1747)

Parliamentary debates ... 1803 to [1820], ed. T. Hansard (41 vols., London, 1812–20)

Parliamentary debates ... [1820–30], ed. T. Hansard (25 vols., London, 1820–30)

Parliamentary history of England ... to ... 1803, ed. W. Cobbett (36 vols., London, 1806–20)

298 *Bibliography of primary sources*

Philipson, L. *An examination of the judgment of the British High Court of Admiralty on the capture of a Swedish convoy* (Stockholm, 1800)

Postlethwayt, M. *Universal dictionary of trade and commerce* (London, 1751)

Pott, J. *Observations on matters of prize and the practice of the admiralty prize courts* (London, 1810)

The proctor and parator their mourning (London, 1641)

Pufendorf, S. *De jure naturae et gentium*, trs. C. Oldfather and W. Oldfather (2 vols., Oxford, 1934)

Report of the commissioners for examining into the duties, salaries, and emoluments of the officers, clerks, and ministers of the several courts of justice..., R. Com. Rep., 1824 (240) IX, 75

Resons for setling admiralty-jurisdiction and giving encouragement to merchants, owners, commanders, masters of ships, materialmen and mariners (n.p., 1690)

Robinson, C. *Collectanea Maritima* (London, 1801)

Reports of cases argued and determined in the High Court of Admiralty (6 vols., London, 1799–1808)

Rolle, H. *Un abridgement des plusieurs cases et resolutions del common ley* (London, 1668)

Les reports de divers cases, Banke le Roy (London, 1675–6)

St. German's doctor and student, eds. T. Plucknett and J. Barton (Seld. Soc., London, 1974, vol. 65)

Salaries and retired allowances to judges, R. Com. Rep., 1833 (230)

Select pleas in the court of admiralty, ed. R. Marsden (2 vols., Seld. Soc., London, 1892, 1897, vols. 6 and 11)

A short view of the Lord High Admiral's jurisdiction (London, 1775)

The statutes at large from Magna Charta [to 46 Geo. III], ed. D. Pickering (46 vols., Cambridge, 1762–1807)

The statutes of the United Kingdom [from 47 Geo. III to 1 Will. IV] (24 vols., London, 1807–30)

[Stephen, J.] *War in disguise or the frauds of the neutral flags* (London, 1805)

Substance of the speech of... Sir William Scott... upon a motion for leave to bring in a bill relative to non-residence of the clergy (London, 1802)

Taylor, J. *Elements of civil law* (Cambridge, 1755)

Trial of Captain John Kimber for the murder of two female negro slaves on board the Recovery, African slave ship... 1792 (London, n.d.)

Trim, T. *Ecclesiastical dignities, ecclesiastical grievances... with observations on Sir William Scott's residence bill* (London, n.d.)

Valin, R. *Nouveau commentaire sur l'ordonnance de la marine* (New Rochelle, 1776)

Vattel, E. de. *Le droit des gens*, tr. C. Fenwick (Washington, 1916)

Vincent, F. *Proceedings in the High Court of Admiralty, held at Justice-Hall in the Old-Bailey on Saturday, March 30, 1782* (London, 1782)

Viner, C. *A general abridgement of law and equity*, 2nd edn (24 vols., London, 1791–5)

Voet, J. *Commentarius ad pandectas*, 5th edn (Hague, 1726)

[Watts, R.] *The practice of the court of admiralty in England and Ireland* (Dublin, 1757)

Welwood, W. *An abridgement of all sea-laws* (London, 1613)

Wheaton, H. *A digest of the law of maritime captures and prizes* (New York, 1815)

Elements of international law, ed. G. Wilson (Oxford, 1936)

History of the law of nations in Europe and America (New York, 1845)

Wynne, W. *Life of Sir Leoline Jenkins* (2 vols., London, 1724)

Zouch, R. *The jurisdiction of the admiralty of England* (London, 1663)

INDEX

prize, neutral rights and duties),
172, 176–86, 201–2; policy
considerations (*see also* High
Court of Admiralty, jurisdiction,
prize, policy considerations), 122,
154–6, 160–1, 163, 171, 181–2,
227, 230–2, 256–7; reliance on law
of nations (*see also* law of
nations), 172, 177–9, 181–3, 185,
193–5, 199, 204–5, 218, 220–1,
251–5, 257–66, 269–71, 280–1;
Rule of '56 (*see also* High Court of
Admiralty, jurisdiction, prize,
Rule of '56), 230–8; territorial
waters (*see also* High Court of
Admiralty, prize, territorial
waters), 176–9, 249, 265, 284;
three mile limit (*see also* High
Court of Admiralty, jurisdiction,
prize, three mile limit), 176, 178,
249; transportation of enemy
troops (*see also* High Court of
Admiralty, jurisdiction, prize,
transportation of enemy troops),
184–5; treaties (*see also* High
Court of Admiralty, jurisdiction,
prize, treaties), 181, 205, 252–5;
visit and search (*see also* High
Court of Admiralty, jurisdiction,
prize, visit and search), 180–3,
254, 264
interpretation of statutes and
treaties, 252–5
as judge of the consistory court, 41,
44–7, 50
judicial administration, 273–9
judicial independence, 223, 264–73
as King's Advocate, 41–3, 45–9, 130,
142–7, 150–2, 176, 193, 204, 227–
8, 271, 287
knighthood, 41
lecturer, 38, 44
member of Dr Johnson's Club, 39
as member of Parliament, 39, 50–2,
218–19, 253–4, 265, 271, 274, 277,
279
member of University Dining Club,
38–9
at Oxford, 32–9, 44, 256
peerage, as Baron Stowell, 40, 44,
52–4
precedent, use of (*see also* High
Court of Admiralty, precedent, use

of; precedent), 47–8, 59, 62–3,
79–80, 93, 94–5, 100, 102–3, 112,
134–5, 143–5, 153–9, 161–3, 165–
6, 170–1, 185, 193, 199, 205, 223,
238–40, 243–52, 256, 258, 262–6,
278
retirement, 58, 243
as scholar, 32–9, 44, 47–8
social life, 54–8
Stowell notebook, 45–8, 59, 151,
154–5, 286–7
wives: Maria Anne Bagnall, 37, 54–
5; Marchioness of Sligo, 55
youth, 32–4
Scott, William, father of Sir William
Scott, 31
Scott, William, son of Sir William
Scott, 31–2, 54–5, 58
seamen, 63–5, 67–79, 164, 180, 255,
274
punishment at sea, 75, 101–3
Selden, John, 112
Sheridan, R. B., 39
Simpson, Sir Edward, 59, 125, 127,
245, 287, 292–3
Simpson manuscript, 59, 68, 100–1,
104–6, 111–12, 125, 245, 286–93
Smith, Adam, 39, 256
The wealth of nations, 256
Snelle Zeylder (*Leeiw*), 136–9, 144–5,
147, 148, 158
Snipe and others, 223
Stephen, James, 117–18, 218, 236
War in disguise, 218, 236
Story, Joseph, 52, 250, 282–3
Summer, Lord, 244
Sutherland, Dame Lucy, 34
Swabey, Maurice, 43
Swinney v. Tinker, 74

Taylor, John, 37
territorial waters, *see* High Court of
Admiralty, jurisdiction, prize,
territorial waters; Scott, as judge
of the admiralty court, in prize
cases, territorial waters
Theodore, 124
Thornton, Robert, 275
three mile limit, *see* High Court of
Admiralty, jurisdiction, prize,
three mile limit; Scott, as judge of
the admiralty court, in prize cases,
three mile limit

Pettyfoggers and Vipers of the Commonwealth,
The 'Lower Branch' of the Legal Profession
in Early Modern England

C.W.BROOKS

For EU product safety concerns, contact us at Calle de José Abascal, 56–1°, 28003 Madrid, Spain or eugpsr@cambridge.org.

www.ingramcontent.com/pod-product-compliance
Ingram Content Group UK Ltd.
Pitfield, Milton Keynes, MK11 3LW, UK
UKHW010350140625
459647UK00010B/966